WHAT OTHERS SAY ABOUT THIS BOOK

Wes Howard Brook, Seattle University, *Empire Baptized: How the Church Embraced What Jesus Rejected* (2016)

Lee Van Ham understands deeply the urgent task before humanity as a species: turning from what he calls a "MultiEarth" to a "OneEarth" consciousness. Drawing upon a wide range of companions on the journey, including Jungian psychology, indigenous myth, personal experience and modern science, Van Ham gracefully and passionately interweaves the call to inner transformation and social/ecological transformation that is necessary to our survival. He gently leads readers step-by-step to begin to put aside ego-based control and move into interdependence with all of creation. It is a challenging, but much needed invitation. Folks overwhelmed by the state of the world and not sure how to respond will find here a solid companion and guide.

Kritika Narula, blogger at "So Many Books, So Little Time," freelance writer, Delhi, India

I had earlier read Blinded By Progress *and adored how our environmental issues were explained through the concept of the Muti-Earth worldview. This book takes it up a notch and shares information at a speed that speaks volumes about the urgency of the situation we are in. It echoes the sentiment of Amitav Ghosh's* The Great Derangement *and is just as commendable an effort to bring the environmental discourse to the centrestage. It is important to view this as a call to action, one which is reaching it's finality.*

Richard Rohr, Dean of the Living School for Action and Contemplation, Albuquerque, New Mexico

It's widely agreed that a massive effort is needed to keep our planet habitable in this century. Less widely understood is how our human species must move beyond ego-consciousness into the greater consciousness centered in the soul, or Self, in order to be capable of that effort. From Egos to Eden clearly shows how the two energize each other, making possible new humans and new societies. It provides a compelling eco-spirituality in which Earth and soul are no longer in opposition, but poles for an integrating Uni-verse. Readers will be guided through the stages of the heroic journey that is ours to make in these decades.

Herman F. Greene, President, Center for Ecozoic Societies, Chapel Hill, North Carolina

Van Ham asks the essential question, "How do humans live on one Earth?" and takes it seriously. This book is the second in a trilogy, the first concerning the illusion of progress and the succeeding one to focus on best practices. In this volume he takes us on the hero's journey of moving from false reality of our current "MultiEarth" industrial civilization to taking on the burden and then the promise of a viable future. He draws heavily on Thomas Berry who wrote that the main difficulty in this journey would not be the physical situation but the "psychic entrancement" of our present mode of development. This is a soul struggle of the highest degree at both the individual and collective levels. Van Ham looks for guidance in the wisdom of indigenous people who preceded civilization and now distance themselves from it. He recovers the meaning of the Garden of Eden as the promise of cooperative balance and what befalls us when that is lost. He takes us on the journey of moving beyond the small self of ego to the larger self that lives in a covenant relationship with Earth and all its beings.

Steve Gehring, corporate attorney, Omaha Nebraska

From Egos to Eden *is a must read for all of us who continue to treat our planet as though we had three others in the warehouse. Lee Van Ham and I have been on a journey together for 43 years. When I first heard Lee speak at a pastor interview session, I knew that his ideas both tantalized and frightened me. Forty-three years has not changed that. He is one of only two or three people throughout my life who can stretch me to uncomfortable spiritual growth and love me through the process.* Blinded by Progress *and* From Egos to Eden *have again done that for me and will do it for all who read these two jewels. Lee's gentle but compelling journey will motivate each of us to a deeper understanding of our Garden and how to preserve it for the next generations of inhabitants.*

Pannell Carr, M.D., Jungian-oriented Spirit-centered counselor, San Diego, California

From Egos to Eden *powerfully informs and champions the earth's present crisis and calls for help, inspiring a needed paradigm shift into greater consciousness. By doing the hard work of illuminating and contrasting the healthy connection that exists between earth and spirit, it offers us a sound, beneficial and soulful path for the healing and regeneration of our civilization.*

Jim Larkin, Interfaith Minister, Berkeley, California

In From Egos to Eden *Lee Van Ham provides a well thought out and beautifully communicated wake up call for humanity to save ourselves and the One Planet we have to live on. Through story telling and history lessons, Van Ham holds up a mirror for us to look into, providing a clear picture of how we have come from the Garden of Eden to the Ego driven world of today and how that phenomenon is creating a demand on our Planet that she cannot meet. The story of human history Van Ham presents, which he calls the "Civilization Project," clearly explains how we have come to live with a "Multi-Earth" mentality that literally requires much more than our "OneEarth" can provide. We are literally living beyond our means as a race, and have been for a very long time. Is there still time to turn this dynamic around? Pick up, open, and read this book to receive a compelling call to action to insure that there is!*

Jeff Edwards, Professor Emeritus, Northeastern Illinois University, Chicago, IL

Van Ham has studied, reinterpreted and brought forth a new old version of OneEarth and that is a good thing. What first opened my eyes in this book is Van Ham's deconstruction of the Eden Myth. Clearly, and supported by researched references, he takes us back to Augustine's version of the Eden myth that is not the original Judea version. What a difference, when you see how the original is far from what we have been indoctrinated to believe. Van Ham submits that Nature's interdependence of all life becomes the renewed version of life.

Gerald Iversen, CEO and Chief Activist at Simple Living Works

Some may read Van Ham's words as "Change or Die!" For those who will hear, he is most emphatically and sincerely saying "Change and LIVE!" Though the subject of the book is "deep," Van Ham keeps it from getting academic. Without being self-indulgent, he connects each of the steps toward OneEarth consciousness to to his own personal story.

FROM
EGOS TO EDEN

OUR HEROIC JOURNEY TO
KEEP EARTH LIVABLE

BOOK II IN THE SERIES
EDEN FOR THE 21ST CENTURY

LEE VAN HAM

From Egos to Eden: Our Heroic Journey To Keep Earth Livable
Lee Van Ham

Published by OneEarth Publishing
3295 Meade Ave., San Diego, CA 92116
http://www.theoneearthproject.com

Author contact information:
lee@jubilee-economics.org

Publisher's Cataloging-In-Publication Data

(Prepared by The Donohue Group, Inc.)

Names: Van Ham, Lee. | Johnson, Hannah, 1993- illustrator.

Title: From egos to Eden : our heroic journey to keep Earth livable / Lee Van Ham ; illustrator: Hannah Johnson.

Description: San Diego, CA : OneEarth Publishing, [2017] | Series: Eden for the 21st century ; book 2 | Includes bibliographical references and index.

Identifiers: LCCN 2016921328 | ISBN 978-0-9911554-2-2 (print) | ISBN
  978-0-9911554-3-9 (ebook)

Subjects: LCSH: Environmental psychology. | Human ecology--Psychological aspects. | Nature--Psychological aspects. | Environmentalism--Psychological aspects. | Eden. | Deep ecology. | Consciousness.

Classification: LCC BF353.5.N37 V36 2017 (print) | LCC BF353.5.N37 (ebook) | DDC 155.91--dc23

Cover artist: John August Swanson
Editor: Nikki Lyn Pugh
Illustrator: Hannah Johnson
Indexer: Noalani Terry
Publishing Services: AuthorImprints.com

"A human being is part of the whole called by us universe, a part limited in time and space. We experience ourselves, our thoughts and feelings as something separate from the rest. A kind of optical delusion of consciousness. This delusion is a kind of prison for us, restricting us to our personal desires and to affection for a few persons nearest to us. Our task must be to free ourselves from the prison by widening our circle of compassion to embrace all living creatures and the whole of nature in its beauty… *We shall require a substantially new manner of thinking if mankind [sic] is to survive."* (emphasis added)   —Albert Einstein (1875–1959)

(The abridged version as it appeared in the *Monthly Review*, New York, 1949)

Also by Lee Van Ham

Blinded by Progress: Breaking Out of the Illusion That Holds Us
Korean edition, Jeeyoungsa Publishing (2015), Seoul, Korea

Blinded by Progress: Breaking Out of the Illusion That Holds Us
(2013)

"Unmasking the Gods of the Marketplace," *Nurturing the Prophetic Imagination*, Wipf & Stock, (2012).

Dedication

To Juanita,
in gratitude for the array of energies, attitudes, and actions
she uses to help move me
from head to gut and heart,
repeatedly reigniting my journey
or correcting its course;
and
for experiencing with her
the rewilding Presence of the natural world,
that often has her exploding in "Oh my gosh!"

CONTENTS

Gratitude for Many Involved in This Book

Sensations of gratitude swirl in my chest as I think of the many who are part of this book's coming together. I thank some of you by name below; others are present in the paragraphs and thoughts in ways I'm not conscious of. I acknowledge with gratitude the mystical, spiritual ways this book came together. Sometimes thoughts entered my consciousness and carried me to where I'd not had in mind to go. They came like a breeze entering from I know not where, carrying a fresh scent. Thoughts congealed during early morning writing times, but they also wondered in while I was engaged in the activities of the day.

The cover art resulted from a friendship that began because our cars were parked beside each other in a parking lot. Following a conference, artist John August Swanson and I were at our cars at the same time and began a follow-upconversation about his workshop (which I'd attended). It shifted quickly to our lives, and became a conversation of the heart. This book resonates with his strong desire, nurtured in his spirituality, to promote wellbeing and justice on Earth. When I asked him about having a piece on the cover of this book, I was excited when he promptly suggested, "Journey into the Forest." I can only hope that the book will be judged as good as its cover.

In a conversation with my daughter, Lauren, I told her that I really wanted an Indigenous woman to write the "Foreword." She suggested Patricia St. Onge and introduced me to her. Lauren is committed to eco-ministry, so she understood well what I was writing about, plus she and Patricia share work on the same faculty so she was in position to make the introduction. Patricia has not only written the "Foreword," she consulted with me, particularly on Chapter Seven, to write in ways that First Peoples felt present with their voices—quite different from merely having a light-skinned, Dutch-American like me write about them. When she suggested I read Robin Wall Kimmerer, *Braiding Sweetgrass*, it happened that I could begin reading immediately because Juanita, my spouse, had a copy. It had been given to her somewhere in the past by Lauren.

Then there's the sequence about how the use of "liminal space and time" happen in the book. Had I not been invited by Lane, my son, into the process of reviewing some of his writing as he worked on his PhD dissertation, and then the book that followed, I would not have known about "liminality," an important concept in this book. In another sequence, Lane also gifted me with a book many years ago, saying, "Dad, I think you'll like this." It was Jerry Mander's book, *In the Absence of the Sacred*. I go back to it again and again to absorb insights into what technology does to us and how Mander holds up the spiritual consciousness of non-technological peoples. A quote from Mander opens Chapter Seven.

The first manuscript of this book needed a lot of work. Nikki Lyn Pugh, editor at As Your Word, worked many hours on that raw version and helped me see what to change in a major rewrite. Other early readers, Jim Larkin, Steve Gehring, and Harry Watkins, added comments I incorporated into the final form. Greg Newswanger got me past some doubts I had in the really early stages by commenting on a rough outline and a few potential chapters. Through his family foundation, Greg also contributed financially to publishing this book.

Several themes in the book called for graphics to visually represent them. None more so than the heroic journey, which gives the book a sense of movement and overall unity. Hannah Johnson was quick to pick up on what I wanted and then patient to work with me when I changed my mind—often! I'm grateful for the opportunity to work with her, a talented young designer and artist, and for the extra punch she gives to this book.

Michael Johnson, my colleague in the OneEarth Project, developed skills as a proofreader in years past while he worked in various facets of the publishing industry. Lucky for me, he "wouldn't think of not proofreading my book!" As a filmmaker, his eye quickly catches how the flow of ideas can be improved. So, in addition to proofreading, Chapter One, in particular, is better because he spotted that I'd hid the main point too far into the chapter.

Linda McKee, a grateful reader of my first book, partially funded this one. After she gave loving attention to her father's passing, she found it fitting to make a donation from his estate to the costs of publishing this book.

My own work of doing what I write about has included regular visits with therapist Dr. Pannell Carr. My spouse, Juanita, helped me see that I needed to be more conscious of behaviors and choices that were sabotaging what I most wanted in relationships and life. I'm grateful to Juanita for this important push (I didn't really want to go to a therapist at the time) as well as countless other ways she has made this book better through conversations we've shared. I chose Dr. Carr because I wanted a therapist with a Jungian orientation. Over many visits together, she guided me into topographies of consciousness where my head's intellect and gut's primal emotions can come together in the intelligence of the heart. Learning to bring my head and gut together in the heart is essential in my own heroic journey to greater consciousness.

Publishing independently of publishing companies has strong advantages, but it also has lots of pitfalls and work. Thanks to David Wogahn, at AuthorImprints, Inc., for keeping current on what works and what doesn't in the rapidly changing world of "indie" publishing. After hearing him make a presentation at a local library, I turned to him to help me with publishing and marketing. He really wants to see an author's work rewarded. His integrity in every aspect is refreshing. For this book's cover, David helped me use 99designs, a company that creates online competition among designers. The cover of this book was chosen from over two dozen designs submitted. I'm grateful to the unknown designer for the bold, blue cover arranged around the artwork of John August Swanson.

Being the kind of reader who appreciates a good index myself, I appreciate the work of Noalani Terry in providing a highly functional index for you, the readers of this book.

Thanks, finally, to all the endorsers for taking time with the pre-published manuscript and writing a few sentences about what they especially value.

FOREWORD

When I read this manuscript, I knew there was an important message in it. Lee Van Ham is grappling with one of the significant issues of our time. How do we live in harmony with Earth and all beings who share this planetary home with us? *From Egos to Eden* is a powerful invitation for people whose lens onto the world is Western and Judeo-Christian to look deeply at the origin story that has so powerfully driven much of Western History. At the heart of this book is a key to finding a pathway from an extractive, late-stage Capitalist worldview to a regenerative, ancient/re-imagined one. By deconstructing a Western, Judeo-Christian understanding of the original meaning of their Creation narrative, Lee opens a crack that shows one more way to grow into the kind of global community that Our Mother, Earth, is demanding, if we're to thrive in the coming generations. The idea that we currently are using up resources at a rate that requires five earths to sustain our lifeways over time is sobering. That framework is very compelling. We clearly don't have more than our one Earth home.

While I read with enthusiasm, at the same time, I felt an increasing discomfort, particularly as I got to Chapter 7, where he discusses First Peoples as guides on the journey. Making my way through each chapter, it became more clear to me that what was creating the discomfort, was the realization that the author hadn't located himself in his own identity as a middle class, White, Christian man. As often happens when White people write, they have strong, yet often unrecognized assumptions about who they mean when they say "we" in their writing. I was reluctant to continue writing the "Foreword." I knew I'd have to share my observation with Lee. We talked on the phone. I was fully prepared for him to say that he'd find someone else to write the "Foreword." I shared my frustration with his articulation of the contributions made by indigenous communities. I asked if he'd read the writings of Native authors, particularly Robin Wall Kimmerer. Most of what he'd read, assuming it was written by Native people, was actually written by White people who "studied" indigenous communities. Sadly, this happens too often, and Lee isn't alone in it. After two intensely wonderful conversations, his response to my critique was: "I haven't heard anything yet that makes me think you shouldn't write the 'Foreword' to the book." A few weeks later, he sent me the revisions he'd made as a result of our conversations and further reading. I was honored to see that he'd taken my concerns seriously.

My initial excitement and hope remained, and even grew, as I read the revised version of the book. I think Lee has done a very good job of letting the voices of the "guides," whether Jung, Korten or Kimmerer, speak in their own voices. At the same time, he brings his own courageous and authentic voice to the discussion. The flow and interweaving of the voices seems organic to me. His understanding of the impacts of that original Judeo-Christian story is clear from the narrative. He also sees that the story of Eden is dangerous as it has been interpreted over time. It leaves its adherents with the belief that their mandate to "have dominion" comes from God. It also reinforces the notion that patriarchy is sanctioned by God. Lee breaks through that historical reading of the stories in Genesis and offers another way to look at them; a way that can be a guide for 21st Century Christians. For those of us who don't adhere to that story, or who have found it the source of much of the destruction in our midst, there is something instructive here as well.

By opening to the possibility that there can be another interpretation of the stories in Genesis, Lee invites us into dialogue with its historical and current power to influence our social institutions and structures—far beyond the "Church." Conquest, colonization, slavery, internment, exclusion and domination by gender and socio-economic status have their roots in the idea of "having dominion." By cracking historical interpretations open, the stories become liberated in two ways. First, they take their place as one (or two, as he points out) stories about the ways that human beings located themselves in the ecosystem of our global community. They can stand with the hundreds (thousands?) of stories that tell us how we came to be members of the planetary household. Take for example, the *Mohawk Creation Narrative*. Because for generations it wasn't written down, it has the delightful and moving elements that reflect the power of oral traditions. While the outline of the story is held carefully, the story is often told with caveats of "some say…(this) and some say… (another)," freeing the listener to pay attention to the heart of the message. That story, which I've come to understand more fully as I'm getting older (my family was colonized and Christianized by missionaries and televangelists), is a story of collaboration and co-creation.

> *When Sky Woman falls, the birds catch her, Turtle offers his back as a landing place, animals offer their lives as they bring dirt up from the bottom of the ocean, which covers the whole planet. When they finally bring the earth, Sky Woman dances, spreading the soil on the turtle's back, bringing the land into being. After two more generations, when her daughter dies, from her body come corn, beans, squash and tobacco; gifts from the Creator to the generations who will come after her.*

Whole books have been written about this story, and there are so many more stories that give us other ways of interpreting the world around us, and help us understand our place in it.

This book, this reading of the Genesis story, which has been so compelling for so many generations, has been instrumental in getting us to where we are now; living in ways that would require five Earth homes to sustain us. Some are planning strategies to take themselves away to other worlds so they can start again. If we don't learn the lessons outlined in this book, no matter where they go, they'll replicate the same problems they've created here. Holding a "one earth" consciousness is a powerful way to move from where we've come to where we need to be.

If the story of the Garden of Eden has informed your way of being, there are important lessons in this book. If it hasn't, the book gives you a peek into how the Western mind was informed by this story. Either way, it's an important contribution to the larger conversation about where we are, and where we want/need to go in order to live as healthfully contributing members of the ecosystem in which we find ourselves. We are more than "stewards" or "guardians" of the land and all beings. We are members of this profoundly interconnected web of life. When we care for the land, we must also care for each other, for we are the ecosystem as much as the rain, the forests, the waters, the animals and the sky. This book is one piece of the map that moves us along the journey home to ourselves.

—Patricia St. Onge (Haudenosaunee)

PREFACE

A big change was set in motion for me the night in 2010 when I spoke on ecological economics to a small audience at a church. During my presentation, one man in the audience caught my attention because he nodded his head in smiling approval of much that I was saying. Afterward, he handed me his card and we agreed to get together.

That's how Michael Johnson and I met. Subsequently, we lunched together several times and discovered that Daniel Quinn's writings had changed both of us. After reading his book, *Ishmael*, we began to see ourselves living as part of Nature's processes, not above them as we had before. That shift in perspective changed how we saw ourselves and the world. In lunch after lunch, Michael and I learned that we shared a mission for living sustainably, lovingly on the planet.

A project took shape between us. We called it the *OneEarth Project* (see http://theoneearthproject.com/). Through it we would contribute to the ecological, economic, and spiritual efforts that were afoot to live within Earth's capacities. So, I went to work writing a book and Michael, an award winning filmmaker, began planning a film.

My first book, *Blinded by Progress: Breaking Out of the Illusion That Holds Us* (2013), waded into understanding more deeply how and why our intelligent species continues to live at a scale that requires more than one planet. As I was writing it, an early reader of my manuscript pointed out that I was actually writing two or even three books. That's how I shifted towards writing a trilogy. I decided to call the trilogy, "Eden for the 21st Century," because the livable Earth we are pursuing is a contemporary Eden of interdependent relationships. We can live inside of Earth's life-sustaining community of all species if we give up dominating the planet.

This second book, *From Egos to Eden: Our Heroic Journey to Keep Earth Livable,* begins with a chapter on how I see Eden as a powerful mythological story for OneEarth living. The idea or archetype of such a Garden lives deep within everyone. As a result, we have an image of a sustainable Earth and are motivated to make that Garden real in our lives and societies. Edenic, or Earth-size, living is not foreign to humanity. Doing it, however, creates a new human, one with greater consciousness than our current MultiEarth civilization manifests. Because creating a new human can sound like stretching for what we can't reach, in this second book I describe the "heroic journey" that increases our reach. All of us can make that journey; the depths of our souls call us to do so as does Earth herself.

In the OneEarth Project, we are on that journey. We know our species can do better than what MultiEarth thought and practice has shaped. We believe that humans evolved within cosmic Creation for a purpose higher than what we are currently living. Our mood is not to scold what we've done, but to swing open the gates to greater topographies of consciousness that we humans can move into. In those topographies, we can step into the capacities we need to keep Earth livable.

Who I Bring to the Book

I'm a recovering member of the Civilization Project that I write about as the perpetrator of Earth's crises. The context and consciousness from which I write are important for readers to know and for me to own. I have not fully extracted my thinking or acting from the heavy presence of MultiEarth civilization. The heroic journey that is the framework of this book is the journey I am on. I am an older Dutch-American male, born in 1940, on a farm in Iowa. My elementary schooling was in a rural country school—kindergarten through eighth grade together in one room. By age 26, I had completed four years of graduate school. My faith journey, that began as fundamentalist Christian, has broadened into inclusive expressions of many spiritual paths. Yet, I am most familiar with the Judeo-Christian stories which have shaped me. Many of them, I believe, have a contribution to make to OneEarth living if we can break them free of their MultiEarth colonization. I am drawn to the rituals, practices, and thought of other paths, fascinated and nourished by their diverse expressions of the One, the Source of life and love. I grew up in the underclass and have carried some of those values into the lower-middle class where I've lived most of my life. I grew up in a practicing, unconscious patriarchy. Though I disavow the privileges that attach to being white and male, they influence me nonetheless as I continue to seek the unity of masculine and feminine in myself and in societies.

These and a myriad of other life experiences will inevitably show through in this book. Influences on my life are reflected in the people I quote and the authors in the bibliography. To an imbalanced degree, they are European-American male authors. Many are inclusive of differences in gender, economics, spiritualities, and worldview. But this is not, as I see it, the same as including more voices of women, First Peoples, or other racial groups.

I want to interact genuinely with the rich diversity of peoples, spiritual expressions, and cultures around me. Yet, because of how our societies are structured and some choices I have made, my life experience has not fully arrived at what I'm reaching for.

I see our planet as continually evolving, humanness being an important embodiment of Earth's creativity. As a human in Earth's continuing evolution, a major part of my work is to expand my consciousness—not in isolation, but interrelated with all Earth's life and activities. I want to get beyond the smaller topographies of consciousness that my ego can control, and into topographies much larger, more Earth-size. In this creative, evolutionary process, at least ten consciousness-changers have factored prominently in my life and in this book:

1. Emptying myself of what I once "knew" and felt certain about. Being open to receiving new information and new perspectives.
2. Re-narrating a story or myth, drawing on a different layer of meaning related to a current situation.
3. Going into Nature to learn and be.
4. Engaging with Wildness encountered in Nature and in my own being.
5. Encountering the darkside—so-called negative aspects of myself, of others and of society that I'd disowned, couldn't be bothered with, just didn't know about myself or others, or didn't want to know.
6. Experiencing "The Other"—all that is beyond understanding.
7. Hearing and telling stories of change, whether in conversation with another person or through movies, books, audios, and spiritual texts.
8. Taking in new information that changed my paradigm or simply how I thought about someone, someplace, or something.
9. Experiencing pain, suffering, and disease. Moving beyond the circumstances surrounding it and growing from it in some way.
10. Loving and being loved.

It seems that I have been interested in transformative change my whole life—this book being my latest expression of it. In college and graduate school, I thought of myself as studying in order to construct an educated framework for a life of working on change. I focused on history, philosophy, and theology, as well as biblical and religious studies. Soon after grad school ended in 1967, I became excited by the human potential and humanistic psychology movement. I adapted it for use in small groups focused on spiritual deepening. I saw how transformative small groups could be. When effectively facilitated, they offer a protected circle to participants. When the group dynamics feel right, we can safely share feelings, deepen human bonds of community, and describe our spiritual journeys. Opinions, dogma, and judgments do not intrude.

In midlife, when I felt as if my own spiritual life had gone stale, the psychology of Carl Jung enlarged my horizons and reinvigorated how I thought about soul and spirit. As my inner world surged ahead, it triggered a restlessness for balancing actions in the outer world. I came under the tutelage and companionship of people who were eloquent peacemakers. They confronted our country's violence in places like Vietnam, Nicaragua, and El Salvador with peacemaking. With reason and passion, they pursued justice in social and economic systems at home and abroad. Such trans-*forming*, in contrast to con*forming*, continues to allure me.

All of these streams of interest show up in this book—personal growth, spiritual deepening, interpersonal community, challenging unjust structures, and advocating alternatives that embody greater economic, ecological, and social justice. Each of these flows as a tributary into my current worldview which has changed from one shaped mostly by civilization's ways to one shaped by Nature's ways.

I realize now that my connections to Nature began early in my life. Born on a family farm in Iowa, my family's activities and income connected directly to the whims of weather. We depended on the rains and snows, the freezes and thaws, the sun and humidity for seeds to sprout and mature, for grain to ripen, and for fields of hay to cure upon mowing. The aromas of a rain shower, of freshly plowed dirt, and curing hay remain unforgettable delights to me. Thunderstorms and wild winds evoked fear and awe. Farm animals decided our daily schedules. The cows needed to be milked in the morning and evening; eggs were gathered twice daily to prevent them from being cracked. These experiences show how Nature was my first instructor in ecology.

The mystery of Nature's ways was real to me from these early years on. As I've continued to learn from her, I also learn how much she conceals. I sense that she holds within her a spirit and an interdependent wholeness that I intuitively consider sacred and holy. Scientific and rational explanations, though I've eagerly sought them throughout my life, do not by themselves describe the experience of living within Nature's ways for me. Nature handles the polarities and tensions of life and death so honestly, sometimes graciously.

Even though Nature has shaped me in more ways than I know, and even though I love Nature and feel loved by her, only in the past decade have I recognized Nature as a worthy, holistic, and integrative center for how I think about life. Doing so has deepened my conviction that OneEarth living is as possible for us as it is necessary.

As I wrote and re-wrote the chapters, changes occurred in me. I moved into consciousness that is taking me further into Earth-size thinking, loving, and living than what I'd previously been able to do. If reading and absorbing this book, or perhaps arguing with parts of it, has a similar benefit for you, I hope to hear from you or read about it in a review. By sharing stories that are conscious-changing we speed along consciousness change in one another. The heroic journey can't happen in isolation.

This book intends to convey my deepening sense of respect for what Earth-size consciousness is and how challenging it is to live there. There's so much challenge in being interrelated with all living things—and so much anticipation and power. It takes living in community to a new level.

Great as I believe the challenge to be, I also believe that living in Earth-size consciousness is completely possible for us. It happens in a topography of consciousness[1] greater than what egos can handle. We can help one another get there by eschewing both sloth and self-righteousness on the heroic journey. Either one can force us off the road. Both goading and humoring one another can keep us traveling toward a topography of Earth-size consciousness. The chapters that follow tell why I believe we can do this. Many already are.

With this added awareness, readers, may you discern more accurately what you read, judging fairly and finding that which makes stronger and more loving your own contributions to the conversations and practices for keeping Earth livable.

INTRODUCTION

This book, the second in a trilogy entitled, *Eden for the 21st Century*, focuses on the enticing, challenging work of changing ourselves and our interactivity with all life. The next book addresses changing society with Earth-size concepts, policies, and actions that empower our households, schools, banks, businesses, and organizations to practice OneEarth living. These two arenas of "how we are" and "what we can do," though separated into two books, inseparably interrelate and reinforce one another. They are part of one unified journey. Like shadow and sunlight, like the darkness and the light that occurs within every 24-hour day, they are pairs in a whole.

To review the inner logic of the *Eden for the 21st Century* trilogy, in Book I, I describe the worldview that has produced our 12,000-year-old civilization as a functional illusion. Why illusion? Because it continues to encourage humans to live by expectations that require multiple planets, even though in reality, we have only one. That illusion continues to shape systems and hearts.

Book II guides our journey into the topographies of enlarged, Earth-size *consciousness*, personally and collectively. Only in those topographies are we able to live OneEarth ways. It takes a heroic journey to get to such consciousness. Chapter by chapter, I follow the sequence of the "heroic journey" as Joseph Campbell classically described it in *The Hero with a Thousand Faces* (1949). The journey begins when we hear the Call to the adventure. What follows is transformative: departure, finding allies, re-wilding our dehumanized selves, passing through the ordeal of changing to a new human, and arriving in OneEarth consciousness. To live in the topography of OneEarth consciousness with some consistency requires images more imaginative and compelling than what MultiEarth civilization uses. One source for such images is the ecologically healthy Garden that lives deep in the souls of all humans. Of all the art and stories that this archetypal Garden has inspired, the story of Eden can help us live OneEarth consciousness in the 21st century once we liberate it from how MultiEarth thinking has locked it up as a story of continuing human failure.

Book III speaks of best concepts and practices for OneEarth living. These get us in step with Earth as she enters a new geological period. Motivated by compelling OneEarth mythology and science's discoveries of the interactive processes that are the heart of all life, we can be part of Earth's evolutionary trajectory into this new era. In that vein, Book III is about the Eden we can choose as a species and what that can be like.

A Summary of Book I, *Blinded by Progress*

To catch you up if you have not read my earlier book, *Blinded by Progress: Breaking Out of the Illusion That Holds Us*, it describes my quest to understand more deeply the powers that keep MultiEarth thinking in charge of our world. Simply put, to live the MultiEarth worldview requires the capacities of multiple Earths; to live the OneEarth worldview requires the capacities of only one abundant planet. (See the "Appendix" for a table that contrasts these two worldviews.)

While it is obvious that we have only one Earth to live on, we continue to use the resources of more than one. What kind of consciousness, unconscious elements, paradigms, and mythology are at work within us that keep MultiEarth ways going? Why have leaders and cultures remained so gridlocked that civilization has been both unable, and often unmotivated, to solve the complex ecological problems before us? Though many good activities are underway, we are reminded of their insufficiency by the Grim Reaper of species extinction who continues swinging his scythe. Only recently has there been a growing sense that the scythe swings for our species as well. How, then, can we be released from the trends of species-death in order to do our part to sustain life among Earth's millions of species?

Faced with the illusions pursued by MultiEarth living, I remembered what Art Lyons, a professor, economist, and community organizer in Chicago, said to me on several occasions: "If we do not make the correct analysis, we have no chance of working on solutions that will really work."

While I applaud the thousands of efforts to be more green and sustainable, I believe all our efforts and decisions need to pass the litmus test posed by two questions:

1. *Does this action fit within OneEarth living or is this action only a more sustainable version of MultiEarth practices?*
2. *Does this action benefit only humans or all the species in Earth's community of life?*

I was seeking honest answers to these questions when I wrote *Blinded by Progress*. They led me to describe five big, interlinking practices where these questions, if asked, will lead us to stronger solutions:

1. Treating MultiEarth economics as religion.
2. Creating economic Frankensteins, for example, corporations with personhood.
3. Shrinking the treasure of humanness, i.e., civilization's dehumanizing ways.
4. Disguising corporatocracy as democracy.
5. Neglecting human population and species imbalance.

Blinded by Progress ended with a deathbed scene from John Steinbeck's novel, *East of Eden*, where a word was spoken assuring us that we have the power to change out of the paradigm that holds us in an illusion. We *can* undergo the tectonic shift in our spirits, cultures, souls, and ways of being, so that our ways of living and the societies we shape are to scale with Earth's capacities. And this brings us to the second book in the trilogy.

What to Expect in This Book

The opening page of this book quotes physicist Albert Einstein (1875–1959) as saying that we need a *substantially new manner of thinking* in order to see ourselves as part of the whole of Nature and the Universe. Without this, he says, we live in a kind of delusion in which we see ourselves as separate from the rest.

MultiEarth's ways spin a mesmerizing delusion. New technologies gush into our awareness with assurances of new convenience and status. Yet, entrancing as MultiEarth living is, this book explains why I believe we can do what we must: break out of the trance. Doing so requires journeying into a larger topography of consciousness where we see Earth-size ways of living as more enticing than we've ever seen them before. In Earth-size consciousness, we can reverse climate change and other ecological crises we've inflicted on ourselves, on Earth, and on other species.

When we doubt that our species is capable of this tall order, it is because we have not yet come to believe how great a change happens to us when we move into larger topographies of consciousness. It is no exaggeration to say that in larger topographies of consciousness we become new humans. Our souls have what it takes to get us there, but civilization has not called us to such greater capacities. Now, however, Earth calls us there. She speaks to us through extremes of weather and changes to fresh water supplies, oceans, and air quality. Her speech calls us to get into our greater capabilities. *From Egos to Eden* guides us on the journey to being new humans, a journey that is at once heroic and completely doable.

Joseph Campbell's book on what he called the hero's journey, *The Hero with a Thousand Faces* (1949), lies in the background of this book through the work of Christopher Vogler. Campbell described how the hero in myths takes the challenging and dangerous journey into greater consciousness, and then returns with the treasure that the folks back home need in order to live in peaceful wellbeing. Upon reading Campbell's book, Vogler realized that myths describing a hero's journey all had essential elements, and that these structure the sequence of the myth's storyline. That discovery led him into giving Masterclasses to movie script writers and producers on using the sequence of the heroic journey to make better movies—ones that move us, even change our lives. Vogler has written *The Writer's Journey* (2007) as a guide for script writers. His succinct summary of the hero's journey is what I have loosely followed in developing the chapters of this book. Key stages in the story are capitalized:

> The hero is introduced in his ORDINARY WORLD where he receives the CALL TO ADVENTURE. He is RELUCTANT at first to CROSS THE FIRST THRESHOLD where he eventually encounters TESTS, ALLIES and ENEMIES. He reaches the INNERMOST CAVE where he endures the SUPREME ORDEAL. He SEIZES THE SWORD or the treasure and is pursued on the ROAD BACK to his world. He is RESURRECTED and transformed by his experience. He RETURNS to his ordinary world with a treasure, boon, or ELIXIR to benefit his world.[2]

I've chosen the "heroic journey" over "hero's journey," in part, to get past the hero-heroine gender language, though the gender issue goes deeper than just the words. Myths dramatizing the hero's journey have mostly grown out of MultiEarth, patriarchal cultures. That orientation has biased them and often exacerbates the wounding that women have already experienced from MultiEarth patriarchies. Consequently, the heroic journey, as I develop it, shuns the patriarchal models that depict the hero as individualistic and anthropocentric. The issues we face in the 21st century require the heroic journey to be about interdependent, interactivity with all of Earth's community of life. This shift calls on the feminine and masculine in all of us and treats our gender differences as two poles of a greater sphere. OneEarth living thrives on the kind of thinking in which dualities like gender enrich and empower a larger whole. Readers will decide whether or not the heroic journey as presented in this book works for both genders as together we pursue life in topographies of greater consciousness.

The first two chapters of *From Egos to Eden: Our Heroic Journey to Keep Earth Livable* set the stage for the heroic journey that follows. Stories and myths guide our life journeys and make sense out of events that defy reason's ability to do so. Movie series such as *Star Wars* and *Lord of the Rings* kindle our motivation to persist against dark powers that overwhelm our egos. Both seek to leave superpower civilization behind for worlds shaped by a new humanity. In *Chapter One* I work with the myth of Eden in the same way. Eden has compelling power to connect us with the Garden, healing the wound of disconnection that happens when we choose MultiEarth civilization. The Garden lives in the human and collective psyche as a universal image of abundance and possibility. Connected with that Garden, we can shape Earth-size living in a way that works for the 21st century.

Making the Garden real on our stressed-out Earth strikes us as daunting work, and is likely even larger than we imagine. By any measurement, doing so is our Great Work as I call it in *Chapter Two*, copying acclaimed author, cosmologist, and self-proclaimed "geologian," Thomas Berry. We need to reconnect with Earth as she regenerates herself and moves on into her next geological epoch. Her Holocene and Anthropocene Eras have provided a geological stability for civilization, a project of ego consciousness. But to join her in her next era means moving from ego consciousness into the larger topography of Eden-consciousness—a journey of unimagined adventure.

This journey begins in *Chapter Three* where we hear the CALL TO ADVENTURE that today comes from both our planet Earth and a person's soul. This Call lets us know that we need to go from where we are to a new kind of interdependence with all things. It's a Call too strong to ignore. It forces us to deal with our

RELUCTANCE and decide for or against. *Chapter Four* sets out what happens if we turn away from the Call. If rejected, the Call's energies don't go away but continue to work from our unconscious. From our underworld, they reshape our lives in polarities of unpleasant behaviors: aggressive and passive, tyrant and weakling, usurper and manipulator. We can see these polarities at work across civilization—too often in horrifying and death-delivering ways.

If, on the other hand, we embrace the Call, we make the conscious choice to move out of where we are, TO CROSS THE FIRST THRESHOLD. *Chapter Five* swings us into departing. We know we can no longer be satisfied with where we've been; at the same time we're not clear how to get to where we're being Called to go. This liminal, in-between state proves to be a highly creative space. It's a state of mind that hangs with us the entire journey, effectively opening us to see things differently as MultiEarth thinking TESTS us and ENEMIES of greater consciousness rise to stop us.

An example of seeing differently happens in *Chapter Six*, on Earth's insurgency against civilization's abuses of her. Instead of seeing Earth's ongoing insurgency primarily as wild forces we need to control, we are able to see them also as forces that reshape us to be people ready for OneEarth thought and action. The ecological crises stressing Earth get us thinking in geological time, not just civilization's rapid time. Earth is helping move us along in rediscovering our interconnectedness to all things.

One of the major graces that happen on the heroic journey is that ALLIES and guides appear unexpectedly. Because MultiEarth civilization does not think of First Peoples as guides for living today, *Chapter Seven* does the unexpected and presents First Peoples as guides who know how to live with Earth-size consciousness. The traditional ways of thought and practice followed by many First Peoples today have survived MultiEarth's onslaught. Their traditions provide an unbroken connection with how our species lived long before the Civilization Project became an upstart aberration, beginning about 12,000 years ago. They provide strong guidance for the knowledge, attitudes, and capacities that all humanity needs in order to live in unity with Earth and her living community.

Chapter Eight brings to us two guides, one with a map of personal and collective consciousness, the other with a map of the topographies of greater consciousness that are the destination of our heroic journey. The first guide, Carl Jung (1875–1961), gives us the essential information on how to move beyond the ego consciousness that has shaped civilization. Jung recognized that we have, not one, but two centers of identity, the ego and the Self. The Self has enormous capacities for living beyond anything the ego can muster. It connects us with the pulse of Earth and makes objectives of the heroic journey possible. The second guide, David Korten, provides a map with five topographies of consciousness. The smaller topographies, Magical and Imperial, produce MultiEarth civilization. The largest topographies, Cultural and Spiritual, produce OneEarth community. The middle topography, Socialized, produces a consciousness that sways toward lesser or greater topographies depending on which is most prominent. This map shows us where we are and where the heroic journey takes us.

The heroic journey *From Egos to Eden* intends nothing less than that we become *new human beings. Chapter Nine* describes rewilding, an essential process in remaking our humanness so that we heal from civilization's dehumanization and become capable of participating fully in Earth's diverse community of life. Rewilding puts us into a different relationship with wildness. Instead of civilizing the Wild, we let the Wild humanize us. Rewilding heals us of the great wound of our disconnection from Nature, a wound that has turned us into civilizers and tamers of Nature instead of lovers and tenders.

Rewilding contributes greatly to our abilities to go into ego's and civilization's underworld where the heroic journey takes us in *Chapter Ten*. The underworld, or unconscious—the INNERMOST CAVE—contains all that our ego and civilization has not wanted or has ignored for one reason or another. So the underworld frightens both the lone ego and the collective egos that create MultiEarth civilization. Going into the underworld involves a death of ego as the center of our identity. We undergo THE SUPREME ORDEAL of metamorphosis. Thereafter, we live RESURRECTED, more from the center of Self, less with ego in charge. This metamorphosis of becoming new humans is the TREASURE of the heroic journey. By it we discover our capacities to live in the topography of Spiritual Consciousness. We are able to join in a renaissance of interdependent OneEarth living that was impossible before our heroic journey.

The more we behave as new humans the more we bring back from the heroic journey. We are able to face what many don't even want to think about: MultiEarth civilization has begun breaking down in apocalyptic fashion. *Chapter Eleven* argues why "apocalyptic" describes our century accurately. Apocalyptic eyes dare to look at catastrophe, and apocalyptic speech can describe it more accurately than most. With a catastrophic temperature rise beyond two degrees Celsius likely, we need to see daringly, and describe accurately, what is happening: nothing less than the breakdown of civilization *and* the breakthrough to what comes next. New humans recognize how Earth is deconstructing MultiEarth civilization and evolving a new Creation. Imagination sees the apocalyptic breakthrough that egos and civilization don't.

In *Chapter Twelve* we arrive home. As the heroic journey concludes, "home" means living in the topography of Spiritual Consciousness. So even if we RETURN to the same physical geography, nothing is as it was before. Everything is new. British poet T.S. Eliot (1888–1965) wrote about such consciousness change in a most memorable way in "Little Gidding," the last of his "Four Quartets" (1945):

> We shall not cease from exploration
> And the end of all our exploring
> Will be to arrive where we started
> And know the place for the first time.

Living in Spiritual Consciousness is an achievement and a gift which empowers us even as the unraveling of civilization leaves none of us untouched. We count on our imaginations to continue connecting us with symbols and myths that renew the enchant-ment and substance of Spiritual Consciousness. We count on our reason to chime in with new ways of thinking. Our future is with Earth. Living in Spiritual Consciousness makes possible the Eden that MultiEarth civilization cannot achieve.

Lee Van Ham
February 2016
Spring Valley, California

SECTION ONE

Changing How We Tell the Eden Myth

Vigorous as is my intention to move on down the road to OneEarth living, challenging questions still pester me: Do I have the consciousness necessary for consistency in such living? Is my consciousness honed in on Earth-size thinking? Is the kind of thinking I'm doing the "substantially different kind of thinking" that Einstein said was necessary in order for us to solve the problems created by the kind of thinking civilization has been doing so far? Where in my life am I choosing convenience and security over a shift to greater consciousness? Am I embracing the consciousness-changers that take me further into OneEarth living even when they disturb my comfort zone?

Such questions hovered nearby as I began this book on moving into greater consciousness. I want to live with greater consciousness, but I also feel anxious about doing so. Greater consciousness inevitably carries responsibilities that lesser consciousness does not.

This first section describes two major frames for the heroic journey described in subsequent chapters: (1) Chapter One, reconstructs a myth that, when lived, brings the changes we need, and, (2) Chapter Two, elucidates our Great Work.

I've come to recognize that we all live by myths (stories) that direct our lives whether we consciously choose them or not. I also believe we can do a much better job of helping one another connect with our Great Work as a species. We've substituted an excessive amount of energy on lesser works that are focused in the values of the Civilization Project. More reward happens when we get involved in the Great Work of keeping Earth livable. I see it as our purpose in Earth's creational, evolutionary processes.

Just What Is the Eden Myth?

Eden is not a utopia lost. It is not a Garden of magical thinking or innocence. It is an evolved, healthy ecosphere that is alive in our conscious mind, and lives even more strongly in the regions of our unconscious. It exists mythologically to guide and shape OneEarth living. In various forms, it may exist biologically and ecologically.

Earth appears intentionally bent on evolving it. We can inhabit it, but only if we have conversations with ourselves and others that frighten the bejesus out of our egos. Only by centering who we are around the larger core of our Self, not our ego, are we able to inhabit Eden. Its bio-systems, deeply real, transcend what our civilization has delivered, or can deliver. Civilization's orientation toward rational proof and thought, helpful as they are, cannot deliver Eden. But as we move beyond rational understandings and embrace the fullness of Earth's ways, we also use our fuller capacities as humans, including employing myth, symbol, and imagination. We then are not only able to live in Eden, we insist on it.

But even as I say this, I do not mean to shrink Eden to historical size. As soon as we name a place "Eden," Eden will be somewhere else. It remains beyond our control, beyond what we can fully embody. It is material and mystery. The heroic journey on which this book takes us increases our capacities to move Eden out of the unconscious and express it in our lives. But Eden is ever developing new potentials in our unconscious minds.

For readers who'd like to see an account of the Eden myth as found in Genesis 2:5–3:24, the following is the version given in the New Revised Standard translation of the Bible.

> In the day that the Lord God made the earth and the heavens, when no plant of the field was yet in the earth and no herb of the field had yet sprung up—for the Lord God had not caused it to rain upon the earth, and there was no one to till the ground; but a stream would rise from the earth, and water the whole face of the ground—then the Lord God formed man from the dust of the ground, and breathed into his nostrils the breath of life; and the man became a living being. And the Lord God planted a garden in Eden, in the east; and there he put the man whom he had formed. Out of the ground the Lord God made to grow every tree that is pleasant to the sight and good for food, the tree of life also

in the midst of the garden, and the tree of the knowledge of good and evil.

A river flows out of Eden to water the garden, and from there it divides and becomes four branches. The name of the first is Pishon; it is the one that flows around the whole land of Havilah, where there is gold; and the gold of that land is good; bdellium and onyx stone are there. The name of the second river is Gihon; it is the one that flows around the whole land of Cush. The name of the third river is Tigris, which flows east of Assyria. And the fourth river is the Euphrates.

The Lord God took the man and put him in the garden of Eden to till it and keep it. And the Lord God commanded the man, "You may freely eat of every tree of the garden; but of the tree of the knowledge of good and evil you shall not eat, for in the day that you eat of it you shall die."

Then the Lord God said, "It is not good that the man should be alone; I will make him a helper as his partner." So out of the ground the Lord God formed every animal of the field and every bird of the air, and brought them to the man to see what he would call them; and whatever the man called every living creature, that was its name. The man gave names to all cattle, and to the birds of the air, and to every animal of the field; but for the man there was not found a helper as his partner. So the Lord God caused a deep sleep to fall upon the man, and he slept; then he took one of his ribs and closed up its place with flesh. And the rib that the Lord God had taken from the man he made into a woman and brought her to the man. Then the man said,

"This at last is bone of my bones
        and flesh of my flesh;
this one shall be called Woman,
        for out of Man this one was taken."

Therefore a man leaves his father and his mother and clings to his wife, and they become one flesh. And the man and his wife were both naked, and were not ashamed.

Now the serpent was more crafty than any other wild animal that the Lord God had made. He said to the woman, "Did God say, 'You shall not eat from any tree in the garden'?" The woman said to the serpent, "We may eat of the fruit of the trees in the garden; but God said, 'You shall not eat of the fruit of the tree that is in the middle of the garden, nor shall you touch it, or you shall die.'" But the serpent said to the woman, "You will not die; for God knows that when you eat of it your eyes will be opened, and you will be like God, knowing good and evil." So when the woman saw that the tree was good for food, and that it was a delight to the eyes, and that the tree was to be desired to make one wise, she took of its fruit and ate; and she also gave some to her husband, who was with her, and he ate. Then the eyes of both were opened, and they knew that they were naked; and they sewed fig leaves together and made loincloths for themselves.

They heard the sound of the Lord God walking in the garden at the time of the evening breeze, and the man and his wife hid themselves from the presence of the Lord God among the trees of the garden. But the Lord God called to the man, and said to him, "Where are you?" He said, "I heard the sound of you in the garden, and I was afraid, because I was naked; and I hid myself." He said, "Who told you that you were naked? Have you eaten from the tree of which I commanded you not to eat?" The man said, "The woman whom you gave to be with me, she gave me fruit from the tree, and I ate." Then the Lord God said to the woman, "What is this that you have done?" The woman said, "The serpent tricked me, and I ate."

The Lord God said to the serpent,

"Because you have done this,
    cursed are you among all animals
    and among all wild creatures;
upon your belly you shall go,
    and dust you shall eat
    all the days of your life.
I will put enmity between you and the woman,
    and between your offspring and hers;
he will strike your head,
    and you will strike his heel."
To the woman he said,
"I will greatly increase your pangs in childbearing;
    in pain you shall bring forth children,
yet your desire shall be for your husband,
    and he shall rule over you."
And to the man he said,
"Because you have listened to the voice of your
wife,
    and have eaten of the tree
about which I commanded you,
    'You shall not eat of it,'
cursed is the ground because of you;
    in toil you shall eat of it all the days of
your life;
thorns and thistles it shall bring forth for you;
    and you shall eat the plants of the field.
By the sweat of your face
    you shall eat bread
until you return to the ground,
    for out of it you were taken;
you are dust,
    and to dust you shall return."

The man named his wife Eve, because she was the mother of all living. And the Lord God made garments of skins for the man and for his wife, and clothed them.

Then the Lord God said, "See, the man has become like one of us, knowing good and evil; and now, he might reach out his hand and take also from the tree of life, and eat, and live forever"—therefore the Lord God sent him forth from the garden of Eden, to till the ground from which he was taken. He drove out the man; and at the east of the garden of Eden he placed the cherubim, and a sword flaming and turning to guard the way to the tree of life.

CHAPTER ONE

Eden's Transforming Power—Lost and Regained

And YHWH God planted a garden in Eden.   —Genesis 2:8

The historical mission of our time is to reinvent the human—at the species level, with critical reflection, within the community of life-systems, in a time-developmental context, by means of a story and a shared dream experience.[3]   —Thomas Berry, *The Great Work*

The changes Earth is making in this 21st century exceed anything we've known in 12,000 years. The ecological crises she's undergoing mean that by 2100 CE she will no longer be home for millions of species. They will have left us. "Gone extinct," as we say. And our species is the primary reason. Massive species extinction is, of course, just one of the events in the ecological upheaval underway on our planet. The destabilizing of our planet is greater than at anytime since civilization began around 10,000 BCE.

What will life be like on our planet in ten, twenty, or fifty years? That's what scientists are trying to project, but the factors of change are complex and defy precise projections. We know that the big changes Earth is making require us to resize our lives and societies from supersize (or what I call MultiEarth) to Earth-size just to keep Earth livable. And that requires us to make a heroic journey to discover capacities of thinking, imagination, and being that civilization has not yet evoked from us. The journey heads us toward reinventing who we are as humans—most especially, becoming able to live in larger topographies of consciousness than the ones that have gotten us into the crises which now threaten us. In these new topographies, capacities in our species that civilization has underplayed or suppressed in its 12,000-year story will become primary and necessary.

Deep within us lives a story that civilization has suppressed, but which has the power to help us on this journey. It urges us to say "Yes!" to Earth's Call. It's a story about living in a Garden—a Garden that lives in our souls as a deep structure and strong potential. The Jewish storytellers called it Eden, meaning "delight, well-watered, and plain." Eden lives in us as an image of a highly livable Earth, a planet with which to be delighted. Much more than an ancient story, Eden has the voltage we need for our heroic journey in the 21st century to keep Earth livable. Eden is numinous—an irrepressible story that helps us know how to live as part of Earth's rich community of life. It's about greater consciousness—a story that unfolds in a topography of larger consciousness than what civilization has yet achieved.

But for many, Eden is a story of human failure, not aspiration. That's why we need to correct how we tell Eden. This great story needs to be set free from its affiliation with an ancient human "Fall," or from an "original sin" so great that we can't recover from it. If we can shed that way of talking about the Garden, then, we won't ignore the images that rise from our souls—images that show us how to fit inside of Earth's capacities as she spins toward her next geological epoch. Before this century is complete we can give a contemporary answer to a question that civilization has been unable to answer: *Can Earth be as whole and livable as Eden?*

From Literal Tale to Mythic Power

From childhood, I heard the story of the Garden of Eden as a literal tale about the first people on the planet. It made sense to me.

Children are, after all, literal, magical thinkers. When my earlier teachers presented Eden in just that way, I was in. Eden was a lush, pristine garden, a beautiful spot where a primitive woman and man lived. And, oh yes, they were naked—a curious detail to even young ears. God joined them every morning for walks among thriving plants and animals, a moist rainforest flush with species. All was quite wonderful until one day, a serpent started talking to the couple. At that point, of course, the story goes bad. My attitude toward snakes went along with it.

But not far into my elementary school years, questions began to arise. I asked my father, "Dad, who did Cain marry?" Dad smiled as he replied, "His sister, I guess. There wasn't anyone else." Later, as an adult, a seven-year-old girl asked me a similar question, "Who took care of Adam and Eve when they were little?" These are sensible questions to ask if Eden provides a literal history. After all, guys don't marry their sisters and people don't just appear as full-grown adults.

Like so many, Dad thought of Eden as the history of the first humans. Such an understanding is a logical step in the development of a child, right along with Santa Claus and other literal, historical understandings of mythology. But there comes a day when we begin to understand how good myths can't be held by history; they convey truth bigger than history.

To be clear, as I use the word in this book, "myth" is a kind of literature that carries truth bigger than what can be conveyed in historical narratives and scientific facts alone. As such, this usage is the opposite of another way we use "myth" in common speech, like when we say, "Oh, that's just a myth," meaning it's not true at all. In what follows, you will see that by calling Eden a myth, I am recognizing that it was intended to empower people with living, transformative truth that is more powerful than anything history can convey.

So it is that as literal thinking of early childhood changes to mythic truth, new ways of seeing and thinking flood our later childhood, teen, and early adult years. We graduate to new understandings of Santa, for example, and develop critical, symbolic thinking that replaces our earlier magical, literal patterns of thought. Oddly, many of us do not update how we understand Eden. It's more likely just to fall from relevance and become "just a story." (Not that I don't at times lapse into seeking childlike magical solutions to complex issues or try to make my way of seeing a situation *THE* way—literally.)

Shaking off the literal, historical version of Eden came slowly for me. Closely associated with that version was an emphasis that Eve and Adam failed an individual test of loyalty. The story revolved around their disobedience: the couple disobeyed God's instructions. There were simple do's and don'ts about which fruit they could eat and, most importantly, the one (the only one) which they were not supposed to eat. The guidelines themselves seemed lenient enough, but the consequence of disobeying them seemed extreme. It was death. Even so, given the teeming abundance available to them, avoiding one tree in the middle of the garden? Pretty easy. Or so it seemed to me as I heard the story. The simplicity only intensified how unnecessary the disobedience seemed to me.

As the story goes, however, the whole order of things got questioned by the serpent, who the myth calls the most subtle of creatures. After making Eve's acquaintance, the serpent merely asked her to look at the pleasantness of the fruit of the forbidden tree, assuring her that despite God's forecast of her death, if she tasted it, her eyes would be open. So she did, and sure enough, her eyes were still open. Then she offered some to Adam. He sampled it as well. Next thing you know they hear leaves rustling. God is walking in the garden, coming for their daily walk together. God calls out, "Adam, where are you?"

The couple felt ashamed. They quickly made a covering of fig leaves and hid from God. But God found them, discerned the truth of what had happened, and expelled them from Eden. Just like that! But it didn't end there. At least not according to a version endlessly repeated over centuries in one of Western civilization's most widely told stories. That version holds that their disobedience passed on to each of us. Like a congenital illness, that sin was passed along generation after generation. The consequences keep us living outside of Eden. Only divine intervention can save us now from our personal, psychological, and spiritual failure.

Popular as that version of the story has been, I've come to see that it fails the crucial test of conveying what its original, Jewish storytellers really intended. They intended Eden to be an uplifting myth with transcending, transforming power. It was an antidote to all the devastation overwhelming them and their people at that time. Eden was a mythic story that brought strength amid their trauma and gave meaning to their humiliation and suffering. The Jews had been torn from their Judean homes by Babylonian soldiers after a long conflict. They were now refugees in a strange land. They were utterly dispirited as they worked to restructure their lives in the foreign empire of Babylon, 6th century BCE. From that abyss, the myth of Eden emerged.[4] Daily, they were exposed to Babylon's culture of domination and, even worse, to versions of a national story that said, "Babylon rules by the desire and design of the deities!" As much as they hated it, the Jews came to recognize a disturbing fact: the Babylonian story was merely a different version of the same imperial story they'd been telling and living back in Jerusalem and Judea. That story had failed them. Why was it working for the Babylonians? Or was it?

For most of my life, I haven't really known quite where or how the Eden story originated. Even when I had stopped thinking of it as history, I had feared that calling Eden a myth would diminish its value. That hesitancy disappeared the more I came to appreciate what myth is, how it gives meaning to cultures and persons, and how it has the power to convey truth too big for history to hold. Once I understood myth in general, and came to know that Eden, in particular, originated as a myth in the abyss of 6th century BC. Babylon, I began to see what a great mistake we make when we reduce the epic-size myth of Eden to a historical or quasi-historical tale.

What a wicked irony that the rich mythology of Eden has been used in the Western world to bring religious sanction to MultiEarth thinking and civilization, whereas the original tellers of the Eden myth used it to challenge the same! So great has been this inverted misuse of the Eden story that overstating its consequences may be impossible.

Elaine Pagels, Princeton University professor known for her work in Early Christianity, goes into how Eden, in a version eloquently expressed by Augustine (354–430), has influenced Western civilization. Though Eden's influence, positive and negative, predates the Roman Empire (27 BCE to 476 CE), Pagels, in her book, *Adam, Eve, and the Serpent*, explains how Eden's influence manifested negatively towards the end of that empire. Speaking of the influence of Augustine, the bishop of Hippo in North Africa, Pagels writes:

> From the fifth century on, Augustine's pessimistic views of sexuality, politics, and human nature would become the dominant influence on western Christianity, both Catholic and Protestant, and color all western culture, Christian or not, ever since. Thus Adam, Eve, and the serpent—our ancestral story—would continue, often in some version of its Augustinian form, to affect our lives to the present day.[5]

At this minute, you and I are living some version of Eden. It may be a version that guides healthy OneEarth choices or it may be a counter version that's holding us in the unsustainable MultiEarth patterns spread throughout Western civilization. We may not know it yet, but we *can choose* which version of Eden's mythic powers we want to influence us. Augustine's version of the Eden myth maintains our captivity to empire and the MultiEarth paradigm. Loving Earth and all Creation today involves us in recovering the power of the Eden myth so that we can be released from captivity to MultiEarth civilization as the Jews were in Babylon. For me, **the recovery of Eden's power begins by exposing ourselves to the charge Eden held among its original tellers.**

The Myth-Generating Abyss of Babylon

The decimation of Jerusalem by the Babylon Empire in 587 BCE, was preceded by more than a decade of domination by Babylon over Judean politics and economics. Despite their weak leadership and widespread economic dysfunction, the Jews wore down the patience of Babylon's greater power with fierce nationalism and rebelliousness to foreign control. The end came for Jerusalem via a 30-month siege. When the Babylonian army finally entered the city, they completely plundered it. The valued treasures of the Temple were taken, deeply violating the sensibilities of people and the traditions associated with that hallowed place. The people, terrorized and humiliated, were sucked down into collective despair. Under the direction of the hostile Babylonian army, 10,000 or more Judeans were forcibly deported, traveling a circuitous land route to Babylon. It was the elite, privileged, well-positioned, and educated who were rounded up and relocated to Babylon. Only the underclass peoples were left behind.

Once in Babylon, the Jews grieved their faraway homeland and the way of life they left behind. In Jerusalem, they had felt exceptional, in large part because they believed their deity, YHWH, would protect them. Had not YHWH inhabited their Temple, now destroyed? They had thought their capitol city and surrounding lands were holy to YHWH. Yet now, all lay in desolation. The gods of the Babylonians had triumphed.

But as they settled near the Euphrates River in Babylon, the Jews began to rehabilitate their understanding of who they were in the world. They reviewed the generations they'd invested in Judea. They reassessed their beliefs which considered their land and capital city a protectorate of YHWH. Their strongest emperor, Solomon, had enslaved many to build that glorious Temple which they had believed YHWH inhabited in special ways. But invoking YHWH hadn't given them the insurance they thought it did when Babylon came up against them. What they'd thought was beyond the reach of foes, the Babylonian army pillaged ruthlessly. The

Babylonians found nothing "sacred" in Solomon's Temple nor any sign of YHWH. The sacred items of worship were quickly turned into the booty of war.

How did things go so terribly wrong? Was YHWH not on their side after all? As they thought back over their story, they remembered that long ago they had been nomads and agrarian workers of the land, living in communities and villages. Over time, many of them had shifted to city-living, centralizing their work and industry. Their cities grew. Then, like the city-states around them, they anointed monarchs to unify them. They became a people with a king, temple, and capitol city. As they saw it, they'd made a lot of progress over those years and were proud of it. But now all those gains had been vaporized by a hostile empire's military. What had seemed so lasting had proved to be utterly ephemeral. Their former sense of identity was now lost; their purpose gone. The hard reality of the moment was that they were no more than captives in a culture with strange language, customs, songs, and stories.

In this psychological and spiritual abyss, they saw themselves in a mirror. It was an unexpected mirror provided by the Babylonian culture. As they heard the Babylonians tell their mythic stories of how their deities made them mighty and gave them the right to rule the world, they felt sickened by such bravado. But the Jews also recognized that the story they'd clung to in Jerusalem was, in fact, the same kind of story. Their version had different people, cities, lands, and concepts of "God," but it had created the same kind of empire. In the mirror of Babylon, they saw how an empire's "official story" gets created to justify the empire and those citizens it privileges. Enemy Babylon was becoming for them a thought-purifying, consciousness-evolving kiln. Inside this kiln, the Jews remembered that they'd left much more than Jerusalem; more importantly, *they'd left Creation*. They had disconnected themselves from the greatest life-shaping story of all. When they saw Babylon doing the very same thing, it shook them out of their collective cultural and religious daze. A substantially new way of thinking was being born within them. The real story of their origins was not about David and Solomon at all.

This eye-opening revelation while in the Babylonian abyss honed their minds and quickened their self-reflection: if the real story of their origins was not about the monarchies begun by David and Solomon, then what was it? where did they come from? who were they really? to whom and to where did they belong? As many of us discover, when we ask the right question, our answers become clearer. So it was that the Jews in Babylon began to search for origins more trustworthy than monarchies and empires. The search proved highly creative and fruitful. They evolved new stories of their beginnings and collected or adapted others. Most memorably for us in the 21st century, they told the Eden story and other episodes that were collected into their book of origins, "Genesis." They reassociated themselves with Creation, and relocated themselves within Nature's interdependence of all life. In so doing they reconnected with the most powerful worldview possible, one that is holistic in its interdependence of all things. One that is infused with a sense of the sacred. Why had they left it anyway? The answer came quickly. They had left it because they had felt that by doing so, they were improving their situation and they would gain more respect among the peoples of the world.

But now they realized how, in fact, their choices had narrowed their consciousness, not expanded it. They'd become intensely ego-centered; they had fixated on generating an imperial-oriented land "just like the others." By choosing to participate in civilization's "homogenized consciousness," they'd let the true and wild movement of divine Spirit get civilized right out of them. They had put a lot of faith in empire-minded David, Solomon, and their successors, but in the process they had lost the grander interdependence that thrives in the larger life of all Creation.

Their abyss experience uncovered springs of life for them, springs they'd forgotten about. Remembering them had taken their physical dislocation from the geography they held dear. Being disconnected from every symbol of identity and from every routine of familiarity, with all the psychic and spiritual pain that brought them, proved to be just the medicine needed to break through to remember the deeper and greater story of their origins than what they'd been living by. What they'd been living had turned to debris—the debris of their own civilization experiment.

They were not only Jews after all; more anciently, they were *Homo sapiens*. They proclaimed as much in Genesis as they daringly and excitedly proclaimed their origins to be in the creational order "way back in the beginning." And so, as the debris was cleared, new stories of the origins of all humanity gurgled up from the spring of their growing consciousness. They now had stories that preceded empires and could outlast any of them. They could see that their stories of "in the beginning," of Eden, and more, helped shape their identity in ways that went far beyond the Babylonian story of origins, called *Enuma Elish*. Whereas *Enuma Elish* told how violence between deities created the world, the Jews told the story of YHWH, who created the world without violence. The Jews rested their story on their belief that speech was more powerful than violence. So it is that in Genesis we read how YHWH spoke the world into being. With poetic repetition, YHWH says, "Let there be...." Each "Let there be" is followed by some creational activity such as the creation of light, sky, vegetation, birds, beasts, marine life, and more. Everything from light to humans came to be through joyful, nonviolent creativity. It's one way the Jewish myth of origins differs sharply from the stories of origins told by dominators.

Through the art of storytelling, and as the artists of this new consciousness, the Jews in Babylon protested Babylonian violence and imperial domination. In the writing of Genesis, the Jews also cleansed themselves from the imperial theology which they themselves had so recently embraced in Judea.

The processes that produced a new mythology of origins included, as I've said, serious self-analysis. They needed to acknowledge how they'd participated in what I call the MultiEarth worldview (see "Appendix" for a table contrasting the MultiEarth and OneEarth ways of thinking) in order to generate mythologies for greater, OneEarth living. They needed to recognize how they'd cut themselves off from the creational OneEarth way of thinking and how they'd forgotten Earth's self-regulating procedures. They realized that they'd been snookered into civilization's way of thinking. They'd fallen for patterns in which humans calculate benefits for themselves by imposing regulations and controls on Earth's systems. By joining in on the heady, egoistic goals of the "civilized" world, they'd lost their perspective on what truly improved life and what did not.

Through this collective self-analysis, they discovered that they'd drifted into huge illusions and how their own grandiosity had replaced Creation's grandeur. They, like so many during the Neolithic Revolution,[6] had not been discriminating enough about the long range implications of the new tools and technologies that comprised that revolution. Most importantly, which worldview did the innovations of the revolution serve? The MultiEarth way of thinking and living or the OneEarth ways?

By not using the two worldviews to assess the new developments, the Jews had adapted to and had adopted the innovations of the Neolithic Revolution just like others had. They had opted for the MultiEarth civilizing and taming of the land. It was an early form of non-sustainable farming; OneEarth agriculture by contrast tends and stewards wildness along with its production of food. They had become calculating humans. Ego-thinking came to be highly rewarded while the greater consciousness of soul-centered thinking was devalued. They had come to favor the efficiencies of uniformity. They had joined others in homogenizing diversity instead of preserving biodiversity. Preserving biodiversity maintains Earth's self-regulating systems that balance populations and habitats of all species, humans included. They had preferred policies that eased private ownership of land in lieu of those which assured the administration of Earth as a vast commons for use by many. They had come to love the concentration of wealth and power more than the distribution of both as practiced by Creation.

The Genesis storytellers recognized how opting for MultiEarth ways had forced them out of OneEarth Eden. With the telling of the Eden story, and claiming it as an essential part of their story of origins, the Jews owned their responsibility for having yielded to the enticements of civilization with its many inherent MultiEarth ramifications. They did so through the characters of Eve and Adam. In those symbolic figures, they acknowledged that they had said "yes" to the enticements. They admitted that the MultiEarth ways had indeed looked good to them, like the fruit growing on the tree of the knowledge of good and evil. The advances during the Neolithic Age, followed by the advances of the Bronze Age, and then the Iron Age (beginning 1300 BCE), had looked to them like highly desirable fruit. They'd bitten into it. Only later would they discover that they did not have the full knowledge of good and evil after all. Their knowledge was a facsimile based on illusion.

Babylon humbled them out of their arrogance. In the larger consciousness they moved into while in that abyss, they appreciated anew that the duality of good and evil was filled with entangling subtleties beyond what their ego consciousness alone could master. A greater consciousness, one able to see the wholeness beyond dualistic divisions, was needed. In the pain of Babylon, the Jews saw how much consciousness mattered. Greater consciousness could hold dualisms in constant creative tension; lesser consciousness, on the other hand, was prone to make ethical choices in which good resided on one side and evil on the other. Ego consciousness simply lacks the ethical muscle to make choices that consistently transcend the dualistic thinking prevalent in MultiEarth thought and practice. Living in Eden's OneEarth ways requires the capacities of a greater consciousness that egos fear, but can, as the following chapters show, come to partner with.

This lack of ethical muscle in ego consciousness is portrayed so clearly when Eve and Adam encounter the Serpent. As the story goes, the Serpent was the most cunning of all the wild creatures—an important reason for picking it for its role in the story. Eve and Adam were not, after all, tricked by obvious enticements that ego consciousness could sort out, but by more subtle ones. When myths present tricky situations like this they often do so with the help of characters perceived to be tricksters—characters who do lots of good but may disregard conventions of culture and relationships. Tricksters excel in moving a story beyond the *status quo* or the general order of things. The Serpent has long appeared as this kind of character in myths because it embodies the kind of opposites that facilitate thinking differently about established norms—even favoring what contradicts them. It was well-noted, for example, that snakes shed their smaller skin, only to emerge with a larger and healthier one. Also, because the eyes of snakes are ever open, waking or sleeping, they suggest being highly conscious—seeing at all times. Modern medicine introduced another opposite: snake venom can bring death, but it is also used in serums of healing. Traits such as these made the Serpent a great fit for Eden's mythmakers.

In accord with its cunning, Eden's special Serpent suggested to Eve and Adam that he was not contradicting the creational order, but adding subtle nuances to the divine coherence of OneEarth ways. He gave voice to that part in all of us which argues our egos into believing they can do more than they can. He held that our ego consciousness could do as much as or more than that greater center of identity in each of us, the Self (see Chapters Three and Eight where I develop the roles of ego and Self in detail). The Serpent spoke of MultiEarth possibilities that would improve Eden, all it took was to change one rule.

As the Genesis storytellers reviewed their origins, they realized, "That's the voice that took us away from the Creation-based way of thinking and living we'd been doing." It was the voice that had spoken convincingly throughout Neolithic times, advancing civilization and turning OneEarth living into an act of resistance to the MultiEarth ways taking over.

So it was that the time in Babylon became a time of healing for the Jewish consciousness. It provided a unique, though unwelcome space in which to shed their smaller consciousness of being people defined by monarchies, temple, city, and land that were exceptionally favored by YHWH. They emerged with a larger consciousness capable of Earth-size thinking and living. In so doing, the Jews of that moment in history rejected the primacy of the human civilization story that continues today, and replaced it with the continuing story of Earth, mythologized in the opening narratives of Genesis. Such consciousness has not, as we can see from history, continued as the primary consciousness of Jews or others. Nonetheless, the historical record should not take our eye off the prize, namely, the enlightened consciousness of all who choose mythologies of OneEarth Creation instead of mythologies of MultiEarth civilization.

How Civilization Took Away Eden's Power

Had the myth of Eden spread out from Babylon, loaded with the full charge it contained when those original Jewish storytellers first wrote it, the MultiEarth Civilization Project we see today would have been challenged at every step by large sectors of humanity, regardless of their religion. Eden would have been told and retold across diverse cultures. It would have instilled the OneEarth way of thinking deeply enough to influence thousands of decisions. But this was not to be. Though Jews, Christians, and Muslims have continued to use the story, they've lost or misunderstood its full significance. Eden has instead been demythologized. Shorn of its layers of mythology, the Eden story does not enter into us with that numinous charge able to transform our MultiEarth worldview, or transcend the unsustainable patterns of ego-centered civilization.

If we don't hear the Eden story in the context of our own version of the Babylonian abyss, we miss that the story radically shuns empire in favor of Creation. Or take away its unabashed preference for the OneEarth paradigm, and Eden shrinks from its systemic rejection of MultiEarth thinking to become an ancient, personal ethics story about falling into sin. Once we reduce Eden from its mythic size, and strip it of its social, economic, political, and cultural meaning, it comes to us as a much narrower, greatly weakened psychological and spiritual tale. Instead of being a mythic-poetic rendition of the beginnings of heaven and earth, providing the story that advocates for an overall paradigm of evolutionary Creation, it gets down-sized to speaking of one species, and its faulty morality.

Even among many well-educated religious leaders, Eden has lost its power to shape and transform systems. As mentioned above, most Christian theologians, at least as far back as Augustine, 354–430 CE, have joined in telling the stripped down version. Even the personal, spiritual meaning that remains has been distorted. Our human species comes out the worse for it, emerging as failed, flawed persons. The myth has been told as teaching that what happened in the Garden (disobeying YHWH by eating fruit from the forbidden tree and the consequences of doing so) was passed on, so that Eve's and Adam's choices became part of a psycho-spiritual birth defect in every human.

Because Christianity has had such a formative influence on Western civilization, and because the reach of that civilization's political and economic superpowers during the past two millennia has been global, the use of the Eden myth as a story that downgrades all humanity into sinful creatures has had an extraordinary impact on how our capacities as humans are understood worldwide. For example, it is common to hear in discussions of economics that greed is so deeply ingrained in humans that it is "natural" for us to corrupt any economic model we use. When such a view gets affirmed with little discussion, it becomes futile to suggest that we can care for the commons through right relationships defined by justice, love, and sharing. "Dream on," we're likely to be told. "Adam and Eve made that impossible." Proponents of various economic models are left to argue whether greed can be controlled best through competitive markets or government controls. Those favoring the capitalist model like to think of the market as a strong and dynamic enough force to hold greed in check through the market's inherent or structured competitions. The proponents of socialism, however, claim that the market is inadequate, especially when dominated by mega-corporations oriented toward unlimited growth and maximum profit. Therefore, they argue, governments need to act as a counter balance and use their power to control greed. Both see their model as the best we can do given our fallen species. Both accept the view of human nature embodied in the personal, psychological, historical meaning of the watered-down version of Eden whether or not they attribute their point of view to the mythology underlying their thinking. Throughout civilization, how we view the capacities of our species determines which economic models we embrace and which ones get batted aside as impossible.

The Roman Empire, 27 BCE to 476 CE, provides a historical example of Eden's tamed version at work. Rome's dominating, modernizing impulses brought the MultiEarth style of urban and industrial living to a new scale around the Mediterranean world. Those imposing Rome's imperial worldview of militarized peace through strength, the *Pax Romana*, did not, of course, have the original context of the Eden myth in their minds or they would have collaborated in structuring a far different world around them.

However, Jesus, a Jew and a contemporary of the *Pax Romana*, got the Eden story right. Though he lived immersed in the first century CE version of the *Pax Romana*, Jesus countered it by living and teaching from an Earth-size consciousness. He claimed that Creation empowered us far more than empires, temples, and civilization could. Many resonated with his appeal to transplant society and life into a bigger consciousness than either Rome or temple religion offered. The temple, though run by Jews, was ever in cahoots with empire. In contrast to their limited ego consciousness, Jesus urged his followers to be rooted in Creation and connect with Earth and her community of life. How connected? Like his own "oneness with YHWH" is the norm he suggested. Living in that greater consciousness, Jesus healed many diseases of body and mind that are symptomatic of the physical and emotional strain we experience when alienated from Creation's community of life. He shifted people out of ego insecurities and into a new form of security and solidarity based on the sharing and cooperation exhibited throughout Creation.

After just a few years of Jesus' Earth-size life and message, the imperial powers of Rome, as well as those running the Jerusalem temple, had been pushed to the limits of what their ego consciousness could tolerate. Given that capital punishment delivered by public crucifixion was Rome's way to handle disrupters of the *Pax Romana*, Jesus was put on a cross. Thereafter, his followers were intermittently and unevenly repressed until around 300 CE, when the empire did a 180 degree turn. It happened when a new emperor, Constantine, had no small need to unite his imperial conquests under one banner. In a decisive military victory, he credited divine intervention. Whether or not he had a vision of a Christian symbol (the Greek letters Chi Rho that he and his men drew on their weapons) is disputed to this day. In truth, he may actually have credited one of the imperial deities. What is not disputed, however, is that Christians had enough popularity amongst the people to get his attention. Through the Edict of Milan in 313 CE, Constantine ended repression of Christians and opened the way for its rapid spread. The sudden change resulted in grave dilution of whatever Earth-centered consciousness still survived in Christianity. Imperial-centered versions of the faith took over (significant versions of which continue to this day). Its texts and theology were interpreted to better accommodate Christianity to empire living. The same thinking that shaped MultiEarth civilization penetrated Christian thought and practice. Without being conscious of doing so, Christians living amid imperial thought and practice became far more intent on doing what fit with civilization's MultiEarth paradigm than pursuing the resistance engendered by Jesus' counter-paradigm. As they shifted, they took Eden with them.

Eden's Power Reduced to a
MultiEarth Morality Tale

Eden endured, of course, but more as a morality tale within MultiEarth civilization than as a myth liberating people and societies for OneEarth living. Like many myths, Eden's meanings and moral influence live in its many flexible layers. Some layers lend moral influence to a particular set of thoughts and practices even if other layers are ignored. This happened to Eden. The story readily lends itself to the three-part structure of a moral tale—(1) a taboo is stated, (2) a narrative tells of violating the taboo, and (3) a climax to the story enumerating consequences of violating the taboo. In the Garden, YHWH said clearly that eating fruit from the tree of the knowledge of good and evil was taboo. The story proceeds to tell us how Eve and Adam directly disobeyed that taboo. Then it details the dire consequences for such disobedience.

Morality tales resonate quickly with us because every day an onslaught of choices between good and evil come at us. Having to make these moral choices makes us wish we had greater knowledge of good and evil. The struggle within each of us to do good takes on great subtleties as evils hide inside the "sugar-coatings" of modern life: convenience, a nicer home, fashionable clothing, quick money, more influence, attracting the people we want as friends, greater prestige, cultural success, and more. More broadly, the word "spin" describes the highly developed form of intentionally sugar-coating courses of action that governments and militaries suspect will be met with popular resistance. Businesses and religions, along with all enterprises and philosophies, often seek the words that bring them greatest impact, rather than seeking to inform transparently and accurately. With these deceptive powers daily before us, from our personal lives to the marketplace and global relations, how can we not empathize with Eve and Adam?

In the MultiEarth worldview, we often hear our moral failures as humans clustered into what gets called "the human condition." Sometimes that condition is traced back to Eden. When this condition is given a historical origin in Eden, its weight increases to fate delivered upon us without our consent. Yet, we must live with its unending condemnation. No wonder it's often called "The Fall."

But the word "Fall" is nowhere used in the Eden story to describe what happened. Furthermore, "Fall" does not appear in any context within the entire Hebrew Bible. Only centuries later did it get used in conjunction with Eden, including a couple of references in one New Testament epistle, *The Epistle to the Romans.* Later on, many Christian interpreters became especially fond of the word.

But, given that "Fall" was not attached to the Eden myth until centuries after it was first told, we have plenty of reason not to use the idea of it in understanding Eden. The Fall effectively shifts emphasis *away* from our soul's inherent, creational drive to grow to the full powers of humanness available in the greater Self. As a process of our human development, it embodies divine action, human evolution, and Christ-consciousness. It, not the Fall, is the core of what it means to be human.

An important reason for why ideas of the Fall have so effectively pervaded civilization emerges when we see how well they have served imperial purposes. The influential Augustine (354–430 CE), the North African bishop in the Roman Empire's later years, is just one of many Christian leaders past and present who have been more inclined to defend the actions of Rome, the U.S., or other empires as preservers of civilized order, than to protest them as anti-Creation. Taking our clue from the Genesis storytellers in Babylon, Eden considers Rome and all other empires as Babylons. But Augustine, and many since, have not functioned with the Earth-size consciousness distinctive to Genesis. Instead, many gifted minds have worked with the theory of the Fall in ways that give empires divine sanction for anti-Creation views. Three such corollary views follow below:

1. elevating civilization's authorities;

2. believing that good can come through selective force and violence, including "just wars;" and

3. reducing the creational status of women.

1. Elevating civil(ization's) authorities—When told as a morality tale, the scale of disobedience in the Garden grows to where it forever prevents our souls from completing their full development. In this theory, only grace from the outside can unite us with God or bring wholeness to our lives. Such grace is not regarded as incarnate in the psyche even though the psyche has evolved via divinely attended creational, evolutionary processes. The spiritual teaching arising around this view is that God offers us the necessary grace, intervening in our sinful lives, which would otherwise remain separate from God and wholeness.

Churches and other religious institutions, along with their rituals and priesthood, have claimed for themselves the role as primary mediators of such grace, but they are not the only ones to do so. Authorities in the civilized world everywhere make similar claims, dispensing graces that sound less religious until we understand that states and economics operate as functional religion. Every leader in government and business proclaims to have the "solutions" for our current human condition. The messages of advertising are quick to point out our condition. They reinforce our feelings of inadequacy thousands of times a day, and tell us that they have just the grace we need. They entice us with products and programs we can buy—all designed to save us from ourselves and from the hardships of our condition. Their grace, too, comes from outside ourselves. The whole MultiEarth worldview is permeated with low views of human moral capacities and with redemptive solutions administered by certain people, institutions, or a transcendent God—but nearly always from outside ourselves.

Low views of humanness are a boon to empires and markets. When how we think about ourselves emphasizes original sin, a propensity to evil, and being basically flawed, our sense of personal and collective weakness makes us gullible to authority figures and their claims to divine origins for that authority. Disobedience to such authority carries consequences; abuse, for example, becomes deserved. How dangerous, then, for Eden to be told as a morality tale of human failure even though one of its layers of meaning speaks of the consequences of disobedience of YHWH. We need to consider carefully the significance of Eden for our view of human nature. If it primarily defines us trapped in original sin, we dangerously elevate civilization's authorities. We also repress the divine power at work in humans by which justice stirs in our souls and calls on us to resist authority wherever it expresses itself unjustly.

Views of human nature that don't use Fall-thinking proceed differently. Not that they minimize our capacity as humans to act diabolically in acts of horrific evil; or ignore the need for grace to enter our lives if we are to fulfill our evolutionary, creational purpose. But the emphasis is more on grace being awakened in the processes of the soul, in Earth's vast interdependent systems, and in sectors of OneEarth society. The divine is incarnated throughout humanity, Nature, and Earth. It is the opinion of the divine that humanness is a great habitat for its radically decentralized, non-authoritarian, and communal ways. Such views reflect the Eden myth more accurately and give impetus to OneEarth living.

2. Believing good can come through selective use of violence and force, including some wars—Another consequence of making the Fall the foundation of our human condition is the thinking that wrongs can be corrected through violence and force if it is selectively and justly carried out. In this line of thinking, it is argued that force becomes necessary because human nature will often do the right thing only if coerced. Whatever percentage of truth lives in this theory, civilization's authorities have expanded it to justify the large-scale use of force. Faith in redemptive violence has prevailed throughout the millennia of our MultiEarth civilization. This follows in the footsteps of the *Enuma Elish* myth of Babylon rather than the Creation myth of Genesis. In *Enuma Elish*, creation occurs from the violence of the gods. In Genesis, creation happens without any violence. But stripped of its power to transform human life and society, Eden becomes little better than another version of Babylon's *Enuma Elish*.

Augustine used ideas of redemptive violence to create his just war theory. It has allowed some hefty configurations of state violence to occur in the name of justice. He sanctioned many acts of the imperial authorities as "necessary" to maintain civilized order. His theological work has continued to be the foundation of today's debates of what makes a war just. Augustine's ideas continue to be used and misused by empires, nuances are created and debated in religious communities, and peace talks among nations continue to measure violence against justice and redemption.

Despite the justifications of force and war that continue, the state of civilization today, as in the past, offers plenty of cause for pause. The notion that violence has redemptive purposes has itself produced far more violence than peaceful coexistence. Civilization's track record shows that there is no "war to end all wars." Wherever the MultiEarth paradigm is affirmed as the system of belief, nations, corporations, and people justify violence in leadership with thoughts such as "We must control and dominate in order to lead." In this vein, everyone sees themselves as the good dominators who save themselves and their clients from the bad dominators. Such thinking has littered civilized history with wars and applied incalculable resources to technologies of destruction. Weapons industries have profited enormously, siphoning off from societies the innovation and resources that could otherwise serve the wellbeing of Earth. While claiming ourselves to be "civilized," our behaviors of savagery have exceeded that of all other species on Earth.

Force and violence, so often justified by seeing humans as fallen, has more often evoked the lower capacities in human nature than redeemed them. **The MultiEarth paradigm has re-narrated Eden as the story of the Fall instead of the myth affirming our capacities for OneEarth living.** To change course and evoke from one another the best we are capable of being, the Eden myth would help us greatly if we told it as its originators did. The enormous capacities we have for cooperation, sharing, awe, and love would not just be used in ethical admonitions or spiritual homilies, but be part of conversations among governments, nations, and businesses. Abuse in families and gun violence in society cannot abide without a strong belief in redemptive violence. By shifting our belief to Eden, conversations and actions function from a new and transforming framework.

3. Reducing the creational status of women—When thought of primarily as a morality story of the Fall of humanity, Eden places a great and unfair burden on women for leading the way into sin. Eve, after all, ate first, then offered the fruit to Adam. As a result, in the Fall theory Eve is regarded as morally inferior to Adam and a seductress of him, leading him to do evil. What a convenient interpretation for patriarchal civilization to take from this myth! The consequences of this radically patriarchal version of the Eden story have been horrific for the treatment of women globally while men continue to use the story to justify their elevated status.

The MultiEarth model for living has milked this definition of the relationship between men and women to its fullest yield. MultiEarth practices continue to be highly patriarchal though some corrections have been made. It is hard to see how the MultiEarth model will ever be able to correct fully this injustice given that domination, conquest, and competition figure so strongly in what it calls success. More likely, just relationships between male and female require a complete change in paradigm to OneEarth thinking where interrelatedness, cooperation, and sharing assure greatest wellbeing. Regaining Eden's original power as a transforming myth would put MultiEarth patriarchy into a tumble and bring healing to men and women.

Another consequence of downgrading Eve has been to denude Earth. Eve, the mythic mother of us all, and Earth, the primal mother of us all, have been treated similarly throughout MultiEarth's patriarchal history. Mother Earth remains valuable primarily for her *use* to us, not for her *being* with us and us with her. This despite that without her we have no being. Patriarchy and MultiEarth thinking continue to see Mother Earth as "it," not "us"—not as the amazing home of our natural cohabitation.

Because Augustine and other religious leaders did not pose the Creation myth as a protest to the ways of Rome's Empire, much of the political, social, and economic context of Genesis was lost. Augustine's astute mind, coupled with his influence as a bishop, galvanized the reduced meaning of Eden and sent it into future centuries as "universal truth." We'd have done better had we appreciated Augustine's views as his personal wrestling with this myth in light of his own life context, especially his unresolved moral guilt and concern for civil order in a weakening empire. But his views became "the Church's view" on many issues.

While quarreling with Augustine's views and their influence, we can also appreciate that he was early on the scene of how Church and Empire would interface. Christianity had been embraced by Rome's Empire barely a century before. Along with the benefits it brought to Christians and churches came the challenges of shifting from theologies of resistance to an oppressive Empire to theologies that could interface with a kinder Empire. Augustine, like many others then and now, struggled with whether, how, and when Christian scriptures and thought fit with empire.

To review the above for emphasis, it's important to appreciate that throughout Western civilization, religious communities have taught Augustine's version and meaning of Eden as core to the faith. Civil institutions, from schools to governments, have taught it as foundational to the best and most civil way of doing things. Both religious communities and civil institutions have done this using the MultiEarth paradigm as their basic way of thought and behavior. Lost was the Creation myth's paramount ability to shape life according to the creational, OneEarth paradigm. *Empire became the lenses through which to see Eden instead of Eden being the lenses through which to see empire.*

Lost completely has been Eden's ability to do the very thing it was created to do: to test civilization's developments from the Neolithic Revolution onward, accepting those innovations and technologies that were to scale with Earth-size living and rejecting the rest. Instead of being a grand myth able to challenge the existing myths of progress and power centralized in corporations, empires, or superpowers, Eden has been used to confirm them. Instead of being a consciousness-changer, Eden has served most often as a MultiEarth consciousness-confirmer. Instead of functioning as liberating mythology, Eden's greatest impact has been as moral tragedy.

Regaining Eden's Power to Transform Us

In the 21st century, most people who know the story of Eden continue to think of it as a story from the past, chronicling the human Fall into sin after briefly experiencing idyllic life. Eden has none of the numinous power of the 6th century BCE when it challenged civilization's pursuit of all things anti-OneEarth, and helped a group of people in despair be reborn to a powerful identity connected with Creation. *What happened in the 6th century BCE can happen again in our time.* We have the ability to retell Eden in its mythic explosiveness. It can be an essential story in the compelling mythology of who we really are: people with the capacities to grow Earth-size consciousness and live as OneEarthers. The myths of modern "Babylons" include the American Dream and the reign of a global capital economy. These myths have no more authority than did the ones proclaimed in ancient Babylon unless we give it to them. Our task is to follow the Jews in Babylon and reject such myths in favor of the Eden myth as they told it.

For Eden to have similar power today—the power to move humanity through a time of transformation beyond civilization to community of life—we must hold firmly in our minds the two paradigms that Eden contrasts: empire and Creation, or MultiEarth and OneEarth. Remember that the original Jewish storytellers were seeking an explanation for how humanity in general, and they in particular, had not been able to resist the great reshaping that the Neolithic Age onward had brought, nor channel its creativity for OneEarth living. With every decade, civilization-shaping had intensified, leading gradually to a new socio-political structure, that of empire. During those decades, agriculture adopted new stone and metal technologies that increased the scale of productivity. The more food available from the farmers, the more cities grew. Cities got stronger through concentrating power and wealth. Inequalities increased. Cultures of eco-regions that had focused on tending those eco-regions sustainably, gradually redirected themselves to serve the cities.

These decades of "progress" screeched to a halt for the Jews when Babylon entered their hallowed Jerusalem, ruthlessly pillaged it, and forced them on a long journey to the Tigris and Euphrates. It was the kind of life-interrupting horror that got them asking, "What got us to where we are?" What they'd thought was progress had turned futile, even fatal as a life-sustaining way of being.

They awakened to see how a paradigm that had been rejected was in fact the superior one. Creation-centered living was superior to empire-centered living. Eden got its power by juxtaposing these two paradigms. The Garden expresses the interconnection of species in a balanced life community; but Eve and Adam's interaction with the serpent expresses the disconnection from and unbalancing of that life community. The Garden is the paradigm of OneEarth living; the Eve-Adam-Serpent agreement is the paradigm of MultiEarth living. Throughout our lives we make many choices for one or the other. Always these choices have consequences.

In the Eden story, the consequences for choosing the MultiEarth paradigm are delivered by YHWH. The mistake in telling Eden as a story of the Fall and original sin is that these consequences are taken as a general sentence upon all humanity. But the original tellers of the story intended something quite different. They intended Eden to shine a bright, clarifying light into our choices so we can differentiate MultiEarth from OneEarth thinking. Sometimes the differences are subtle and not apparent to us. The curse Eden says YHWH delivered to Eve, Adam, and the serpent is not a moral pronouncement on all humanity, but a strong reminder of a whole matrix of consequences we set in motion every time we choose MultiEarth ways. In this way, the curse upsets the thinking that MultiEarth living is all about progress and convenience as it claims to be; the curse names many of the difficulties inherent in MultiEarth ways, difficulties that eventually overwhelm all involved.

The details of that curse that were already obvious to the Jews in Babylon in the 6th century BCE have only increased since. Every century shows new configurations of what happens when we compound choices made out of MultiEarth consciousness. As the Jewish storytellers saw it, it's not that the fruit of the tree is not delicious and beautiful, it's that its juiciness contains elements that later on sour and poison eco-regions we've come to count on for our lives. The fruit is not finally digestible by species, by eco-regions, or by Earth's life-systems. It destroys life.

Because Eve and Adam chose MultiEarth ways of thought and practice, they could not stay in Eden. They opted for patterns of thinking connected to civilization rather than Creation. Saying that they chose to eat of "the tree of the knowledge of good and evil" is the myth's way saying they chose the consciousness upon which civilization is based. It is a consciousness of dualisms. Civilization measures things in terms of this vs. that, bad vs. good, and other polarities; Eden's more expansive consciousness sees beyond the polarities of life and makes choices based on a larger whole within which polarities interrelate creatively. How we get to Eden-consciousness is a multi-phase process which this book describes as our heroic journey.

The consciousness chosen by Eve and Adam was not the consciousness awakening among the Jews in Babylon, and it need not describe the choices that prevail in our lives. Eden, when its power is regained, springs us free from such fatalistic understandings of what happened in the Garden and liberates us to move into greater

consciousness. Three types of experiences, as they repeat themselves in our lives, illustrate how the regained power of the Eden
myth can change us and our world each day. All three require us to
increase our awareness:

1. Become aware that greater consciousness requires disobeying lesser consciousness;
2. Become aware of who the Babylonians are today;
3. Become aware of Sacred Presence in all Creation.

**1. Become aware that greater consciousness requires disobey-
ing lesser consciousness**—We cannot cross into topographies of
greater Earth-size consciousness without violating some of the
rules of smaller consciousness. Unlike Eve and Adam who started
from OneEarth consciousness and moved to MultiEarth consciousness, we have been living immersed in MultiEarth consciousness
but need to move to OneEarth thought and practice. So we must
disobey the guides who taught us the rules of MultiEarth civilization. At times this will feel wrong; we may be called rebellious. But
it is wrong and rebellious only when measured by MultiEarth civilization's norms. Obeying OneEarth ways means disobeying many
MultiEarth ways.

Changing paradigms has many parallels to the normal maturing processes in our lives. For example, we can't mature in consciousness as adults by docile obedience to norms that guided us in
childhood. One day my pre-teen son, a devoted comic book reader
and collector at the time, said to me, "Dad, I think you'd like this
comic book." "Why?" I queried. "Because good and bad are mingled
in the same characters," he replied. His ethical views were developing. He was seeing how complex situations require flexibility
even as we struggle to maintain integrity. Simpler absolutes from
younger days no longer suffice. Similarly, we can't live with ecological assumptions that no longer fit how to live on our planet. We
need to become adult ecologically.

Though it can get dicey, when we transcend good-bad dualisms,
it's a sign we're operating in a larger topography of consciousness

where humility, awe, mystery, wonder, and love have to come through for us. I use the phrase "topographies of consciousness" rather than "stages" or "orders" of consciousness because it feels more organic to me, more like we are actually changing location to somewhere different in our internal geography. Changing consciousness is a trip! On the journey we adjust to new relationship patterns, roles, incomes, and ideas. Our bodies change. Spiritually we awaken to stimuli we hadn't even noticed before. We abandon earlier ways of thinking about God because they're too small; we find larger ones or skeptically wonder if such exist. In topographies of greater consciousness the "word of God" will sometimes contradict the "word of God" we heard in lesser consciousness. We come to truth and beauty differently in larger topographies of consciousness from smaller ones. Different parts of our psyches come alive; others quiet down. The parts that come alive sometimes live by different rules than the parts that had been louder. Meaning gets attached to experiences that once meant little. We often contradict our earlier selves when we roam greater topographies. It can be upsetting; it can be liberating. Some people won't understand us; others will be eager to accompany us. What was once either-or, may now be both-and. In larger topographies, love, justice, and mercy operate more from an integration of heart, gut, and mind. There's no universal formula; it's a messy meet-up with the unknown.

The Eden myth, framed in the large topographies of Creation, was not available to the Jews when their topography of consciousness was circumscribed by civilization's imperial thinking in Jerusalem. Supporting their monarchy and practicing temple religion kept them from hearing the Call to topographies of larger consciousness. Their consensus of what was true and good back in Jerusalem was exposed in Babylon. What they thought YHWH had sanctioned in their homeland, they now overthrew. They no longer believed that YHWH sided with temple and monarchs as they moved into their emerging, larger consciousness. They came to believe instead that YHWH was more interested in Creation-based living. In this way, their journey into the greater, creational topographies of consciousness necessitated disobeying what they thought YHWH had said to them in smaller consciousness.

Translating their experience into the situations and language of today, we must disobey the truths that implement MultiEarth's civilization, even the ones we've taken to be "of God," in order that we might obey the Divine voice that calls us to Earth-size thinking and living. This type of disobedience goes with a growing consciousness in which we form a new identity centered in both Creation and our greater Self. This is the Great Work we undertake in the following chapters—a Great Work of breaking away from superpower cultures as we develop the richness of creational cultures.

2. Become aware of who the Babylonians are today—Core to reclaiming Eden's power for today is to recognize who the modern Babylonians are. Once we've identified them, Eden can help us undercut the mythologies those Babylonians tell about themselves. In the long run, Babylonians do not stay in power because they have the mightiest military or most dominant economy. They retain power because enough people believe in their mythology. When enough of us move into greater consciousness, we see the falseness of their myths. Then we switch our beliefs to a creational paradigm, and their power diminishes.

Not that the Jews in ancient Babylon suddenly overthrew an empire once they'd put Eden "in the beginning" of the collection we call "Genesis." But these stories did give them an identity as solid and grand as evolutionary Creation itself. It shifted their mythology of origins and the very foundation of all they held sacred and true. They no longer staked their identity on creating an empire that would be a superior model among empires. We can appreciate how big a shift that is when we consider how wide and deep the belief persists in the U.S. that we are *the* model of democracy for the world; that we are an exceptional nation. But the Jews in Babylon realized that exceptionalism misleads all who live by it. It thrives in topographies of ego consciousness. Its arrogance justifies injustice;

its claim of moral superiority prevents us from moving into the topographies of greater consciousness where we need to live. The Jews had given their heart and soul to creating a better empire, an exceptional one. But all they'd accomplished was to prove that the MultiEarth paradigm of civilization was simply stronger than their model. They didn't create an exception to the paradigm at all, only proved its extraordinary powers. The paradigm *itself* was the issue, they discovered. So they shifted paradigms from MultiEarth empires to OneEarth community of life. By doing so, they created a myth of origins that trumps empire and superpower consciousness to this day.

Eden, a myth for all times, has never been any more relevant than now. It resonates today as all of Creation cries out for humanity to rediscover that our true identity is with her, not with the MultiEarth forces arrayed against her. When we recognize who the modern Babylonians are, we figure out clearly who to believe and who not to believe. In that light, being a citizen of the U.S., where superpower status, exceptionalism, and MultiEarth economics are vigorously pursued, I recognize my need for Eden's powers. Believing in Eden's ways convinces me to withdraw my belief in my country's MultiEarth and exceptionalist mythologies which support domination of others, threaten species, and selfishly over-extend Earth's resources. Eden moves me to put the fullest trust I can muster in Creation's ways, the ways of OneEarth living.

3. Become aware of the Sacred presence in all Creation— Wherever the Eden myth regains power in our lives and communities, our consciousness senses the presence of the sacred everywhere. Eden's mythology is highly *panentheistic*—not pantheistic, but "pan-en-theistic." The "en" between "pan" and "theistic" makes a huge difference in meaning. Pantheism, without the "en," describes all things as sacred, but circumscribes the sacred *inside* of the material world. It lacks transcendence, so is a bit flat compared to panentheism. "Theism," on the other hand, without the "pan" or "en," indicates a transcendent "Other" apart from—even distant from—the material world. "Theisms" fumble in the task of integrating the transcendent with the everyday world where dualisms like material and spiritual, human and divine keep life divided. Just as improved lenses improve our eyesight, panentheism perceives that all of the material world has the numinous Presence of the sacred infusing it. Equally important, panentheism remains open to "otherness"—even when it's so immense that it far exceeds what human reason and empirical research can fully comprehend. Panentheism holds that we can experience this "beyondness," that doing so connects us most wonderfully with the Universe, providing the welcome sense that we belong here. Across cultures, "God" may be the most common word used to describe that which is beyond or mysteriously within. But the experience itself remains beyond all words.

Mechtild of Magdeburg, a 13th century German Rhinelander who broke with the paradigm that dominated culture and religion on issues of patriarchy, hierarchy, and distant transcendence, offered a succinct statement of the power of panentheism when she said: "The day of my spiritual awakening was when I saw, and knew that I saw, God in all things and all things in God."

Panentheism helps us bow to the Mystery it recognizes as flooding the transcendent Cosmos we're part of. It also helps us recognize that divine Presence inhabits what's right in front of us. Approaching all things with a panentheistic orientation fosters relational cooperation, appreciation, and respect among all beings throughout Earth's community of life.

Panentheism loves reason along with all other ways of knowing. As a panentheist, I am broadening my appreciation for those other ways—including ones I have too often treated as inferior to logical reasoning and intellect. The intelligences of my belly and heart, as well as my spouse's sensitive energetic knowing, give me nonstop opportunities to consider how everything around and within me offers a sacred Presence that defies total analysis. While affirming science's methods in our search to know, panentheism also encourages other intentional activities as methods in that search. These include meditation, prayer, reflection on teachings, chanting and song, tending relationships, working for justice, tending to the land and waters, immersing ourselves in Nature, and many more. All can connect us to the Sacred Presence in surprisingly direct ways. Our Cosmos and Earth are awash with the sacred, communicating always, but in various ways. Being in that communication loop requires us to live mindfully and to discern what we can through all the ways that we come to knowledge.

Advance in living panentheistically may take us deeper into our Self identity and our own resources; it also deepens our appreciation of how groups, "tribes," and ecospheres are a locus for advancing our direct experience of the sacred interdependence of all things. Panentheism frames how we sense the sacred in all things, and all things in the sacred; it does so more holistically than either pantheism or theism can.

Seeing the world panentheistically meshes with the interdependent democracy that thrives in Nature's community of life. Nature concentrates power only to sustain the species or ecoregion, not for a species to conquer beyond its needs. In Nature, power gathers to promote social function, cooperative balance, and species wellbeing. Divisions between "us" and "them," in which "us" is beneath "them" or "us" is human and "them" is divine, are minimized. Human and divine, oneness and diversity all enhance one another, and one does not displace the other. Polarities coexist and complement one another.

First Peoples who live their traditional ways express a panentheistic worldview. They seek to balance polarities and all relations with Nature more than they expect to resolve them. That point of view fed their healthy suspicion of civilization's ways and nurtured them in OneEarth thinking.

These three areas of awareness—(1) disobeying ego consciousness to move to greater consciousness, (2) identifying the Babylons in operation today, and (3) using the panentheistic frame to see the sacred Presence in all things and all things in that Presence—all demand much of us. They will reward us with new capacities to live planet-size lives. When a well-told Eden mythology ripples out with the power to generate such increased awareness, we "reinvent the human," as Thomas Berry urges us to do (see the quotation at the head of this chapter).

To sustain the reinvention in daily practice requires inhabiting a greater topography of consciousness *and an underlying story*. The Eden myth, when we can feel its regained power in us and in our culture, can do the job. Truth is, the full weight of a sustaining story rarely rests on one myth. Cultures evolve many. OneEarth culture is no different as the following chapters will show.

Conclusion: The Myth That Takes Us Beyond Civilization

A misunderstood Eden cannot serve humanity well. To accelerate the relocation of our species into topographies of greater consciousness, we need the stimulus that potent OneEarth myths provide. Eden has that kind of explosive charge when told with the genius of its authors. It can drastically change how we see things. With that new vision moments happen where we say, "Oh, I now see how we can move out of the dark sequences of MultiEarth civilization and into shaping sustainable societies." These societies follow the models of Nature, Earth's own life-sustaining systems and bioregions.

That Eden helped Jews in the 6th century BCE protest Babylon's story of divinely ordained empire assures us that it can do the same today. Such protest is necessary if we are to move beyond MultiEarth civilization because so many contemporary superpowers, wealthy nations, and corporations presume to deserve divine blessing, or think they are administering God's ways in the world. What is necessary is to regain Eden's power by translating it to fit our current situation.

I opted to take on that task in this opening chapter to this book for two reasons. First, I am chagrined that Eden has been used inaccurately to foster MultiEarth views of human nature and egoistic thinking, the very paradigm it was intended to protest. Second, I believe that it has the power to energize our relocation into OneEarth views of human nature and Creation-centered consciousness.

The following chapters will move us beyond the limited view of human nature expressed in the punchless versions of Eden. An Eden accurately told portrays us humans as a messy and creative mix of dark and bright, but quite capable of heroic journeys into the topographies of consciousness where OneEarth living is possible if not inevitable.

The further we move into such larger topographies of consciousness, the clearer we see that Eden's mythic power is neutered in the MultiEarth consciousness. At the same time, we also become more able to retell Eden with the charged meanings and messages that its symbols have radiated since its inception. It's a bit of a loop. When Eden regains its power, Eden helps us move into greater consciousness; and from the vantage point of greater consciousness, we see more clearly the difference between a lackluster Eden and a numinous one.

Once it regains its power in our consciousness, Eden becomes a prime exhibit and mover on how the abundant, creational order stirs imagination and innovation. Myths seeking to validate MultiEarth ways compare poorly to Eden. Only myths that protest MultiEarth civilization can inhabit the same field of power as Eden.

I believe that our yearning for a sustainable Earth community of life can be realized, and that Eden's storytellers hold their own among all the wonderful artists who provide countercultural images, songs, and myths imagining OneEarth ways. All of these contribute images and symbols that provide the mythic crunch to reverse climate change and to do our Great Work in the 21st century—a work we turn to in the next chapter.

Ponder, Discuss, Act

1. How would *you* describe the aims of Eden's original storytellers?

2. Contrast the MultiEarth view of human nature with the OneEarth view? How does Eden mythology factor into those views? What's your view of human nature?

3. Of the following emphases given to the telling of the Eden myth, which ones have you heard (or even told) most often, and in what situations?

   • The tragedy of human failure passes on and on
   • The morality tale about disobedience
   • The role of male and female
   • The consequences of personal sin
   • The "Fall" into different consciousness or from innocence to consciousness
   • The "Fall" into sin
   • The tempting choice of MultiEarth living
   • The interdependence of living within a OneEarth community of life

4. What images of the archetypal Garden rise into your imagination?

5. In your everyday life, do any of the images you have of Eden influence you?

6. In what ways do images of Eden generate OneEarth living for you or others? Do you have a particular activity, like meditating or being in Nature, that connects you to Edenic Oneness? If so, what is it? If you don't, what is an activity that you might like to try?

CHAPTER TWO

Our Great Work: Going Beyond the Civilization Box

The Great Work now, as we move into a new millennium, is to carry out the transition from a period of human devastation of the Earth to a period when humans would be present to the planet in a mutually beneficial manner. This historical change is something more than the transition from the classical Roman period to the medieval period, or from the medieval period to modern times. Such a transition has no historical parallel since the geobiological transition that took place 67 million years ago when the period of the dinosaurs was terminated and a new biological age begun.[7]   —Thomas Berry

It is far easier to walk in shoes too small for us than to step into the largeness that soul expects and demands.[8]

—James Hollis, psychotherapist

Our Great Work in the 21st century is to reverse climate change and to reshape our societies to live *within* our planet's generosity. This task requires the "reinvented human" of Chapter One and a heroic, cooperative effort. Change, both within us and around us, must be to scale with the enormity and complexities of the forces threatening life on our planet. Our *inner changes* must take us into greater and deeper topographies of consciousness. Our *outer changes* must accelerate all the actions of relationship with Earth that can reverse climate change and restore the health of our planet's land, water, and air.

Said in another way, our Great Work is to leave the "Civilization Project" of the past 12,000 years. That project has approached Nature with the intent to tame and control her, to civilize her. The project understood humans as "naturally" prone to barbarity, so we too need to be tamed and civilized. But our heroic task today requires us to proceed quite differently. We need to come closer to mimicking Nature than civilizing her. Our civilizing activity turns Eden into dark tragedy; our Great Work rediscovers Eden's enlightening possibilities to undergird the new relationship we need with all species, and with ourselves.

The inner and outer activities of this Great Work reinforce one another, each causing the other and each resulting from the other. That synergy increases as we join with all who are engaging in this work. In solidarity, we become able to do what the Civilization Project has not and cannot accomplish—reshaping our lives and social systems to fit *inside* Earth's eco-systems. Difficult as this change is proving to be, we are fully capable of doing it. Its epic size need not deter us if, in solidarity, we engage upon *our* Great Work equipped with myths as eloquent as Eden, with science's best data, and with determination to continually ask of all human decisions: Does this decision get us to OneEarth living, or does it merely revise MultiEarth versions?

Simultaneously with *our* Great Work, the Earth is engaging in *her* Great Work as well. The grand Cenozoic Era, 65 million years in duration, is coming to an end. A primary indicator of this enormous geological transition, one that remains too much out of our awareness to have stirred us to sufficient action, is the massive extinction of species that is currently underway. That extinction has already become the 6th largest in Earth's 4.5 billion year story, and continues to spread to 200 more species *every day*. Earth's evolutionary and creative imagination is evolving into a new era. This era is as yet unnamed, though I like the name Ecozoic Era,[9] used by Thomas Berry, Brianne Swimme, and others. It denotes that Earth's continuing evolution has a bias that does not favor the Civilization Project. Her self-regulating systems, as they evolve, reveal a bias for balancing imbalances and behaving interdependently—a creational process favoring OneEarth ways that Eden expresses mythologically.

Of these two Great Works, ours and the Earth's, we can be sure that Earth's is well underway. Evidence is building that our species, too, is stepping up to our responsibilities, though, so far, we lag far behind the speed and scale of change Earth requires. That does not detract, however, from the growing numbers of us whose choices show that we've undertaken the Great Work. What is needed is for humanity and Earth to move along synchronistically in their respective Great Works. Then the "Great Change" to the Ecozoic Era will metamorphose along its natural course, unprecedented and unpredictable though it may be. We humans will leave behind our brave but immature MultiEarth Civilization Project, relocate ourselves inside Earth's eco-systems, and venture fully into the responsible maturity of OneEarth living.

As stated above, the Great Change must happen in our souls as well as in society. Whichever one leads, the other must always follow. The negative and positive poles of a battery illustrate the interaction needed in order for the energy of change to be produced. Much like the battery produces energy powerful enough to generate electrical transformations, so the inner and outer poles of psyche and Earth generate the power to transcend MultiEarth devastation and secure the future inhabitability of our planet. These great energies of soul and Earth impact one another and transform the societies and cultures that we've shaped. They move us beyond ego-centered consciousness enabling us to live in the consciousness of our greater Self. They also move us out of civilization-centered consciousness so we can live centered in the greater consciousness of ongoing Creation.

Across the centuries, some individuals have demonstrated what such greater consciousness looks like. We often hold them up as examples for us all. However, collectively our human species has yet to move there. That "big move," as Thomas Berry says in his book, *The Great Work*, is now an inspiring possibility for humanity! Berry, a priest and cosmologist, liked referring to himself as a "geologian," because, for him, geology, cosmology, and theology could not properly be held in separate departments or disciplines. "Geologian" perforates the borders of such compartments. Though he well knew civilization's inclination to divide knowledge into separate compartments, he intentionally blurred those borders. Berry expressed his views within the context of Earth and Cosmos, not civilization and history. History and civilization were too confining for the worlds he explored, too subject to being spun about according to the bias of the author. The Cosmos, Berry firmly reminded us, tells the only story that has no larger context. It is its own context. No story of civilization or any other story at all fits that claim. Because of how it dwarfs other stories, the cosmic story has the size to guide us into Earth's next era. Clearly then, our Great Work must proceed in conscious awareness of the cosmic story.

Our Move into Earth-size Consciousness

I want to make two obvious statements regarding the size of our Great Work. First, our Great Work is bigger than we may think. Second, the more we know, the bigger it becomes. The epigraph to this chapter cites Berry saying clearly that our Great Work is larger than anything we have done in our lifetimes; even larger than what humans have done in the entire history of civilization. The empires of ages past and the superpowers of today have given expression to amazing human cultures. Such achievements, however, shrink in scale when compared to the challenge of moving to Earth-size consciousness, and to its corollary: adjusting to Earth's move into a whole new geological epoch.

Even when we extend the history of civilization back to the Sumerians by the rivers Tigris and Euphrates in the Fertile Crescent, or to the Omo River Valley of Africa, there is still no precedent for what our work is now. Our work answers the Call jointly extended by Earth and the deep Self to move out of all MultiEarth forms of progress, development, economics, and patriarchy, as well as all hierarchical rule by the wealthiest and most powerful. Such forms work in ego consciousness, but are too immature, too spiritually and psychologically undeveloped, to work in Earth-centered consciousness. When we respond to Earth and Self, following their urgings into greater consciousness, we mature and develop into OneEarth thinking. We change how we live, not because it makes life easier or more convenient, but because of a priceless prize: it connects us with our evolutionary, creational purpose as a species. Earth and Self jointly define our Great Work and help it happen.

Our Great Work moves us out of the current structures of MultiEarth civilization—including MultiEarth models of economics, finance, recreation, entertainment, religion, education, business, enforcement, and government. We move into topographies alive with OneEarth thought and practices. Even if we resist such a move at first, we soon discover that our souls inherently long for it. Our souls shrug off ego consciousness and feel the liberation of being able to assume greater responsibility for relationships of caring and sharing throughout Creation. The further we get into the larger topographies of consciousness into which our Great Work takes us, the more ready we are to leave behind orientations focused on "me and those like me." Our dormant capacities to cultivate feelings of love for all species awaken. Awe and amazement become valued avenues for gaining knowledge that differs from what a strict scientific approach can deliver. Practices of humility and spirituality are also more present in the topographies of consciousness required for our Great Work.

In *The Great Work*, Berry exhibits enormous capacity to speak of all the ways that human activity and inventiveness throughout the 20th century were devastating Earth; yet he spoke with visionary possibility, not despair. He deeply believed that we humans could make the meta-changes in consciousness necessary to undertake the Great Work. As he saw it, both we and our children had a special role:

Our own special role, which we will hand on to our children, is that of managing the arduous transition from the terminal Cenozoic to the emerging Ecozoic Era, the period when humans will be present to the planet as participating members of the comprehensive Earth community. This is our Great Work and the work of our children.[10]

By the end of his life in 2009, Berry saw that Earth was already well into the terminal centuries of the current Cenozoic Era. The Cenozoic, along with the Mesozoic and Paleozoic Eras that preceded it, comprise the three periods of Earth's story in which animals have lived and evolved. Each of the transitions between these eras extended for millennia. During these transitions, the first phase was marked by great die-offs of species as Earth's inhabitability underwent radical deconstruction. Some species partially adapted, but only a small percentage were able to adapt to the full scale of changes that transpired between each era. Each die-off phase was followed by centuries and millennia during which new species emerged through the patient, creative, evolutionary process.

These previous phases of die-off and new emergence lasted millennia, and provide the context in which Berry understands what's happening in Earth's story today. Berry stretches our minds to reach for Earth consciousness. When our consciousness is shaped by Earth, we can see ourselves in transitional roles that are highly different from what our egos and MultiEarth thinking conjure for us. In Earth consciousness, civilization and egos are secondary. Creation and Self are primary. Not only are we in Earth's unfolding story, we are planet-inhabiters in the Universe's incomprehensibly vast unfolding. With the kind of Earth consciousness that Berry exemplified, we get beyond any feelings we might have of being too small to correct and heal what MultiEarth attitudes, corporations, and economic models have done.

Having defined the scale of our Great Work, and having professed belief that we and our children have the capacities to undertake it, I want to describe further the process by which we can move into

Earth-size consciousness. Getting there involves us in a back and forth dance between inner and outer change. *Inner changes* involve becoming ever more aware of the workings of our soul. Getting to know our ego and other aspects of ourselves is like getting to know other people in life. First we make one another's acquaintance; then we may move into functional relationships. But it takes time and intention. The better we get to know our egos, the more we see that they are not capable of Earth-size consciousness. They are too small a center of identity for that kind of awareness, thinking, and living. So when we journey into greater topographies of consciousness, our egos get worried. They feel afraid, send us warnings, and work to get us to turn back. Our egos undergo a kind of ego-suffering because they must come to acknowledge, albeit painfully, that they cannot be the center of the greater identity our Great Work requires. For that, a larger center of identity is needed. That center is Self, which I've already introduced and am eager to say more about in following chapters.

Outer changes involve us in promoting policies that can shape OneEarth structures and systems. Personal practices matter, but policies are essential to scale OneEarth changes up to Earth-size. As we learn of more Earth-size structures and systems, we use them. By being alert to both practices and policies we give our beliefs legs and a public voice. We change individual behaviors and also the systems that impact the behavior of whole communities and regions. By owning practically and publicly what is going on with us, our inner changes get translated into visible Earth-size actions. Bringing our inner and outer worlds into congruence can take us to moments where our emerging consciousness clashes with the reigning practices in organizations and relationships that we are part of. In such moments we develop discernment and skill in engaging disagreements that arise in our Great Work.

The inner and outer changes of our Great Work need also to synchronize with Earth and the huge changes she continues to make. She continues to invite us to disrobe from supersize grandiosity and put on Earth-size grandeur. That invitation has turned into *the* imperative of the 21st century. We have tarried so long in small topographies of consciousness, and so repeatedly turned from Earth's ecological messages, that the warmth of her invitation has taken on the heat of imperative. As her messages have increased in volume, more of us scurry to change practices and policies, acknowledging that Earth's changes determine ours. The humility she forces upon us opens us to different ways of thinking. Many businesses, campuses, and local governments now seek to reshape themselves to fit Earth's context. Some investors, who see the declining future for the fossil fuel industry, have begun withdrawing funds and investing in sustainable energy sources. These actions are responses to Earth's imperative. Awareness is spreading that to opt for the MultiEarth status quo is to choose the path of an endangered species.

By undertaking our Great Work, we acquire the consciousness to be sure the changes we make are at a scale right for our planet. We alertly synchronize with her. I make it sound like a well-choreographed transition to an Ecozoic world is underway. In fact, we already see the harshness and cruelties of the transition— unprecedented species extinctions, damaging weather extremes, polarized ideologues vying for leadership, violent struggles for energy, decades-long droughts, displacement of people escaping rising oceans and ecologically triggered conflicts. All of these severely challenge the adaptive capacities of MultiEarth practices, systems, and thinking. Being a global leader in a MultiEarth business or amassing wealth only to show success in MultiEarth ways becomes smaller in significance when put in the context of Earth's imperative.

Our planetary home, and its presence in our consciousness-expanding Cosmos, is the irrefutable context for all of us, all species, all business, all religion, and all education. Many elected and appointed officials in our countries talk and vote according to a story that does not fit what's happening on our planet. Both their ideology and actions fail in the OneEarth paradigm. But when we proceed with clear planetary and cosmic parameters, we can be confident that our Great Work will get us where we need to go. It presents itself as a daring, faith-evoking alternative to the Civilization Project which, instead of being our Great Work, has so far been our immature and lesser work.

Civilization: A Project of Immature Consciousness

What we've been fashioning throughout the history of the world—at least as most of us have learned that history—is called "civilization." Given all that our species has invested in it, I've resisted saying that MultiEarth civilization has been a project of immature consciousness. Yet such a conclusion is confirmed by the two consciousness maps I introduce in Chapter Four. Neither of them finds our civilization within the topographies of mature consciousness.

To see the immaturity of MultiEarth civilization we need go no further than how it shapes dominating ways of living that are beyond the means of Nature and feels justified in doing so. Living beyond our means does not line up with maturity. A more mature consciousness shapes collegial ways of living within Nature's generous limits and admits that our civilized systems have been "living on the dole." Civilization has not paid its own way nor taken responsibility for its theft from Earth, from other species, or from disadvantaged humans. Instead, civilization has glorified super achievement, especially when the devastations such achievements continue to exact can be hidden. So to sing the praises of MultiEarth civilization as a success story is possible only within MultiEarth, immature consciousness. From an Earth-size perspective, the Civilization Project has been more illusion than success, though calling it that can feel shocking in the extreme. What our species has pursued for millennia, and much of what we've worked so hard to achieve personally—often with simple, worthy intentions of improving life—is now being exposed by Earth herself as not only unsustainable, but as unable to fulfill the purpose of our species as well.

Gambling is one way to talk about it. Casino gambling is not my thing, so I can readily walk past the gaming machines in the

Las Vegas airport. But I do expect to see Lady Luck walking among those machines. Her tempting, smiling invitations and lures will, she hopes, tip the balance in us humans so that we'll believe in our luck to win against the odds. Civilization, based on MultiEarth living, has similarly counted on Lady Luck. Over the centuries, so many human choices that changed the direction of ecological relationships assumed we "owned the house." We gambled that Lady Luck would reward us and that our take came without strings.

But the immaturity of such magical thinking is now being exposed. Earth is showing us decisively that we don't own her—and that we can't. Instead we *owe* her, and the total is far more than we can pay. But we're hooked. Even though we hear what science has been telling us for decades about industrialized climate change, overpopulation, and using up Earth's resources, when it comes to giving up MultiEarth ways, we continue to believe in Lady Luck.

As far back as 10,000 BCE, Lady Luck began enchanting us to civilize Nature if we want to win big. From that time on, we humans opted for civilizing tendencies that had not been our way before then. Enough data has been dug up by anthropologists and paleontologists to show us the early formations of civilization 10,000–12,000 years ago, following the last glacial period. Geology has dubbed the period that followed the ice, the Holocene Epoch (Holocene means "entirely recent").[11] With the massive movements of ice ended, climates and geographies stabilized.

Of all the "modernizations" in human behavior and culture that happened over subsequent millennia, none was more significant than the change in agriculture. By domesticating plants and animals instead of hunting them in their wilder, natural habitats, food was produced in greater quantities. Farming moved from tending Nature's production and extracting from her to managing tilled plots. Though tilled plots yielded increased amounts of food, the revisions in farming that came along with tilling also limited variety, biodiversity, and nutritional values. Nonetheless, more production meant more changes in how people shaped society. With agriculture providing the food they needed, people moved to towns and cities where they devoted themselves to different kinds of crafts, skills, and city-building. That movement of population into cities and out of rural ecology and culture separated more and more people from Nature. They became more involved in shaping lives and societies that advanced the civilizing values of the MultiEarth worldview. Once agriculture began practices focused in production instead of stewardship of the commons, the Civilization Project was off and running. Human, animal, and plant life would never to be the same again. British historian Gordon Childe (1892–1957) called this time of unprecedented activity a revolution—the Neolithic Revolution. It was a slow moving revolution by today's standards. Significant changes in agriculture and city formation that began as early as 8000 BCE, took until 2500 BCE to spread into most inhabited areas.[12]

Histories of civilization praise the changes in farming and city-building during the Neolithic Revolution as progress; but there were strong downsides, and these increase when we view the Revolution from topographies of OneEarth consciousness.[13] As regions began refocusing themselves from rural culture to new social and economic patterns shaped by city-centers, all people were not empowered equally. Occupations became more specialized; but because some proved more lucrative than others, they shaped new divisions. The worth of human labor, far from being regarded as having equal value whatever the task, began to be calculated according to hierarchies of value and merit determined partly by what people wanted, but also by the policies of those with the most power. Power and wealth circulated in ways that separated societies into economic classes. Nature lost out to those who calculated that there were more benefits in controlling and abusing her than to be stewards of the balance she brought to life-sustaining eco-regions. These trends muscled their way into strategies of dominance. Those who rode the trends effectively dominated the community, set the standards of right and wrong, and determined what had more value and what had less.

Another huge change in the Civilization Project came in the 8th century BCE when money was invented.[14] It was a timely invention and a great boon to economic advance as the rural-urban equation continued to change. Occupations continued to diversify and each occupation had its own products. But there was no quick way for people to exchange their products for others they needed in their families or occupation. To facilitate easier exchange, the products each occupation made needed a widely accepted form of measuring their value. Money supplied that measure once people could agree on its value. The coins received for a product were trusted to have value for subsequent purchases.

To grasp the degree of change that money made in the civilization story, we need to recognize that up to this point in civilization, the primary way you could get a product you wanted was if you had a product that was wanted by the person from whom you wanted to make a purchase. But from the 8th century BCE onward, money empowered you to make purchases regardless of your own product. Having money became more reliable and powerful than having product. Whereas before you gained market-access only if your product was in demand, with money in your pocket, you had access to any of the products of the market that you had enough coins for.

But many downsides came with the invention of money, especially when seen from the larger consciousness of an Earth-centered and Earth-size paradigm. Skill at adding and subtracting money to calculate profit, appraising value, and making financial deals grew in value, even though they were increasingly abstract compared to an economy mimicking the transactions made within Earth and her community of life. Calculating money successfully took precedence over cultivating relationships even though relationships across Earth's community of life are the basis upon which money can benefit anyone. Transactions often focused so much attention on profit that appreciation of the craftsperson, or the wellbeing of an eco-region, was forgotten. The abstraction from life which money made possible continued to increase over the centuries to where today we have economic transactions in which products called derivatives are traded even though what they are and what they do is not understood fully even by their creators or regulators. Not to be overlooked as a downside of the invention of money is how it changed humans psychologically and spiritually, making us far more calculating in our choices of what has value and what does not. Though MultiEarth civilization cannot function without this invention, money is also a major contributor to the unraveling of its Civilization Project.

As the civilization story proceeded beyond the Neolithic Revolution, we *Homo sapiens* became increasingly dominant over all other life forms. Using advances in technology and amassing economic power, our species configured a world divided into the dominators and the dominated. Earth and Nature, having long ago lost out as the context for the decisions that guided human ways, suffered reckless domination. Instead of the context, Nature became a subtext for humans and our accelerating MultiEarth practices. No longer Mother Nature, she became an "it," not a "her." Humans determined "its" value according to their criteria of Earth's usefulness. As a result, humans moved into the position of Earth's chief predator, relinquishing our evolutionary purpose to live within Earth's community of life as a species able to increase consciousness about interdependent living.

Today, the 12,000 year civilization story continues to provide the frames in which the governments of the richest nations, executives of global corporations, and voices of corporate media see our global situation. MultiEarth's businesses and governments are largely led by those who see the Civilization Project as *the* story of human history, and the most important story one can tell about our human progress. Current MultiEarth-inspired leaders of the Civilization Project show only reluctant willingness to see our unfolding crises in frames of Nature's ways and Earth's story. The larger frames of geological epochs lie well outside the frames of civilization and its smaller topographies of consciousness. Such Earth-centered frames are also missing from most religious institutions and the curricula of academia, though inspiring exceptions can be found.

Given the pressures upon leaders to act from a topography of ego consciousness, we can wonder how many of them are even able to move into the larger topographies of consciousness where they can use such epochal frames as the Cenozoic and the Holocene? The powerful and wealthy within governments, militaries, and corporations continue to picture 21st century realities inside frames small enough so that they can manage them. Epochal frames aren't manageable. Moving beyond the Holocene Epoch, for example, requires a maturity of consciousness beyond the capacities of the topographies where ego reigns. So it is that the conversation in the public arena has been, and continues to be, limited to the frames that human civilization can handle. As a result, and as the maps of consciousness in Chapter Four will show, the consciousness that controls public discourse remains too limited to get us in sync with the great movement underway in Earth's unstoppable unfolding. For that, we need to use cosmic or geology's epochal frames as well.

This sketch of the story of civilization from the Neolithic times to the present is not complete without noting that many people have persistently resisted the civilizing powers that have carried the day and lived with a different consciousness. Though we cannot tell their story here, we can note their determination not to be engulfed in MultiEarth ways. Among them we find far more interested in naturalizing humans than in civilizing Nature. Showing appreciation for their resistance and joining them in carrying it forward moves us along in the Great Work. It is the work by which we move with Earth to end the Civilization Project. The most effective way to end the project happens as we create, from a larger topography of consciousness, the alternatives that carry us toward a new epoch, the Ecozoic Era.

Anthropocene: Geological Epoch
of Our Immature Work

Dutch chemist Paul Crutzen is a scientist who does use the larger frames of geological epochs, and they've served him well, enabling him to see civilization's advances through Earth-size lenses. Crutzen, who shared a Nobel Prize in Chemistry in 1995 for his work in atmospheric chemistry (specifically ozone formation and depletion), had been aware for some time that the activity of humans has had such enormous impact on the planet in the past couple centuries that it exceeded all definitions of the Holocene Epoch. He and other scientists recognized that we'd moved into a new epoch. Crutzen created a bit of drama one day at a scientific conference when he interrupted the speech of the conference chair, because the chair kept referring to the current geological epoch as the Holocene. Crutzen blurted out, "Let's stop it! We are no longer in the Holocene. We are in the Anthropocene." The audience sat in stunned silence immediately following Crutzen's surprise interruption, but during the coffee break that followed the chair's speech, the Anthropocene was all the buzz.[15]

In 2002, Crutzen made his case for the Anthropocene (*anthropos* is Greek for human) to his scientific peers with an article in *Nature*, an international weekly journal of science. He suggested the 18th century as the beginning of the Anthropocene because of the rapid acceleration in technological industrialization that started at that time. Scientists using Anthropocene to name our current epoch continue to work on how to calculate just how massive our species' impact is on the planet. One example comes from biologist E.O. Wilson, who calculates that the human biomass is 100 times larger than any other species that's ever been on Earth.[16]

Because transition to a new geological epoch needs to show a change in fossil records, one of the key questions is: Does the human impact on Earth create a change in what the fossil remains of this era will show? Geologists are increasingly convinced that the answer is "Yes." They cite as evidence: the rapid leveling of forests, the massive damming of rivers, species extinctions far higher than during the past 500 million years, and the destruction of coral reefs in the ocean unlike anything since the last mass extinction 67 million years ago. The geological record now being laid down will show all of these Earth-reshaping changes. These factors also move scientists beyond dispassionate reports to speaking urgently about what our species is doing. Such urgency, they realize, is actually required in order for their reports to be accurate. The data describe an urgent situation! And it comes smack up against the wealth and power of industries, stock markets, and governments who, therefore, resist the changes the scientists urge based on the data. This is all the more reason why Crutzen and others want to use the word "Anthropocene." They want to name the size of the human role in transitioning Earth's story into a new geological epoch. They want explicitly to implicate our species—we, the *anthropos*, are fully responsible for the current geological devastation. The term "Holocene" does not implicate us, but protects us from responsibility for the epochal changes advancing across our planet.

The debate about the naming of this new epoch continues. Some are even proposing that the entire Holocene epoch needs to be renamed Anthropocene—so intense has been the impact of *Homo sapiens* on this chapter in Earth's story. Wherever the conversation among scientists goes, we seldom hear Anthropocene or any other geological language from the lips of world leaders or media voices who frame so much of the conversation of our civilization. Leaders in politics and media continue to use the smaller frames of human history to describe what is happening and decide how to respond. But their frames of understanding are too small to manage Earth's epochal changes, or to lead us onto paths of Earth-size action. As a result, they, along with a large proportion of the global population, tumble into less and less ability to read the signs of the times accurately.

The global superpowers who have led the planetary devastations that brought us into the Anthropocene have been the European countries, Soviet Union, the United States, China, and

Japan. All of them did so while functioning as empires extracting goods from around the world in the name of improving or protecting life. During the 20th century, the U.S. took the mantle and decisively succeeded the various empires of Europe and elsewhere. Europe's nations had colonized the maps of the Americas, Africa, and wherever else they could during the centuries of their dominance. But in the 20th century, these colonies were given independence. At least that was the language used. What truly happened was that the political colonies ruled by nations with colonial power morphed into economic colonies ruled by corporations. Colonization through corporate rule has been the preferred approach of contemporary empire as designed in the West by the U.S. and in the East by the late Soviet Union. China, now in ascendancy, also shows a preference for its own version of imperial economic and business dominance. Whether as political or economic colonies, the succession of empires, with all their merits and flaws, continues to be the dynamics of the day and sets the agendas of politics, economics, militaries, business, education, religion, and culture.

These MultiEarth superpowers, both countries and corporations, have been the prime players in such an antagonistic devastation of Earth that her geological systems have been set into epoch-changing motion. Earth's story has been ignored in superpower discourse. But what's important to note for our Great Work toward Earth-size living is that civilization's long historical arc of advancement, development, and presumed progress is being challenged—not just by people on the outside of power and wealth, or by competitive nation states aspiring to greater power, but by Creation herself. It is apparent that Earth, not *anthropos*, will have the major voice in the 21st century on how power, wealth, people, and species will be organized on a single planet. Earth is protesting superpower economics more loudly than environmental activists ever can. Her message? "My life-support system is stressed beyond my limits. You're killing the bioregions without which no one can live." No civilization has had to deal with this message on a global scale before. We are in a geological epoch named for us *Homo sapiens*, but it does not flatter us. It further exposes the egoistic smallness of the consciousness of MultiEarth living. Doing our Great Work takes us into topographies of greater consciousness where we can cooperate with Earth's more expansive, life-sustaining, evolutionary processes.

Our Great Work Exceeds the Achievements of Civilization

Though many people regard the achievements of human civilization to be the masterpiece of our species, those remarkable achievements do not approach in scale or consciousness our Great Work which moves us into a new Earth epoch. To better understand the scope of our Great Work, it is important to see how it differs from the achievements of MultiEarth civilization. As the gorilla, Ishmael, in Daniel Quinn's bestseller[17] points out, we need to look behind the drama of human civilization in order to recognize that it is only a project within the greater human story by which we live to our fullness.

The consciousness it takes to sort out what serves our Great Work and what serves civilization is colored by the time, money, and effort we invest in learning and living civilization's ways. As individuals our investment is for a lifetime, but as a species we have invested in civilization for millennia. As a result, our species is more inclined to defend civilization with our dollars and drones than to reassess it and declare that it has been, to a large degree, a universal mistake. Yet, difficult as it is to do so, we're past the time to admit that our civilization story is more like a Greek tragedy than a heroic myth.

The ancient Greek tragedies dramatized the great intentions of egos. The lead characters proceeded boldly, but without full awareness of the unconscious dynamics lurking within their souls. With considerable insight, the Greeks portrayed these dynamics as gods at work, exercising their autonomy over human wills. In modern psychology, these gods have morphed into powerful archetypes in our psyches. Either way, the results are the same. Whether gods or archetypes, they repeatedly override the intentions of our egos, spice up our choices with unexpected benefits or devastating betrayals, and put us into our various modern day tragedies.

In the Greek tragedies, the gods, working behind the scenes, took the lead characters into behaviors that sabotaged the very goals they wanted to achieve. Similarly, the gods of civilization (archetypes of the unconscious) have worked within us to sabotage the entire Civilization Project. Wanting to improve life, we are heading for death. Egos have acted unaware of the enormous powers operating from their hiding places in the unconscious. The power of the archetypes act upon human egos and the more ego there is, the more they get to play. Earth, on the other hand, is acting through her natural self-regulating ecosystems. Both now conspire to bring us to civilization's undoing. Only by moving into a greater topography of consciousness can we achieve the discernment we need to extract ourselves from civilization's achievements—accomplished amid her tragedy—and connect with our Great Work.

Having gotten off course, our species must now, with equal parts humility and steadfast focus, redirect ourselves to the Great Work that gets us in step with Earth on her cosmic journey. Undisputedly, when contrasted to civilization, Creation continues as both the older and future system by which life is ultimately arranged. Earth's inhabitability, now and throughout this century, depends on our ability to make a major recalibration in how we live—and to make it quickly.

This Great Work involves us in the details of changing how we think about everything. Changing all of our mental default settings requires far more intention than changing our accounts when we get a new credit card. Just as important as changing the details is changing "the big picture." What is typically considered the big picture is no longer nearly grand enough. When we give a closer look to the big picture descriptions coming out of MultiEarth thinking, we can see that they aren't big enough to break us out of the

Civilization Project tragedy. But the epochal and cosmic frames for the big picture of Earth-size living can break us out of the Civilization Project.

Being committed to our Great Work also engenders suspicion about all explanations generated by the powers that keep MultiEarth civilization in charge. These "official" stories, the stories of the "winners" in the civilization drama, seek to persuade us that the ones on top belong there. They offer justifications for the actions of MultiEarth powers. When adroitly told, we can be taken in by these explanations and emulate their stories. They may succeed in anesthetizing our capacities to redirect ourselves to Earth-size thinking. But healthy suspicion regarding the stories that keep civilization in place come with living in the greater topographies of consciousness into which our Great Work takes us.

Doing our Great Work joins us to the interconnectedness of all things where we experience the bonds of interrelationship as a treasure of living. Civilization's MultiEarth agenda has pushed that treasure into the collective unconscious. Therefore, our Great Work, both personally and collectively, is to raise awareness of this treasure above the surface again. Faithfulness in this work synchronizes our deepest Self with the evolving dynamics of Earth and Universe. This holistic work is psychological, spiritual, and practical. It changes the choices we make in our daily lives. We get meaning doing activities we didn't bother with when under the influence of MultiEarth ways. To be faithful to our Great Work we need to make the case for how our species comes into meaning and significance through holistic interrelationship with all that pulses on Earth and beyond. Earth-size understandings eschew the disconnections permeating MultiEarth civilization: divide to control, analyze the parts in order to understand the whole, search for the ultimate by splitting even tiny atoms into their tiniest particles, create specialties in professions, sever employees from a company so its stocks will rise, and all the rest.

Another test to sort our Great Work from the work of the Civilization Project is to ask, "What news matters most to us? How do we rank the relative importance of events?" In our Great Work, Earth events matter even more than world events. We want to know the geological time as well as Greenwich time. When the BBC tells us about "The World Tonight," we want them to put what's happening among humans and nation states in the context of what's happening in the eco-regions and Earth's geology. We live in an awareness that the biggest questions are not being generated in civilization, but by Creation and the interplay between Earth and her inhabitants. Stories about the stock markets, which corporations earned most, or what the president or prime minister said need to be framed by what Earth had to say and how we're investing in Earth so as to add to our natural wealth, not only our financial wealth.

While profits and economies may grow or contract, what we most need to hear is about efforts to steward Earth's natural wealth so continuing habitability can be assured for all species. Stock markets have left unanswered the vital question: how can Earth be expected to handle more economic growth and a burgeoning human populace if her natural wealth continues to decline? Fully reporting "the world tonight" places that question front and center. If framed by the natural world, not just the civilization world, "the world tonight" will report on how the exponential increase of *Homo sapiens* requires space, food, and water that bullies other species out of their habitats. OneEarth news cannot be framed only within the Civilization Project.

It's news, is it not, that our MultiEarth practices are being rejected, not by another military power or terrorist group, not by liberals or conservatives, but by Earth herself? Day by day, Earth's speech makes herself clear: she will not be finessed nor overpowered by us. Her 4.5 billion year commitment to bring about life—conscious life—will continue on her own geological clock. She will puncture our illusions as if they are a circus balloon. She is on a marvelous course to correct the imbalances our civilization has produced but is all thumbs when it comes to correcting them. Earth faithfully does what is her Great Work to do. By framing the news according to the Great Work, Earth's and ours, the conversations change about stock markets and climate change. Our responses get us beyond what civilization can muster.

Another aspect of our Great Work is the radical community it requires with all of life. We need, for example, to buttress one another in the challenging belief that we can do better than the Civilization Project. In the face of daunting struggles and intermittent failures, it can be hard to hang onto that belief given how it requires tectonic shifts across the globe in how our species thinks and acts. This is not to minimize that our Great Work has an unmistakable individual choice and intent to it. But its accomplishment is all about connecting in actions for the common good. All of us who believe that our human capacities can do better than the Civilization Project often find ourselves paddling vigorously against major cultural, economic, and religious currents who are skeptical or flatly disagree. MultiEarth's influence is hard to break.

We also need to help one another see how Earth is our ally. That her dynamism seeks cohesion of purpose with all her creatures has not been sufficiently a part of daily consciousness for most of us. She is challenging us to reassess our choices that have built the Civilization Project. Earth pleads with us to fulfill our evolutionary purpose instead. Making our lives, businesses, education, and faith this Earth-centered has not yet become our default setting. It's Great Work to get there and requires lots of us contributing.

Calling this work our Great Work strikes deep at the yearnings inside of us. It awakens energies that want to rise up to the task, even if this *magnum opus* takes us into experiences where it feels like earth-moving equipment is reshaping the landscape of our souls. What we've doubted human nature could do, what we've thought was beyond our human reach, has appeared that way to us because of the topographies of smaller consciousness in which we've been living. In the following chapters, the heroic journey will guide us to topographies of consciousness where who we are coincides with OneEarth practices. In our Great Work, we live these practices. In doing so, none of us need rise in the morning doubting that our lives matter.

Conclusion: Humility and Muscle in Our Great Work

The same description of our Great Work by Thomas Berry that heads this chapter best summarizes the size of what we are about. Unprecedented in civilization's history, we have to turn to Earth's history to find a parallel:

> The Great Work now, as we move into a new millennium, is to carry out the transition from a period of human dev-astation of the Earth to a period when humans would be present to the planet in a mutually beneficial manner. This historical change is something more than the transition from the classical Roman period to the medieval period, or from the medieval period to modern times. Such a transi-tion has no historical parallel since the geobiological transi-tion that took place 67 million years ago when the period of the dinosaurs was terminated and a new biological age begun. So now we awaken to a period of extensive disarray in the biological structure and functioning of the planet.[18]

Changing psychologically and spiritually to an Earth-centered con-sciousness, and changing socially and economically to be part of Earth's community of life, are twin poles in our Great Work. We cannot expect Earth to be deterred from her evolutionary trajec-tories. She will fulfill her mission to evolve life that can live to a higher stature of consciousness than civilization currently exhibits. The Anthropocene epoch, just like the Holocene before it, will soon be eclipsed with a sequel. It will be more mature. We are part of the possibility of this moment as well as all the suffering accompanying such an intense transition. On the one hand, we are contributing to the greatest extinction of species within the last 65 million years. On the other hand, we are called to the great, unprecedented conversion that is making obsolete the civilization models developed over the past 12,000 years. Earth is proving to be a consciousness-changer beyond what we have heretofore appreciated.

No modern culture has yet mustered the consciousness to transition from one geological age to another. Only pre-civilization humans came close when they transitioned from the Pleistocene Epoch, marked by repeated glaciations, to the Holocene Epoch, marked by the launch of the human Civilization Project. Even the dislocations experienced by our ancestors at that time do not measure up to the transition that is our adventure now. Nonetheless, those humans, however inferior we might have previously assumed them to be, give evidence that our species has the capacity to get into the larger paradigm of Earth's evolution, a prerequisite for us to participate in the OneEarth story.

Evolutionary, creational powers have put within us a great consciousness muscle. Underused, it remained undeveloped during the endless succession of MultiEarth advances in the 12,000-year Civilization Project. But as soon as we exercise it, the muscle awakens and develops to its full strength. Using it risks opening our hearts and minds to a paradigm of Spirit, Earth, and Self too big for our ego's comfort zones. This paradigm is bigger than family or nation, but it is just the right size for OneEarth living. To participate in the alchemy of this civilization-transcending transition, we need to overcome the media's misdirection, which remains mistakenly focused more on collaborations and alliances between nations and transnational institutions than on either Earth's patterns that sideline those events, or imaginative human innovations that show our readiness to live a OneEarth paradigm.

We humans need to hurry into a new and safer consciousness with the same urgency as if we were outracing a wildfire. Throughout the history of civilization, we have been telling our story as one of ascent and progress. We continue to pride ourselves in being smart, alert, and wide awake. But the truth is that we have had our eyes open inside a particular bubble. Because of the limitations of that enclosure, civilization is only now coming to see the flames threatening to overtake us, sped along by the high winds of growth economics and ego bluster. What began as a "controlled burn" to make the ecology of life better has gotten out of control. Future geologists may well describe the Anthropocene Epoch as the age in which the human species lost control of its impacts on Earth. Devastations resulted and many were wrapped in so-called super achievements that blinded the species to their impacts.

A major hurdle preventing our Great Work is mustering the humility to acknowledge the immaturity and smallness of consciousness that has given us the civilization we're so "proud" of. The CEOs, presidents, economists, central bankers, and Wall Street company directors along with educators, religious leaders, and all the rest of us when we're caught up in MultiEarth consumption, live inadequately aware that the consciousness of the day is as yet too small, too immature to live inside our green Earth. OneEarth living requires that we become more conscious than what our civilization shows.

Around the globe, MultiEarth models are still advertised as "the best way to go," and millions follow in hot pursuit of that "best." Most national policies and international agreements grease the way for such pursuit, often penalizing alternatives. MultiEarth thinking irrationally predominates in the major decisions being made, even as OneEarth living is recognized by many as the obvious and only viable road to travel for sustainability. As a result, now early in the 21st century, human consciousness roils with conflicting energies. More and more people know that our species must change. Quickly. We also know that our elected national leaders have become more gridlocked than big city rush hour traffic. Just as problematic for us are growth-based business and financial leaders who remain addicted to an economic model beyond Earth's capacities. They have yet to heed Earth's ecological warnings that they must change from this intoxication with the MultiEarth spirits of expanding money and power.

Simultaneously, the numbers of people and entities grow that are engaged in the Great Work of our species, learning as we go.

We work toward a tipping point where human consciousness shifts exponentially in favor of life for all species.[19] We know that those in charge remain fervently devoted to a paradigm which Earth's own Great Work is currently rejecting. Despite rhetoric that makes it seem as if they have the only way through our current crises, it is their imprisonment in the gilded cage of MultiEarth success that is most striking. As leaders deliver less and less, the dreams of hope they hold out disappear like mirages in the desert. Their failures quicken alternatives among all of us whose imaginations have become awakened and ready for action. Empowered by how we see Earth rejecting their ways, many of us are reconnecting with Earth. In doing so, we are also reconnecting with our own deeper Self. We increasingly recognize how Earth's wisdom influences our daily direction and that our internal restlessness parallels Earth's intent to *move on*. We've already been working to align our souls with Earth's evolution out of the MultiEarth economy and story treasured by Western civilization. As OneEarth living gathers new adherents, from individuals to businesses and academics, the brooding of the Spirit gestates new powers of life.

The conviction that we can do better lies strong in me as does the sense that, as mentioned above, we're heading toward a tipping point. Both of these sentiments will be expanded upon in the chapters that follow. My conviction is not diminished by the failures of the past. Instead, I'm inspired by our Great Work to move into a new Earth-size, Earth-centered edenic consciousness and practice. The Call to such a heroic journey beckons all of us. We have not chosen it, as Thomas Berry says, but we have been summoned nonetheless. It is to that Call that I turn in the next chapter.

❀

Ponder, Discuss, Act

1. What was the history of civilization as you learned it during your school years? How has your understanding of civilization changed during your adult years?

2. Describe "our Great Work" in your own words. Invite others to dialogue with you about this and compare notes.

3. What widespread efforts for OneEarth living seem especially significant to you? Why?

4. Where do you see groups of people holding together both the inner and the outer impulses for our Great Work?

5. What are your responses to the following sentences:
   - As her volatility increases, Earth is proving to be a major consciousness changer.
   - Scientists are leading us in learning to read Earth's complex signals accurately.
   - Interestingly, the more intent we become on moving into an Earth-size topography of consciousness, the better we become at reading her signals.
   - Like any relationship, our relationship with Earth improves as we center her in our consciousness.
   - Our relationship with Earth goes a long way to determining how free we are to move into a topography of consciousness where OneEarth living is foremost.

6. Describe how you are engaged in the Great Work right now? and, what other way of engagement would fit well with your values?

SECTION TWO

The Call to Live in Eden

The concept of being "called" has been part of my life since boyhood. It implanted in me the idea that greater forces than my own choices, or my parents' choices, or money, mattered in shaping what I did, and who I could become. At one time or another, I have sensed a Call to a particular vocational choice, an action, or a way of being. In this book, I describe Call as what I hear Earth and Nature saying to us through ecological crises. Synchronized with Earth's Call comes an inner Call to "grow up," and move into a greater, Earth-size consciousness. The consciousness that favors MultiEarth ways is too small for what's astir today on our planet, or stirring in me. Together, Earth and soul are telling me that I can be more than what I yet am, and that I can live more interactively with Earth and her life community than I do.

I capitalize the word "Call" to emphasize that throughout my years I've understood this phenomenon as connected with Divine sources. Call has to do with the Voice of The Holy, the holistic. It is an invitation to use capacities within me that are able to bring greater wholeness to my personal being, to my relationships with others, and to Earth and her ecospheres. This invitation comes in a tone of grace. It believes in me so strongly that I'm inspired to act, and to see if its confidence in me just might be true.

The two chapters of Section II peer into the anatomy of Call. I answer key questions that arise: How do we sense that we're being Called? Why might we hesitate to embrace Call? What happens when we turn from it? Chapter Three opens with how Bilbo Baggins, in "The Hobbit," was Called to a heroic adventure. Bilbo's experience reveals the strong paradoxical quality of Call: it triggers emotional upset in us while also affirming that we are capable of doing more than we think. Call tells us that we are expected to move into topographies of consciousness greater than we had ever imagined possible for ourselves. This expectation is part of the package of being human, a species researched and designed by evolution's patient procedures. Said another way, this expectation is a hovering Presence of the Holy that fusses with us to become more fully human. The ball is in our court. Will we consent?

Given how upsetting Call can be, how disrespectfully intrusive into plans we have for ourselves, it can hardly be a surprise that turning away from it happens often. Doing so, however, has disturbing consequences, individually and collectively. The freight of the Call, if we decline it, has to be carried somewhere. And so it goes into our bodies or into unhealthy expressions of our being. It manifests in bullying, usurping, and dominating; or, conversely, in withdrawing, behaving passively, and manipulating. Chapter Four provides an introductory exposure to how, when we refuse the Call to the heroic journey and our Great Work, we abort our own psychological drives to greater maturity. We behave outwardly in ways that generate pathologies of chaos, greed, and superiority; we destroy people, other species, and Earth.

Since all of us have these negative capacities within us, I could not write this chapter without having my own pathologies rise up like monsters to stare at me. They remind me of countless moments in which I have not shown up or taken responsibility, or, conversely, turned verbally aggressive. I bow to acknowledge my respect for the psychological and spiritual monsters that made this a most challenging chapter for me to write. But I have no intention of letting them prevail. Heeding the Call is far too important to me.

❀

CHAPTER THREE

The Call into Earth-Centered Consciousness

The Great Work before us, the task of moving modern industrial civilization from its present devastating influence on the Earth to a more benign mode of presence, is not a role that we have chosen. It is a role given to us, beyond any consultation with ourselves. We did not choose. We were chosen by some power beyond ourselves for this historical task.[20]   —Thomas Berry, *The Great Work*

UNLESS someone like you cares a whole awful lot, nothing's gonna get better. It's not.   —Dr. Seuss, *The Lorax*

Bilbo Baggins loved his life in the Shire. The overwhelming forces mounting in the greater world of Middle Earth did not interfere there. Risks were minimal; beauty abounded; comforts and privileges were secured by the Shire's community. What a great, idyllic place to live!

Such is the opening scene of the 2012 epic fantasy film, *The Hobbit: An Unexpected Journey*, directed by Peter Jackson, and based on the book by J.R.R. Tolkien. But Bilbo's life was about to be changed. A Call to a heroic journey beyond the Shire, and beyond what he thought himself capable of, was about to intrude. To follow Bilbo in his Call to adventure is to bring to consciousness our own feelings about the moment we are in. Our species is now summoned to a journey as epic and mythic as the one Tolkien portrayed.

Bilbo Baggins' Call to Adventure

One particular day, while the Shire was enjoying its usual sense of wellbeing, Bilbo recognized that a stranger had come among them. Being a hobbit of good manners, Bilbo asked him, "Can I help you?"

"That remains to be seen," the stranger replied. "I'm looking for someone to share in an adventure."

Bilbo had zero interest in biting at the bait of such an invitation. "An adventure?" he queried disinterestedly. "Now I don't imagine anyone west of Bree would have much interest in adventures. Nasty, disturbing, uncomfortable things. Make you late for dinner."

At that point Bilbo wanted to twist away from any further encounter with the stranger. He awkwardly checked his mail, pretending to pay no further attention to him. Then he excused himself curtly with "Good morning!" and walked away.

But the stranger wasn't to be dismissed. He hooked Bilbo into further conversation and broke through Bilbo's resistant consciousness shaped by comfort, privilege, and satisfaction. Shortly, Bilbo discovered that he had been engaged by the famous wizard, Gandalf.

Now, Gandalf lived and thought in a larger consciousness than did the people in the Shire. He therefore knew that, despite appearances, all was not well with the Shire. In truth, all of Middle Earth was under great threat from evil powers who had intentions to control the land. All inhabitants, including those of the Shire, would be ruled by these powers unless they could be challenged and disarmed. Bilbo had no idea! This world-changing conspiracy was underway outside of Bilbo's smaller consciousness.

As he and Gandalf continued talking about "the adventure," Bilbo had an increasingly visceral reaction. Suddenly, he fainted.

Then, as he began to recover, he actually began inching closer to accepting Gandalf's invitation.

"Can you promise that I will come back?" Bilbo queried, seeking some assurance that he'd be safe.

"No," Gandalf replied, disappointing him. "And if you do… you will not be the same."

Though the answer was not comforting, Bilbo was highly intrigued. A war was raging inside him. One side wanted all this disturbance to go away. But another side, one that actually wanted adventure, was boldly muscling to the fore. It was then that Gandalf reminded him of his family lineage: one side Baggins, the other side Took. The Baggins side was known for valuing security, orderliness, and simple elegance. The Shire was their kind of place. The Tooks, however, took to adventure. They thrived on risk. In effect, Gandalf's Call to adventure disturbed Bilbo into seeing how he'd gotten all one-sided. It was time to go to a new level of living and embrace both sides of his family heritage. He needed to do this for himself, but as Gandalf would lead him to see, all of Middle Earth also needed him to get beyond his myopic, Shire-shaped consciousness and grow to his full self. From there he would see his world differently. No longer would he be satisfied to think of just himself and the Shire; he would see himself as part of a larger world and as doing a greater work. Gandalf's Call would take him into greater consciousness, changing who he was and how he understood the world.

But all that lay in a future unknown to Bilbo and not predictable even by Gandalf. In his present moment, Bilbo just needed to resolve his inner war: Baggins or Took? He knew he needed to own both. It was the only way he could be who he truly was. Opening to his Took side, he overcame the fear of his Baggins side, and prepared for the adventure.

From there Tolkien's story takes us on a heroic journey, first with Bilbo Baggins in *The Hobbit*, and then with Bilbo's distant cousin and chosen heir, Frodo, in *Lord of the Rings*. Their adventures unfold into a large and Great Work. When Frodo succeeds Bilbo, he and his companions undergo an initiation into a greater sense of Self and a greater sense of their world—just as Bilbo had before them. Their life-purpose expanded, their lives took on meaning they'd never imagined, and in the process, they inspired fuller lives among other inhabitants of Middle Earth as well. Though their fears and risk-aversion never went away, and though discomforts were often intense, both Bilbo and Frodo mixed these uncomfortable states into a new balance that increased their courage, love, and fulfillment. Companions accompanied them; kindred spirits provided hospitality along the journey; and spiritual powers met them when they needed them most.

The purpose of their journey was the destruction of the "one ring," a master ring of power crafted by Sauron, a dark lord, to control the other rings of power: three held by Elves, seven held by Dwarves, and nine held by Men. During the adventures of the Ring, the seven are swallowed by dragons or regained by Sauron, the nine (along with their human owners, now the Nazgul) are back in the control of Sauron, but the three remain held by the Elves. If Sauron were to reacquire the "ring to rule them all," not only the Elves but all of Middle Earth would be controlled by him. Only Frodo and his companions could prevent this. But to do so, they had to persevere through danger-filled forests, blizzards, and encounters with ferocious orcs (goblins) on their journey to return the ring to the place where it was originally forged: Mount Doom. If Frodo kept the ring, it would corrupt and destroy him. If he dropped it into the fires of Mount Doom, it would be destroyed and the threat of world domination averted.

The drama on Tolkien's Middle Earth parallels the drama on planet Earth. Here fierce and enormous corporate powers, compulsively and deliberately, grow bigger and more dominant as they strategize ways to impose themselves on Nature and all nations. Their "rings" include patenting genes, which gives them ownership of agriculture and life itself; negotiating global trade agreements, which guarantees their profits and economic control of countries; and "buying" elected officials, which gives them the power to legislate and rule from behind the scenes. With these they expand MultiEarth ways across civilization. They appear unstoppable. They dazzle us with the wizardry of technologies and new economic tools. They rival the best dark wizards of Middle Earth.

But rising up everywhere across the MultiEarth preeminence, OneEarthers are answering the Call to live according to Nature's paradigm. Our determination grows in the face of MultiEarth excesses. Increasingly, we are joining our efforts to live inside of Nature's dynamics, inside of Earth's self-regulating bioregions. These powers of Nature continue to reveal that they are too big for MultiEarth to finally gain power over them. They show that MultiEarth powers can never get the "fourth ring." Nature refuses to be fully controlled.

Even so, our Call to live within Nature's paradigm is as demanding an epic as the heroic adventures of Bilbo, Frodo, and

Our Heroic Journey to Keep Earth Livable

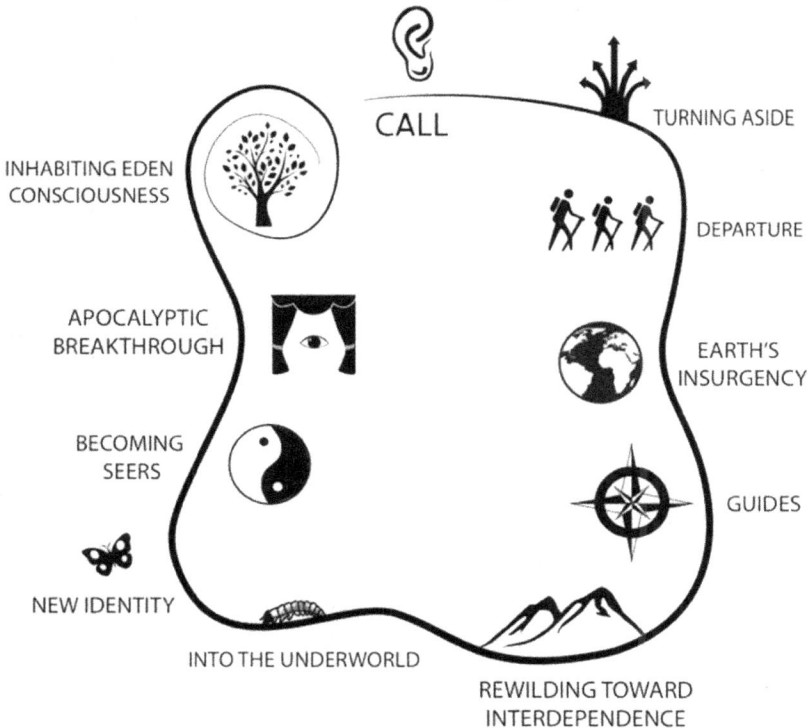

CALL

TURNING ASIDE

INHABITING EDEN
CONSCIOUSNESS

DEPARTURE

APOCALYPTIC
BREAKTHROUGH

EARTH'S
INSURGENCY

BECOMING
SEERS

GUIDES

NEW IDENTITY

INTO THE UNDERWORLD

REWILDING TOWARD
INTERDEPENDENCE

their companions. It takes us into our fuller capacities as a species. Getting there is no casual stroll inside our comfort zone. Rather, we are being summoned to conduct a complete makeover of who we *Homo sapiens* are in the world—our psychological identity, our spirituality, our social policies, our way of conducting business, our educational assumptions and processes, our cultural expressions, and our relationships with all species. Everything undergoes change when we shift from MultiEarth to OneEarth ways. Even our "radical individualism" and "us-versus-them" thinking has to change to a larger sense of Self and "all-of-us-together" thinking. As this shift to interconnectedness and cooperative thinking expands among us, we can be sure that Gandalf has come into our "Shire."

The Anatomy of Call

When I asked a friend why he was an attorney, he replied, "I am called to be one." His education in a Jesuit school had made him quite aware that "voice" and "vocation" are linguistically joined (Latin "vocare") and that the voice within was a holy encounter, a Call to vocation, an inner voice not to be ignored. He has sought to be faithful to that vocation amid the rampant ethical challenges placed before him by clients, the system of justice, and peer expectations.

Without knowing it, he articulated how I understand Call. To me, Call has the kind of impact on us that helps shape our life choices. It lodges within as a living and corrective presence. It brings meaning to our work that cannot be written into a job description. Because it's an integral activity of our souls,[21] experiencing Call is inescapable for every human. We can, of course, be so oppressed by poverty or wealth, or so caught up in expectations of culture, family, and living standards, that we're too distracted to recognize the voice that conveys Call to us. To recognize the voice of Call, we need to be attentive to what stirs within us, and what prompts the stirring. We may be stirred by another person, a particular story or book, other living things, Earth, or other sources. Sometimes Call comes through the configuration of gifts and interests we've been given. We may like our Call; we may shrink from it. Our family may like it or try to dissuade us from pursuing it. The economy may reward it or force challenging financial circumstances upon us. But Call is the kind of phenomenon that requires response.

Given the many voices appealing to us, including conflicting ones, it's a good idea to "test" the Call. By that, I mean to bring it into conversation with others, and to try it on for size in our activities in the world. It's been said that if what we're thinking is Call doesn't smack of being too big, or even impossible, then it's not Call. Testing Call makes external what can sometimes be too internal; it makes collective what can be too egoistic and individualistic. In such testing, Call may be confirmed or redirected. Others may resonate with it and strengthen it, even join in, sharing in the work to which we are called.

When these basic descriptors of Call are applied to the choices confronting our human species, we can see that our choices are a personal and collective Call to shift paradigms. The challenge before us to move *out* of MultiEarth lifestyles, MultiEarth economics, and MultiEarth ecology, rings and reverberates as a Call *into* living OneEarth ways. We are called away from civilizing Nature and into living within her. The Call may feel welcome, unwanted, impossible, or some of all three. It is an invitation to a heroic journey that changes who we are to such a degree that we no longer want to be where we've been. On the journey, we find ourselves becoming what we never thought possible. The tasks of this Call are our Great Work, as described in Chapter Two. The motivation to say "Yes" to it does not come from pleasing others or making money. Our "Yes" comes from a mix of dynamics that we experience as summons, compelling invitation, impossible, and inescapable imperative!

In the 21st century, no human can be deaf to this collective Call to Earth-centered living. The voice rises from our souls, and comes at us from Earth through her weather, oceans, and lands. Soul and Earth speak with one voice. They add resonance to one another like octaves played on a keyboard. Their resonance even lives in the construction of the words "ecology" and "psychology." The"-logy" ending to the words derives from the Greek "logos," meaning "word" or "voice." Thus, ecology is the voice of the "eco-," or "oikos" in Greek, meaning "house." Because *oikos* refers to any house, from a personal habitat to the whole inhabited Earth, "ecology" is then the voice of Earth, our common home. Similarly, psychology is the voice of the soul. Though ecology and psychology are typically thought of as far apart, the construction of the words links them in the sense that they each have a voice. Their voices are like magnetic north and south poles in the anatomy of Call. Magnetic poles, though apart and different, cooperate to form unified electromagnetic fields which provide the energy for everything electric in our world. Ecology and psychology function like that in the anatomy of the Call; they energize our move into Earth-centered consciousness.

The "Earth Pole" of the Call

The vital importance of electromagnetic fields to our world would not happen without the unifying cooperation of a magnet's polar opposites. Likewise, the Call to our Great Work happens through the cooperation between our psychologically dynamic Self and our ecologically dynamic Earth. The ecological or "Earth Pole" is the outer, visible terminal of the Call, and the psychological or "Self Pole" is the inner, invisible one. The two interact to generate the oomph for moving us into new topographies of consciousness that are larger, more mature, and more able to accept both the weight and the deep joy of OneEarth being.

Because our species has created a civilization that has numbed us to the great energies generated by the Earth-Self polarity, we've thrown ourselves into the multi-millennia project of civilizing everything we can, bringing it under our control. Not thinking of Earth's ecology as having voice and speech, we have designed technologies that override many of Earth's ways of talking—the natural signals by which she tells us that she resists our ways. Most of the time, Earth's deep geological, oceanic, and atmospheric dynamos have remained quiet enough for us to put Earth's speech out of our daily consciousness. We've been schooled to think that the advance of human progress puts Nature and Earth in our service. Civilization's subjugation of Earth continues to bring forth amazing new products and possibilities that we could not have imagined a few decades ago—or maybe even last month. So it happens that civilization, dependent on the resources and capacities of multiple Earths, has greater influence on how we think and act than our one and only Earth does.

But Earth has not gone into a coma, nor have her ways been superseded by civilization's progress. The evolutionary process of 4.5 billion years continues with full vitality, adapting and resiliently responding to every impact, be it the asteroid from the Cosmos that destroyed dinosaurs 65 million years ago or the single dominating species of *Homo sapiens* that is destroying habitability today. Earth has been moving beyond MultiEarth's civilizing inventiveness as surely as superbugs evolve to move beyond the powers of antibiotics and pesticides. Earth is making it clear that our models of civilization squeeze her much too tightly. Asserting her wildness, she's breaking out of our constraints.

Like Gandalf to Bilbo, and more emphatically than at any time since the arrival of *Homo sapiens*, planet Earth is holding us accountable. She is urging us to accomplish our primary purpose. When we do not listen to Earth, we miss our primary purpose and we get the current global reality which cannot survive Earth's ecological and geological powers. As mentioned previously, in terms of geological stages, the baton of Earth's story is being passed to that new era which Thomas Berry called the "Ecozoic." MultiEarth consciousness has not yet come to terms with how Earth is signaling the end of the Cenozoic Era. As humans, we have to do a lot of remodeling of our minds and life patterns in order to get in step with what Berry saw happening:

The Cenozoic is the period of biological development that has taken place during these past 65 million years. The Ecozoic is the period when human conduct will be guided by the ideal of an integral earth community, a period when humans will be present upon the Earth in a mutually-enhancing manner. The Cenozoic period is being terminated by a massive extinction of living forms that is taking place on a scale equaled only by the extinctions that took place at the end of the Paleozoic around 220 million years ago and at the end of the Mesozoic some 65 million years ago. The only viable choice before us is to enter into an Ecozoic period, the period of an integral community that will include all the human and non-human components that constitute the planet Earth.[22]

The Earth Pole of our Call to the heroic journey comes from this nearly unfathomable evolutionary change Berry saw as being well underway on our planet. Let's turn now to its complementary opposite, the "Self Pole," which brings an inner-outer balance to our Great Work by getting us beyond ego to the larger identity center we all have in our soul's anatomy.

The "Self Pole" of the Call

Just as civilization has dulled our alertness to the dynamics of Earth, so also it has numbed our awareness to the extraordinary dynamics within us. Because our egos, not our Selves, have designed civilization, we have no accurate sense of what is possible when what inhabits our Self Pole gets activated. Egos cannot comprehend or imagine the capacities of Self; egos fear them. Self's capacities are too big for egos to manage. In subsequent chapters (especially Chapter Eight), I will describe more fully the powers and potentials of the Self Pole. Here I want only to recognize the role Self plays in the Call to move us into Earth-centered consciousness. Self can recognize the elements that comprise Earth-size, or OneEarth, living and see their full potential. Egos lack the capacity to do so. This explains a lot of why our human response to climate change has been so inadequate, why we unnecessarily send species into extinction, and why our choices continue to put life in jeopardy around the globe. The smaller consciousness of our egos can cause what's happening, but can't manage it. We need the wholeness-seeking powers of the Self which egos shun.

Unless the latent capacities of the Self Pole are activated in us, there is nothing in us sufficiently capable of interacting with the Earth Pole to generate the energy for our change to Earth-centered living. Earth counts on us to evolve to our fuller evolutionary capacities—especially to move our identity from ego to Self. When we get a new phone or credit card, we can activate their latent capacities with a simple phone call. But to activate the Self Pole we need to develop psychologically and spiritually beyond the relative immaturity that MultiEarth civilization expects of us. Civilization values the ego thinking that pushes us to move up in the hierarchy of power, control, and wealth. But Earth calls us to center in an "all-of-us-together" kind of thinking. It's a conversion that comes more quickly and easily to some of us than others.

But whatever time and effort conversion takes, getting there means getting to know and center in the deep Self. It's an amazing alternative to the identity center that ego provides. The Self center's extraordinary capacities include being able to do Earth-size thinking. It eagerly goes beyond the confines of ego's civilization. Self knows that civilization cannot be our ultimate destination. Operating from the identity center of Self, we can turn civilization into a learning time, and make it a stepping stone to Earth's Ecozoic Era. Self consciousness can reverse the damage of the ecological and species imbalances that have resulted from pursuing civilization's beliefs. The events of the current Anthropocene Era call on us to leave ego as our primary center of identity, relocate our center to the Self, and be clear with our ego that its purpose is to serve the Self. Doing so gives the Earth Pole a partner in the Self Pole—a duo able to energize our move into the OneEarth paradigm.

Not that our egos will cooperate easily with such a transition. Insecurity, inadequacy, and the need for control prevail in ego-centered thinking. To compensate, our egos exhibit an inflated sense of their own value. But underneath, they have inklings that they cannot match the extraordinary capacities of Self. Learning to reassure our egos that they too have a role, and to love them into cooperating with Self, becomes an important task as we embrace the Earth-Self Call.

To Whom the Call Comes and How

The Invitation[23] from Earth and Self comes to all of us. This strong Invitation from Earth and Self rings like an alarm beside the bed of MultiEarth civilization. It's most unwelcome. Civilization doesn't want to wake up to Earth and Self. Nonetheless, the Invitation finds resonance in our psyches. Latent aspects within us awaken. Parts of us have been waiting for just such a signal to rise up and break out of civilizing confinement. These potentials in our psyches long, by evolutionary design, for maturity just as surely as a seed longs to sprout from the soil and grow to its full intent. Awakened by the dynamics circling the globe during these Anthropocene decades, the potentials in our psyches are aroused to say "Yes!" to the Call and make the heroic journey into OneEarth consciousness. With a ready partner in the Self Pole, Earth's unswerving intent to continue with her 4.5 billion years of evolution makes the Call to OneEarth living real; its achievement possible.

Instead of seeing the activity of Earth and the activity of the soul as separate spheres entirely—a perspective assumed in MultiEarth thinking—the Earth-Self Call embodies a profound interconnection between these two spheres. If we hear only the Earth Pole, we may focus in environmental activism. Or, hearing only the Self Pole, we may focus in personal growth. It's the integration of the two that's special about the anatomy of the Earth-Self Call. The full Call heals the wounds caused by the excessive separateness MultiEarth ways have imposed on us. Separating us from Earth,

Your Call to the Heroic Journey of Earth-size Living

Earth and Self join in inviting *you*

to participate in our planet's move into the Ecozoic Era;

to cross over into topographies of consciousness that are
Earth-size and Spirit-infused;

and to intentionally live conscious of our interrelationship

with all of Earth's community of life.

This Invitation calls you to your fullest capacities—

An identity capable of OneEarth living.

MultiEarth has assigned us sovereignty over her; separating us from Self, MultiEarth has limited us to ego consciousness.

Earth and Self know the same tunes. Like a jazz duo, they play many riffs, but the core Invitation to greater capacities of being and action carries through. The Call can cause nights of tossing and turning. It can slow us down with an illness that gives us time to consider it more thoroughly. It may erupt with outward behaviors that cause us to lose our job, bring changes to our place in our families, or redirect our goals in school or work. Careers embarked upon can be disrupted. Relationships may be challenged. But, whether undertaking the Earth-Self Call proves bumpy, or relatively smooth, it comes with great love and takes us on the path that is ours to walk.

We are wise to give full attention to all that this Invitation stirs up within us. This Call—let me state it with italicized emphasis—*does not come only to gurus of consciousness, to prime ministers, spiritual masters, leaders of ecological organizations or businesses, or people who are well-educated. It comes without prejudice to all humans.* Throughout the dozen millennia that the Civilization Project has been in existence, some in the past did see—with visionary and prophetic imagination—what Earth is now awakening in all of us. But today the Self must become the center of identity for our species—first for a numerical tipping point of ten to twenty percent, then for all. It's how our species is designed to partner with Earth. If only the exceptional respond to the current crises, the Great Work cannot be accomplished.

Given the unresolved issues of gender in our species, I want to emphasize that the Invitation comes to women and men alike. Well, not exactly alike. Each gender has both a similar and also a specific energy with which the Invitation is engaged. The dominance of patriarchy in recent millennia messes with the heroic journey as it is undertaken by both women and men. Moving along on the journey requires that we think of masculine and feminine energies not only as genders, but also as archetypes within all of us. Thought of in this way, the mythic journeys of both heroes and heroines join together helpfully for all of us. The feminine and masculine energies move us along on a journey too big for any of us alone or any gender alone. But as both energies come together in the center of the Self, they can interrelate in a holistic way that patriarchy has prevented. Patriarchal rule in the MultiEarth global culture has egoistically divided the archetypal feminine-masculine unity into polarized pathologies of genders. The Call to the heroic journey includes healing the wounds and pathologies of that division. A new holistic integration of the two cannot come quickly enough. We need the masculine and feminine energies interacting fully, archetypally and interpersonally, in order to accomplish the greatest work our species has yet been summoned to undertake. Wherever the journey moves differently for men and women, the differences will enrich both of us when we function in a consciousness of interrelating much like the poles of Earth and Self interrelate in the Invitation and journey.

Another familiar separation that is healed as we move along on this heroic journey is our scientist and spiritual parts. The Earth-Self Invitation is carried to us from sources where mysteries of Spirit infuse all that science can observe and know factually as well as all it can never know. The mighty forces of our planet and our deep Self join to push us out of zones controlled separately by spirit or science, and into where we see and understand those zones as a single larger space. We come to know this space when we open ourselves to using imagination and reason together. MultiEarth consciousness favors a division between these two. But OneEarth consciousness facilitates interaction between our scientist and spiritual domains. As a result we perceive possibilities which either acting alone does not comprehend. For example, the rational consciousness of science, which our egos have favored, commonly regards Earth as inanimate and without consciousness. But the Self delights in connecting with all that remains unexplained and contradictory for the ego—a venture of spiritual openness to possibilities. In an act of spiritual curiosity, Self welcomes what comes leaping out of the boxes in which egos arrange all that we know or think we know. The boxes of contained and scientifically tested knowledge need the open fields of images and imagination in order to consider whether an inanimate Earth might not be just a construct of ego-thinking. By bringing science and spirit, reason and imagination, together, Self-consciousness can open us to consider whether and how Earth may be animate as she interacts with all life in ways ego-conscious never considers.

Botanist Robin Wall Kimmerer (Potawatomi), Distinguished Teaching Professor of Environmental Biology at the State University of New York, Syracuse, speaks of the "grammar of animacy" and how the language she hears in the woods from plants and waters conveys animacy, whereas the language she hears in the biology lab names each part after seeing it intimately. One is the language of subjects and being, the other of objects and observation. She tells of the impact on her when she first discovered that her Indigenous

language has a word for the life force that pushes mushrooms up
through the soil:

> I honor the strength of the [botanical] language that has
> become a second tongue to me. But beneath the richness of
> its vocabulary and its descriptive power, something is miss-
> ing, the same something that swells around you and in you
> when you listen to the world. Science can be a language of
> distance which reduces a being to its working parts; it is a
> language of objects. The language scientists speak, however
> precise, is based on a profound error in grammar, an omis-
> sion, a grave loss in translation from the native languages of
> these shores.
>
> My first taste of the missing language was the word
> *Puhpowee* on my tongue. I stumbled upon it in a book by
> the Anishinaabe ethnobotanist Keewaydinoquay, in a trea-
> tise on the traditional uses of fungi by our people. *Puhpowee*,
> she explains, translates as 'the force which causes mush-
> rooms to push up from the earth overnight.' As a biologist,
> I was stunned that such a word existed. In all its technical
> vocabulary, Western science has no such term, no words to
> hold this mystery. You'd think that biologists of all people
> would have words for life. But in scientific language our ter-
> minology is used to define the boundaries of our knowing.
> What lies beyond our grasp remains unnamed.[24]

Science hesitates to use language for the animacy of Earth. So it is
that the Invitation comes through the language of science *and* the
language of spirit. It arrives as a grace that our Self can receive, and
that our egos are forced to think about even if it overwhelms their
capacity. To use poetic, spiritual language, it connects us with the
One, the Source, the Wholeness who lives in the Cosmos and in
whom the Cosmos lives; it connects us to the One who lives in our
souls and in whom our souls come alive. Call can come to us quite
logically and reasonably. But its fuller dimensions are also primal.
It comes through science and from sources beyond what science

speaks of. While Call is sometimes scientifically precise, it can also be poetic, mystical, even wordless. Earth and Self spare nothing in their desire to deliver their Invitation to us. They want us to move to our greatest capacities.

A Personal Experience with Call

The weeks of my chemotherapy stretched into five months. With five-day treatments every four weeks, my months divided into two bad weeks and two pretty good ones. But the bad weeks, which included throwing up every evening, dragged me deep into depression. During those days, just loading or unloading the dishwasher felt like a full day's work. Across many hours, I was slowly learning how to do nothing—a hard lesson for me. I'd already had to take a leave of absence from my work as pastor of a congregation; now any activity seemed too much. More than I knew, I'd attached my worth to a life of doing, doing, doing. But during the "bad weeks," just trying to read or put thoughts into sequence was futile.

One morning during those weeks stands out. It was winter 1996–97. December, or maybe January. I was home alone, enveloped in an unwelcome nothingness, when a thought formed in the barren landscape of my mind. Given that my ego had seemed unable to form a thought, the clarity of this arrival surprised me. I turned my attention to it, knowing it had come without any agency on my part. Clear as a spoken voice, it said, *Lee, not someday, but now!* I knew exactly what it meant.

During the several years prior, I'd become interested in organizations working to undo injustice with just alternatives. When announcements of events on economic justice came in the mail, I read them as if they were a letter from a lifelong friend. But then I would ask myself, "If I did participate in this event, how would I translate what I learned into value for this congregation? How could this congregation participate in this justice work?" Most often those questions stumped me. Then, with some pangs of psychic pain, I would reluctantly lay the announcement aside, adding it to a stack of papers on my desk. "Someday," I would promise myself.

Up to that point in my career, I had continued to believe that congregations were, or could be, a strategic and primary change maker, a space where subgroups in a congregation could be little think tanks generating alternatives to a culture shaped by corporate-ledeconomies and superpower thinking. But the Voice that spoke in me during the chemotherapy-induced depression punctured that belief. I was coming to see that congregations tend to be much better caretakers of the casualties of corporate-led economies and superpowers than agents for changing social and economic systems. Valuable as it is to bring care to all who suffer wounding from today's systems, I knew that this was no longer my Call. I was being moved to make changes in the system itself.

Relatively few congregations in my experience have proved up to the challenge of organizing alternative communities that make addressing systemic change their mission. Wonderful exceptions exist. Martin Luther King, Jr. was certainly able to mobilize religious leaders and a percentage of congregations to address issues of worker and racial justice. But even during the civil rights movement, from the Montgomery Bus Boycott (1954–1955) to M. L. King's assassination in 1968, only a minority of congregations, black as well as white, fully engaged. White pastors in cities felt helpless when white members moved out of the neighborhoods of their congregations and black families moved in. Changing neighborhoods emptied out many white congregations at the time. Congregations weren't institutionally flexible enough, nor interracially conscious enough, to adapt. The emptied buildings were left standing in neighborhoods that now had far less money, different culture and music, different lifestyles, and more people living at the margins of social-economic systems than at the center. The Voice I heard telling me "not Someday, but now" had me thinking that my time of working in a congregation was ending.

Not that I didn't know of exceptional congregations. Some effectively combined humanitarian caring, spiritual empowerment, and witness for systemic justice. Certain congregations in Tucson, Arizona, continue to stand tall today as they tirelessly work for just immigration policies. They show remarkable persistence and effectiveness in their humanitarian work and advocacy for migrants crossing the U.S.-Mexican border, driven by the economic injustices of NAFTA (North American Free Trade Agreement) and other policies. U.S. economic practices toward Mexico and Latin America continue to undercut the economic viability of hundreds of thousands of small, family farmers as well as village economies. As a result, many Latin Americans reluctantly make the choice to provide for their family by heading north. In some villages it's practically a rite of passage into adulthood for youth to seek work in the U.S. despite multiple life-threatening risks they take crossing the border. Some who cross in the Tucson area benefit from the work of involved congregations. Kudos to those congregations and to congregations everywhere that are able to connect justice to spiritual practices. Included are congregations advocating for Fair Trade, LGBTQ rights, living wages, ending the death penalty, and greater care of Creation in general.

Typically, congregations and faith-based schools and organizations are comprised of people with a broad spectrum of political views. This makes institutional involvement in changing systemic injustices nearly impossible without surfacing feelings that divide the participants into factions and threaten the institution's future. With such high stakes, the tendency is to limit mission to so-called "spiritual matters." That position, though it appears to be neutral toward systemic change, actually supports the reigning political and economic systems, including their injustices. But for me, it had become impossible to separate spiritual matters from the rest of the world; I had come to believe that the spiritual infuses all the rest.

Regarding ecology, too few congregations have thought out their worldview sufficiently enough to be able to align themselves with the Earth-size and Earth-centered patterns of ecological justice. When their mission, building, caregiving, and education do not get shaped by a OneEarth paradigm, then MultiEarth practices win by default. OneEarth practices get expressed only fragmentally. Though every such fragment matters and has an impact, what languishes is the integrated teaching required for the mass scale of change that we need at this time. To further emphasize my point, the word "church" derives from the Greek word *ekklesia*, and means to be called out of imperial civilization into creational living. Simply put, the challenge of living up to the meaning of the word "church" lies beyond what congregations shaped by MultiEarth living can do.

So it was that my experience of "church," including 30 years as a pastor, became a questionable arena for me as I thought about how to act on the clear Call, "Lee, not Someday, but now." Cancer had awakened me with a start! I began to think of my illness and chemotherapy treatments as a "kiln of transformation." The lucid clarity of that Voice in the otherwise emptiness of my being, commanded my attention. I could not imagine doing anything other than to rearrange my life and comply. It was not a suggestion; it was an imperative! Without questioning, I began to plan for a change in life direction. Economic justice themes would no longer be lost in a stack of papers on my desk. They would be front and center. I knew that what I had been doing had gotten me to where I was. I wanted to go in a new direction, and the Voice I heard while in the transforming kiln made that direction clear. As soon as my chemotherapy treatments ended and my strength returned, I set about changing what I said I'd do "Someday" to doing it "Now."

That was early 1997. By August, 1999, I had resigned from my position at my church and retired from pastoral ministry. I was 58. Juanita, my spouse, had retired the previous year from working in a global corporation—a work environment she had come to recognize as toxic for her. We agreed on important choices as we transitioned into lives structured by our respective Calls. One choice was to move out of our home in the suburbs into an intentional community in Chicago. Since our incomes from work were coming to an end, we developed a budget to live on less than half of the slightly-more-than $100,000 we had earned together. It was surprisingly easy, inclined as we were to live materially in what someone has called "simple elegance."

As life continued, the Earth Pole was activated for me and nothing less than the force of Earth herself amplified my inner Call. Increasingly I turned toward Nature as the center of my spiritual nurturance. I craved learning more about her species and felt a deepening sense of awe as I became aware of their interdependence. Earth's Voice spoke to me in transcendent, sacred ways through stunning beauty and endless intricacies that left me in awe. Her behaviors also disturbed me. As Earth acted out through extremes of weather, carbon-burdened air, acidifying oceans, and dying soils, I heard her crying out against MultiEarth ways. As I learned more and more about her cry, I heard other species join in. I was coming to see that a huge cast of actors is livestreaming a dark documentary on abuse, torture, and murder. Today, the human takeover of natural habitats races ahead. Biocide increases. As we displace species from vast regions of habitat, we show some mercy by arranging reserves and zoos for survivors. Though the work of reservations and zoos to preserve diversity of species is heroic, its magnitude is not keeping pace with the rate of extinctions, poaching, or habitat destruction. The Voice I heard via all these means enlarged my Call. What had been focused in economic realms has morphed for me into a Call that sees economics inside the parameters of the environment. Such an "ecological economy" inverts the MultiEarth economies that see ecology as merely a subcategory of the overarching topic called "economics."

Why the Earth-Self Call Requires a Heroic Journey

In a baseball game, a hero gets the game-winning hit in the last inning. In a movie, a heroine stands up to the powers that be, overcomes the odds, and makes the key difference as she helps good triumph over evil. But it's in mythology that heroes and heroines take on their most profound significance. Consider a myth in which the hero and heroine leave their familiar environment and travel into an unfamiliar region in search of some benefit on behalf of the people and culture called "home." Perils await. All too soon adversaries intervene in surroundings that are unknown. They rise up to do all in their power to prevent the mission from succeeding. The hero's or heroine's lack of essential power becomes obvious. Success in their mission appears unlikely; even their survival is threatened.

But a secret wisdom comes to life in the struggle. Each time the hero or heroine acts in full submission to the task, risking completely who they are in their ego personalities, ways open up for them to continue the journey. Ego consciousness, as it was before they took the risk, was not capable of seeing what opened up to them following the risk. New allies also emerge with each new challenge. This pattern repeats itself along the heroic journey. Each repetition grows the consciousness of the hero and heroine. They move into new topographies of consciousness with expanses beyond anything ego knew or could know when the journey began. As their consciousness grows, the powers of the hero and heroine increase. More of their capacities become known to them. But, of course, the next challenge makes even the newest capacities seem insufficient. And the pattern repeats again.

In the subtitle of this book I say that our challenge is to keep Earth livable. In the face of MultiEarth practices that continue to put more greenhouse gases and particulates into the air every year, keeping Earth livable means radically changing MultiEarth civilization's thinking and choices. The exponential explosion of the human species in the 20th century from 1.5 billion in 1900 to 6 billion by 2000 and continuing to over 7.3 billion currently[25] has caused more impacts on Earth's species and our planet's carrying capacity than what we've accurately calculated. If we'd have had the equivalent of a biofeedback machine to give us immediate feedback on what the rapid expansion of our species was doing, we'd have been more likely to make some different choices. But most of the indicators we have used to measure our activity have encouraged the growth of our species into the current damaging imbalances. The rapid numerical increase of our human species at the expense of other species continues even though it is agonizingly unsustainable. Without moving into a topography of consciousness beyond what egos can handle, we cannot keep Earth livable. Only through metamorphosis into the capacities of Self identity can our species align with our living planet's ways. And that metamorphosis requires a heroic journey.

Weighing Our Response to the Earth-Self Call

It's quite possible that some of us feel we've already gone on a heroic journey. After all, it's taken a lot to get to where we are. Let's give it a round of applause. It's equally possible that the Call to the heroic journey comes more than once in a lifetime. Life has a way of presenting new crises that require more of us than what we can handle. Said another way, choosing to identify with Self rather than ego always smacks of the heroic. It's a recurring choice that takes us on psychological and spiritual quests. The growing pains can be severe as our lives twist in new directions and reconfigure where we didn't even know we could go. We do not get to where we can say, "There! I'm done now." If we do, we'll be surprised by developments that announce, "There's more to come." Change is more primary than stasis.

Unlike other experiences of great change and turning to which the Voice calls us, the Earth-Self Call includes our planet as a pole of the whole. The Earth Pole makes all the difference in giving this heroic journey the weighty task of keeping Earth livable. The Earth-Self Invitation requires us to weigh questions like:

- How can I tell whether I need greater consciousness than what I have in order to be an integral member in a OneEarth community comprised of Earth, other species, other humans, and my own soul?
- On what do I base my belief that OneEarth living is reachable?

- If everyone were doing as much as I'm doing, would the human ecological footprint[26] fit on our planet?
- What additional choices am I willing to make to align my lifestyle and ecological footprint to fit OneEarth living?

Our answers need to be good enough to hold off the baying, skeptical voices inside and out that say dismissively, "You're talking about utopia. It's never going to happen. We'll never get beyond the greed and selfishness of humans. You're way too optimistic about what flawed humans can achieve. We have to be practical." But, of course, the most practical we can be is to be in step with the planet. It's cynical and defeatist to think we're here as victims of ourselves incapable of opting for greater consciousness able to shape Earth-size living.

In the 1960's, a committed group of young people who sang and strategized for a different and better world wrote a well-conceived plan called the Port Huron Statement.[27] It concluded with these words: *"If we appear to seek the unattainable, as it has been said, then let it be known that we do so to avoid the unimaginable."* Their statement fits perfectly our situation in the 21st century.

As is, unimaginable breakdown in Earth's life-generating systems is underway. We weigh our response to the Earth-Self Call knowing that we have become a humanity of planetary misfits, not "good fits." The universal Call for humans in the 21st century is how to shape lives and societies that fit on this planet along with the other species. The questions continue to roll towards us: Can we see ourselves *inside* of Earth's 4.5 billion years of awe and wonder? Or will we continue, as we have throughout the Holocene-Anthropocene epochs, to construct a destructive platform of living *outside* of her truth? Will we continue to believe in our divine right to progress by extracting from Nature on the cheap and dumping what we can't use for profit? Or will we move to a greater consciousness in which we need Nature's wildness more than we need to civilize and use her? How willing are we to submit our thinking to radical revision—to re-think how we understand ourselves? To re-think our relationships to Earth and all her inhabitants? Renowned physicist and theorist Albert Einstein (1875–1955) made such re-thinking central when humans made nuclear weapons for the first time. He said: "The world we have created is a product of our thinking; it cannot be changed without changing our thinking."[28] The Earth-Self Invitation is to go on a heroic journey that changes our thinking in a world where ecological crises have multiplied in size and number beyond anything we've ever known.

Vaclav Havel (1936–2011), a literary dissident from Czechoslovakia, and later the president (1989–1992) of the Czech Republic, saw the gravity of our planetary situation and urged us into a revolution of consciousness: "Without a global revolution in the sphere of human consciousness, nothing will change for the better… and the catastrophe toward which this world is headed— the ecological, social, demographic, or general breakdown of civilization—will be unavoidable."

Havel knew from his own experience how a revolution in thinking could impact everything else that gets called "revolution." During the hard years when Czechoslovakia was an oppressed satellite of the USSR (Union of Soviet Socialist Republics), the superpower of the East and arch-rival of the U.S. at the time, Havel practiced bold, public dissent. With pen and action, Havel gained international attention as he protested the severely constricted freedoms imposed on his country. It was part of his heroic journey to be involved in freeing his country from superpower domination. Dubbed "The Velvet Revolution" (1989)—a revolution of consciousness more than force—it concluded with Havel being elected president.[29]

Havel's call for revolution translates for us into a clear RSVP to the Earth-Self Invitation: "Yes! We're in!" The young people who affirmed the Port Huron Statement in the U.S. of the 1960's, and Vaclav Havel in Europe a couple decades later, had the flashes of consciousness needed to live believing that a better world was achievable. They are being echoed in this century. The World Social Forum, which began in 2001, has served as a venue for how to construct a world different from the one being constructed by MultiEarth globalization, the World Trade Organization, neoliberal economics, and the rule of transnational corporations. Today the slogan, *otra mundo es posible* ("another world is possible"), sustains groups of Mexico's Indigenous peoples and many others around the globe who boldly, creatively organize sustainable societies autonomous from the superpowers of globalization.

It's not being dramatic to say that the stakes couldn't be higher for us as we respond to the Earth-Self Invitation. If we agree to it, we leave whatever security the *status quo* can give us. If we complete the journey, we'll trade ego's civilization consciousness for a transcendent consciousness that can open us up to a story as big as Earth and Cosmos. It's a story sure to reshape us into new beings, capable of new relationships with all Creation. But if we decline the Invitation, then we cannot expect Earth to be inhabitable for children already born or those to come. Parenting, grandparenting, and caring for all children in the 21st century and beyond includes being on the heroic journey to which Earth and Self call us. Only through our "Yes!" to the Call will we experience the metamorphosis into new beings capable of deconstructing the MultiEarth world and reconstructing our lives and societies into OneEarth living.

The Earth-Self Invitation fits well the definition of Call which holds that a Call needs to feel impossible. That our soul's inner drive can be inspired by the sheer impossibility of the Earth-Self Call may astonish us, but it also holds our salvation. The next two chapters explore more fully the consequences of saying, "No!" (Chapter Four), and the anxieties of saying "Yes!" (Chapter Five).

Conclusion: Our RSVP to the Earth-Self Call

Throughout this chapter, I have emphasized that we can move beyond the ego-identity that stops us far short of our fullest capacities as humans, and our responsibilities among the species in Earth's community of life. Because we've been shaped in an ego-centered culture, many of us lack faith to believe that we can transcend what we're doing and get on with OneEarth living. Egoistic world-views have shaped civilization and do not recognize our innate capacity to live something greater. But the Earth-Self Call does. In the U.S., our national and cultural mythology is to be a leader of civilization, not to move into topographies of consciousness that transcend it. Changing out of that mythology, and moving beyond the ego-centered inclinations in us that our culture reinforces so aggressively, is our *magnum opus.* Our children cannot live in an inhabitable Earth if we do not undertake the journey to which we are called.

In my case, nothing short of cancer uprooted me from an earlier expression of my Call, rewiring me for a new direction. I simply was not conscious of the many energies at work within me that required changes which I was not inclined to make. Most recently, the Earth-Self Call has me wondering: "Am I living in the topography of consciousness necessary to express OneEarth living?" My inner voice says I need to go further into the topographies of consciousness where my thinking and living become more Earth-size. I need to become more aware of what in my own unconscious prevents my journey into topographies of greater consciousness, as well as the potentials and powers there that want to move me along. The psychological pressure within me to move beyond what my ego center can do is joined by the geological and ecological pressures around me. Together, these pressures comprise a spiritual union extending a most formidable and unavoidable Call.

Egos may talk of greener living and caring for the planet, but ego-centered consciousness is too small to break out of MultiEarth living. Ego consciousness cannot be expected to get us beyond the "Great Illusion" that I described in *Blinded by Progress: Breaking Out of the Illusion that Holds Us* (2013). That illusion keeps us living beyond the capacities of our planet even though there is no Planet B. The heroic journey can break us out of that illusion because it combines inner and outer change at a scale that fits the needs of our planet. If we make only the outer changes of the Earth Pole of the Call, they will soon be coopted by ego-centered thinking. If we make only inner changes of the Self Pole of the Call, they will not embody themselves on the planet, and the cycles of civilization will continue on a deadly path. Together, the Earth and Self Poles get us to OneEarth thinking and living.

Of all the species, we have the greatest potential for consciously moving into OneEarth topographies, but it requires us to use the Self identity center. It's a capacity and a destiny that brings joy along with an equal portion of responsibility. If we turn from such a destiny we add to Earth's crises, as the civilization story shows. Earth is holding us and the civilization we've created accountable. We cannot escape that our Self center of identity has developed capacities to replicate faithfully Earth's cooperative, unselfish behaviors. Our ego center of identity did not evolve such capacities. During the Holocene-Anthropocene Epochs, our consciousness got mired in ego-centered immaturity, like waterfowl mired in an oil slick. As a result, our consciousness needs a good cleaning in order to swim and fly into Self's greater consciousness. By accepting the Earth-Self Call to our Great Work, the heroic journey, we can get there. Still, doing so involves us in a major psychological-spiritual passage—a dying to one identity (ego) and a rising to a new one (Self). The resulting new consciousness turns inside out the way we think in the MultiEarth view. Instead of being here to rule Earth, we move to respect her reign, one in which we participate as part of a radically democratic way of living.

The compelling power of this Call resides to a significant degree in recognizing its origins. With origins simultaneously deep in our souls and in Earth, its primal sources cannot be surpassed. Furthermore, it echoes in the cry of all the species suffering drastic loss of habitat. We cannot decline this Invitation without unwanted consequences for ourselves and all of Earth's inhabitants. To say "No" to the Call, we decline Earth's great grace; a turning away from the evolutionary purpose she gifted to our species. Said another way, to refuse declines the sacred, the Divine image that is both in our souls and in all of Creation. The wholeness toward which our souls congenitally aspire is aborted before it can be born.

Conversely, by accepting the Earth-Self Invitation we step into an astonishing moment of initiation that expands our capacities to think, imagine, and act in ways that fit the gift of our planet.

The Earth-Self Call to the heroic journey is a weighty summons. Earth, a complex self-regulating system of sub-systems, will, of course, continue whether we agree to the heroic journey or not. She will recalibrate herself for continuing evolutionary processes even if our human species fails to convert from our ego thinking, ethnic identities, and imperial-centeredness. The changes now happening in Earth's soils, oceans, and atmosphere point to where our ways are at odds with life itself. The judgment Earth is currently passing upon MultiEarth's Civilization Project moves ahead, and it moves at her pace, not the pace of the ego consciousness in charge of climate summits or economic policies of central banks. Whether or not to say "Yes" to the Earth-Self Call is not a debate between political parties or a debate between business and environmentalism. It is a debate with Earth. She determines the agenda and the time at which it must proceed.

The very actions of Earth that judge the Civilization Project to be terribly out of sync with her capacities also assure us that Earth's preference is to gracefully regenerate life as it can be—a planet characterized by interdependent wellbeing. Earth is telling us plainly, "You are now where the road divides. Which route will you take? Will you just keep doing the same thing as long as you can? Or will you take the heroic journey to live with me and regenerate the community of life?"

By choosing the heroic journey we become active participants in a great transition from one geological era to another. There's been nothing like it since our ancestors transitioned from the Pleistocene Age to the Holocene-Anthropocene. In addition to the potential for apocalyptic breakdown of the Civilization Project, cooperation and productivity beyond anything MultiEarth achievement can imagine will happen. When this consciousness evolves widely, well beyond outstanding examples of spiritually evolved beings and isolated societies, we will come to a tipping point, tipping toward

Ecozoic living. Underused parts in our psycho-spiritual DNA will flower. Once activated, they can provide us with an expansive consciousness which knows how to live centered in the Ecozoic world. We will move into a wide practice of the OneEarth economy, a OneEarth Community, and a living democracy. Nothing utopian is intended by this description. It simply affirms that the greater consciousness of which we're capable enables us to engage in all the struggles and joys that a OneEarth life and society portends.

Ponder, Discuss, Act

1. Bilbo and Frodo Baggins had their lives interrupted by a "call to adventure." How has your life been "interrupted" by a Call you could not ignore?

2. In your experience of Call to the heroic journey, what anxieties and affirmations do you experience?

3. Reread the Earth-Self Invitation. Describe to yourself or others how you are hearing the Call from Earth and Self at this time in your life. Put yourself into Earth's experience. How would you express a Call to the human species to press ahead on the needed heroic journey?

4. What is your RSVP to Earth's Invitation? What action can you take as part of your RSVP to the Invitation?

5. How has your consciousness, or what your life is about, shifted as a result of having entered into the Great Work?

6. If a couple wanted to engage you in a conversation on whether or not they will choose to have children given the challenges of the 21st century, how does the Earth-Self Call to OneEarth living impact your response? Consider, for example, the contrasts in rearing children according to the MultiEarth or OneEarth worldviews (see also the Table in the "Appendix").

CHAPTER FOUR

Turning Away from the Call

The hero, as [Joseph] Campbell puts it, is the 'man of self-achieved submission'—a submission to 'what is.' When you submit to being, you attune to what the world asks of you: the hero's 'call to action.' But Campbell characterized the tyrant as the 'man of self-achieved independence'—and that independence is a separation from being, a refusal of the call.[30]   —Philip Shepherd

In their bipolar dysfunctional system, Tyrant and Weakling—usurper and abdicator—need each other to remind themselves of their other half.[31]   —Robert Moore and Doug Gillette, *The King Within*

If you bring forth what is within you, what you bring forth will save you. If you do not bring forth what is within you, what you do not bring forth will destroy you.   —Jesus, *Gospel of Thomas*

Perhaps some people follow the Call immediately, but resisters predominate. So much within us does not like Call; that wishes it away. As the sense of Call gets too strong in us to ignore, various arguments of resistance line up: "I must be responsible the way civilization says to be. I must provide security for myself and my family." Or, "This Call rode in during an emotional experience; it's not to be trusted." Or, "I'll ignore the Call until it moves on? I'll erect boundaries around my comfort zone and 'do good' where I am." Or "No! I'm not following this Call-voice. I'm letting it know who's boss. I have other plans."

Ego consciousness feels uneasy as soon as it's confronted with something as big as the Earth-Self Call. Egos

- fear the unknown into which the Call inevitably takes us.
- don't want to risk the sense of security they've managed to achieve, even if it is an illusion.
- fear parents and other loved ones will frown on choices that we make to heed the Call.
- fear lower incomes or loss of retirement and health benefits will result if we follow the Call.
- want to be in control, and don't want to recognize the greater powers of Earth and Self to direct life and societies more holistically.

But the Earth-Self Call does not give in to ego's arguments. The Voice comes from places beyond ego's domain. Its ecological, psychological, and spiritual charge of energies put unsettling, though ultimately empowering, thoughts into our minds. The Call can distract us by day and awaken us from sleep at night. It may persist gently or come upon us with the force of the angel who surprised Mary in Nazareth with the announcement she was to bear a special child. If we follow Mary's response to Gabriel, we will risk our ego security and social acceptance for a greater identity beyond ego's knowing. But we may also choose not to walk Mary's path. We can just admire her from a distance, can't we? For ourselves, we'll choose security. We just want to live life as we imagine it. We'll leave to Mary the kind of Great Work she did.

As happens so commonly, security and control seduce us with their comfortable familiarity and promise of a future planned in ego's favor. Sticking with the *status quo* brings a sense of being in charge. Call? No thanks. We're with Bilbo: life in our shire is good. Life in the larger world is too big for us to have much impact there anyway. We know what we need to know, thank you very much, and are satisfied to leave well enough alone. And, if it turns out that life is less than we once hoped, then we'll take comfort in the accomplishments we've achieved and the love we share with family and friends.

But…. And this is a big "but."

Saying "No" to Call Energizes the Tyrant in Us

The "but" I speak about is this: we can decline the Call *but* the numinous energies of the Call don't die just because we decide to ignore or decline it. We may think that it's a case of *out of sight, out of mind, but* it's *not* out of our lives! Saying "No" to the Call means we don't go on the heroic journey, *but* the energies of the Call live on in us undercover. And not in positive ways. Their intended purpose having been declined, the energies of Call become tyrannical and unconscious. Since the energies are stronger than what our ego can handle, our outmatched egos must now deal with those energies as tyrants living in the unconscious rather than as the indefatigable energies fueling the Self on the heroic journey.

In his book, *New Self, New World* (2010), Philip Shepherd explains much of what's happening in the world today as the result of widespread rejection of Call among our species. As Shepherd sees it, over the millennia of civilization, the intelligence center of our species moved from the belly to the head. As it did, the integral relationship between belly and head, body and mind, unraveled. Intelligence became less and less embodied; more and more abstract. Since Call and the heroic journey are primarily embodied experiences, not abstract ones, the journey to which we're called involves us in re-embodying intelligence. From the Call that begins the journey, all the way through to the reward and return, the heroic journey depends more on embodied intelligence than on thinking it out in the head, though both come into play. If we rely on head knowing alone, we will turn aside from the heroic journey, arguing with embodied intelligence that we've found a shortcut or a superior way.

This separation of head intelligence from body intelligence manifests prolifically in the scenarios we live in the world today.

Refusing the heroic, the experience of the tyrant controls so many lives:

> In mythic terms we are the tyrant who won't become the hero. We receive the hero's call but refuse it, because we believe ourselves safe and secure.... Myth warns us that when we indulge our tyrannical tendencies, we inherit the tyrant's lot in life. We have no security of being, and so we live with the tyrant's anxieties. We try to fill the emptiness of our being, and so we suffer the tyrant's greed and restlessness.... In identifying so closely with the tyrant, we have even come to share a tyrannical ideal of freedom, which is the ability to disconnect.... Thanks to our disconnection, we have also inherited the tyrant's rampant fantasies.... We've gone mad. I can't believe politicians are still talking about the necessity of economic growth—as though the planet were going to grow along with us.... Our current crises are a product of our hallucinations, which arise directly from our broken relationship with the body.[32]

The dissociation between our minds and bodies extends to how we think up lifestyles and economic-social structures that are separated from the planet-body on which we depend. The pathology of this separation from the natural world shows up in the endless stream of one-sided decisions that institutions and inhabitants make against Nature. These decisions need the balance that body intelligence brings. Head intelligence, acting alone, proceeds as if the world didn't need the bodies of plants, people, or planet. When we structure life and systems on head intelligence separate from Nature's body, we behave as executioners of bodily life everywhere across our planet. We may avoid the Call to the heroic, but the consequence animates a tyranny of planetary death.

Another dangerous illusion we see when head intelligence dissociates from its embodied partner, is "self-made" people. The presumption is that being "self-made" is strong, showing how to achieve greatness on our own. Mythologist Joseph Campbell boldly tackles that notion, along with its cousin, "rugged individualism," showing that neither can be signs of greatness in a world where interconnectedness is a primary rule of Nature. Civilization repeatedly confuses the achievements of the dissociated tyrant with the achievements of the interdependent heroic.

In *Hero with a Thousand Faces*, Campbell writes:

> The inflated ego of the tyrant is a curse to himself and his world—no matter how his affairs may seem to prosper. Self-terrorized, fear-haunted, alert at every hand to meet and battle back the anticipated aggressions of his environment, which are primarily the reflections of the uncontrollable impulses to acquisition within himself, the giant of self-achieved independence is the world's messenger of disaster, even though, in his mind, he may entertain himself with humane intentions.[33]

MultiEarth civilization's stories of self-made men and women, far from being worth emulating, are stories of "the world's messengers of disaster"—people of disembodied intelligence. Seeking to be independent, individualistic, and self-made are immature, egoistic imitations of the full capacities we move into when we shift our identity to Self. When we look beneath the luster of the "self-made stories," as Shepherd and Campbell help us do, we see that concentrations of power and wealth, whether in individuals or societies, result, in large degree, from decisions made when body and head intelligences have lost their interconnectedness. Self-made people have become pathologically dissociated from the innumerable sources that have flowed into their lives, not the least of which is a MultiEarth paradigm that brought them favors. Such is the unconsciousness of tyranny. The Civilization Project exemplifies the tragic imbalances and inadequacies thought to be justified when we function with such unconsciousness.

The distribution of wealth in today's economy is another prime example of head-body dissociation, global economics being almost totally a product of head intelligence. Shepherd specifically links wealth to the tyrant's control of the Civilization Project, not to the heroic journey that achieves OneEarth living.

> Wealth is the primary means within our society for achieving the tyrant's independence, and we not only long for that kind of independence—we see it as a measure of personal value, freedom, security and choice. We have been raised to believe that the pursuit of personal gain is our birthright—as if the goals of the tyrant supplied our purpose for living. The seductiveness of that belief obscures our true birthright, which is harmony and the spirit of service that enables it; it is a birthright that requires a soul's journey, a transformation of consciousness. Wealth is not a catalyst for such a transformation, but a deterrent to it. The tyrannical independence made possible by wealth has as its prime goal the *avoidance* of transformation, the maintenance of the status quo of our mistaken identity.[34]

In MultiEarth civilization, even when persons of wealth feel eager to do good with their wealth, more philanthropy serves to advance MultiEarth thinking and living than it does transformation to heroic, OneEarth ways. MultiEarth wealth more often prevents than facilitates the greater purpose of our species to live with transforming consciousness and democratic interdependence with all species and bioregions.

In contrast to the disembodying of intelligence that happens in the MultiEarth world, OneEarth cannot happen without re-embodying intelligence of the head and integrating it with belly and heart intelligences. Embodied, OneEarth consciousness thinks of wealth ecologically as well as economically. Wealth resides more in ecospheres than investment portfolios. Our body intelligence tallies wealth in terms of what flows through the ecospheres, nurturing life's bonds of interconnectedness. The animals and plants of an eco-region do not inspire us because they exhibit "self-made" achievement, but because they exhibit participation in astonishing webs of relationships that exceed what our heads understand. Our belly intelligence transforms our understanding of wealth and how to work with it. As the heroic journey progresses, wealth looks nothing like the wealth that tyrannically prevents transformation.

Meeting the Tyrant's Opposite

The tyrant is not the only archetypal energy awakened when we reject the Call. It's polar opposite, the weakling, is too. Archetypes have a bipolar structure, which explains why we so often act one way and then, later, act the opposite. To better understand the tyrant-weakling phenomenon, we need a more detailed picture of the Self than what we have so far. The pioneering psychological work of Carl Jung (1875–1961) redrew the map of our souls, showing new and different structures from anything that his predecessors had discovered. He came to see that our psyches had anatomies comprised of what he called complexes and archetypes. These, he discovered, were universal throughout our species.

A contemporary Jung scholar, Robert Moore, has extended Jung's ideas—especially regarding the Self center of identity. A post-graduate training analyst with the Jung Institute of Chicago, Moore calls himself a "cartographer of the soul" and has developed a neo-Jungian map of the deep structures of the psyche. His map shows the bipolar composition of the four archetypes that he regards as the essential anatomy of the Self: King, Warrior, Magician, and Lover. The names of these archetypes tilt to the masculine because Moore was working on masculine psychology at the time. But he believes the structure of the Self to be the same for women. They can be renamed for use in feminine psychology.

Doug Gillette joined Moore to write a set of books about these archetypes. They describe the dark behavior of these archetypes in immature masculinity, as well as their beneficent behavior in mature masculinity.[35] Immature, unhealthy masculinity is common in patriarchal societies. Moore and Gillette help us see clearly how differently the world gets shaped by healthy, mature expressions of the archetypes of Self compared to unhealthy, immature expressions.

The Moore and Gillette book series goes on to speak of the Self center of identity in terms of the *potentials* and *energies* of the four primary archetypes in addition to the *structure* they give to the psyche. These three—structures, potentials, and energies—provide meaningful ways to talk about the Self center of identity. As *potentials*, archetypes hold the possibilities of our fuller capacities as humans, capacities which go unused in smaller, ego topographies of consciousness. As *energies*, archetypes fuel our journey into those larger topographies where the fuller capacities of our potential can develop muscle and become effective. Understanding our archetypes as structures, potentials, and energies helps us get to know better the powers within our Self. It's the kind of Self-knowledge that encourages us to look beyond our inadequacies, and come to trust that we can work collaboratively with others to increase Earth-size living across our planet.

Adding further to our Self-knowledge, Moore and Gillette spell out how the four archetypes behave in both their unhealthy bipolar activity and in their healthy integrated activity. In their healthy behavior, each contributes to making the heroic journey possible:

- The King/Queen establishes mission, direction, and goals that shape our response to the Earth-Self Call, then stewards these throughout the heroic journey.
- The Warrior in both genders serves the King/Queen by bravely engaging fears and conflicts we face while on the journey. Warriors do so assertively and nonviolently. Their motivation stays clearly focused on fulfilling the mission of the King/Queen.
- The Magician in both genders tends to the metamorphosis of the journey, combining together non-rational, rational, imaginal, and empirical elements. He/she mixes the elements in ways that are mysterious to egos but which changes hearts, minds, worldviews, and behaviors. As a skilled alchemist of

the soul, the Magician is in the thick of our transformation. Whether we feel pain or joy, the processes brim with surprise and a sense of the sacred.

- The Lover activates inherent potentials and energies for cooperation, empathy, and relationship. As a result, we unfold, blossom-like, into embracing the interrelatedness of all things. The power of the Lover brings to larger topographies of consciousness dimensions of love our egos cannot know or express. The Lover brings a different kind of chemistry to the interrelatedness of all life than what egos imagine as even possible.

When these four energies interact synergistically, we experience capacities that we doubt to be possible while living in ego consciousness and the civilization it shapes. A Self with these four archetypes functioning well pursues heroic change without becoming inflated. When we live from such Self identity, we can stand up to the daunting odds with which MultiEarth civilization challenges our OneEarth intentions, and, joining with Earth, we can prevail. Whether or not our life choices look desirable to ego-centered people matters little to us. We know that ego-controlled identities can only catch glimpses of the Self's levels of function, and those glimpses happen only in a peak moment or on a "good day."

But here's the kicker, and with it comes the explanation of what happens when we turn away from the Earth-Self Call. The Call is stressful! Overwhelmingly so. The four major archetypes of the Self serve as engines of enlightenment and OneEarth living only when they function in health. Under stress or fatigue, the archetypes express their dark polarity. One side of that polarity overwhelms the ego with far more energy than it can handle. The ego inflates. Exploitation and dominance—both characteristic of the tyrant—result. Alternately, when the other side of the polarity takes control of the ego, it disengages. The energies of the archetypes are withheld and ego has no zip to challenge the unfairness that harms Earth, other species we need, or excluded members of society. We then sabotage our own intentions and let down or even betray people we love.

The energies in the polarized state are invariably excessive. *Inflation* of energy makes us act with exaggerated potency: ego assumes it's in charge and that its ways can prevail, whatever the situation. *Deflation* results in acute impotency of action: ego feigns innocence, makes excuses for itself, and steps back from accepting responsibility for our behaviors. Both inflation and deflation happen because ego tries to handle archetypes without Self's help. But it can't. Ego identity's most helpful role is as a subsidiary to Self identity. When ego becomes inflated with archetypal energies only Self can handle, aggression results. The King/Queen usurp control in MultiEarth's dominating fashion; the Warrior becomes combative and violent, even savage, in crushing dissent; the Magician arrogantly pursues her/his changes acting as if they're good for all but manipulating them to advantage some over others; and the Lover becomes grandiose in thinking she/he is greatly admired by many, loves being well-connected, and develops addictive relationships that overflow boundaries.

Conversely, when ego becomes deflated of all archetypal energies, passivity results. The King/Queen abdicate responsibility for MultiEarth's failures, making excuses for their part; the Warrior acts like a victim of circumstances that treated her/him unfairly; the Magician can't effect change or impact, acts dumb, confused; and the Lover becomes emotionally numb, claims little need for close relationships or spiritual connection, closing down rather than risk learning she/he is not liked.[36] Even when we stretch to put the best face on these behaviors, the energies and potentials of polarized archetypes can do no better than MultiEarth civilization. Even when MultiEarth discussions and decisions try to do better, or try, for instance, to be greener, the efforts are often sabotaged by the bipolar behavior of unconscious archetypes that egos can't handle. Consequently, the paradigm change that Earth and Self call us to is not undertaken.

Each of Us a Tyrant and Coward—Really?

As I sat listening to a gifted black preacher speak one January at a breakfast in memory of Martin Luther King, she began, predictably, with her greeting and courtesies. But then she said, "I have a hard saying for you today." As we all wondered what she had in mind, she proceeded in a style I greatly appreciate: she interacted with her audience until the voices responded, "Go 'head, sistuh. Let us hear it!" Having gotten their permission, she proceeded to speak boldly.

Though I'm unable to get your permission before you read this, I will, nonetheless, alert you that a hard saying follows: *unless we make the heroic journey to greater, Earth-size consciousness, we will fluctuate back and forth between weakling and bullying behaviors, between behaving as predators or as those abdicating our responsibility for our planet's habitability.*

This hard saying works broadly in our lives, families, businesses, campuses, governments—across civilization. To take a simplistic example, during my high school years, I loved playing basketball. But my play was terribly inconsistent. I would play well one game, then mess up the next. The mess up typically happened as a result of basic errors. I was baffled by how this was happening and stopped trusting my abilities in the game. Since I didn't get this corrected during my playing years, I never could contribute my best to the team.

In ways far more significant in life than high school basketball, I've been baffled by moments where I couldn't connect with my own inner power to fully show up as my fuller Self. I have often remained quiet in challenging situations, unable to "show up" with what I feel and think. As a result, I've betrayed relationships and underperformed in jobs. But then, the opposite has also happened. My silence in one moment can flip and show up as a stubborn, even petulant, gotta-be-right kind of person. Such tyrannical behavior reveals my hidden hurt or annoyance, not a healthy kind of personal power. The weakling withdraws; the tyrant attacks. Only the maturing Self navigates life and uncertainty with a more integrating, balancing spirit.

Over time, these flip-flop patterns of weakling-tyrant behaviors just seemed to be me. But feedback, both loving and hostile, told me that I was confusing, even angering, people. I was certainly frustrating myself. I came to understand that not showing up on the one hand, or having to be right, on the other, were both ego strategies that I was employing in order to avoid responsibility for my own feelings and behaviors, especially in tense situations. I constantly played out these strategies in my mind because head intelligence was my default setting. I used it far more commonly than my belly intelligence. I now know that whenever the pattern of weakling-tyrant appears in my life, it means that I am off my path and unable to follow the Call of do the Great Work. Of course, I often recognize it only after I've hurt people or not shown up in a situation where I had a useful contribution to make. I doubt that truly owning our behaviors as either weakling or tyrant ever gets easy. Tricky, disturbing stuff, this becoming more aware of *all* of ourselves. But, immeasurably rewarding too.

Though I've opened the door for you to see what's going on within me, what's happening there is universal in our species. No one avoids tyrant-weakling behavior despite our desire to be mature and capable. Consider our role as predators on the planet. As *Homo sapiens*, few of us think of ourselves as predators despite how the civilization we tout and brag about dominates other plant and animal species, coercively controls weaker countries, and plunders the planet. Not that we don't fall victim ourselves to predation by other species. Venomous spiders and snakes bite, microscopic viruses infect and kill, and bears and large mammals take lives. Our biggest predator, though, is our own species. The many ways we kill one another further reveals the pathology and tyranny that results when egos reject the Earth-Self Call, but then become possessed by the bipolar archetypal behaviors of the Self. Under the sway of unhealthy, tyrannical archetypal energies, we kill one another through wars and violence. Accidents from vehicles, machines, medicines, and other inventions take thousands of lives annually even though we've invented them for purposes to improve life. In all of Nature, no species has wielded the powers of predation more lethally than we have. Though our culture saves the word "tyrant" for particular nations whom we deem to be our enemies, or for ruthless dictators we want to demonize, to deny the tyrant archetype at work in us is a sure way to avoid moving into greater topographies of consciousness. From Nature's perspective, as well as the perspectives of many of the world's subjugated peoples, the tyrannical powers embedded in MultiEarth practices are coming into full view through global climate change and the crises endangering most other species of the planet.

At the other end of the spectrum, we are familiar with weakling deflation. All of us know the difficulty of standing up to power, or following through on what we believe. Dissociated from the energies of our Self, we cannot bring ourselves to go against our parents' plans for our lives, or rearrange our lifestyles to take a cut in pay, or leave a job with greater prestige, or make other sacrifices in order to follow the Earth-Self Call even when following that Call will keep our planet livable for our own children, not to mention the other forms of life on which our own lives depend.

It's not hard, of course, to name tyrants who ruthlessly step on and destroy others, or who rule corporations with little heart for the workers and environment, or lead military dictatorships. We can also name cowardly doormats who become passive when challenged, are averse to risks, and let down those around them as a result. It is much more difficult for us to see how either one describes *our* behaviors—and most difficult when we're in the behavior. Yet, it is a law of the psyche that turning from our Great Work strengthens in us the passive-aggressive activity of coward and tyrant, weakling and bully, excessive compliance and stubbornness. None of us is exempt.

Even if I'm tempted to turn from the Call, I certainly don't want to choose tyrant or weakling. I'd like to argue for another option. But, truly, none of us has a choice in that matter. The structure of the psyche is as consistent as are the constellations among the stars. I might as well ask Orion to put his belt on another way or ask the handle of the Big Dipper to attach itself to the other side of the dipper's cup as to argue with the structure of my soul. It's far more fruitful to deepen my understanding of what happens in my soul than to pretend I can rebuild it or ignore it. Awareness allows me to work creatively with those moments in my life when the heroic is happening, or, alternately, when tyrant or weakling possess me. Every such moment presents me with a new opportunity to move into topographies of greater consciousness. If such moments reveal me as cowardly and as avoiding responsibility, or as assuming authority that violates other persons and species, then I am being shown how I've gotten off the path of our Great Work as a species. Recognizing what's happening, I can once again choose to get on the path to greater consciousness. The better we come to know the archetypal structures, energies, and potentials of our souls, the more able we are to stay with the Great Work our species is called to.

Bullies and Cowards among Nations and Transnationals

What happens when we turn from the Call personally, also happens collectively. In many instances, the U.S. government stands by weakly as tyrannical regimes in Latin America, the Middle East, and Africa corruptly enrich themselves while in power, and disappear or murder their opposition through death squads they secretly support. No matter how many people such regimes kill, how much damage they do environmentally, or how repressive their laws are toward employees or Indigenous peoples, the U.S. likes them as long as they keep their region stable for "our interests"—meaning for U.S. corporations to extract resources and for the U.S. to be geopolitically dominant in the region. Calls for these countries to honor human rights sound good, but carry no expectation of compliance.

The U.S. cowardice of silence ends, however, when a nation turns against what we want for that region. Then we turn bully. Even if the nation in question has chosen leaders through democratic elections, we will demonize those leaders and undermine their power in every secretive and overt way we can. The democratically elected presidency of Salvador Allende in Chile (1970–1973), and the Iraq Wars of the two Bush presidencies provide glaring examples. Allende initiated policies to keep resources and assets in Chile that were leaving through multinational corporations without fairly benefitting Chileans. In response, the U.S. demonized Allende, assassinated him surreptitiously, and vigorously supported the strong-armed dictatorship of General Augusto Pinochet who succeeded Allende.

More U.S. bully energy initiated two wars in Iraq (1990–1991 and 2003–2011). The U.S. justified these, in part, because Iraq's President, Saddam Hussein, was deemed to have turned on us. He was no longer a friendly dictator, but an enemy whose threat and powers we exaggerated to justify our military attack. We feared a weakening of our control over "our interests" in the region. We stirred up war fever and invaded. In this case the "interests" we were seeking to secure were the region's rich oil fields.

When acting as bully, the U.S. does not accept responsibility for its dishonesty, injustices, or dirty tricks. Our speech is always of democracy and freedom. Yet, when a leader or party arises in one of the countries in our self-declared "sphere of influence," we stop at nothing to defeat them. It must be noted that some of the leaders and groups we treat this way speak and act with greater consciousness than we do. Some of them are in the throes of choosing a more heroic path of freedom and self-determination for their country than anything we have in mind for them.

These are examples of how the archetypes of weakling and tyrant, not hero and heroine, rule the world. They are part and parcel of the MultiEarth consciousness manifesting in the Civilization Project that holds us in its archetypal bondage. Not that U.S. behaviors are unique in this regard. We see the tyrant-cowardice behaviors in most countries of the world. But instead of being a leader set apart, the U.S., with all its power, has not answered the Call to the heroic; instead, it repeats the archetypical, bipolar patterns of power made familiar across the sweep of civilization.

The same bully-coward polarity thwarts international action in the face of the mounting global ecological catastrophe. Economically or politically strong countries—Britain, France, Japan, India, Germany, China, Russia, the U.S.—are not stepping into the consciousness able to provide the heroic leadership being called for by Earth and the souls of people everywhere. All explain why they can't take action to the scale that Earth says they must. Bullying and cowardice alternate in statements from climate summits with strong countries insisting on control of decision-making while small or poor countries are treated as expendable.

As with nations, so with transnational corporations. ExxonMobil, Shell, ConAgra, Monsanto, Goldman Sachs and hundreds of others continue to bully their way around the global economy, reporting bully profits at the expense of Earth and all her inhabitants. Yet, these large, economic powers are immature weaklings when it comes to being responsible for the devastation they bring to species and ecospheres. They cowardly take their business to countries with the weakest environmental laws and slackest enforcement. Though bullying their way as transnational mega-powers—many with budgets larger than countries—they become weaklings, abdicators, cowards, manipulators, and deceivers in the face of Earth's ecological judgments on their business models. They are unable to sustainably steward the ecospheres of their operations, or involve the inhabitants in primary financial benefits. They are unable to lead the heroic journey to a OneEarth economy because they are too lame to measure success by anything other than growth, a measurement that fits only MultiEarth thinking.

How the darkside of the archetypal King/Queen, Warrior, Magician, and Lover operate among transnational corporations gives us more understanding about their behavior in the world than just saying that they are ego-driven. More than ego is at work among transnationals. Their corporate egos are possessed by energies, shaped by structures, and pursue potentials that arise from the immature behaviors of archetypes in the corporation's soul. These energies, structures, and potentials are unhealthy, immature expressions, not healthy, mature ones, because transnational corporations consistently turn away from the Earth-Self Call to pursue business with the great purpose of advancing Earth-size ways. Turning away from greater consciousness and Earth-size purpose redirects how the King/Queen, Warrior, Magician, and Lover work in the transnationals. These archetypal powers of the corporate soul could make possible a heroic journey to transformation in the world. But the inability of transnational corporations to step up and embrace the Earth-Self Call turns the primary archetypes of their identity away from the heroic and toward the bipolar, underworld expressions which now devastate the planet. Not only do their managers turn from the Call that would make their business enterprise become what it needs to be, they also deny the potentials of the Self as having any feasibility in our world. Consciously or unconsciously, their egos know that any serious attempt to put themselves in the service of the Great Work is certain death for their corporation in the current global economy. So they function from the darkside instead. They are not willing to risk the redistribution of power and wealth, nor the loss of shareholders, that transformation involves.

As nations and transnationals continue to reject the Earth-Self Call, the energies that continually put the Call before them go into their underground and become stronger. When these energies surface, they erupt outside of official protocols and controls; they become a dominant force throughout the government or business. Nations and transnationals choose most of their leaders from among persons functioning in the topography of ego consciousness similar to the corporate ego. All involved need to function within the MultiEarth paradigm. Some candidates for leadership appear gentler than others; some are more shamelessly blunt. But few exceptions get elected or appointed. As a result, bully-weakling archetypal energies reign throughout the departments, management, economies, and governments of the world. Dissent and whistleblowing are punished. With such "possession" of the systems of government and transnational business, collective egos and archetypes block the heroic journey for many who could otherwise be encouraged to embrace the Call. In every way, when the tyrant and the weakling are in charge of our collective choices as a country, a business, or a society, our options in relationships and actions are diminished, putting the Great Work out of reach and Earth's community of life at risk.

Civilization: A Result of Turning Away from the Call

It's a hard saying to consider, but in the context of the above framework, the human Civilization Project must be viewed as a product of turning away from the Call, not of fulfilling it. Ego thinks of itself as in charge. At the same time, it cannot embrace the Call without surrendering control and serving the greater identity of Self. Furthermore, ego operates without sufficient awareness that its choices are being greatly distorted by the archetypal presence of tyrant-weakling from the unconscious. The result, when we spread ego control across the millennia in which it has refused the Earth-Self Call, yet remained in charge of the Civilization Project, is our present MultiEarth conundrum.

Looked at in this way, we can see that the MultiEarth project is destined to die. The Self-Earth collaboration takes us into territory where MultiEarthers simply cannot maintain control. The tyrannical aggressiveness of our species has littered history with violence while claiming the highest of causes. Our cowardly withdrawals from the heroism of moving to fuller consciousness have been justified by ego-thinking platitudes like "we can't expect too much from flawed humanity" or "we want to take care of the environment but we need more time." Such postures of low expectation and procrastination are tactics for abdicating responsibility. Martin Luther King, Jr., wrote, *Why We Can't Wait* (1964),[37] to refute abdication and prod assertive action during the civil rights movement. What he applied to civil rights for minorities in the 1960s applies to ecological rights for all species today.

Neither combative, arrogant bullying, nor innocent-acting abdication gets us down the road to the fullest purpose for our species. Up to now, we simply have not understood how the archetypal powers function well enough to break out of them personally or collectively, and so the MultiEarth Civilization Project has continued. But because this *status quo* has so clearly become a culture that our planet is rejecting, we need to reckon more effectively with these archetypal powers.

Accepting the "hard saying" about what happens when we turn away from the heroic journey is like having a bad dream. The benefit of the dream comes to us only when we work with it using two basic dream axioms. First, our dreams are about us, not about the people in the dream. Second, the interactions in our dreams represent interactions between different parts of ourselves. We'd much prefer thinking that our bad dreams are as irrelevant as they are unpleasant. But what our egos call "bad dreams" forcefully bring to our awareness what we've been pushing away. The dream tells us what we need to know in order to move in the direction we most need to go.

Civilization is a bad dream. The tyrant, weakling, and heroic archetypes are key characters. Civilization's bad-dream crises are jarring us into seeing that we remain captive to our archetypes unless we move into greater consciousness. The better we recognize how the tyrant, weakling, and heroic behave in civilization and in us, the quicker the curtain opens for us on a new drama in which we move beyond civilization. We come to see our predation and domination as what we do when the tyrant is in charge. When the weakling is in charge we go along with domination in order to get along. We are too cut off from our psycho-spiritual energies to speak and stand for our truer values. Seeing the truth of the hard reality that tyrant-weakling archetypal energies control many of our behaviors as individuals and in our collective endeavors becomes the launch pad for stepping away from civilization and into the heroic journey.

The consciousness that has shaped the multi-millennia human Civilization Project does not have the healthy archetypal power to move into topographies where new ways of thinking shape life. Unhealthy archetypal power prevents doing so. MultiEarth civilization cannot survive in a consciousness where healthy archetypal powers enlarge our consciousness to make the interconnected "we" our rock-bottom way of thinking and behaving instead of the dissociated "I;" or when the primary way we work with wealth is through the commons of "all of ours" instead of the ethnic protectionism of "ours" or the privatization of "mine." Though some citizens within MultiEarth civilization live in the consciousness of healthier archetypal powers, the culture as a whole—including those who lead and drive MultiEarth civilization—remains in smaller topographies of consciousness where archetypal powers of tyrant-weakling hold captive our species. The heroic journey remains beyond MultiEarth capability.

The MultiEarth Civilization Project specializes in shaping egos to be in charge, not in deconstructing them in order to serve the larger Self center of identity and reshape society to OneEarth living. That's why the majority of people with wealth and power in MultiEarth civilization speak more from ego than Self identity as they tell about their hard work, ingenuity, skill, and knowledge— all meritorious reasons for being "at the top." Some speak more consciously and give tribute to family and certain social privileges the system provided, but few show the consciousness of how heavily the social and economic system tilts in their favor. Those who do become convinced that they must make changes. Some walk away from fortunes and other advantages to reconstruct their lives around causes that take them on the heroic journey. Many stories—from Francis of Assisi to John Robbins of the Baskin-Robbins families—tell of such new identities. The prevailing culture may even extol them individually for their "good deeds." But praise does not translate into building alternatives to the structures that keep MultiEarth privileges in place.

Breaking with MultiEarth civilization requires all of us to avoid self-deception about where we are in the topographies of consciousness. If we aren't on the heroic journey to grow consciousness and to translate it into society, then we must admit that we are mucking around somewhere along the spectrum of ego's pretensions and archetypal captivity. But if we can recognize when we are alienated from psychic and spiritual powers (weaklings) or inflated by them (usurpers), then we are operating with new consciousness and can break with civilization and turn back to the Call.

Cain and Abel—A Turning Away Story

In my previous book, *Blinded by Progress*, I described in greater detail the civilization that resulted as our species, since 10,000 BCE, has usurped and abdicated our way to the present. In that book, I introduced the biblical myth of Cain and Abel through John Steinbeck's novel, *East of Eden*, a 20th century story placed in the Salinas Valley of California. Steinbeck's novel was a modern elaboration of the Cain and Abel myth in which Steinbeck wrestled with whether or not we humans really had the capability to choose out of the Civilization Project. In the Hebrew version,[38] dating at least as far back as the 6th century BCE, Cain was the prototype for MultiEarth living and manifested the archetypal energies of the tyrant-weakling. Abel, meanwhile, was the prototype for OneEarth living and manifested the archetypal energies of the heroic. When Cain realizes that his offering to YHWH, the unnamable Divine Presence,[39] is not favorably received, but Abel's is, he becomes angry.

Like Cain, those stuck in MultiEarth ways expect to set the norms for behaviors across society. They set those norms according to what serves their goals, which many also see as God's goals. Meet these norms and you merit reward; fail to meet the norms and you lose out. They believe their way is best for everyone. But now all of Creation is rejecting MultiEarth norms while embracing OneEarth ways. MultiEarthers act in Cain-like ways: they become angry, go into denial, and engage in self-justification of their choices. All such behaviors express the tyrant-weakling archetypal energies of self-achieved independence instead of the heroic energies of self-achieved interdependence.

When an angry, rejected Cain was warned that evil desired to have him in order to master him, the myth speaks to how the archetypal tyrant-weakling energies desire to master MultiEarth believers. Devoted MultiEarthers partake in a risky venture. They are addicted to more. "Growth is good," they say, and greed, they believe, can be managed through the Market. However, given the heavy-handed manipulation of markets today, a more honest conclusion is that they believe greed is good and can best be managed by global corporations, central banks, various huge financial institutions, and trade agreements. Other MultiEarthers believe government also has a significant role to play in managing human greed. But any plan to manage greed while egos are in control holds no promise for OneEarth living because greed is a kind of archetypal possession of the ego by the tyrant-weakling. The tyrant takes and the weakling calls it good. Loving more takes over, masters us, and tyrannically rules.

Cain, out of anger but also with premeditation, murdered his brother Abel, then tried to distance himself with denials: he said he hadn't killed his brother nor did he know where he was. After all, he wasn't his brother's keeper. The denials resonate with the behaviors of MultiEarthers. In the great oil explosion in the Gulf of Mexico in 2010, death came instantly for 11 people and unknown numbers of animals, plants, and micro-life. For 87 days the crude flowed into the Gulf before the well could be capped, expanding the injury and death in the waters and along over 100 miles of Louisiana shoreline. The petroleum corporation, BP, denied the risks of their deep-water drilling and denied massive killing of species through the crude that spewed into Gulf waters. They used a highly-toxic chemical to disperse the oil so the slicks would not be visible on the surface but sink to the bottom instead. BP sought every way possible to limit its "keeper of the Gulf" responsibilities. They exemplify the MultiEarth business model of powerful corporations that extract from Earth as much as they can as cheaply as they can, and that includes avoiding as much responsibility as they can for damage. In the Gulf, coastal residents complain that they did not receive compensation for the wealth held naturally in their ecosystem. Instead, they inherited the damaged ecosystem that remained after the wealth of the resource was gone. Though large, BP's compensation payments were far below actual costs. Both full compensation and full payment of cleanup would add costs to the corporation involved in the extraction so, as best they could, the corporation externalized these factors from their business equation.[40]

The leaders of civilization have not looked at themselves through the prism of the Cain and Abel myth or its equivalents. But to do so helps us with our choices. Think of Cain as the prototype of MultiEarth civilization and Abel as the prototype of OneEarth ways. Cain turned from the heroic journey he was called to and moved into the tyrant-weakling alternative. Cain embodies the mindset of the civilizers of every generation as they commit to the unsustainable "progress" of the Civilization Project. Today's MultiEarthers live and die by the contemporary version of the Cainite worldview. The OneEarth heroic orientation of Abel continues today to be too much for civilization's mindset to handle. For all who turn away from the Call, Abel's ways of living must be slain.

Turning Back to the Call

Turning from the Call need not be our final choice. If we are able to feel the impact of our tyrant-weakling behaviors manifesting across civilization, we may well want to go another way. We see the damage done to relationships and Nature by egos alternately possessed by inflated archetypal energies they can't handle and then deflated because they have no idea how to access archetypal energies. The cycle brings so much destruction and pain. But without a mature Queen/King, neither we nor nations or corporations can set responsible goals to correct ecological and population imbalances. Immature Warriors can get mean when adversity strikes or, alternately, make excuses and be no-shows. They may give allegiance to supremacy types of nationalism and win-at-any-cost economic growth. Unable to connect with healthy archetypal energies, they cannot fight for ecological health or defend Nature's commonwealth for all. Immature Magicians conjure quick fixes, economic bubbles, and rituals for narrow economic and religious orthodoxies. They fear making mistakes too much to be able to guide the transformations that involve us in the Great Work. Immature Lovers swing back and forth between being flooded with feelings and connecting addictively at one end, or being unable to feel and connect at the other. They cannot love with a holistic love that includes Earth's full community of life and the sacred Presence that infuses it.[41]

If we get our fill of such tyrant-weakling living, giving the Earth-Self Call another chance can make a lot of sense to us. That said, tyrant-weakling behaviors never go away completely. They have ways of reappearing in our behaviors even when our deep desire is to be fully immersed in the Great Work. But the recurrence of tyrant-weakling behaviors need not discourage us. Each recurrence provides an opportunity to strengthen our choices for Earth and Self. The further we proceed on the heroic way, the more we develop our holistic, spiritual muscles. Philip Shepherd, in his book *New Self, New World*, cites mythologist Joseph Campbell as emphasizing that we become heroic to the extent that we continue to practice "self-achieved submission" to the greater, unifying purposes of life. This differs from the tyrant's practices of "self-achieved independence" which disconnect us from those purposes. Weaklings tend to behave as innocent about those purposes or as victims of circumstances making it impossible to participate in life's greater purposes (see the quotation at the head of this chapter).

Because our society continues to be so focused on independence—a keystone in MultiEarth thinking and behavior—the Call from Earth and Self to move away from independence to the fuller maturity of interdependence upsets the habits of thinking throughout our culture. The spotlight of U.S. culture shines on the individual, from the individual salvation of religions to the self-made icons of business, from sounding battle cries of political revolutions to providing security through retirement plans. To embrace the Call, though an individual choice, is a choice away from individualism. It is a choice to submit to the greater interdependence at the core of Earth's life community. As such, turning back to the Call takes us into a deepening love.

Conclusion: Taking in the Hard Saying

The hard reality that this chapter presents can take a while to integrate into our thinking. But the more we do so, the more liberation blossoms within us. The archetypal structures, potentials, and energies of the awakened tyrant and weakling give us "ah-hah" moments of insight into the powers that shape us and our MultiEarth world.

Turning from the Call gives the green light to personal irresponsibility and to the bully-coward, aggressive-passive polarities filling our days and planet. Externally, to refuse the Earth-Self Invitation intensifies the environmental, geological, psychological, and spiritual forces that drive the current epochal changes across our planet. Internally, refusal fragments our psyches' anatomically. The energies of our psyches separate from one another and hole up in various compartments. Separated, these different parts fail to communicate with one another. From this wounded place, we cannot mature or create a mature society. Instead, we become passive or bluff with bravado. We are no longer able to achieve the psychological and spiritual maturity necessary for OneEarth living.

A tragedy takes over. The wholeness toward which our souls congenitally aspire is aborted before it can be brought into the world.

This chapter emphasized that what happens personally and individually, also happens collectively. Consequently, these behaviors dominate the key decision points in the personal lives of our species, the leadership and culture of business, corporations, finance, religion, government, education—all the sectors of society. The better we recognize the wide range of tyrant-weakling behaviors, the better we know what we're up against in the journey to move beyond the entire, multi-millennia Civilization Project. We can see that it's not only about history, it's also about the influence of the archetypes.

How do we take in the hard saying of this chapter? By acknowledging our own tyrant-weakling behaviors and taking responsibility for them to where we correct the damage we've done as best we can. That breaks us out of the civilization that holds us under its influence and readies us to begin the heroic journey.

The story of tyrant-weakling civilization differs like night and day from the story that the heroic archetype writes. Weaving ourselves into the heroic story changes our worldview and the societies we in turn shape. Our thinking flips over from the assumption that MultiEarth living is the way of greatest advantage and leads us on a path able to see in Earth and Self those deeper, more fulfilling advantages we have yet to claim. Earth and Self call us to so much more than what civilization has envisaged thus far. We turn next to that "so much more" to discover how to get there and what it looks like.

Ponder, Discuss, Act

1. How have you experienced turning away from the Call in your own life? What were the results in terms of external manifestations and internal feelings?

2. A behavioral shift often opens our eyes to new ways of thinking. But new ways of thinking also lead to changed actions. It's a testimony to the interconnectivity of everything. How does perceiving your soul (psyche) as having heroic as well as tyrant-weakling structures and capacities lead to new action? Conversely, how do the actions of the heroic as well as the tyrant-weakling create a new way of thinking for you?

3. How does the fact that humans have mostly resisted the Call to the heroic journey impact your understanding of what civilization has accomplished and the "so much more" that we are capable of?

4. What action looms before you as a result of reading this chapter?

SECTION THREE

Journeying Toward
Eden-Size Consciousness

In case Chapter Four's discussion of the consequences of turning away from the Call felt depressing, you'll like Chapter Five better. It roils with the excitement, anxieties, and uncertainties that come with embracing the Call and taking the first steps on the heroic journey. Once we depart on the journey, we overcome the inertia of civilization's familiarity and firm up our personal commitment to explore the unknown. We head into new ways of thinking. We seek to be aware of what we've mostly ignored. We take another look at what we've rejected. We get a feeling that a new moment has come for us, and that if we don't take a chance on this moment, we will miss out on the deeper purpose for which we have come into the world.

A part of the chapter that holds special interest for me tells about the in-between space of having left where we've been, but not yet arriving at where we are headed. Liminal space is another name for it. In that space, I feel uncertain about my path. But for all I don't like about its uncertainties, liminal space has opened me to thoughts and paths I wouldn't have otherwise considered, or even thought possible.

Chapter Six describes Earth as the primary consciousness-changer in the world today. Nothing civilization is doing changes what and how we think more than what Earth is doing. I hear Earth speak through the traumatic ecological crises: "Lee, you and your species are destroying what has taken millennia to evolve. Stop! Look! There's such a better way to go!" The more I look at Earth, the more clearly I see the "better way." I'm inspired to act and to believe that we are capable of making the changes needed for Earth-size living. Why would she have evolved us to be less?

CHAPTER FIVE

Embracing the Call:
Farewell to the Familiar

We let go of an attachment to illusions; this is departure.[42]

—David Richo

The art of letting things happen, action through non-action, letting go of oneself, as taught by Meister Eckhart, became for me the key opening the door to the way. We must be able to let things happen in the psyche. For us, this actually is an art of which few people know anything. Consciousness is forever interfering, helping, correcting, and negating, and never leaving the simple growth of the psychic processes in peace.[43]

—Carl Jung

We are literally hypnotized from infancy by the cultural milieu in which we are immersed; we see the world the way we are enculturated to see it. A prime task of adult life is to become dehypnotized, "enlightened"—to see reality as it is.[44]

—Willis Harman

As for labeling someone a whistleblower, I think it does them—it does all of us—a disservice, because it "otherizes" us. Using the language of heroism, calling Daniel Ellsberg a hero, and calling the other people who made great sacrifices heroes—even though what they have done is heroic—is to distinguish them from the civic duty they performed and excuses the rest of us from the same civic duty to speak out when we see something wrong, when we witness our government engaging in serious crimes, abusing power, engaging in massive historic violations of the Constitution of the United States. We have to speak out or we are party to that bad action.   —Edward Snowden

Rope swings moved to a whole new level for me one morning while on a visit to my friends, Greg Newswanger and Juji Woodring, in the Heathcote Community, Freeland, Maryland. After breakfast, Greg and Juji suggested, "Let's walk over to our neighbor's place and play on his swings." We set out through a patch of forest and shortly arrived at the neighbor's home. We were warmly welcomed to a living room with a rope swing dangling from the center of a high ceiling beam. Without any coaxing, the neighbor and "swing master" hopped on the swing and playfully demonstrated his love for swings as he made large circles around the room.

We chatted about his swings and were soon inspecting others he had around the yard. Finally, he introduced us to the grand-daddy of them all. It was a single long, thick rope that dangled from a tree branch about 50 feet in the air. Big knots tied at the bottom of the rope were its "seat." The idea was to take the rope in one hand, walk over to a ladder built against a tree, climb up that ladder rope in hand, and launch your swing ride from that high perch. But the ladder was mischievously positioned so that it was not possible to get onto one of those big knots at the end of the rope swing without jumping from the ladder, rope in hand, and pulling yourself onto the knot-seat while swooping downward in midair. Soon Juji stood at that very spot on the ladder where she needed to jump onto the swing—or decide to walk back down the ladder. "Wow!" she called out. "You really have to commit yourself at this point!"

Then, taking a few seconds to collect her wits, she overcame her inner turmoil and made the commitment. Swoosh!

Swinging into Departure

I took the next turn up the ladder. Juji was right. As much as I wanted to move from the security of the ladder onto the rope swing before launching, there was no way. I looked down. The ground looked to be 100 feet below (really more like 25). The moment of truth came for me just like it had for Juji. I grasped the rope tightly, put my trust in my arms to pull me securely onto the rope-knot seat *after* I pushed off from the ladder, and *while* I was on my way down. I made it! Quite easily actually. Suddenly, I was into an exhilarating ride of long arcs—down-up, back and forth—until the pendulum I was riding came to a stop. But the turmoil of emotions I had felt at launch time on the ladder had nearly prevented me from launching. There had been that moment when I had to stare down fear and let it know I had every intention to defy it. From then on, it became quite possible, and I had a swing ride unlike any I'd had before.

Similarly, fear doesn't go away when we commit to embracing the Call; it just loses its control over us. All the messages of childhood continue with us as grown-ups, telling us that we are vulnerable and can succeed only at the will of the big and powerful forces of the world. We know well how that world has its ways of getting its "pound of flesh." No wonder, then, that our friends and family may feel afraid for us when the Call takes us beyond what they understand. Instead of encouraging us to live our own, deeper life, they may make it more difficult for us. Messages come at us from all sides, urging us to be secure and "happy" instead of encouraging us to respond to the Call that gives us our deepest satisfaction, and connects us to that for which we're here.

It's true, of course. When we step toward new and greater topographies, into larger shoes and spaces, we face ever-present dangers. When the people we know and love are ruled by fear themselves, they may lose confidence in our judgment if we move beyond where their sense of safety ends. As long as we live inside their comfort zone, we are doing "what's right." But if we move beyond it, which is where Call inevitably takes us, then they don't understand us, see us as foolish or wrong, and may well distance themselves. We are fortunate if we have relationships that encourage us to live the heroic mythology of our own soul and of the grand Call of Creation.

Be that as it may, ultimately we need to take responsibility for ourselves, override the chatter of others, as well as our own internal conflicts, and opt in favor of what we hear Self and Earth saying: *Come, move into fuller capacities. Come to the size consciousness for which you're evolved. Tell your ego to choose maturity over security.*

In a book aimed at helping adults let go of the false illusions we cling to and "hop on the swing," David Richo writes, "To cooperate with the call is to let go of illusions and integrate whatever happens with personal work. What a plight for us humans: our plight is to let go and take hold at the same time!"[45] Or, in Juji's words, "Wow! You really have to commit yourself at this point!"

To embrace the heroic—a synergy between the deep drumbeat of Earth and the yearning of our souls—puts us on the path of metamorphosis instead of conformity. To choose a life incurably drawn to walking into greater consciousness may violate the boundaries of home, parents, congregation, work, and nation, but it will be the life that is ours to live. The journey of the heroic takes us *out of* MultiEarth ways and ego consciousness while simultaneously taking us *toward* Earth Community and Spiritual Consciousness.

Embracing the Earth-Self Call, truly taking it in and being taken in by it, shifts us profoundly to where we feel pain in how MultiEarth choices disturb Earth's balancing ecosystems. The data and alarm of scientists that previously glanced off of us, now penetrate our consciousness and strengthen every step we take on the heroic journey. The knowledge of ecological crises presses into our souls. There the archetypes of the Self rearrange themselves to act according to the Call. The immoral significance of what MultiEarth living is doing clicks in for us and forms the conviction that being in deeper harmony with Earth is a moral act that must not wait any longer. Whatever kept us in lesser consciousness and bound us up in the security of the familiar has now been pushed to the rear by aroused, heroic, archetypal energies too long repressed in us.

We want to get moving. We're determined to get past the thresholds of our souls and societies where sentinels protect the powers that be and keep us from changing. Whether these sentinels be the norms and mores of society, friends who do not want us to go against the group, the prohibiting complexes within us, or those who sow doubts that Earth's climate convulsions are anything more than cramps she cycles through from time to time, we're moving on. Whether by stealth or confrontation and struggle, we're determined to balance initiative with disciplined timing as we leave our comfort zone and head into the journey. Whatever fear we had about unknown territory before has now been overridden by the pain of staying put, and the anticipation of discovery in new topographies of consciousness! What resistance we had to the Invitation has turned to determination to go all the way with it.

By now we know that the risks and costs of resisting the Call are far greater than accepting it. If we resist Earth's ways to correct imbalances in her ecosystems, we will invest energy in what is futile, economically ruinous, and morally wrong. If we resist the deep psychic processes of our soul, we will pay the cost with illness, with the plague of immaturity throughout our middle and senior years, and with the sense of having strayed from, and fallen short of, the best we can be and do.

So off we go. The MultiEarth illusions have lost their luster. We're choosing the OneEarth story. With both courage and fear lending their energies, we head into the unfamiliar.

Deconstruction: Traveling in the Land Between Here and There

Feeling certain that the MultiEarth space can no longer be our space, we set out to test ourselves: how will we do what is necessary to live the OneEarth worldview? How strong is our belief that OneEarth ways will be sufficient to shape life on our planet?

Scientist and novelist C.P. Snow once said, "Between a risk and a certainty, a sane man [sic] does not hesitate." He was urging the West in 1960, to take risks to limit nuclear weapons during the years of the out-of-control arms race with the Soviet Union. Snow's point was that nuclear destruction, whether through intent or accident, was all but certain if the U.S. and Soviet Union continued building nuclear arsenals, transporting them, and posturing with them.

Half a century later, with massive destruction unfolding through ecological crises, we can adopt Snow's comment to renew his appeal for sanity among humanity. As nations come together in climate summits, instead of doing the least possible, leaders must act sanely and take the risks necessary to avert the certainty of global catastrophe. So far, the risks taken are insufficient to avoid the catastrophe being delivered by a combination of an extractive growth economy, systems and policies that intensify the immoral and unsustainable rich-poor divide, crescendoing changes in climates, and technologies driven more by profits and war than by planet and peace. Humanity's lifestyles, households, and workplaces must, like the nations, choose the sanity of greater risks given the certainty of catastrophe without doing so. As the Cenozoic Era exits the stage, it is certain that MultiEarth ways are ending with it. The more humanity feels this great change now destabilizing the foundations of civilization, the more sanity displaces illusion among us. The number of MultiEarthers distancing ourselves from MultiEarth ways is growing, even though we may not yet be clear on how to shape a OneEarth way of life. Early on the heroic journey, we move into this "no longer, but not yet" space—no longer caught up with MultiEarth thinking, but not yet fully into the OneEarth consciousness where we're headed.

We know that clinging to where we've been will not make the Cenozoic Era stay, nor will intensifying MultiEarth ways strengthen their endurance amidst Earth's rejection of them. Too many heads of states and institutions, legislators, and business leaders continue to say otherwise. But Earth is already well along on her move into a different space. She's begun an exodus of unfathomable proportions. Deciding to join her earlier rather than later is the saner of options for us.

Our human inclination tries to leap over this in-between time. We wish we could get on the swing to the new destination of OneEarth living before we leave the launching ladder we're standing on. But the infrastructure for OneEarth living is only partly in place at this time. More OneEarth consciousness and practices need to develop among us and spread with speed of a good news video that goes viral. Nonetheless, we can already opt for many practices tilting toward OneEarth living. We can choose to eat low-meat, organic, and locally sourced diets. We can choose to use credit unions and financial services other than mega-size banks. We can choose to consume less and accumulate only our fair share. We can choose locally owned businesses and farms as our sources for what we buy. All of these can increase OneEarth wellbeing and help us participate in the interconnections through which Nature thrives.

Though we can resist these choices for reasons such as convenience or cost, the more we exit MultiEarth habits of thought and living, the more such reasons wane. The further we go into this in-between space, the more we want to live the "not yet;" we want to make as much of it real as we can. If we leap over this in-between space and time, or try to hurry through it to the next thing, we do not deconstruct enough of our old ways of thinking and acting to truly embrace the new "not yet." Instead, we will contaminate the new with our old patterns of thought and behavior, and the heroic journey will be sabotaged.

A Zen story describes the process of leaving where we've been as emptying. Nan-in , a Japanese Zen master during the Meiji era (1868–1912), once received a visit from a university professor who came to inquire about Zen. Nan-in served his visitor tea, pouring the cup full—and then continuing to pour. The professor watched the overflow until he could restrain himself no longer. Agitated, he exclaimed: "Stop! The cup is overflowing. No more will go in!" To which Nan-in replied, "Like this cup, you are full of your opinions and speculations. How can I show you Zen unless you first empty your cup?"[46]

The professor hadn't thought of the step Nan-in directed him to take. He needed to enter in-between space, and there empty his mind of the consciousness he'd brought with him to that moment. Spiritual teachers of all religions refer to "emptying" as a requisite for living life more fully. Some call it the "Way of the Negative" because it requires that we negate one mindset in order to make room for another.[47] Our ego resists such negation. Why should it need to lay aside some of its proudest achievements in thought and deed? Ego consciousness fears the empty, barren nothingness that the "Way of the Negatives" prescribes. But OneEarth consciousness cannot be added onto MultiEarth consciousness. It is a replacement. Getting there requires emptying; entering nothingness.

Paradoxically, there is *something* within the nothingness. The essence of the Negative is to better discover the Self, and how to make it the center of a new and more capable identity. Into the emptiness comes that other world we seek; it seems to do so spontaneously, unsummoned. Truth is, it has been there all along, but our cup was already full. The Self was unable to enter our spaces of consciousness because we'd been fully occupied by the smaller, MultiEarth world. Though we can empathize with the professor's desire to have the best of both worlds—to hold onto the academically focused consciousness he had while at the same time adding on a Zen consciousness—such an approach cannot work. Zen belongs to a different worldview altogether. It becomes available only when we leave ego consciousness behind for a reconfigured identity within the Self. OneEarth consciousness requires this kind of emptying because it is not ego size. When Self-identity guides us, as it does in OneEarth thinking, it requires ego to let go of MultiEarth thinking, to travel the Way of the Negative.

One evening at a small dinner party, I was in a situation that shows how impossible it is for us to receive a new story when our hearts and minds are filled with the one we are living. A woman invited a handful of us to dinner in her nice suburban home west of Chicago to celebrate the academic achievement of a mutual Filipino friend. Our friend had gotten a PhD despite the difficulty of writing a dissertation in English. Her friends, however, were mostly in the Philippines, so she had only a few of us to celebrate this achievement with her. We appreciated so much that our host had taken the initiative to make this celebration happen. Around the dinner table, I was asked to give a bit of an update on the organization I was with, Jubilee Economics.[48] Soon our conversation turned to how rich and poor countries relate to one another and our host interjected, "What I'd like to know is how can we bring them up higher economically without taking ourselves down?"

Because I had talked about an economy that is more fair than the prevailing one, eyes turned to me to make the first response to the host's pertinent question. So, I said, "We can't. But all of us can live in the abundance of enough, sharing in Creation's great generosity."

The difficult part of my answer was "we can't." Except for our honored guest and her husband from the Third World experience of the Philippines, the rest of us were firmly shaped by the MultiEarth, First World worldview. We lived with more than our share. The assumption of our host, and some other guests, was that the answer lay within the parameters of economic growth, not constriction or redistribution. This assumption is not surprising. It's a widely-proclaimed tenet of American-style capitalism that we can overcome poverty through economic growth for everyone. But it's a tenet that does not hold true on the journey into the greater topography of Earth-size consciousness. Along the journey, we must empty ourselves of the MultiEarth story, a primary shaper of our lives. It feels like giving up our identity—how we think of ourselves religiously, financially, socially, and much more. It's true: deconstruction of ego identity, even when gentle, still takes us apart.

At first blush, such shaking up and emptying out feels wrong. It's such a counter-intuitive thing to do for all who've been living the overarching story of human civilization. That story heralds progress and ascent, development and growth, innovative technology, and "being in charge." Though this civilization story is no more than 12,000 years old—barely more than 5% of the total time that *Homo sapiens* have been on the scene—one of the great accomplishments of this story is that we think of it as THE NORM. As such, the story tricks us into a tragic self-delusion of exactly where we fit into the great story of Earth. Our version of the story puts us in control. Less euphemistically put, we are the bullies of the planet rather than its tenders. Though our version of the story has shaped some parts of human existence to achieve great good, it has also misled us in ways that are tragically disastrous. On the long path we've taken, we've built success upon success until the path became a road, and the road became a superhighway. But will MultiEarthers—especially those in strategic positions of global wealth and power—continue to drive this fast, multi-lane road with eyes pinched shut and foot pressing down the gas pedal?

This MultiEarth story grips us. The fingers gripping us are our possessions, the expectations of our job and friends, the beliefs of religious institutions we respect, and the seductions of our consumer habits. Moving into the in-between space, we cross into a larger, unfamiliar topography of consciousness where we become able to curl back the MultiEarth story's fingers from our lives. As we move farther beyond what's been THE NORM, we can begin to hug a new, OneEarth normal, and be surprised to meet up with people who are also there.

Elevating "in-between" to Normal

It was in a conversation I had with my son, Lane, long enough ago that I can't remember when, that he called this in-between space "liminal space." I hadn't heard the term before. Lane went on to tell me about the work of Scottish cultural anthropologist Victor Turner (1920–1983) who had made "liminal space" his special interest. Turner spoke of all other points in history as either pre-liminal or post-liminal, thus putting *liminality* at the heart of a society's current experience. I took to the word immediately. It was so interesting to think of each moment as a liminal moment, rather than thinking of liminality as something unusual that happens occasionally.

Following Turner's thinking, being in liminal space is not abnormal, though it may at first feel so. It certainly feels different from what we'd thought was THE NORM. What we want to avoid is having egos, our own or those of other "helpers," rush in and fix our uncertainties. What we most need is for Self to have whatever time it takes to bring us to a more capable identity and an Earth-size consciousness. Earth's changes will proceed, of course, through her own liminal space, sharing with us her tremors and evolutionary course. But for all our eagerness to quickly fix everything, and to do so before MultiEarth civilization fails further, liminal space asks for different behavior. In liminality, we can say plainly and confidently: "We don't need a completely new social-economic system in place before we make our farewells to a growth economy that needs multiple planets to continue. We can place our trust in the ways of Earth and Self to bring us to the 'not yet' of OneEarth's community of life."

In liminality, we begin to think thoughts beyond the questions that our ego consciousness was concerned about. We discover more about how the larger identity center, Self, tackles the questions and proposed solutions arising in liminality. Ego-centered consciousness does not do well with liminality; larger topographies of consciousness centered in Self, on the other hand, find liminality alluring and essential. Functioning from Self, we can reach for things like Eden, which egos don't even try doing, dismissing such as impossible.

Liminality's uncertainties produce a truck load of anxiety for egos. In ego consciousness, we rush for relief, doing whatever we can to normalize life as quickly as possible. Before deconstruction can fully happen, ego thinking returns to the familiar, usually in a slightly reconfigured form that suggests a change has been made. This behavior, of course, totally interferes with the capacities of Self to do its heroic Great Work. To hurry through liminal time to some new, post-liminal way is more likely to result in new guises of MultiEarth ways, not the exodus from them that we need. Hurry-up-through-liminality has been the usual pattern across the history of the Civilization Project. When a revolution succeeds, the revolutionaries all too often and too quickly become like the oppressors they replaced; the revolutionaries simply have not emptied their cups of ego consciousness to get beyond the old way of doing things. Their revolution does not include what former Czech President Vaclav Havel called a "revolution of consciousness." As a result, the revolutionaries cannot follow through on their intent and promise to start something truly different. For that they must journey into greater topographies that embody the Earth-size consciousness of the greater Self.

Our own nation's story follows this pattern all too closely. U.S. colonies broke free of the clutches of the world's greatest empires of the time only to form a nation that would itself become the world's greatest empire, the global leader of MultiEarth economic domination of species and Nature. Those who came to this land from Europe had cups too full of the past and of their own egos to learn OneEarth ways being practiced among Indigenous Peoples. Their revolutionary zeal gained independence from colonial masters, but did not gain, or even seek, interdependence with all species. Hurrying through liminal times, and seeking to normalize life as quickly as possible, they missed the sign that says, "Your Great Work This Way!" In life's departures, liminality is where we discover directions for life that do not appear in the "normal" of civilization. In liminality we have the opportunity to go beyond civilization. Getting "back to normal" misses that important opportunity. Thanks to Turner for telling us to put on the brakes and recognize the gifts in liminality.

Turner's perspective also provides a new frame for the liminal time our planet is in as it leaves the Cenozoic Era. Thinking liminally, leaving the Cenozoic takes us all into a time of uncertainties beyond what we can know. The geological processes are in motion for epochal evolutionary activity. Based on past geological changes that include mass extinctions like we're now in, the current massive, geological-ecological-spiritual passage will likely continue for a couple of centuries or more. That's Earth time for configuring a new geological era.

For Earth, the Cenozoic is now pre-liminal space. Unlike ego's fears, Earth fearlessly enters a period of geological liminality. The Invitation from Earth to us is not to cling to the Cenozoic, but to align ourselves with the transformational energies of liminality and benefit from them. To fight her is futile. Joining her in liminality is our only real choice. And that means journeying heroically to Self identity and larger topographies of consciousness.

Where Earth goes in this liminal geological time is partly determined by the consciousness with which we live. If we embrace the Earth-Self Call, and make it our responsibility to move into topographies of consciousness devoted to Earth-size living, then Earth's actions will be less traumatizing than if we avoid or delay responding to the Call. To remain in ego consciousness is to assure that we will not cooperate with Earth nor cope well with what happens. But from within topographies of Earth-size consciousness, and by living from the identity of Self, we can heroically devote ourselves to reverse the instabilities our activities have put into the climate, oceans, soils, and species. Much of this reversal can be set in motion during the first half of the 21st century if we move into liminal space and rearrange our lives, societies, and economies to do what we already know we must do. If Thomas Berry's vision comes to pass, then Earth is heading for an edenic Ecozoic Era. Whether Earth can move to such an era soon or only over many centuries depends, in part, on the consciousness with which we live.

There is no sugar-coating of liminality that can ease ego's fears of being in such space. Whether irrational or rational, being afraid is what egos do when their control is in jeopardy. The uncertainties and size of changes that happen in liminality beg for new constructs. That eagerness for new constructs in the face of losing the former ones produces the highly transformational environment in liminality. In his doctoral dissertation (later revised into the book,

A Common Humanity), Lane Van Ham speaks of the great creativity and transformations that happen in liminality. In particular, he describes how previous mental borders between people, as well as boundaries between countries, can be transcended when we experience new communities—ones considered impossible while in pre-liminal thinking.

> The unformed, unconditioned character of this 'betwixt and between' moment is often marked by the temporary suspension of status hierarchies, presenting a 'model of human society as a homogeneous, unstructured *communitas*, whose boundaries are ideally coterminous with those of the human species'. Turner says *communitas* 'may be said to exist more in contrast than in active opposition to social structure, as an alternative and more liberated way of being socially human, a way both of being detached from social structure—and hence potentially of periodically evaluating its performance.[49]

Joining with an "unstructured *communitas*" that contrasts to MultiEarth civilization without actively opposing it gives us an important strategy. The heroic journey is less about protesting and defeating MultiEarth structures than about creating workable OneEarth alternatives. Leaving, or being stripped of, how we thought and lived within the MultiEarth paradigm, we are highly motivated to live in a new story and new community. Exodus from a MultiEarth story because it's lost its power for us, frees us to join with others and look at the OneEarth story with new interest. It becomes a story, not only for our survival, but for how we jointly want to live. In a liminal "tribe" where all are getting used to new topographies of consciousness, the OneEarth story can sink into our cells and bellies. We recognize the Earth community of life as where we belong. The uncertainties of liminal space throw us off balance enough for us to consider and embrace many OneEarth perspectives that before we ignored and cast aside.

In liminal space new ways of thinking pop up faster than sparks from a flaming wood fire. Everything that was gets re-examined. Everything new gets considered. Our sense of right and wrong, good and bad, beliefs and assumptions, all get messed with. A new sense of the sacred and holistic Presence arises. New criteria emerge for us. We no longer trust the criteria we used in MultiEarth thinking. The deep examination that we give to everything arising during our between and betwixt experiences makes the *communitas* of which Turner speaks indispensable. Our Self attracts new colleagues, friendships, and loves. It's part of moving from individualist, independent patterns to being part of the interdependent community of life that becomes indispensable as we proceed on the heroic journey.

Befriending "The Other"

Perhaps the most inclusive way to talk about what we encounter in liminality is to call it "The Other." Is there any better, catch-all name for all that the consciousness of egos, in their ethnic and imperial-thinking, reject, ignore, or simply can't fathom? So, by definition, once we go beyond ego consciousness, we unavoidably meet up with "The Other." Little wonder that as Earth leaves the Cenozoic Era, we face lots of "The Other."

The Other changes constantly. It is numinous and pulses with an archetypal mix of energies, potentials, and pitfalls—a mix way beyond what ego consciousness can sort out. That's why when nations, courts, schools, parents, and persons live circumscribed by ego consciousness, they enforce rules against The Other, consider it inferior, and believe it's their duty to protect us all from it. But as we get beyond ego control in liminal space, new capacities begin to emerge for us, and meeting up with The Other connects us with the very energies essential to fueling the journey initiated by the Earth-Self Call. Significantly, the reasons which make The Other a menace in ego consciousness are the very reasons why greater consciousness eagerly explores its facets. To ego, unable to break from MultiEarth living, The Other appears as unorthodox and heretical. It trespasses on ego's love of convenience and rational explanations by intruding as inconvenient and irrational. But what appeared unorthodox, heretical, inconvenient, and irrational before, looks different in liminal space. Some of what had been rejected by the MultiEarth worldview, and had scurried off to hide from the influence of ego and imperial consciousness, resurfaces as true and essential for OneEarth living.

The Other contributes greatly to moving our identity away from ego and imperial limitations toward the greater capacities of the Self as a new center. As The Other overwhelms our ego, with its ethnic and nationalistic preoccupations, we are forced to grow our relationship with our greater Self. In liminality's highly transformative space, our emerging new identity can take in truth too big and too paradoxical for what the more limited ego can do. Charles Dickens' character, Ebenezer Scrooge, in *A Christmas Carol*, gives an example of liminality's transformative power. When on Christmas Eve the spirits visited Scrooge and took him into liminal space and time, he was able to see, feel, and think in ways that he could not or would not before. He was moved beyond ego-centered boundaries into his generous, compassionate, and joyful Self.

Such power of the spirits is also part of Jung's map of our psyches. Jung used the word daimonic to describe the mingle of holy and demonic that can be encountered in territories of The Other. During the Hellenistic empire, Greeks referred to lesser gods as *daimons*. These weren't the major gods of Mt. Olympus, but ones that, nevertheless, directed much of human life from their hidden quarters in the unconscious. Daimons operated outside of ego controls, pushing humans toward both good and evil. Artists testify to the presence of the daimonic when they describe one of their artistic achievements as having been generated from beyond their ego capacities. Sometimes these results have been conjured through mind-altering drugs. Nonetheless, they are daimonic in that they are ego-transcending and often a mix of holy and demonic.

Most importantly for Jung, daimonic described the elemental force that seeks to drive us irresistibly to greater consciousness. He found this force in every human and group he studied. This force takes us on the journey to which Earth and Self call us, but does not necessarily heed social mores in its determination to bring us to the fuller consciousness of OneEarth living. Whether or not the daimonic elements behave according to social norms, they serve us well by connecting us with The Other as we say farewell to the familiar consciousness of ego and empire.

The daimonic Other also hovers near and inhabits every organization, business, campus, congregation, nation, and culture collectively. Any individual or group who identifies themselves only with their conscious mind in ways that suppress, exclude, attack, and dominate what is The Other to them is operating from a less invigorated consciousness than what OneEarth living requires. Only in Self, by (1) encountering Other's energies as they present themselves, (2) opening to their possibilities and dangers, and then (3) integrating them into our own conscious living, will our consciousness expand and mature to make sustainable inhabitation of our planet possible.

Befriending The Other in liminal space is one of life's most transforming experiences, every time it happens. The resources of The Other are just what we need to move beyond today's MultiEarth civilization. Exiting the consciousness of civilization, liminal space provides a dynamic, ever-changing realm beyond anything MultiEarth ways give attention. These vast topographies of greater consciousness can never be plumbed fully, not even by the most heroic of journeys. Such vastness is a good thing in this case. It provides a limitless alternative to anything the powers of ego civilization can fathom.

A final word of caution about how the daimonic mingles evil with good. Eruptions of the daimonic are to be expected as we move into greater consciousness. Even so, some eruptions can have such a powerful mix of evil and good that we can need a community, or persons with advanced experiences and knowledge, to accompany us through them. Though I have sometimes talked of ego as an identity center we must leave behind, what we really need is for ego to submit to Self. With the help of Self, ego can tolerate growth in consciousness and benefit from it. The ego-Self partnership develops capacities, in conjunction with a community and persons with advanced experiences and knowledge, to sort the gold from the remaining waste when the daimonic of The Other overflows. The chapters that follow give us more opportunities to befriend The Other, and for the ego-Self partnership to garner experiences in sorting the vast resources of The Other that are so essential to the heroic journey.

Conclusion: Reaching for What We've Not Yet Been

A collection of 71 table talks attributed to the 13th century Iranian poet Maulana Rumi includes this brief story:

> A king sent you to a country to carry out one special, specific task. You go to the country and perform a hundred other tasks, but if you have not performed the task you were sent for, it is as if you have performed nothing at all.[50]

By making our departure, we're heading for the country to which the king has sent us "to carry out our one special, specific task." We have said good-bye to an ideology of civilization which we no longer believe in. We've come to believe, instead, that we humans are capable of growing into consciousness that makes it possible to live capacities for harmony and peacemaking previously unknown to us. We reject the line of thinking that says we are by nature just too greedy, too slothful, or too anything else to journey to these OneEarth capacities that others are already living. We accept responsibility for how our lesser, egoistic thought and behaviors have contributed to the failures of the great Civilization Project, but we do not accept that the Civilization Project is the best our species can do. It is simply the best we were able to do while we chose to stay in the small topographies of consciousness that the ego controls. It is from such topographies that we have taken our departure.

A story of two Indian monks reiterates where we have been and where we are going. The two monks were walking along when they came to a stream. They saw a young woman trying to cross the stream. But uncertain of the depth and the strength of the current, she turned back, afraid. Monk protocols prohibited touching her. Nonetheless, the older monk picked up the young woman in his arms, waded into the water, and carried her to the other side. As he set her down, she smiled and expressed her gratitude. The two monks continued on their way. Many miles and hours later, the younger monk said to his older companion, "I can't believe that you touched that woman and held her close all the way across that stream." With a smile, the older monk replied, "I set her down hours ago. Are you still carrying her?"

The behavior of the younger monk illustrates that leaving the MultiEarth story and economy behind can be a challenge. **Yet, getting the MultiEarth consciousness *out of us,* and the OneEarth consciousness *into us,* is essential to our success in our Great Work.** The older monk shows the results of the heroic journey which we have begun in this chapter.

We can admit it: the story of human civilization has filled our cup. We have drunk too long from the tasty, false elixir of the MultiEarth story and its grand tales of advance and progress. As the civilizing powers of one group after another chose to create some kind of empire, humanity has become too drunk with the wine of MultiEarth ways and too foggy-minded to see that other ways are possible. All of that changes when we leave ego consciousness and swing into liminality en route to greater topographies of consciousness.

As I reiterated in this chapter, even groups who rebelled against controlling powers and sought liberation from them, proceeded over time to establish their own control in attempts to consolidate *their* power. For millennia, as each controlling reign gradually over-extended itself and became vulnerable to a successor, that successor, rising with revolutionary promise and energy, evolved a new form of essentially the same controlling model. Civilization has been repeating the same choice over and over while expecting a different outcome. We cannot break the cycle because we do not depart ego consciousness, and its proud creation is the Civilization Project.

The history of the United States doesn't break the pattern, but confirms it. Whatever the original intent of the American Revolution, the U.S. central government and corporations that jointly run the country today hold a global concentration of power and wealth able to exercise imperial control. Essential to that control are the systems that extract harmfully from land and sea, displacing, harming, and killing people and other species in the process. The systems prey on populations and countries with less and redistribute assets from the vulnerable to the more secure. Some have benefited from this system through the years; greater numbers have been excluded; all of us have been wounded by it.

Our exodus from this imperial cycle within the MultiEarth consciousness cannot be accomplished if we do no more than protest its ideology and stop using the empire's socio-economic structures. To truly leave empire behind and change out of the current civilization story to another, we need a more holistic exodus than ever before—one whose external departures from MultiEarth living also happen deep within the souls of humanity. We are heading for a new and greater consciousness where we will discover capacities we don't yet have. The older monk demonstrates the capacities that become available when we truly leave one way of thinking and live immersed in another. We will continue this journey in the succeeding chapters.

Ponder, Discuss, and Act

1. What has been one of your more significant experiences of emptying an old habit or belief system from your life? What changes did this make?

2. Describe some time you have spent in liminal or in-between space. What were your feelings? How were your priorities or values rearranged?

3. Compare the feelings you may have had at a time when you were not able to embrace the Call with the feelings of embracing the Earth-Self Call? What were the outcomes in your life of embracing the Call and not embracing the Call?

4. Describe a time you have befriended The Other despite the inconvenience or wishing it wasn't necessary.

5. Consider the story of the two Indian monks. Describe a time when you behaved like the younger one and a time you were more like the older one. What was your state of mind in each circumstance? What was the outcome?

6. What aspect of this chapter are you most ready to act on?

CHAPTER SIX

Earth's Insurgency
Is Reshaping Us

The earth will not be ignored.   —Thomas Berry

It was only when science convinced us that Earth was dead that it could begin its autopsy in earnest.
    —James Hillman, 1926–2011, psychoanalyst and philosopher

What the inventive genius of mankind [sic] has bestowed upon us in the last hundred years could have made human life carefree and happy if the development of the organizing power of man [sic] had been able to keep step with his technical advances.[51]   —Albert Einstein

E
arth is trespassing on civilization. She is an insurgent undermining and terrorizing the will of the Civilization Project's powers that be. Along with Earth's millions of species, we humans also experience the consequences and suffering. After seeming to serve the MultiEarth worldview over past millennia, Earth now shows that she has been doing no such thing. MultiEarth civilization has tried to one-upEarth's interconnecting systems throughout the millennia of its development. But now in the 21st century, it must face up to the failures of its systems and thinking. If we look at what Earth is doing from the perspective of the ego consciousness that has directed MultiEarth's project, Earth is an insurgent and presents an enormous threat. But from the perspective

of liminal space, heading toward OneEarth's larger topography of consciousness, we sense Earth calling us, with urgency in her voice, to a heroic OneEarth configuration of life. Whatever topography of consciousness we are in, Earth's insurgency is underway, ready or not.

Earth: "Here I Come, Ready or Not!"

"One, two, three, ... TEN! Here I come ready or not!" I was playing the timeless game of hide and seek with Connor and Lilly, our grandchildren, when they were ages five and two. They had disappeared behind some bushes somewhere in the commons of our condo complex. I peered behind a tree, then a bush, and a stairwell. Each time, saying in a fairly loud voice so they could hear, "No, Connor and Lilly aren't there. I wonder where they could be?" Shortly, I would hear a giggle emanating from somewhere and I knew it was time to "find" them. Hiding, fun as it is, can get boring quickly at that age. Being found is more exciting—even more than running to a hiding place.

Though we think of Hide and Seek as child's play, we don't stop playing it after childhood. The stakes just get higher as we grow up. Every misdemeanor and crime committed is a game of Hide and Seek. Someone hides. Someone tries to find. Countries play complex versions of Hide and Seek with one another. Armies militarize it, and the U.S. Central Intelligence Agency and their counterparts in other countries engage in highly sophisticated spy games. But the highest stakes game of Hide and Seek that our species has ever played is the one we're playing with our planet. In that game, Mother Earth has called out, "... nine, TEN! Here I come ready or not!" And we are being FOUND!

For centuries—although it's only seconds measured in geological time—Earth closed her eyes while our *Homo sapiens* species, evolved from her womb, scurried for places to hide the true costs of our MultiEarth lifestyles and economic systems. Though we didn't think of it as playing Hide and Seek with our Great

Mother, in truth, that *is* what we have been doing. Living with a MultiEarth worldview, we designed an economy and chose lifestyles that paid only part of the true cost of our carbon footprint and the hundreds of other by-products of industry that have gone into our waters, air, and soil as waste from our processes of productivity. We mastered the mathematics of hiding the full ecological cost of products, entering only some of them into our accounting ledgers and computers. While much, even most, of the total cost of many products goes unaccounted for in ledgers, those "externalized" costs do get paid somewhere, even if we don't pay for them when we checkout with our purchase. Land, oceans, rivers, and atmosphere pay; uncompensated and under-compensated laborers pay; and communities whose health is compromised pay. The true costs of our land use, resource extraction, waste disposal, and food production have been externalized into such hiding places as the gap between rich and poor, the dead zones in the Gulf of Mexico, the plastic gyros in the oceans, the obesity and starvation of people, the extinct and threatened species, the dangers and poverty of low-income neighborhoods, and the luxuries of wealthier ones.

Earth, however, is no longer closing her eyes. She's exposing our hiding places to the full light of day. Ready or not, the reduced prices offered in our economies are being raised to the full price— not in the checkout line, but in the rapidly growing costs created by the havoc of a destabilizing climate, used up soils, exhausted fish and marine populations, and warming, acidifying oceans. Earth does not practice clever accounting. She follows honest, interactive biospheres. Though the biospheres have shown elasticity, stretching like a rubber band, the limits have been reached. Snap back is underway. Our best recourse is to get honest with Earth, with one another, with other species, and with ourselves. No more Hide and Seek with Mother Earth. She is going forward using her natural accounting and will create new forms of life with or without us. We can expect the life that emerges, when it does, to reverently cooperate with her magnificent beneficence.

Each decade of this century calls for our imaginations to be on high alert, fully attentive for what comes next. Bidding farewell to the 12,000 year-long story of human civilization—the primary tale by which we have understood ourselves and our place in the world—we are in accelerated learning of the greater story that Earth is authoring. Politicians, CEOs, and military generals will continue to spin their stories, but compared to what Earth is doing, all of their compositions and orations are focused in relative minutiae, rearranging actors and actions in the story of MultiEarth civilization. If we look to *them* for our story, we are really stuck. None of them can shape a story to silence what Earth is telling us. It is our good fortune that Earth's Call will take us into a greater consciousness than what superpowers and wealth could ever deliver, and that our Self resonates with our planet.

Humans before the Civilization Project

Earth's story proceeded for over 4 billion years before it came to the chapter in which we humans had a part. Just how humans arrived is a complex part of her story that has unfolded over the last 2.8 million years.[52] New details are constantly being discovered, so the human story continues to change. Many say that *Homo sapiens* (the first human ancestors with anatomies like a modern human) emerged approximately 200,000 years ago in the Omo River valley of what is today Ethiopia. On the other hand, our origins could be traced, as some students of fossil records propose, to multiple areas, not just one. Either way, we humans have a long, fascinating story. And yet, it is minuscule compared to the 4.5 billion year Earth story. Such a comparison of scale gives us reason to proceed with considerable humility when we are tempted by plans to civilize Earth.

Even shorter is the time when what we call "culture" first appeared. Tool use is one of the indicators anthropologists use to determine when a culture begins to form. When did this first happen? Though in use for 2.8 million years, well before *Homo sapiens* emerged, tool use increased greatly beginning about 50,000 years ago, or 150,000 years after the emergence of *Homo sapiens*. Verbal language, another important indicator of culture, did not appear in the fossil record, of course, but it presumably was in place a long time before written language, which appeared a mere 5,000 to 6,000 years ago.[53]

Geologists, anthropologists, and paleontologists continue to uncover and read the revelatory text of Earth. Their careful and self-correcting readings and interpretations of Earth's story, lavishly shared through many publications and online articles, continually reveal more to all of us who want to know the intricate interconnecting dynamics of human life on our one-planet home. Despite the important revelations with which Earth continues to reward our scientific studies, most modern human beings put such discoveries into a category called "past history." Not much from this evolutionary timeline makes it into the stories of modern individuals. "What use is it?" we wonder.

This attitude works against us, however. We've taken so much pride in our modern achievements, and the assets we've personally or collectively accumulated, that we're especially blind to how the evolutionary story of Earth and human life reshapes our story as modern humans. We have come to assume that we evolved to a higher level of consciousness and capacity than those primitive peoples of so long ago. Any of *those* peoples who have survived in the jungles are relics of past times, fascinating to learn about in *National Geographic*, but irrelevant to living in today's world. The assumption is that these primitives will die out or be brought into modern times. What could they possibly teach us with their low tech, simple, nature-based lifestyles, hunting and gathering for survival?

But by calling them "primitive" and "uncivilized," we emphasize the inferior status these humans have in our MultiEarth consciousness. Our culture's complexities convince us that we have developed far beyond them. But there is reason not to dismiss them from modern relevance. In light of how modern culture has exceeded Earth's carrying capacity, whereas primitive cultures by and large did not and do not, our assumptions about them smack of elitism and prejudice more than wisdom. To get at what I mean, consider that the word "primitive" has strong positive connotations when linked to words like "primary," "primal," and "foundational." Similarly, the word "uncivilized" can refer to not being boxed in, tamed, or repressed. Do not many of us chafe at some of the restraints that seek to train and channel our innate, primal creativity? Many of us seek therapy to reconnect with the primary, instinctual intuitions that get schooled and civilized out of us. Arguably, it is our primitive capacities and those least civilized parts of us—the intelligences of our bellies and hearts more than our heads—that can best resist and undo the civilization that is carrying us beyond what our planet can handle. Our belly and heart intelligences are far more immediately connected with Earth than is our head intelligence. Whereas head intelligence feeds egos and civilization, the added intelligences supplied by belly and heart inform Self in its greater OneEarth capacities.

If we're willing to set aside our feelings of superiority regarding the primitive and uncivilized, we can get to know an enduring tradition of human behavior that incorporates primal and untamed energies. People of such tradition have continued OneEarth living in varying degrees, despite the aggressions of the rest of humanity. With an air of superiority, MultiEarthers marginalize and persecute such living as "marginal existence" and backward. Nevertheless, such traditions continue to be stewarded by many First Peoples and others who decide to live simply on Earth. Our Great Work cannot be sustained without wisdom from primal, primitive sources. We have made far too many mistakes with the opportunities that the Holocene Epoch gave us for us to show any arrogance toward primitive sources. After an epoch in which we wasted our truest powers as humans and laid waste to Eden, we can be grateful that OneEarth consciousness has ancient and new practitioners, despite how severely MultiEarth thought and activity have battered and abused it. Chapter Seven focuses on how the traditional ways of

Earth's First Peoples can help humanity reverse the climate change and species imbalances that haunt us today.

Earth, Today's Primary Consciousness Changer

Though OneEarth consciousness is growing around the globe, MultiEarth consciousness still holds most seats of power, designs and implements most policies, and decides how the majority of life on the planet lives and dies. MultiEarth consciousness comes at us from all sides. It shapes us through money's power, crafted messages spun by think tanks, corporate control over what gets projected onto TV screens everywhere, the dogmas of many religions, and the majority of educational campuses. All tell us what we need to do to be successful in the MultiEarth Civilization Project. At this moment in time, however, none of these authority centers holds the position of primary persuader and shaper that Earth does. Her ways have displaced the others as the biggest consciousness changer, though not all acknowledge being displaced. Earth is forcing MultiEarth thought and strategies to deal with her.

The cry of ecospheres being exploited and the Call of Earth to move to Earth-size living are reshaping our consciousness. Questions we hadn't needed to think about until the relentless advance of ecological crises, and answers we have not found easy to hear, continue to upset our egos and call us into bigger consciousness. Simply put, Earth's insurgency is a life-saving revolution. It invalidates and undoes MultiEarth civilization while taking charge of bringing into being the OneEarth paradigm focused in Earth's community of life. The MultiEarth paradigm can't see it that way, of course. The only revolutions it can handle are the ones that are ego driven and remain inside the MultiEarth ways of thinking. But Earth is breaking with that paradigm. What Earth is doing brings her alongside what Self is doing in our psyches. Together, this duo moves us into a larger topography of consciousness, where we continue learning how to make the Earth-size story our own. The magnificence of Earth's story, its agelessness, and its interconnection with the workings of the Cosmos inevitably "Wow!" and delight Self. Mystery and Spirit are common, though never commonplace. The better we get at thinking like Earth and knowing her story, the less likely we are to slip back into MultiEarth thinking and lose our way on the heroic journey.

Running Our Lives by Earth's Clock

A key to living Earth's story is her unique sense of time. We're well aware of how clocks and calendars run our lives in the civilization story. In Earth's story, a different clock becomes important. What time is it according to Earth's clock? Looking at the geological clock, if the 4.5 billion years of Earth-life were placed on the face of a 24 hour clock, hominids would have arrived less than two minutes ago and human civilization less than two seconds ago.[54] Think of it! Human civilization and all the proud achievements of the MultiEarth paradigm over the last 12 millennia have been here for less than two ticks of the second hand on Earth's great clock.

That's why in liminal space we cannot continue to measure time only as it's done in human civilization. When we travel across time zones, if we forgot to make the adjustments in our timepiece, we will soon be out of sync with other people. Similarly, if we measure time only as civilization does, we do not know what time it is on our planet. The periods of time measured in civilization are simply too short to give us the full sense of the correct time for responsible living on Earth. Earth's evolutionary time, once of interest mostly to geologists, paleontologists, and anthropologists, has catapulted itself into great importance for us all. Even civilization's clocks and calendars need now to be followed within the context of Earth time. Only then do we know whether or not what we're doing is on a schedule to keep Earth inhabitable. The schedule for change set at climate summits means little if it lags behind Earth's schedule of change. Any changes we make to reign in civilization's growth economics or ecological excesses cannot get us to Earth-size living if they do not put us on Earth time.

The eras of the geological clock have special significance for OneEarth living given that they can tell us how we *Homo sapiens* lived for hundreds of thousands of years WITHIN the story of a single planet. For over 800,000 years on Earth (perhaps even over 2 million years), humans did not threaten the carrying capacity of Earth. We fit in with how Earth sustains and regenerates life. But now for the 12,000 years of the human Civilization Project, the civilizers have been living as renegades, outside of Earth's community of life. Yet these twelve millennia are just a staccato note in the musical eons of Earth and Cosmos.

When we read only civilization's clock, we forget that all of civilization has happened during only the Holocene and Anthropocene epochs. The geological clock tells us what a special time the Holocene marks, how it stands out because it brought a different, post-glacial climate. Temperatures and Earth's self-regulating systems became relatively stable. As this stability settled in, changes in the behaviors of the human species accelerated, including how we measure time. More and more humans relied on calendars, clocks, and deadlines. Geological time was taken for granted the more humans entered into what became the massive project of civilization.

Choices based on civilization's time increased civilization's control over Nature. Doing something faster than Nature became a tool of domination. It's dizzying how technologies aim for speed, farms hurry animals to market, and stock markets around the world make big trades within split seconds. Parts of civilization now proceed at a pace measured in nano seconds. Our processes race ahead of our ethical reflection. Profit, not rightness, determines the speed of life. Nature's cycles have less and less influence in the Civilization Project. But Earth's insurgency is taking back time from civilization's usurpation of it.

Rebalancing civilization time with Earth time, upsetting as it is for some, comes as welcome news for people wanting to give more credence to Earth time and the traditional wisdom held within it. Many rural, nomadic, and subsistence lifestyles have been negatively impacted by civilization's fast clocks. So too are the species who encounter blockages in their migratory patterns. Their "clocks" are thrown off enough to interfere with where and when they go for food, water, and breeding. All that lives within Earth's cycles has encountered great negative bias from civilization clocks. Little wonder that humans inclined toward OneEarth ways have viewed the Civilization Project with great distrust, and animals have experienced dreadful reductions in their habitats and populations.

Learning how to tell time on Earth's clock is no longer an elective, but a requirement. The future story of Earth will continue to unfold according to Nature's cosmic clock. Though learning where we are in geological time can rattle us, not doing so is becoming catastrophic. So much human effort in civilization goes into controlling time. But when we step through the doorway into liminal space and time, it's as if we walk into a world of geological giants after playing in a sandbox with civilization miniatures. Earth's clock tells time up to 4.5 billion years ago when an enormous and expanding Cosmos was the womb from which our planet was born. Just writing that number reminds me that I cannot truly fathom such a span of time. To put it in a scale I can almost comprehend, imagine teaching a child how to count to 100. As they learn, we patiently sit and listen, smiling as they proudly take us past 70, then 80, 90, and finally "One Hundred!" But we can't listen to them count to one billion. Were they to count one number each second without stopping, it would take them nearly 32 sleepless years to get there. To count to 4.5 billion would take over 140 years.

As recently as a century ago, Earth was thought to be only 1.6 billion years old. Geology has changed that. But it's still a young science, having edged into being taught as a scientific discipline for the first time in the 18th century. Then in the 20th century, the Earth sciences went through a growth spurt. Like a child growing into larger sizes, knowledge of Earth grew beyond the early scientific categories in which it was arranged. New knowledge required a larger calendar, one that could show a chronology with additional divisions into eras, periods, and epochs.[55]

Take for example, the Cenozoic Era, the era which we are now leaving. It is subdivided into two periods, the Tertiary and Quaternary, which are subdivided into seven epochs—eight with the addition of the current Anthropocene. Not until the tail end of the sixth epoch, or about 200,000 years ago, did our *Homo sapiens* ancestors appear. That epoch, called the Pleistocene, was the time of the latest glaciation. Then after the largest glaciation receded, Earth eased into the Holocene around 12,000 years ago and civilization began.

Today it is common for civilization to function with amnesia regarding the recentness of its presence as part of Earth's majestic trajectory. Putting our civilized selves into the geological calendar heals our memories. When Earth is the context for our lives, and not only a source for the commodities of our profits, then we think about life in larger spans of time. How we think about time determines whether or not we can live in a larger topography of consciousness. The oft-quoted First Peoples practice of the Iroquois Nation urges us to make decisions with the next seven generations in mind.[56] Civilization Project time has not been guided by such solidarity with the future.

To help us make Earth's story and calendar our context, David Brower (1912–2000), founder of Friends of the Earth and first executive director of the Sierra Club, told a version of Earth's 4.5 billion years story that framed it in a single work week or, as he said, "Six Days of Creation."

David Brower's Sermon:
It's Healing Time on Earth

I thought it would be useful to do an exercise in perspective relating to time. Squeeze the age of the Earth, four and a half billion years, into the Six Days of Creation for an instant replay. Creation begins Sunday midnight. No life until about Tuesday noon. Life comes aboard, with more and more species, more variety, more genetic variability. Millions upon millions of species come aboard, and millions leave. By Saturday morning at seven, there's enough chlorophyll so that fossil fuels begin to form. At four o'clock in the afternoon, the great reptiles are onstage; at nine o'clock that night they're hauled off. But they had a five hour run.

Nothing like us appears until three or four minutes before midnight, depending on whose facts you like better. No Homo sapiens until a half minute before midnight. We got along as hunter-gatherers pretty well, but the population couldn't have been very big; for those of you concerned about how many hunter-gatherers the Earth can sustain, the range I've heard is between five and twenty-five million people. Then we got onto this big kick: we wanted more of us, we wanted to push forests out of the way so we could feed more people. We wanted to shift from hunting and gathering to starch and thereby start the first big energy crisis (because the greatest energy shortage on Earth is of fuel wood). So we got into agriculture one and a half seconds before midnight. That recently. By the next half-second, we had been so successful that the forests ringing the Mediterranean Sea, for example, were reduced to the pitiful fragments that are the Cedars of Lebanon. That was in one halfsecond. At about the end of that half-second—we're now one second before midnight—after all this time of life being on Earth we began to invent religions.

If I could go back to a point in history to try to get things to come out differently, I would go back and tell Moses to go up the mountain again and get the other tablet. Because the Ten Commandments just tell us what we're supposed to do with one another, not a word about our relationship with the Earth (at least not according to any of the translations I've seen so far). Genesis starts with these commands: multiply, replenish the Earth, and subdue it. We have multiplied very well, we have replenished our population very well, we have subdued all too well, and we don't have any other instruction! The Catholic church just put "stewardship" in its vocabulary within the last seven or eight years!

So here we are now, a third of a second before midnight: Buddha. A quarter of a second: Christ. A fortieth of a second: the industrial revolution. We began to change eco-systems a great deal with agriculture, but now we can do it with spades—coal-powered, fossil-fuel-powered spades. We begin taking the Earth apart, getting ideas about what we can do, on and on, faster and faster. At one-eightieth of a second before midnight we discover oil, and we build a civilization that depends on it.

Because we all relate to a work week, Brower's compact version gives us a sense of how brief human life and civilization have been within Earth's total story. He called it a sermon.[57] It's a healing one—bringing healing to our severe wound of separation from Earth and her measure of time.

Making Earth's Story Our Primary Story

David Brower knew that Earth is our primary story. He'd moved into a topography of consciousness that knows Earth is in charge. Thomas Berry, 1914–2009 (see Chapter 2), also lived in such con-sciousness. With the strength of that consciousness, Berry capably challenged civilization's propensity to spin its own story as more important than the story of Earth. He did not accept civilization's habit of treating Earth's story as the background scenery for what matters most. His expansive understanding of both civilization and the Universe permeate his writings—a wonderful result of his life-long scholarly work aimed at piercing the assumptions, while also incorporating the wisdom, of human civilization, world religions,

Indigenous spirituality, different cultures, and the evolutionary story of Earth.

Earth's Story in Six Days

Day 1: Monday (4.5-3.75 Billion Years)
12 am Creation Begins
Formation of Earth and moon
Rain appears.

Day 2: Tuesday (3.75-3 Billion Years)
First signs of life
Simple, single-celled life
First oxygen-producing bacteria emerge
Photosynthesis invented

Day 3: Wednesday (3-2.25 Billion Years)
Life comes aboard, with more and more species, more variety, more genetic variability.
Photosynthesis releases flood of oxygen (late in day)
Oxygen-loving cells emerge.

$$CO^2 + H_2O \xrightarrow{chlorophyll} glucose + oxygen$$

Day 4: Thursday (2.25-1.5 Billion Years)
Millions upon millions of single cell species emerge and leave.

Complex cells with nuclei emerge.

Day 5: Friday (1.5 Billion-750 Million Years)
Single cells begin to transition to multi-cellular life.

Cells begin to reproduce sexually.

Strands of genetic memory combine.

Day 6: Saturday (750 Million Years to Present)

7 am	Fossil Fuels Form	30 sec. to 12 am Homo Sapiens
4 pm	Dinosaurs Appear	1½ sec. Agriculture Invented
9 pm	Mass Extinction of Dinosaurs	1 sec. Invention of Religions
11:56	Appearance of Human-like Animals	1/3 sec. Buddha is Born
11:59		1/4 sec. Christ is Born
		40th of a sec. Industrial Rev.
		80th of a sec. Discovery of Oil
		12 am PRESENT

*Adopted from David Brower's Sermon: It's Healing Time on Earth and other sources.

In the last decades of his life, Berry became a leading voice for what he called the "New Story." It regards the Universe as the rightful and only context for any 21st century story able to adequately serve as "our story"—the story we tell to explain what makes sense and what doesn't, what matters to our wellbeing and why, and what we live for. Berry rejoiced in the Universe story's ultimacy and grandness that made it the story within which *all* other stories happen.

Civilization has never been able to live with a consciousness big enough to align with Berry on this way of thinking. Its egos have ever created more self-serving stories to explain everything. Though these smaller stories serve MultiEarth civilization's purposes, they are unable to bring us into the Earth-size living that is our only sustainable alternative in the 21st century. Recognizing how the old stories keep humans in our egos and permit Creation to be exploited, Berry aimed for a *new* story able to shape consciousness and life for the next geological era, a story able to fulfill the tall order of moving us into the Ecozoic Era. Switching stories is part of being in liminality. Once we disavow the stories that build identities limited to egos, ethnic groups, nations, and globalizing powers of control, our Self identity eagerly welcomes the larger story of Earth and Universe.

New visions expressed by civilization's governments, businesses, or economics always fall short of being the kind of new story that was Berry's aim. Even the most visionary pronouncements, when they remain within civilization's MultiEarth paradigm, cannot provide the thrust to carry us into the consciousness where Earth's story shapes lives and societies. Only the new, Earth-centered story can guide us in the scale of transformation necessary to take our species out of the MultiEarth civilization and reinsert us into Earth's community of life.

The New Story not only gives us a frame as big as the Universe, and a storyline that moves us from the ego identity center to the center of Self, it also speaks of Earth as organic and living. That counters what most of us have internalized through the MultiEarth perspective where Earth is thought of as inanimate and mechanistic.

But among the diverse voices of science, some descriptions of Earth's macro, life-like functions are emerging. Continued study of the self-regulating systems of the oceans and atmosphere show

behaviors akin to living organisms. Everything from the magma of
Earth's core to her outer atmosphere constantly innovate adap-
tations to fit evolving situations. Geology interacts with the biota
(Earth's animal and plant life) in ways that both are impacted.

The scientific inquiry into an animate Earth has been advanced
since the 1960s by debate about the Gaia hypothesis, first proposed by British chemist James Lovelock when he was working on
a NASA (National Aeronautics and Space Administration) project
regarding life on Mars. The theory was co-developed by microbi-
ologist Lynn Margulis (1938–2011), distinguished for her work on
the interactions between unlike species (symbiosis) and the role
of that interactivity in biological evolution. She sought to connect
the Gaia hypothesis to her work on how microbes affect the atmosphere and layers of Earth's surface. As scientists continue to test
the Gaia hypothesis, some parts get more credence than others.
Whether Gaia is best thought of as metaphor, scientific hypothesis, or both continued to be discussed at four different Gaia conferences between 1985–2006.[58] Some criticisms have fallen away
and new ones have emerged. But even its skeptics acknowledge
that the hypothesis has sped up a lot of scientific inquiry into a
field that was moving more slowly and lacked the comprehensive
frame for thinking about Earth's interacting systems that the Gaia
hypothesis puts forth.

The Gaia hypothesis exemplifies the perception of many scientists that a version, or versions, of a living Earth better understands
our planetary home than proceeding as if its systems interact as
inanimate mechanisms. It links to Greek mythology that expressed
an animate view of Earth, mythology that tells of the primordial
goddess, Gaia, who gave birth to Earth and Universe. (An alternative spelling, Gea, is the prefix in words like "geology," and shows
tacit openness in this discipline to Earth as animate.) In addition
to being the Great Mother archetypally, Gaia is personified plan-
etarily as the Earth Mother. To speak of Earth as our nurturing,
life-giving Mother has long been the relational language used by
Indigenous peoples and some others like Francis of Assisi. Seeing

Earth as our Great Matriarch makes it natural for us to express feelings of affection, appreciation, and connection. The language of science speaks to our head intelligence, but relating to our planet as Mother Earth better expresses the intelligences of our heart and gut. When the intellectual intelligence of the head and the instinctual, primal intelligence of the gut can meet in the core emotional and relational intelligence of the heart, we can value science, metaphor, myth, and emotion for their respective contributions to a greater consciousness without having to choose between them.

As a botanist and a member of the Citizen Potawatomi Nation, Robin Wall Kimmerer works with these intelligences explicitly. Fluent in scientific language, she decided to learn her Indigenous language. It was then she discovered that 70 percent of the words of her native tongue are verbs, whereas in English the verbs comprise only 30 percent of the words. That means that in Potawatomi speech, 70 percent of the words have tenses and are conjugated. It is the language of a culture focused in being and aliveness, allowing for highly nuanced descriptions of relationship and interactivity—a widespread trait of Indigenous languages generally. It helps them express their worldview. Nouns and verbs differ for animate and inanimate referents, whereas in European languages the distinction is made according to masculine and feminine gender. And just what do the Potatwatomi people address as animate or as inanimate? As she learned the language, Kimmerer learned the answer:

> Naturally, plants and animals are animate, but as I learn, I am discovering that the Potawatomi understanding of what it means to be animate diverges from the list of attributes of living beings we all learned in Biology 101. In Potawatomi 101, rocks are animate, as are mountains and water and fire and places. Beings that are imbued with spirit, our sacred medicines, songs, drums, and even stories, are all animate. The list of the inanimate seems to be smaller, filled with objects that are made by people. Of an inanimate being, like a table, we say, *"What* is it?" And we answer *Dopwen*

yawe. Table it is. But of apple, we must say, "*Who* is that being?" And reply *Mshimin yawe.* Apple that being is.[59]

Kimmerer goes on to point out that such "respect for animacy" is not possible in English where "you are either human or a thing. Our grammar boxes us in by the choice of reducing a nonhuman being to an *it*, or it must be gendered, inappropriately, as a *he* or a *she.*"[60]

She also addresses the issue of anthropomorphizing plants and animals. In one of her field ecology classes, she and her students were in a conversation about using animate language about all they were observing. Students came to see how English speaks and thinks about Nature with disrespect compared to Indigenous languages. As one student asked rhetorically, "Just because we don't think of them as humans doesn't mean they aren't beings. Isn't it even more disrespectul [than anthropomorphizing other beings] to assume that we're the only species that counts as 'persons'?" Kimmerer simply adds, "The arrogance of English is that the only way to be animate, to be worthy of respect and moral concern, is to be a human."[61] The paucity of animacy in the grammar of European languages is reason enough why Indigenous languages must be kept alive. A grammar of animacy helps correct exploitation and move an as-yet-livable-planet into an Ecozoic Era with Earth's life community in sustainable balance. Getting there involves using languages that speak accurately about *beingness* in forms that aren't just human. If only humans can be *shes* and *hes*, then all other beings must be *its*. But such language doesn't fit the understanding many of us have of the beingness around us.

Language is also an issue when it comes to expressing our feelings for the planet and for the attention we sense receiving from the planet. Though the scientific contribution of Gaia and Mother Earth may be unclear, their value as metaphor and myth in describing our relationship to Earth must not be understated. Nor need we be shy about using relational language even if it lacks scientific consensus. Relational language moves us out of objectifying Earth, a behavior that has made it easier for civilization to destroy her life processes. Versions of animacy increase feelings of connection, which, in turn, influence how we treat Earth. Relational content helps us feel Earth emotionally as well as understand her intellectually. It is with our heart and gut intelligences that we feel *for* our planet, and *with* our planet—interactions that increase our knowledge of her many interrelations in this time of great ecological stress. Her groaning, cry, and Call, the emotional and relational language of MultiEarth destruction, stir us to respond. It's that emotional bond with Earth that moves us to make the decisions necessary to keep Earth livable. When we live in the consciousness able to think of Earth as the archetypal Great Mother, who cares enough to provide for us and discipline us, then deep love rises in us. We feel the intimacy of OneEarth interrelationship.

Growing a OneEarth interrelationship heals the wound of disconnection that has contributed so greatly to MultiEarth's tragic objectifying of our planet. When we live in the topography of consciousness where our interrelatedness with Earth predominates, then parched land saddens us. New rains that water soils and seeds lighten our hearts. When we sense Earth's systems interacting dynamically with each other, and see how all the species living on or near her crust do so as well, our hearts move into wonder and awe. Earth's multi-faceted, evolving story shows her doing what we describe in human terms as acts of beneficence, grace, forgiveness, and fierce mercies. We offer gratitude.

But the feelings arising from interrelationship cannot exclude the inexplicable horrors of earthquakes, hurricanes, and droughts that put life in jeopardy. Interrelationship with our planet does not provide a tidy solution to our ecological crises. What it does is bring a way of thinking and acting that no longer objectifies Earth but lives symbiotically with her. Our relationship is no longer from a consciousness *within* Earth where thinking *about* Earth is primary. We have moved into a consciousness where the primal, raw emotions from our gut respond to the planet as do the more integrated, refined emotions of our heart. As these join with the thoughtful reasons of our mind, we are more able to be in the kind of messy interrelationship with our planet that just may keep her livable.

Thomas Berry's New Story for humans to live by (instead of the MultiEarth story) introduces us to "the dream of the Earth." Most of us haven't thought about Earth as dreaming. After all, inanimate objects don't dream. But in Berry's New Story, the living Earth has a dream. It is bigger than the dreams our egos have about living in civilization's story. Only Self can resonate with Earth's dream. As is true with Earth's Call, Earth's dream overwhelms our egos but animates our Selves. Earth's dream is ego's nightmare, but for Self, it awakens those greater capacities of humans that ego identity can never help us reach. For the MultiEarth Civilization Project, Earth's dream is a massive problem beyond ego solutions, but for OneEarth living, it's a guiding vision. In Berry's own words:

> The time has come to lower our voices, to cease impos-ing our mechanistic patterns on the biological processes of the Earth, to resist the impulse to control, to command, to force, to oppress, and to begin quite humbly to follow the guidance of the larger Earth community, for this is the larger dimension of our being. Our human destiny is inte-gral with the destiny of the Earth....
>
> I am concerned with the Earth not as the object of some human dream, but with the Earth itself and its inherent powers in bringing forth this marvelous display of beauty in such unending profusion, a display so overwhelming to human consciousness that we might very well speak of it as being dreamed into existence. Our own dreams of a more viable mode of being for ourselves and for the planet Earth can only be distant expressions of this primordial source of the universe itself in its fullest extent in space and in the long sequence of its transformations in time.[62]

Science and Religion in the New Story

Berry recognized that the way he spoke about the New Story some-times stirred resistance in both the religious and scientific communities. He looked at how religion and science have for some time been telling different stories. Historically, when science displaced religion as civilization's primary authority during the 18th century, each gradually, and unfortunately, claimed separate spheres and began speaking different languages. Too often they sparred with one another. But the cutting edge today happens where science and religion are discovering complementary roles in a larger, unifying way of thinking and living.

Speaking from the scientific community, Einstein affirmed in his later years that "all religions, arts, and sciences are branches of the same tree."[63] Berry spoke of how the Earth story that science has been telling more recently combines the physical and the psychic, the material and the spiritual, matter and energy:

> The most notable single development within science in recent years... has been a growing awareness of the integral physical-psychic dimension of reality. The scientific community is possibly more advanced than the religious community in accepting the total dimensions of the New Story.[64]

Overcoming the wall of separation between religion and science generates new understandings and interactions. Science had not wanted to deal, for example, with whether or not Earth has consciousness through its own innovating systems. Religion had not wanted to deal with how the physical world evolves life that transcends earlier forms. But both science and religion need to find their way out of the MultiEarth paradigm.

Religion has too long reduced its focus to the psychology of personal change, the personal relationship with the Divine, morality, and healing the interpersonal wounds of relationships. More outward looking religions have struggled for right relationships in society, the economy, and the environment. With this focus on the psychological, relational, and social realms, religions restricted themselves to "redemption-thinking," i.e., how humans could find a redemptive, healing way of dealing with their own sin as well as personal and structural evil in the world. Creation-thinking, i.e., the larger story of how to live interrelated with all of Creation and why, has, until recently, been largely ignored by religions.

"But the earth," Berry said, "will not be ignored.... The dynamic of creation is demanding attention once more in a form unknown to the orthodox Christian for centuries."[65] Amid our severe ecological breakdown, the usefulness of any religion hinges on its capacities to offer spiritual paths in which Creation is not only the primary locus for experiencing the Divine Presence, but also for an integral way of shaping economics, education, politics, business, and all of life.

For its own part, science has mostly given up on maintaining that its findings are objective. To observe an object is to trigger a response in it. The relationship between observer and object becomes the primary locus of attention for understanding the world, not the object itself. No thing can be isolated and known as pure object. Nor is it any longer thought to be important to proceed with scientific investigation in that way. More important for our pursuit of truth is that we perceive the processes in which everything is interrelating. Science continues to distance itself from a mechanistic way of thinking in which objects are like parts of a machine in motion. More frequently now, science proceeds along an organic way of thinking in which the interactivity of parts show they are subjects initiating and responding, not just objects moving about.

At the forefront of this transition from a mechanistic Universe to an organic one was British mathematician and philosopher, Alfred North Whitehead, 1861–1947 (see Chapter Ten below). He redirected the pursuit of understanding reality away from the concentration on matter and objects, to process and relationships.[66] Many in science recognize that the earlier endeavor to look at everything as "object," insisting that true knowledge focused on matter and that knowledge of matter could be objective, was flawed. Paleontologist and popular science writer Stephen Jay Gould, 1941–2002, emphasized, "Science is not a heartless pursuit of objective information. It is a creative human activity, its geniuses acting more as artists than as information processors."[67] The artist-scientist recognizes that whatever she is observing is changing not only according to its internal processes but also because it is being observed.

Berry considered it highly important that science was shifting toward seeing how all objects have their own subjectivity. Venturing to call it consciousness, Berry saw human consciousness as having evolved from a variety of consciousness forms throughout the Universe. For him, the unfathomable mystery of the total Universe is a macro form of consciousness. Or said differently, it is an interdependent embodiment of all forms of consciousness, from the simplest cell or particle to the most complex.

This consciousness of the Universe, the mystery of being itself, was long ignored by science—a neglect that contributed to an incredible assault on planet Earth. Berry rejoiced to see a balanced subjectivity emerging in science, one combining mystery and numinosity with intellectual rigor. On a parallel track, some strands of religion have been coming to embrace Creation as an evolving, continuous, revelatory story of life, planet, and Universe inhabited by the divine and, paradoxically, inhabiting the divine. For both science and religion, some older stories in which they lived no longer account sufficiently for our experience of Earth. The New Story, a cosmic Earth story with psychic and physical strands intertwining, is being written by Earth, Self, and other species as co-authors.[68]

Earth's insurgency is a game-changer of overpowering magnitude. Resisting it is futile and suicidal. Better to look for the severe mercy that hides in Earth's reactions to the multiple ecological crises we humans are causing around the world. The severity comes in the suffering and death involved in Earth's insurgency. The mercy comes in that the same suffering and death speak like a mother who cares deeply about what's happening. "Look what's happening," she says to us. "With all the love I have, I ask you to change. Move quickly, please."

Conclusion: The Story That's Reshaping Us

As Earth's insurgency presses in on us, Earth's story gets more and more of our attention. In recent years I've been reading more about Earth, watching Nature movies, paying new attention to urban wilderness, and immersing myself in wilder places. Nothing in my life-experience has changed my thinking and acting more than learning about what Earth is doing.

When I took a geology course in college, I had no thought that this subject would change how I saw myself in the world. Being a humanities student, I was simply fulfilling a science requirement. But that geological primer gave me a peek into evolutionary time and processes—even to where I thought of my life as a nano-second in that story. But once I got my course grade, my science require-ment had been met, and I stopped focusing on Earth's story. The humanities, as I studied them, were defined by the civilization story. I've been caught up in that story for most of my life, treating it as if it were the Big Story.

But Earth's insurgency is changing all of us, ready or not, as she discourteously intrudes upon civilization's egos. Ecological pressures have laid open the shallowness of much in our econom-ics and politics. They have exposed the MultiEarth assumptions in many of our models of business and in the frameworks of aca-demic and religious thought. We clearly need a different and bigger story to live by. Earth and the Universe show us that what we've been treating as the main plot is actually a subplot. The Earth and Universe as the main plot in the story have fathomless powers to get us unstuck from an egoistic, MultiEarth civilization. Geology and cosmology are no longer side disciplines for geeks, but essential contributors to the story that is already shaping our communities, work, households, bioregions, and lives.

This is why the New Story Thomas Berry began working on as early as 1970, has been so inviting for me. When we get inside the perspective of Earth, see it scientifically and religiously, we are better able to see what it means to our heroic journey. The New Story, mingling fun and fulfillment with bigger-than-life struggles, tells us we can go to where we did not know we could. In liminal topography, in-between where civilization is but not yet to the OneEarth ways we aspire to, Earth's insurgency, so disruptive to civilization, is more our ally than our foe. She can help us go to topographies of consciousness where we've never yet been—ones where we interrelate with her beyond what we've been doing and cooperate with her for reciprocal wellbeing.

Ponder, Discuss, and Act

1. In what ways is Earth's insurgency reshaping your life? The life of your region? The lives of those you regard as your kindred spirits?

2. How do you schedule your life choices according to Earth time as well as civilization's calendar and Greenwich time?

3. What feelings and thoughts stir in you as you ponder David Brower's sermon: "It's Healing Time on Earth?"

4. Illustrate how you are integrating both science and spirituality in your own life. Where do you continue to feel them at odds? Try talking about Earth's unfolding as a continuing process that is both evolutionary and creational.

5. How is the New Story taking shape for you? What are its impacts in how you think and act?

SECTION FOUR

Guides for Eden's Larger Topographies

Ａll the schools I attended, kindergarten through grad school, educated me in the consciousness of MultiEarth civilization. Then, out in the job world, I strived to be "successful" by those standards. I compromised. I chose the lesser of two evils. I committed myself to jobs and projects through which I expressed my values as best I could. Through it all, my soul wanted something more.

So I sought out books, speakers, conferences, and conversations which pressed into different expanses beyond what I knew. Interested in healing, I took a new look at shamanism and how the world's First Peoples understand Nature. I tried to understand episodes in which First Peoples, intent on practicing traditional ways, clashed with MultiEarth civilization, sometimes violently. The more I learned, the more I saw the continuing egoistic pride and ethnic or cultural prejudice of MultiEarth's attitude and actions toward First Peoples. I recognized that MultiEarth civilization has never stopped vanquishing First Peoples. With that awareness, I became more interested than ever in First Peoples because I saw that their traditional ways are rich in the Earth-size living that all humanity needs to practice today. Not that every Indigenous person practices OneEarth living. But those who continue in the traditional, Earth-centric ways of their ancestors are in the continuous stream of OneEarth living that predates the MultiEarth Civilization Project and carries into the present.

Their persistence, even after centuries of engaging with a civilization that treats their ways as inferior, amazes and inspires me. The colonization of the minds of Indigenous children at boarding schools, where their culture was displaced by European language, dress, and customs, is a most egregious "civilizing" strategy used by the U.S. Today, First Peoples continue to strategize ways to resist MultiEarth civilization—a way of living they are sure will fail—and practice their traditional ways. Some, after getting lost in civilization for a while, make great efforts to reconnect with their living traditions. They and their traditions, I learned, live—meaning that they can change, adapt, yet, persist, by creative stubbornness to retain some of their languages, symbols, songs, dances, and rituals. These traditions, although differing in specifics based on their particular tribal culture, are all based on their *belief that Earth shapes them in the ways of the Great Spirit. Wherever First Peoples live their traditions, they benefit, not only themselves, but all of us. With them, our joint quest for OneEarth living intensifies.*

Chapter Eight tells of two who've guided me into Earth-size consciousness. One, Carl Jung, through psychology; the other, David Korten, through economics. When I first encountered Jung's ideas, a rite of passage began into a new way of understanding myself. My ideas about human nature were reframed when I learned that "ego" and "Self" were different centers around which the elements of our identities cluster. Once I knew I could become a person centered more in the greater Self, I also recognized that I was far more ego-centered than I'd thought!

Korten's conviction that a new, Earth-size economy is possible if we change our story and consciousness adds confidence that we can make the changes we need to make. His "orders of consciousness," which I adapt as topographies of consciousness, show us which topography we're in and where we need to go.

These maps and guides take us into topographies of consciousness that are not only beyond the limitations of the ego, they are also beyond the limits of what any of us can explore fully within a single lifetime. They draw me onward even as they guide me on the heroic journey. I just can't stay where I am.

CHAPTER SEVEN

Guides for Earth-Size Living: First Peoples

Traditional people of Indian nations have interpreted the two roads that face the light-skinned race as the road to technology and the road to spirituality. We feel that the road to technology.... has led modern society to a damaged and seared earth. Could it be that the road to technology represents a rush to destruction, and that the road to spirituality represents the slower path that the traditional native people have traveled and are now seeking again? The earth is not scorched on this trail. The grass is still growing there.[69]   —William Commanda (Mamiwinini; Algonquin), Canada, 1991

Even minimal contact with the native peoples of this continent is an exhilarating experience in itself, an experience that is heightened rather than diminished by the disintegrating period through which they themselves have passed. In their traditional mystique of the earth, they are emerging as one of our surest guides into a viable future.[70]   —Thomas Berry, *The Dream of the Earth*

The opening pages of the book, *In the Absence of the Sacred*, illustrate a widespread, unthinking prejudice non-Indigenous peoples express to and about Indigenous peoples. Author Jerry Mander tells how his editor initially dismissed the relevance of a book he proposed on Indians. To the editor, a book contrasting First Peoples with technological peoples was a nonstarter: "Indians? Oh God not Indians. Nobody wants a book about Indians.... They're finished. Indians smindians.... Mander, you're some kind of goddamn romantic."[71] Mander's editor expresses well the posture of the MultiEarth paradigm which has positioned itself as superior to the paradigm of Indigenous people for up to 12,000 years.

Showing all the eloquence of his advertiser background, merged with his activist experience, Mander, born to immigrant Jewish parents in New York, writes of the wisdom of First Peoples:

> Contrary to our prevailing paradigms, which assume that indigenous peoples throughout the world wish to participate in our economy, many Indians do not see us as the survivors in a Darwinian scenario. They see themselves as eventual survivors, while we represent a people who has badly misunderstood the way things are on the earth. They do not wish to join the technological experiment. They do not wish to engage in the industrial mode of production. They do not want a piece of the action. They see our way as a striving for death. They want to be left out of the process. If we are going over the brink, they do not wish to join us.
>
> Throughout the world, whether they live in deserts or jungle or the far north, or in the United States, millions of native people share the perception that they are resisting a single, multi-armed enemy: a society whose basic assumptions, whose way of mind, and whose manner of political and economic organization permit it to ravage the planet without discomfort, and to drive natives off their ancestral lands. That this juggernaut will eventually consume itself is not doubted by these people. They meet and discuss it. They attempt to strategize about it. Their goal is to stay out of its way and survive it.[72]

Mander exposes key assumptions in the thinking of technological peoples to where, not only does much of the technology lose value, but the thinking behind it becomes unconvincing. Mander has us wondering why the Civilization Project created by technological peoples gave up invaluable wisdom extant among native peoples worldwide. In the liminal space of the heroic journey we see how grievously wrong it is for the MultiEarth worldview to think that First Peoples are relics of the past in a modernization energized by what's called "irreversible progress," an egoistic phrase to absolve the bad moral choices involved in establishing MultiEarth globalization. Insecure egos do not admit this error easily. Such mind-changing moments happen, however, when the alchemy of change so prevalent in liminality does its work. There we can empty ourselves of chunks of MultiEarth thinking. We can overcome prejudices and recognize interdependences we've previously denied.

Writing this chapter comes at a time in my own journey when I am coming into the consciousness to *see* First Peoples and *hear* them in their own voices. Most of my life I've "known" First Peoples only in the voices of others writing about them. Patricia St. Onge (Haudenosaune), author of the "Foreword," is a guide to me in making this important shift. She showed me how in an earlier manuscript she felt talked about, but not there; and how important it is to speak of First Peoples in the present, not only the past, and of their participation in the struggles of now. She changed the tone and tense of this chapter and book.

The first voice in this chapter is that of William Commanda (Mamiwinini), spelling out the contrasting worldviews as separate trails, one of technology, the other of spirituality. Then I tell the story of two European-Americans: Jerry Mander writing a book on Indians, and his editor who with incredulity and raw prejudice shows how thoroughly confined he is to thinking in the MultiEarth paradigm. Mander goes on to write a book contrasting the technological and spiritual paths that Commanda distinguishes.

Hearing and Seeing First Peoples in the Here and Now

The organization I am part of, Jubilee Economics Ministries (JEM),[73] continues to lead delegations of U.S. people and Mexican nationals on trips of experiential learning to Indigenous Peoples (aka First Peoples) in southern Mexico, mostly to the state of Chiapas, but also Puebla and Oaxaca. Between 2000 and 2004, I participated in three such delegations to Chiapas, the southernmost state of Mexico and least developed, where 36% of the population is Indigenous and over a million (27% of the state's population) speak their Indigenous language.[74] Through these repeated delegations, relationships continue to develop with Indigenous groups. One group often visited were Tzotzil people who, after displacement by paramilitary violence, created a new village, Nuevo Ybeljoj, high in the beautiful Chiapan Highlands.

The primary purpose of our visits is to increase international solidarity which increases respect for and protection of the Indigenous Peoples under threat of paramilitary and military actions because of their resistance. Those of us in the delegations from the U.S. and other parts of Mexico benefit enormously as we learn how Mayan peoples of that region have struggled, and continue to struggle, for their culture, traditions, and identities in the face of the same MultiEarth Civilization Project which we resist, though, by comparison, too weakly.

On one visit a group of Mayan men and women elders convened a meeting with us. A village elder whose name I didn't get, queried our three-person delegation: "Each morning I wake up," he began, "and ask myself how I can live in resistance today. How do you live in resistance?" We squirmed. Not that we didn't resist, but emotionally our resistance felt a bit lame given what they were teaching us about theirs. It was a pregnant moment brought about by repeated visits to this community by delegations led by JEM. A level of trust had grown.

Once MultiEarth's NAFTA (North American Free Trade Agreement) went into effect, on January 1, 1994, paramilitary violence and military presence sought to coerce their submission to government policies that gave transnational corporations access to the resources of their land. They knew the JEM delegations came in a different spirit, one of learning from them and accompanying them in their dissent; they saw us, Mexican nationals and internationals, as partners who could carry their story to a larger audience. Delegations have often been overwhelmed by the generosity of the Mayan welcome received, including a willingness to share their traditions, rituals, religion, work, and ongoing struggle of resistance to corporate, MultiEarth encroachments.

They wanted us to know how their human rights are violated by the military and paramilitaries. They showed us how they struggle to make alternative economic choices to the MultiEarth neoliberal economics[75] promoted by the state government and transnationals. After 500+ years of resistance, they continue to see MultiEarth civilization as a long project that will come to an end because it carries within it the seeds of its own destruction. For them, MultiEarth civilization never did receive the imprimatur of the Divine or any sanction that makes MultiEarth ways eternally inevitable. Our conversation revealed what an astute understanding of neoliberal globalization and NAFTA they have—much deeper than many of us in the U.S. The Mayan elder's question comes back to me often: "How do *you* live the resistance?" It is such an inclusive question. Is it not right that we all resist the MultiEarth paradigm? His question corrects the false MultiEarth notion that First Peoples are yesterday and outside of the issues of the day. These Tzotzils are here and now, living a resistance that humbles and inspires every JEM delegation. They set a high standard on what resistance to MultiEarth civilization means, and inspire delegations to step up stronger in daily practices of OneEarth thinking and living. Their Indigenous ways and voices convict delegates in a most gratifying way. What guides they are for the heroic journey! Maybe it's okay that I never did learn the elder's name. Through him I hear thousands of other voices speaking, revealing the broad and deep quest underway for OneEarth living.

When I first visited the Mayan villages, what I saw did not mesh in my consciousness with what I heard the inhabitants saying. On the one hand, I saw their homes made of bare boards and corrugated roofs. But then I heard them develop sophisticated strategies to resist neoliberal economics and globalization. I came to a new consciousness in which I appreciated how seasoned these travelers are. They understand how global forces, driven by corporations, affect their lives and their Indigenous culture and identity. They resist knowing their lives can be at risk. I had not thought before of neoliberalism and globalization as practices of genocide. But Indigenous peoples in Mexico, old to young, see and feel that to be the devastation being delivered to them.

In Tzajalchen, another village in Chiapas, a young man's eyes doubled in size as he talked to the delegation I was in about NAFTA.[76] He said it is the latest practice of genocide toward them by governments and corporations. Free trade agreements give corporations power to transcend governments when the issue at hand threatens their profits. Trade agreements do not consider the historic treaties made between colonizing governments and the sovereign nations of First Peoples; in some cases, First Peoples are relocated from lands that corporations want access to for the resources discovered there. Relocation onto reservations, a tactic so well known in U.S. history, is not a thing of the past. Corporations have dislocating authority, whether legal or corrupt. They do not plan to fully compensate First Peoples or respect their Earth-centered, sustainable practices. When First Peoples are forced into relocations and rule changes, their traditional practices of sustainable living can be severely altered. Their cultural and soul identities, so connected to the land on which they live communally, suffer.

On another day, I joined a "walk of return" in which peoples who had left their communities because of paramilitary harassment and death threats were returning. Could they trust they were safe? Yes, because there'd been months of meetings to talk about what happened to divide their village, what they actually differed on, and what the whole village agreed was their common vision and work. A ceremony of welcome was planned in each community for the displaced persons being welcomed back to their villages. When the "walk of return" arrived at the village, there were ceremonial enactments and speeches. One young Mayan man, in the course of his speech, contrasted their way with that of the U.S. While the U.S. transnationals and government use great power to intrude, divide, and repress, they had refused that way and come together in talks, rebuilt trust, and overcome the odds. They'd overcome great distrust and violation; they'd found a way to recreate their community in peace.

The abilities of the Mayan peoples to understand their struggle for life in terms of big-picture issues happening in the world today give snapshots of Indigenous Peoples worldwide, showing them as guides for Earth-size living today, not just in some storied past. Their efforts of resistance to the Civilization Project get concessions from governments and corporations that allow their traditions to shape Earth-size ways. Were European-Americans and non-Indigenous citizens of nations to bring Indigenous Peoples into consciousness, inspiration and guidance would flow for the heroic journey to OneEarth consciousness and practice.

Globilization Clashes with Indigenous Peoples

Many clashes between Indigenous peoples and the Civilization Project lodge in the reach and reign of transnational corporations. Corporations were vehicles by which Europeans created the empires of Western civilization, invading First Peoples' lands everywhere and establishing colonies with structures of extractive, growth economics and political, legal control over regions. Colonization has evolved to globalization. Shaping the world according to MultiEarth thought and intents continues. Corporations that at first served the rulers of European nations have come to transcend the nation-state structures of government and now, not only make the rules for extracting resources and managing trade, but also adjudicate them.

Many efforts aim to make corporations more socially responsible and function with greater consciousness. Scott Klinger,
consultant, activist, and author, has served as an intermediary
between corporations and First Peoples in negotiations where corporations are seeking access to resources on First Peoples' land.
A European-American with a deep desire to bridge differences,
his work has made him conscious of many flashpoints between
MultiEarth and OneEarth worldviews as they surface in the negotiations. In what follows, Klinger introduces himself within the
context of the MultiEarth-OneEarth tussle in his world. Then he
tells three stories of Indigenous peoples in the struggle with corporations—one from the 17th century conflict between the Dutch
West Indies Corporation's settlement of New Amsterdam and
the Lenni Lappe People; the other two from more recent events.
Scott's own desire is to see life reconnected beyond "the Wall," a
metaphor based on the first story below.

* * * * *

When I was a boy growing up in Cleveland, I remember trips to the
shores of Lake Erie as most undesirable experiences. The instinc-
tive longing of young children to splash and play in the cool waters
of a lake were quickly tempered by the sight of dead fish, some
with two heads, all with seeping tumors, and the smell of their
rotting flesh on the shore.

Recently I returned to Cleveland, to that same spot I so often
went to as a child. I found other children swimming where I had
earlier grieved. The Lake is much cleaner; life has gotten much
better, right? Maybe.

Those steel mills and iron ore processing plants that laced the
Lake with fish-killing toxins a half-century ago have long since gone
on to Korea, China and Eastern Europe. Pollution in Cleveland is
way down, but what about pollution in the newly industrialized
cities of Asia and other parts of the world?

I have worked much of my adult life in the broad area of
corporate social responsibility. I have watched the corporate

sustainability movement grow from asking a few awkward and imprecise questions to elaborate reports which measure and manage seemingly endless inputs and outputs of the manufacturing process.

Yet, when I step back, I don't see the sustainable world that I would expect, given the level of effort that goes into better, more environmentally sustained management. I think the roots of my disappointment go down to the purpose of the corporate sustainability movement. Ultimately, the purpose is really to reduce unsustainability, not to create a more sustainable world.

The corporate world, by and large, fully embraces a worldview based on managing and controlling. Thus, the corporate sustainability movement is often based on bringing technology to bear in creating better ways to manage material consumption and undesirable outputs such as pollution. None of this is a bad thing. Earth is better off for these efforts to improve stewardship of resources. *But it is not enough. These efforts continue to operate within the context of a MultiEarth economy.*

A different sustainability movement can be seen around efforts to support local agriculture. Rather than being built on a manage-and-control model, it is based on the listen-and-adapt tradition more commonly seen in Indigenous economics. Local farmers come to know their land, their soil, and the changing climate that affects them. They adjust their plantings to protect and preserve the soil. In contrast, the industrial agriculture model simply applies more chemical inputs to push the land to grow so they can make the most profit in the market. The consumer accustomed to industrial agriculture assumes they will get strawberries or sweet corn year around. But consumers committed to local agriculture know that his or her response will be to adapt to what the land has to give. Sometimes there will be an abundance, and sometimes far less. Sometimes so much of a favorite food will come that we grow weary of it. At other times, we need to find a substitute or shift a menu because none of a particular food item is available.

Story #1 (Lenni Lappe)
Land Is Sacred, Not Real Estate for Private Ownership

Four hundred years ago, a small group of Dutch colonists settled on the southern tip of Manna-hatta Island, a place named "the hill island" by the Lenni Lappe Indians who called the island home for centuries. The Dutch set to work building houses, shops and roads. They also built a wall—actually more of a fence made of wood. It ran the narrow width of the island. The wall divided their civilized settlement from the wild world beyond. It offered protection from the Indians who lived outside of it. It defined the private property they had claimed exclusively for themselves.

That tiny settlement of New Amsterdam (founded in 1624) was the humble birth of one of the greatest cities on earth, New York City. And the simple wooden wall defined what is today Wall Street, the center of global finance. If you walk down Wall Street today, you will see wooden markers in the cobblestone, symbolizing the path of that first wall.

The story of the Dutch colonists is far more than the story of the birth of a great city and a powerful financial market. It is the graphic story of the creation of a MultiEarth economy on this continent. It is the story of people with a MultiEarth orientation meeting and coming into conflict with peoples who lived in a OneEarth way.

Archeologists tell us several things about the way the Dutch colonists lived. First, they dumped their garbage over the wall— an early "not in my backyard" response. Second, they exploited the land beyond the walls of their settlement in order to sustain themselves. Forests were cleared for fuel wood. Newly cleared land beyond the wall was planted with crops for humans and forage for cattle. Slowly the earth was altered to meet the needs of the growing and thriving colony.

The Dutch colonists of New Amsterdam, like all early settlers who invaded lands of Indigenous Peoples, were motivated by two powerful goals. The first was simply to survive. The second was to generate a profit for those who had funded their trip to establish a colony. It was this latter motive that eventually pressed the colony beyond the confines of the Wall and far into the world beyond.

The Lenni Lappe Indians had a different approach to life, however.

At the time of contact with the MultiEarth people of Europe, the Lenni Lappe occupied a large part of what today is New Jersey, Delaware, and the land between the Delaware and Hudson Rivers, including Manhattan and Long Island. They spent their days hunting and gathering, respectfully using what Earth had in abundance. Their lives were adapted to the environment that was their home. When Earth provided extra, the Lenni Lappe took this harvest and traded it with other Indigenous Peoples living in the region. Trade connected the Lenni Lappe beyond their ancestral home, but they, like most other Indigenous Peoples, placed little value on expanding their borders.

The Lenni Lappe did not believe in private property, a value brought to North American shores by the MultiEarthers. They did, however, believe in gifting, in crafting ceremonies, and in holding rituals in order to be certain that the wealth of the community circulated in ways that benefitted all. The oft-told tale about the sale of Manhattan by the Lenni Lappe to the Dutch likely traces to a conflict over the understanding of property and its proper use. According to the Smithsonian Institutions' Museum of the American Indian:

> At that time Indians did everything by trade, and they did not believe that land could be privately owned, any more than could water, air, or sunlight. But they did believe in giving gifts for favors done. The Lenni Lenape—one of the tribes that lived on the island now known as Manhattan—interpreted the trade goods as gifts given in appreciation for the right to share the land.[77]

The Lenni Lanape OneEarth Peoples of four hundred years ago understood land as a gift to be shared. The Dutch MultiEarth colonists believed land was to be privately owned with exclusive use rights. This example offers two contrasting views of land that continues today.

Story #2 (Menominee)
Sustainable Forestry for Eons

In Northwest Canada, fields of natural gas were discovered beneath pristine wilderness, land sacred to the First Peoples of the region. The Canadian government put the development rights for the land up to auction. They were purchased by an international oil company. Immediately upon obtaining rights to the land, the oil company placed a gate along the access road. They did so because their safety rules required that others be kept from an area where industrial development was beginning. But their actions conveyed a sense of exclusivity that was foreign to those who used the land for hunting and sacred ceremonies for hundreds of years. When conflict arose over the gate, the oil company listened and, upon understanding the First Peoples' view, removed the gate.

But the conflict over land and its use continued. Developing the gas beneath the land would require the drilling of hundreds of small gas wells, maybe more. The thought of their land being pocked by oil wells drew significant protest from many in the community. Some within the MultiEarth perspective did not understand the concern. One petroleum engineer explained, "No one lives within 60 miles of the proposed development; do you care what happens 60 miles from your backyard?" Few in MultiEarth culture have a 60 mile long backyard. But for many OneEarth Peoples, such broad swatches of land are quite commonly thought of as a backyard, not to be owned by one, but to be enjoyed and to be sustained by all.

The oil company continued to try to make its project acceptable to the community, suggesting that after fifty years of development the land would be restored and they would move on. Still, they found more conflicts. MultiEarth peoples in the corporate world live their lives according to their watches, or at least their quarterly calendars—quarterly intervals being the time frame in which they must report earnings to shareholders. But OneEarth Peoples have a much longer sense of time, counting the rings on the trees, rather than consulting watches, in order to mark time. And whereas the corporate people with MultiEarth minds spoke about increasing the value of the land by maximizing its development, OneEarth Peoples saw the goal of development as protecting the productive value of the environment so that it continues to produce over the eons.

Development expert Rebecca Adamson (Cherokee), calls this development framework the Production-Protection paradigm:

> From the Indigenous paradigm of protection and production, production and protection, evolved complex conservation regimes whereby you protected the land because it produced for you and it produced for you because you protected it. This is in stark contrast to the [MultiEarth] practice of protecting small plots of land, while removing the vast rest from protection, a paradigm which has led to the unprotected earth shutting down its productive capacity.[78]

The Protection-Production paradigm is easily seen in the forestry industry. For many years, the dominant business model in the timber business was clear-cutting old growth forests, then either replanting monoculture forests as industrial tree farms or moving on altogether. With the rise of the environmental movement and the reality that old growth forests were almost completely depleted, the MultiEarth mindset of commercial deforestation began to shift toward sustainable harvesting practices. Such practices were far from new, however. They had been practiced by Indigenous Peoples for thousands of years, and commercially by the Menominee Nation in Wisconsin for more than 150 years (shortly after the tribe signed a treaty establishing its reservation). Today, Menominee Tribal Enterprises, a commercial enterprise of the Menominee Nation, carefully selects logs for harvesting, picking those that would properly thin the forest and preserve the diversity of species. It is important to the Menominee not to turn the forest into a wood factory, but to maintain it as a diverse habitat for plants and animals, as well as a place of recreation and enjoyment for tribal members. "Sustainability means living on interest, not drawing down capital. The idea of sustained yield of natural resources is far from new: it means, for example, harvesting trees at a rate within the forest's capacity to regrow."[79]

Story #3 (Yawanawa)
Saving Sacred Forest in the Amazon

Another example of the Protection-Production paradigm is found deep in the forests of the Amazon, in the communities of the Yawanawa people. In this story, a corporation from the MultiEarth culture was able to adapt and learn a OneEarth approach to business.

Located two airplane flights and a two-day canoe ride from Brazil's capital of Brasilia, the Yawanawa faced growing pressure because illegal logging practices were encroaching on their land. Their remote location and loss of traditional means of subsistence led them into deepening poverty and loss of culture. Because the Yawanawa lacked medicine to treat some seriously ill members, they had to leave the community for medical care. Such was the case with a young tribal member named Tashka who moved out of the community as a young man in order to receive long-term care for a medical condition. Tashka's illness meant he grew up comfortable with two cultures. As he reached adulthood, he left the forest and traveled to the United States for college. While there, he remained an active advocate for his community. When things in his community grew more dire, the elders sent for him, asking him to return and be their leader.

It was clear to Chief Tashka from the start that his tribe needed other ways to support themselves in a changing world. So in the early 1990s he took the opportunity to travel to the World Social Forum held at the opposite end of Brazil. There Tashka met representatives of the US cosmetics firm, Aveda. The beauty products firm was interested in natural products to bring color to its offerings. Taska returned home, discussed the proposal with his community and together they arrived at a red berry from the uru-kum tree, used by the Yawanawa as a decorative body paint. The berry grew in abundance in their forest land, and if they could document that the forest had economic benefit for the tribe, they could be more successful in enlisting the government's help with illegal loggers. The Yawanawa and Aveda reached an agreement specifying the amount of berries, the price that would be paid, and the point of delivery. Nothing more.

Months after the berries were being successfully harvested and delivered, a team of Aveda's leaders arrived to learn more about their business partners' lives. One of them asked how many jobs had been created because of the partnership. Confused, the Yawanawa asked, "Jobs?" They replied that there were no jobs, only culture. To show their business guests what they meant, they led the MultiEarthers deeper into the forest where they found the OneEarth Peoples singing as they harvested and processed the berries. Production led them to be able to protect their forest so it could continue to produce. Their renewed connection with their land, in turn, deepened and renewed their culture.

On a return visit, Aveda representatives got to see first-hand what the Yawanawa did with the money they earned from their commercial venture. The village sported a centrally located phone, so it was no longer necessary to make a long canoe trip to convey or receive information of importance. There was also a small health clinic with a refrigerator for medicine, so future sick children (like Tashka had once been) could stay in the village and receive treatment.[80]

* * * * *

These stories indicate why many non-Indigenous people have been turning to First Peoples for guidance on the heroic journey to live Earth-size ways.

"Seasoned Travelers" on the Heroic Journey

The "Introduction" to this book includes a nutshell overview of the chapters showing how they track with the essential elements of the heroic journey outlined by screenwriting consultant Christopher Vogler. This chapter is at the point of the journey when, as Vogler says, "the hero comes across a seasoned traveler of the worlds who gives him or her training, equipment, or advice that will help on the journey. Or the hero reaches within to a source of courage and wisdom."[81]

The experiences of oppression, domination, and injustice described above make First Peoples primary among the "seasoned travelers" especially able to help on the heroic journey today. As already said above with reference to the Mayan Peoples of Chiapas, the emphasis is on *today*. MultiEarth thinking puts First Peoples in *yesterday*. But many First Peoples today have extraordinary wisdom in how to scale types of technology to fit with Earth's natural systems, plus the spirituality, to be co-creators of Earth-size living. I emphasize *co-creators*. The MultiEarth paradigm, if it shows interest in First Peoples, does so not as co-creators, but as sources from which to "borrow," appropriate, take, and steal whatever First Peoples' wisdom and practices can advance profits or other benefits in MultiEarth living. Thinking of First Peoples as equals in an interdependent community with all of Creation is not part of the MultiEarth Civilization Project. However, travelers on the heroic way get to where the MultiEarth's paradigm perforates; then non-Indigenous peoples are able to see and hear First Peoples as colleagues and, in many ways, guides on humanity's journey. Whenever the shift happens, a coup of consciousness overthrows MultiEarth dominance in the consciousness of the traveler. The coup makes it possible for non-Indigenous peoples to see and hear First Peoples as peers and guides on the heroic journey—quite an inversion after being schooled and "civilized" in a MultiEarth consciousness marked by explicit and implicit racism regarding them. The coup is one of the jaw-dropping surprises that happens on the heroic journey. But it cannot happen in the consciousness of MultiEarth civilization. This necessary coup of consciousness happens only as we move into liminality and the larger topographies of consciousness.

Without the coup, MultiEarth civilization continues as always, blind and deaf to First Peoples. Vine Deloria, Jr. (Standing Rock Sioux), 1933–2005, a professor, lawyer, theologian, and activist, did much to change how non-Indigenous people in the U.S. think about American Indians. His book, *Custer Died for Our Sins* (1969), was one of the books that explained the rise in the 1960s and 1970s of what he called Red Power. American Indians discovered that they were taken more seriously by the U.S. public when they enacted their messages and worldview. Consequently, they thought out strategic public actions, such as occupying the island of Alcatraz (1969–1971), a former U.S. penitentiary, in the San Francisco Bay. They were acting on a treaty which said that federal lands no longer being used could be claimed by Indians. A year later, some Indian groups organized a cross-country caravan they called the "Trail of Broken Treaties,"[82] which concluded in Washington, D.C., where they tried to give a 20-point position paper to the government. When President Nixon refused to meet with them, they occupied the Bureau of Indian Affairs building in Washington, D.C. (1972). Many non-Indians were taken aback by such actions, a reaction that revealed the lack of consciousness among most U.S. non-Indigenous people regarding the continuing impact of oppression in the experiences of American Indians. Deloria, of course, understood the oppression and saw the activism as one way for Indians to escape the stereotype non-Indigenous people held of Indians. By these actions, Indians insisted on being engaged in the here and now as living, contemporary humans.

In his subsequent book, *God Is Red* (1973), Deloria continues with how essential it is for Indians and non-Indians alike that the stereotype be broken. As long as the stereotype continues, the oppression of Indians continues:

The tragedy of American Indians—that is the Indians Americans love to read about—is that they no longer exist except in the pages of books. Rather the modern Indians dress much the same as every other person, attend pretty much the same schools, work at many of the same jobs, and suffer discrimination in the same manner as other racial minorities. One can assume that, for all practical purposes, American Indians are the same as the other oppressed groups in American society.... According to this mythology, all of the oppressed peoples share more in common as victims than they do as individual groups with the mainstream of American society.

This simplification overlooks the obvious historical facts.... The cultural and social worldview of American Indians derives from a completely different background than that of every other group in American society. Where other groups suffer deliberate discrimination and oppression, American Indians are the only group whose oppression comes primarily from an effort to help them change into replicas of the white man. Where blacks and Chicanos dare not enter, Indians are dragged by well-intentioned people who cannot leave them alone.

Thus it is that the cherished image of the noble redman is preserved by American society for its own purposes. If most literature on Indians and many of the recent books reflect nothing else, it is that there exists in the minds of non-Indian Americans a vision of what they would like Indians to be. They stubbornly refuse to allow Indians to be or to become anything else.[83]

The stereotypical Indian is not available as a seasoned traveler to guide anyone on the heroic journey. MultiEarthers who seek the wisdom of First Peoples need to get on the heroic journey and go far enough to where their consciousness involves them not only in confessing to the horrible error of conquest, but also in leaving the MultiEarth paradigm to seek the common ground of OneEarth living.

There's far more reason for the common ground approach than MultiEarth consciousness knows. The First Peoples Worldwide website presents statistics accumulated by the United Nations that tell a different story about First Peoples today than MultiEarth civilization has any consciousness about. According to the UN, there are "approximately 400 million Indigenous people worldwide, making up more than 5,000 distinct tribes."[84] About 70% live in Asia. Some populations have declined dramatically, become threatened, or gone extinct. Others are recovering or even expanding their numbers. Though they represent only 6% of the world's population, 90% of the cultural diversity of the world is found among them. They inhabit over 72 of the world's 196 countries and hold 20% of Earth's land mass. Surprisingly, "that land harbors 80% of the world's remaining biodiversity." Few people shaped by MultiEarth education and thinking have any idea that First Peoples are doing anything other than hanging on to viability by a thread. There is no sense in the Civilization Project of the strength of Indigenous resistance to MultiEarth ways; nor of the resilience and adaptations with which they maintain traditional culture against overwhelming odds; nor the wisdom of their voices as they speak to the issues of the day with the depth of understanding that oppression gives to people.[85]

The Problem of "False Indians"

When the primal desire to live OneEarth ways arises in MultiEarth people, those energies, essential as they are for change, can make missteps. One misstep sometimes taken is to become a "false Indian," people who claim Indian ancestry when they have none or give inaccurate descriptions of their associations with Indians. Such claims are the more onerous because they so commonly benefit the person making the claim, giving them "minority person" status when that advantages them or turning it into a career of giving seminars, writing books, and starting groups around ancient wisdom, shamanic healing, drumming, and more. Misappropriation of another's ethnicity for personal gain is a confusing and maddening kind of theft.

Though falsely claiming connections with First Peoples is not to be excused, it also reveals how deep the desire is to reconnect with Earth-size consciousness and living. There are Self's ways and ego's ways of going about it. The heroic journey is about coming to Earth-size consciousness in ways authentic to one's true Self, to be more fully who we are, not someone else. The aim is that everyone be OneEarth peoples, not First Peoples. The primal energies that rise in us who long to reconnect with what the Civilization Project severed us from need our attention. They rise from the archetype of the Human and can carry us to live humanness more authentically than civilization permits. The rituals, ceremonies, spiritualities, and wisdom of First Peoples embodies some of the primal in ways that appeal. But the yearning, when managed by Self, does not translate into becoming First People, but along with First Peoples to be OneEarth peoples, all according to our own authentic and diverse ways. Toward that end, First Peoples are trustworthy guides because so many have for centuries been living in resistance to the MultiEarth Civilization Project. They have generations of experience in adapting to Earth in an ongoing evolution of OneEarth living. The point is not that non-Indigenous people are incapable of teaching important things learned from Indigenous people. But that all of us, when we travel the heroic journey from ego to Self, come to the larger topographies of consciousness in which each of us finds how to be authentic humans, integrating the primal, the intellectual, and the heart, into a human able to live within Earth's interdependent community of life.

The Seven Fires of the Anishinaabe Guide Us All

It's hard for MultiEarthers to believe that traditional First Peoples have not wanted to be involved in the Civilization Project. But

First Peoples have steadfastly trusted the worldview of their traditions as the better way to live with Earth. So the secession of the Civilization Project from Earth-size living, that has been going on for 12,000 years or so, has had its persistent resisters. We can only wonder today what living in the community of life on Earth would be like if the Civilization Project would have been resisted more widely.

First Peoples' mythology abounds with stories of living in ways that center in Earth and Spirit. The Anishinaabe peoples have a compelling story of the Seven Fires. Robin Wall Kimmerer (Potawatomi) tells the story of this series of prophesies and wisdom messages in a chapter of her book, *Braiding Sweetgrass* (2013). Kimmerer has a foot in the Indigenous world and another in the world of science, teaching botany, ethnobotany, ecology, and Indigenous environmental issues. At State University of New York, Syracuse, she is Distinguished Teaching Professor and also the Director of the Center of Native Peoples and the Environment. In *Braiding Sweetgrass*, Kimmerer tells how her people, Potawatomi (meaning "people of the fire") have lived through seven eras, being guided by seven prophecies called the Seven Fires. The Potawatomi are one of three peoples who comprise the Anishinaabe, the other two being Ojibwe and Odawa (Ottawa). They number 600,000 to 700,000 in the U.S. and Canada today.[86] The three became known as the Three Fires Confederacy. It was during the Fourth Fire, she writes, that

> the history of another people came to be braided into ours. Two prophets arose among the people, foretelling the coming of the light-skinned people in ships from the east.... The first prophet said that if the offshore people, the *zaa-ganaash*, came in brotherhood, they would bring great knowledge. Combined with Anishinaabe ways of knowing, this would for a great new nation. But the second prophet sounded a warning:... These new people might come with

brotherhood, or they might come with greed for the riches
of our land.[87]

The Fourth Fire prophecy included a description of those who
would come

> with black robes and black books with promises of joy
> and salvation. The prophets said that if the people turned
> against their own sacred ways and followed this blackrobe
> path, then the people would suffer for many generations.

The turn to Christian religion and the MultiEarth ways of the
"light-skinned people" who came "in ships from the east" led
them into the grievous Fifth Fire era when they became severed
from their lands, language, and ways of interdependence with all
Creation.

> Indeed, the burial of our spiritual teachings in the time of
> the Fifth Fire nearly broke the hoop of the nation. People
> became separated from their homelands and from each
> other as they were forced onto reservations. Their chil-
> dren were taken from them to learn the *zaaganaash* ways.
> Forbidden by law to practice their own religion, they nearly
> lost an ancient worldview. Forbidden to speak their lan-
> guages, a universe of knowing vanished in a generation. The
> land was fragmented, the people separated, the old ways
> blowing away in the wind; even the plants and animals
> began to turn their faces away from us.

By the time of the Sixth Fire the deep losses compounded to where
even their children were turning away from the elders. Loss overwhelmed her people. From the deep abyss of the Sixth Fire came a
message of a future when there appeared to be none.

> The time was foretold when the children would turn away
> from the elders; people would lose their away and their
> purpose in life. They prophesied that, in the time of the

Sixth Fire, "the cup of life would almost become the cup of grief." And yet, even after all of this, there is something that remains, a coal that has not been extinguished....

They say that a prophet appeared with a strange and distant light in his eyes. The young man came to the people with the message that in the time of the seventh fire, a new people would emerge with a sacred purpose. It would not be easy for them. They would have to be strong and determined in their work, for they stood at a crossroads....

Now we live in the time of the Seventh Fire. The Anishinaabe prophecy saw it as a time when many elders as well as the young would make great effort to pick up the pieces of their traditions, language, ceremonies, and religion that had been scattered.

In this time, the young would turn back to the elders for teachings and find that many had nothing to give. The people of the Seventh Fire do not yet walk forward; rather, they are told to turn around and retrace the steps of the ones who brought us here. Their sacred purpose is to walk back along the red road of our ancestors' path and to gather up all the fragments that lay scattered along the trail.

Fragments of land, tatters of language, bits of songs, stories, sacred teachings—all that was dropped along the way. Our elders say that we live in the time of the seventh fire. We are the ones the ancestors spoke of, the ones who will bend to the task of putting things back together to rekindle the flames of the sacred fire, to begin the rebirth of the nation.

And so it has come to pass that all over Indian Country there is a movement for revitalization of language and culture growing from the dedicated work of individuals who have the courage to breathe life into ceremonies, gather speakers to reteach the language, plant old seed varieties, restore native landscapes, bring the youth back to the land. The people of the Seventh Fire walk among us....

A second vision of the Seventh Fire braids into the Anishinaabe story "all the people of the earth" in a prophecy that is startling in how it moves beyond the traumatic domination imposed by the "light-skinned peoples" who came in "ships from the east" to recognize that all peoples on Earth have come to the path that divides into two utterly different futures.

> The Seventh Fire prophecy presents a second vision for the time that is upon us. It tells that all the people of the earth will see that the path ahead is divided. They must make a choice in their path to the future. One of the roads is soft and green with new grass. You could walk barefoot there. The other path is scorched black, hard; the cinders would cut your feet. If the people choose the grassy path, then life will be sustained. But if they choose the cinder path, the damage they have wrought upon the earth will turn against them and bring suffering and death to earth's people.

Thinking about the image of the crossroads, Kimmerer leads us to the possibility of the Eighth Fire.

> I don't fully comprehend prophecy and its relation to history. But I know that metaphor is a way of telling truth far greater than scientific data. I know that when I close my eyes and envision the crossroads that our elders foresaw, it runs like a movie in my head.... I see the people of the Seventh Fire walking toward the crossroads with all they have gathered. They carry in their bundles the precious seeds for a change of worldview. Not so they can return to some atavistic utopia, but to find the tools that allow us to walk into the future. So much has been forgotten, but it is not lost as long as the land endures and we cultivate people who have the humility and ability to listen and learn. And the people are not alone. All along the path, nonhuman people help. What knowledge the people have forgotten is remembered by the land. The others want to live, too.

The path is lined with all the world's people, all the colors of the medicine wheel—red, white, black, yellow—who understand the choice ahead, who share a vision of respect and reciprocity, of fellowship with the more-than-human world....

But of course there is another road visible in the landscape, and from the high place I see the rooster tails of dust thrown up as its travelers speed ahead, engines roaring, drunk. They drive fast and blind, not seeing who they are about to run over, or the good green world they speed through. Bullies swagger along the road with a can of gasoline and a lit torch. I worry who will get to the crossroads first, who will make the choices for us all....

Our spiritual leaders interpret this prophecy as the choice between the deadly road of materialism that threatens the land and the people, and the soft path of wisdom, respect, and reciprocity that is held in the teachings of the first fire. It is said that if the people choose the green path, then all races will go forward together to light the eighth and final fire of peace and brotherhood, forging the great nation that was foretold long ago.

Supposing we are able to turn from destruction and choose the green path? What will it take to light the eighth fire? I don't know, but our people have a long acquaintance with fire. Perhaps there are lessons in the building of a handmade fire that will help us now, teachings gleaned from the seventh fire. Fires do not make themselves. The earth provides the materials and the laws of thermodynamics. Humans must provide the work and the knowledge and the wisdom to use the power of fire for good. The spark itself is a mystery, but we know that before that fire can be lit, we have to gather the tinder, the thoughts, and the practices that will nurture the flame....

I don't know how the eighth fire will be lit. But I do know we can gather the tinder that will nurture the flame, that we can be *shkitagen* [a fungus that grows softball size on birch trees and has uncanny capacity to hold a smoldering fire for a long time] to carry the fire, as it was carried to us. Is this not a holy thing, the kindling of this fire? So much depends on the spark.

The Seven Fires of the Potawatomi make it easy to see where the Civilization Project entered the prophecies. My own ancestors and history are in the ships of the east that arrived during the Fourth Fire and chose greed over brotherhood. I feel shame about how the MultiEarth worldview rolled across the Great Plains in covered wagons and uprooted First Peoples who'd lived there for centuries. The "settlers" believed it was their right to move First Peoples onto reservations, severing them from their identities like a bayonet cutting a cord—the Fifth Fire. I inherited that MultiEarth story. It has taken me decades to realize how apocalyptically wrong it is. I have some acquaintance with dispirited First Peoples living in the Sixth Fire, and then, struggling to find a new identity and daring to express themselves in ways that they were seen and heard, often in ways that light-skinned people found incomprehensible. Now, responding to the Earth-Self Call to the heroic journey, I see myself walking the path of the Seventh Fire, seeking the companionship of OneEarth peoples, nonhuman peoples, and Earth. The Seven Fires offer a most helpful frame for the journey to guide reconnection of all peoples who choose the OneEarth path.

Conclusion: The Key First Peoples Hold

Many First Peoples in the Americas speak of the 500+ years of resistance, referring to the invasive arrival of Christopher Columbus in 1492 and all that followed after. Early on in their clash with the European invaders, First Peoples recognized that they could not change that worldview or defeat the civilization it shaped. Nonetheless, First Peoples believed deeply that their worldview was more enduring than what the MultiEarth worldview brought. That left them with the overwhelmingly daunting challenge of developing a way of resistance, primarily nonviolent, in which they did not lose their beliefs, traditions, culture, or identity. First Peoples have both failed and succeeded in this daunting challenge. By responding to the Earth-Self Call, we end the MultiEarth paradigm that has made the incredibly long resistance necessary and move into reconnecting with one another and interconnecting with Earth's full community of life.

Arguably, this chapter could be the first chapter of this book. It would show that First Peoples carry the torch of continuity passed on from our pre-Holocene ancestors who lived Earth-size ways. The choice for the Civilization Project came in hundreds of little decisions early in the Holocene and since. All of these decisions resulted in further seceding from the Earth-size story humans are capable of living. What is most remarkable about First Peoples is how many tribes have done what huge segments of *Homo sapiens* found impossible to do: resist entering the MultiEarth worldview.

This trilogy of books on "Eden in the 21st Century" is about how the majority of *Homo sapiens* seceded from OneEarth living and how, in the 21st century, we must find new unifying ways to live inside the planet. We need to follow our soul's and Earth's desire that we reconnect with interconnectedness. Without it our species and millions of others don't survive. First Peoples in the Americas not only resisted the MultiEarth worldview, including its most accelerated and hostile aggression during the last 500 years, but persisted within a living tradition that continues to evolve beyond ancient hunting and gathering forms to incorporate updated aspects of culture. Yet, at its best, it maintains vital forms of OneEarth living.

In the Great Work of our heroic journey, we become colleagues with others who live OneEarth consciousness as their default way of thinking. First Peoples have waited centuries for the MultiEarth Civilization Project to run its unsustainable course. They now see it ending. As humility displaces MultiEarthers' certainty and arrogance, First Peoples are primary among those who can guide

MultiEarthers home to a different way of being. Together we can move into the OneEarth Community in a new era shaped by the larger topographies of consciousness that call to us all.

In 1977, at the United Nations Conference on Indigenous Peoples, the Haudenosaune presented "A Basic Call to Consciousness, the Hau de no sau nee Address to the Western World." The Haudenosaune, also called Iroquois, gave their assessment of what has happened in the Western Hemisphere and offered themselves as partners and guides in the changes necessary to keep Earth livable. Their emphasis on "spiritualism" as "the highest form of political consciousness" includes them, as they importantly claim, "among the world's surviving proprietors of that kind of consciousness." The sense of the sacred in their consciousness guides us into the greater topography of consciousness able to keep Earth livable.

> We feel that the Native peoples of the Western Hemisphere can continue to contribute to the survival potential of the human species. The majority of our peoples still live in accordance with the traditions which find their roots in the Mother Earth. But the Native peoples have need of a forum in which our voice can be heard. And we need alliances with the other peoples of the world to assist in our struggle to regain and maintain our ancestral lands and to protect the Way of Life we follow.
>
> We know that this is a very difficult task. Many nation states may feel threatened by the position that the protection and liberation of Natural World peoples and cultures represents, a progressive direction which must be integrated into the political strategies of people who seek to uphold the dignity of Man. But that position is growing in strength, and it represents a necessary strategy in the evolution of progressive thought.
>
> The traditional Native peoples hold the key to the reversal of the processes in Western Civilization which

hold the promise of unimaginable future suffering and destruction. Spiritualism is the highest form of political consciousness. And we, the native peoples of the Western Hemisphere, are among the world's surviving proprietors of that kind of consciousness. We are here to impart that message.[88]

Ponder, Discuss, and Act

1. Jerry Mander exposes social Darwinism as common in the U.S. and throughout the world. According to this tenet of MultiEarth thought, civilization advances beyond that of First Peoples in such a way that First Peoples ways will gradually become extinct. What are your thoughts about such a statement? How has social Darwinism slipped into your thinking? Where do you see such thinking at work in the world?

2. In the Seven Fires, where do you see yourself?

3. In reviewing Scott Klinger's segment with the three stories of Lenni Lappe, Menominee, and Yawanawa peoples, which bits of history and thought are most important to you in moving further into OneEarth ways?

4. Where do you see partnerships happening between First Peoples and others on an exodus from the Civilization Project?

5. Going forward, how do you see First Peoples giving guidance to your own journey into making Earth's story the one you live by?

CHAPTER EIGHT

Guides for Earth-Size Consciousness: Jung and Korten

The experience of the self is always a defeat for the ego.[89] —Carl Jung

An individual has not started living until he can rise above the narrow confines of his individualistic concerns to the broader concerns of all humanity. —Martin Luther King, Jr.

The 20th century brought us new, more scientific understandings of our psyches, especially the great impact of our unconscious on our conscious lives. Prior to the Civilization Project's ascendancy, humans handled the enormously powerful dynamics of the unconscious by telling stories featuring mythological characters or embodying those characters in ritual and dance. Many First Peoples continue this highly effective way of working with unconscious powers. But the Civilization Project gradually displaced such use of myth, symbol, and ritual, preferring logic, reason, and, finally, the scientific method instead. Use of myth, symbol, and ritual continued but primarily to confirm the powers and ways of civilization, not to work with the powers of the unconscious world.

The preference for logic, reason, and science has now swung the pendulum far into the presumption that myth, symbol, and ritual dance are inferior ways of working with the unconscious realm. We are not conscious enough to hold the two, science *and* myth, in creative and ambiguous tension. So now our psyche's great unconscious dynamics, far from having been left behind, find ways to control our lives and sabotage our ego's best conscious efforts. It's one of the soul's strengths, and devilish ironies, that the more control our egos seek over our lives, the more the great energies about which our egos remain unconscious act out autonomously.

The Civilization Project is a result of this conscious-unconscious interplay. Egos propose and depose, acting in control. But energies from the unconscious, acting out autonomously, continually expose civilization's vulnerabilities and failures. Earth's insurgency continues to reveal energies that ego has sought to ignore and repress, but which are showing themselves to be so much larger than anything egos can control. Whereas the Self can work with Earth's insurgency creatively, egos kick "real solutions" up the road for later attention while justifying their inadequate responses. Egos avoid becoming fully conscious of climate change, soil depletion, deforestation's destructions, and the release of carbon, methane, and nitrous oxide into the air because these overwhelm the capacities of ego civilization.

Internally, egos cannot control the primal energies of our psyches. Consequently, greed, corruption, violence, and exploitation continue while ego resists yielding to Self and the more holistic powers with which Self acts. Ego thus prevents the better responses we are capable of making to the current crises of ecology, species imbalances, war, border disputes, and ethnic nastiness. By moving into topographies of consciousness where Self is preeminent and ego behaves as a sidekick, the energies of Earth and psyche become powerful engines of human and planetary transformation.

Three simple maps in this chapter show us topographies of consciousness beyond where our ego goes. These maps, along with guides who have explored these topographies, become essential to the Great Work of our heroic journey. Had Frodo not known the direction to Mount Doom in Middle Earth, or gotten guidance from Gandalf, he would have failed in his adventure. With GPS, perhaps getting lost geographically is about to become a thing of the past. But getting lost in the unconscious remains a real and frightening possibility. Unrolling a map or three of consciousness, and projecting our journey into the regions shown on the maps, gives us an initial sense of orientation to these unexplored locations in our psyches. The three maps in this chapter orient us to where we are, where we've been, and where we'd like to go—the basics. More detailed "maps of the human psyche" can be readily found online that suggest ways of looking at the world of the unconscious, including the structures and archetypes of all that remains below the surface, and how these relate to evolving greater consciousness. If someone can create a reliable "Consciousness Positioning System," a reliable GPS for our inner world, that would indeed be a welcome app!

Picturing How Our Consciousness Grows

During the 1970s and 1980s, when I worked extensively in adult education, a question persisted: "How can we tell if people are growing?" Some forms of knowing could be tested and measured, but true growth, or transformation, was in a different realm. I came to realize that linear models don't fit how our minds, spirits, and psyches move. Personal growth simply doesn't proceed in straight lines.

I remember sitting in a circle where a woman expressed great frustration because an issue that she thought she had dealt with years ago had recently reappeared in her life, and done so in a rather monstrous way. She was so discouraged.

"Have I not made any headway at all?" she asked herself aloud in the group. She wanted to be done with the issue and was down on herself for not having moved on. She now doubted that it was possible for her to put it behind her. It obviously had the power to reappear at times and in guises of its own choosing. Flooded with anxiety, she asked, "Why can't I control my life better?"

We're all familiar with the longing to "be done with" noxious issues of life. I've certainly wanted to put behind me all the shaming experiences and painful moments that float in and out of my memory. Yet, these memories pop up at will, it seems. When they do, they can affect my moods, suppress my abilities, and put toxins into my relationships. Putting the past behind is possible, apparently, only to a point. But I began to recognize a benefit in these spontaneous recurrences from the past. When they reappear, however they manifest and in whatever guise, they do not come to defeat me, but to provide a new opportunity for growth. They are engines for the very thing I seek, greater awareness. "Why not then treat them as friends," I thought, "rather than intruders? Why not consider that they are companions in our lives, ever reappearing along the way to prod our growth into the next stage of consciousness and understanding?"

With this new realization, I needed a new map. A linear map of growth interpreted these intruders with an "Oh damn! I thought I had dealt with this earlier in life." But a different kind of map could recognize that no reappearance is ever the same as the previous one; and each reappearance provides the very energies we need for transformation of consciousness. These visitations from the complex energies of our unconscious are exactly what we need to get us to Earth-size living.

So I changed maps. I began to picture enlarging topographies of consciousness without suggesting that the smaller topography had been left behind. A circle came to mind in which uneven ripples went out from the center to represent enlarging consciousness (See the "Ripples of Growth" graphic below). Because the anxieties we experience in transformational growth typically cluster around certain themes, I pictured those themes as wedges in a ripply-edged pie, widening out from a center point to the circumference. The world beyond the outer crust of the pie continues to push in, arousing first one wedge, then another. As it does, we gain new opportunities for psychological and spiritual growth.

The Ripples of Growth

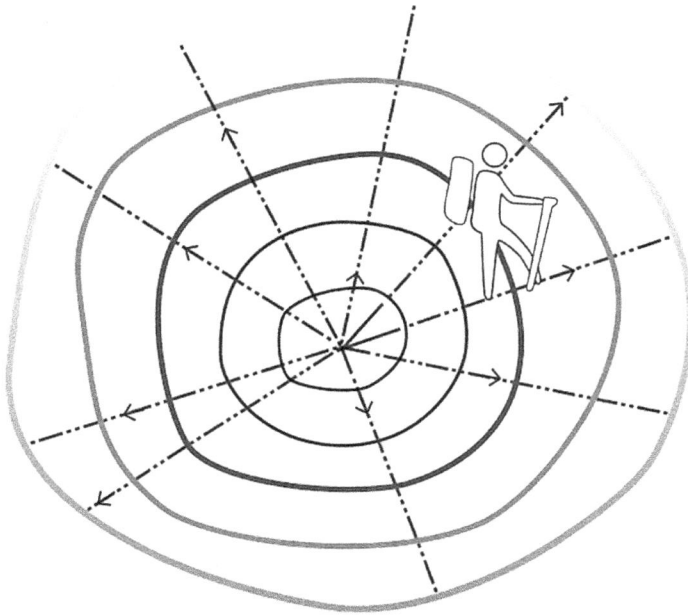

Take the universal experience of overwhelm as an example and name one of the wedges "overwhelm." As we push outward into the unknown, expanding our consciousness, the wedge widens and lengthens at the outer circumference of the ripply-edged pie. Overwhelm presses in from the unknown and reappears in ever new forms. We may have panic attacks or find ourselves paralyzed in daunting moments. In transformational growth, we do not expect to rid ourselves of overwhelm. We do, however, recognize in each fresh experience of overwhelm an opportunity for greater consciousness about the roots of overwhelm in our lives and how it influences us in recurring moments. We know that lots of the overwhelm of the moment is comprised of experiences from earlier in life when we did not yet have the emotional equipment or the right guides to point the way. But now we are older and have both. We can speak kindly to the Child within us and reassure her/

him that, despite the size and surprise of whatever the overwhelm experience of the moment may be, she/he need not cower or fear. We now have resources to deal with overwhelm more thoughtfully, kindly, and decisively.

So when we move to the outer circumference of our consciousness, where life rubs up against us and we once again feel "old" feelings rising, we can proceed on the heroic journey by greeting those energies in the freshness of a new moment. We relate to them with courage in the belief that we are now capable of a more mature choice than we previously made. It's not that our insecurities have gone away or that our hurts don't get exposed. But we've embraced the Call and we're on the move. As a result, we minimize responding like weaklings or tyrants as we have done in the past. Instead, we follow a map of expanding consciousness, and bring updated capacities of Self into relationship with experiences of overwhelm, insecurity, and hurt.

Painful intruders from our past are not repeats to be repressed, but new opportunities for transformation. As the circle expands and the wedge grows larger, we have capacities to befriend the intruder that hurt us before. We are in a new moment of life. The intruder has returned, but now our attitude is not of facing a monster, but a partner in the process of moving into greater consciousness.

We won't always succeed in doing this, of course. But each time we do, the experience reconfirms that befriending our demons is kissing the beast and discovering its beauty. Francis of Assisi discovered as much when he touched and kissed a leper, whom his upper-class upbringing had taught him to despise. When he violated that prohibition, his consciousness of the world grew bigger. He began to see all species and living things in the Cosmos as his sisters and brothers. He befriended what he had previously shunned. For all of us, befriending what we keep avoiding, working around, fearing, or fighting, doesn't just bring us new information. It brings us transformation of consciousness as well. The next two guides in this chapter offer maps of the soul that help us "picture" the transformation of consciousness. They make visible the foreign, little-known topographies into which the heroic journey takes us.

Carl Jung's Daring Explorations of the Unconscious

Carl Gustav Jung (1875–1961) swam upstream throughout his 85 years of life. As a psychiatrist, he was a devoted scientist—a profession that would certainly put him in the mainstream of the 20th century. But much of his research was at the margins of what science regarded as legitimate. He studied dreams, alchemy, astrology, Eastern and Western philosophy, cultural mythology and literature. Whatever the paradigm of modern scientific inquiry excluded held special interest for him. Early in life, he saw how the dominant paradigms ignored valid questions and left out important data when that data did not relate to the paradigm's narrowed field of inquiry. He experienced this as an inquisitive boy with theological questions that his father, a Lutheran pastor devoted to a particular creed, could not answer satisfactorily; he experienced more of the same in psychiatry and science. It was in these marginalized, neglected, and rejected areas where Jung often found the sources of healing and wholeness for his patients and the world.

Jung came to recognize that everything a paradigm left out lived on in the unconscious mind—not neutrally, but actively. It didn't just hang out in the unconscious, it thrived there. Our unconscious minds are, he realized, a great zoo of energies that our rational egos do not want to deal with. These energies appear as the actors and symbols in our dreams; they contribute, albeit unconsciously, to the choices we make about the material stuff, art, people, and symbols we bring into our lives. They inhabit stories whose characters or plots we imitate. We think of ourselves as making rational, informed choices about finances, business, jobs, music, family, and religion, but remain unaware of how much various energies from our unconscious influence the assumptions and myths below the surface of our choices. In moments of awareness, we feel baffled at how the very matters that seem most irrational are the ones that influence our lives, work, and society the most. Jung saw that in order to understand human behavior, and to consciously choose new ways of living, we need to give lots of attention to the unconscious world.

Jung first came to my attention when I was in my late 30's, during a several-day event I attended at a multi-faith center outside of Des Moines, near Colfax, Iowa. Up to that time, I'd given little attention to understanding the role of symbol and myth in our lives. My level of consciousness about such matters fit perfectly the observation of French philosopher, Paul Ricoeur (1913–2005): "In our time we have not finished doing away with idols and we have barely begun to listen to symbols."[90]

In this unlikely location in the farm fields of Iowa, I heard guest leader Morton Kelsey[91] frame a worldview according to Jungian thought. My mind, having grown overweight with rational and logical thinking through an out of balance diet of philosophy and theology, began to reel as I listened. At the end of his first presentation, I went to my room, flopped on my bed, and thought, "A whole new world has sailed into my ken." Most significantly, in the world as Jung described it, the rational and symbolic were merely opposites of one greater whole. It was a new way of thinking that began to heal in me the inner split between the rational and symbolic—a continuing process. But in that moment of new beginning, I felt a "Hooray!" I'd discovered a guide for this journey.

Over the next years I continued to expand my understanding of Jung, recognizing the revolution of consciousness he presented. I attended more events led by Kelsey and read his books along with those of other Jungians—John Sanford, June Singer, Robert Johnson, Emma Jung, Robert Moore, Maria von Franz, and Jung himself. When I moved to the Chicago area, I made regular visits to the Jungian Institute to check out cassettes by Robert Moore, Murray Stein, and others. This extensive diet revealed the hunger in me for a worldview in which Spirit was recognized as a given, integral to all processes. Too long my diet had been out of balance, monopolized by a rational worldview that considered Spirit unnatural.

Before being exposed to Jung, Kelsey, and the like, I could offer the world of Spirit no more than its own compartment along-side, but separate from, large sectors of my life that were all about reasoned approaches to family, religion, science, business, and politics. Spirit was sometimes present in those sectors, of course, and many individuals in those sectors certainly professed faith. But Spirit's integrative, transcending powers were limited to intermittent interventions in life. Bringing Spirit out of its compartment in my mind so it could have an integrative, border-crossing presence in my daily life happened in this new worldview where the rational and symbolic came together, not in a worldview shaped primarily by reason. To have Spirit dialogue with other areas of life is not the same as when Spirit saturates life, actively infusing and transcending all rational and non-rational compartments.

To me, Jung shines as one of the 20th century's outstanding guides for our heroic journey. He traveled the journey for himself. He understood that the heroic journey requires us to trade security for the anxieties of all that is uncertain. But in the liminal uncertainty of the journey, the trade we've made pays off when our unknown capacities evolve to their fullest.

Jung's Map to Our Greater Capacities

In previous chapters I have already been using one feature of Jung's map of the psyche, the feature showing, not one, but two centers of identity. Named ego and Self, the two centers help us differentiate between what is and what could be. What seems impossible to attain, even when we think of pushing our ego into greater and greater effort, becomes possible once we realize that the capabilities of Self are expansive beyond knowing. Such is the case, for example, with the crises we face in the 21st century. We know we need different and greater capabilities to get beyond the consciousness that has given us MultiEarth civilization, but we doubt that humans operating with ego identities can do it. Jung's map shows us another center around which we can configure identity, one that connects us with powers that make Earth-size living possible.

It was through explorations of conscious and unconscious realms within himself, his patients, and the various cultures he visited and studied that Jung came to see how the ego is much the smaller of the two centers of identity despite its central position in the conscious world. "Self," or as Jung called it, *Das Selbst* (The Self), is by far the larger. The Self is not only a center of identity, but also, paradoxically, the whole of our capacities and potentials. It includes not only our consciousness and ego center, but also our vast unconscious. Configuring life around the Self has a kind of borderless feature to it. Not only is Self immeasurably larger than the ego, its attitude toward the unconscious is 180° different. Whereas the ego, separate from the unconscious world, tries to hold it at bay, the Self is anatomically connected with it and ever engaged with its energies. The boundaries and limits we'd come to place on our possibilities with ego in charge open to new lands and waters with Self. Seeing these two centers on Jung's map leaves us asking, "How do we bring the ego-Self potential from the map into our lives?" The answer lies in the heroic journey.

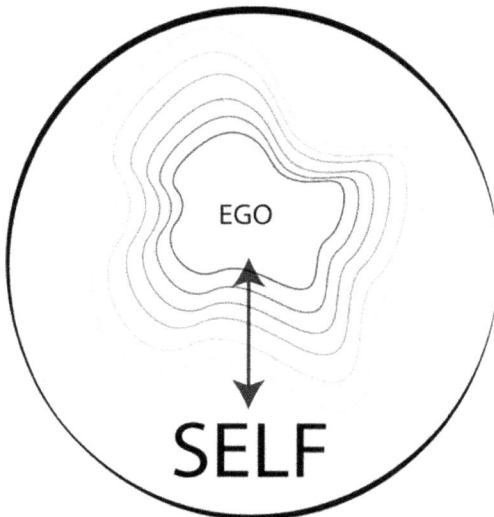

Along with the two centers of identity, Jung's study of the psyche revealed that our unconscious minds have structures which he called "complexes" and "archetypes." Complexes are a composite of experienced memories, unconscious elements, and an archetypal core. A complex of "mother," for example, includes our experiences with our mother and mother figures—both what we remember of them and those which are in our unconscious. But it also has an archetypal core of Mother Earth and the Great Mother who births and nurtures all. These psychic structures are loaded with energies, potentials, and pitfalls. Without these psychic engines we cannot live; with them we live an adventure that mixes conscious choices with unconscious influences. Our rational minds perceive only some of what the complexes and archetypes bring into our worlds. It's essential, therefore, that we value and develop our non-rational capacities in order to make headway on the heroic journey to greater understanding of being more complete humans in a New Story and new Earth epoch.

Continually studying the complexes and archetypes in his patients and on his visits to other cultures, Jung came to perhaps the greatest consciousness-changing conclusion of the many he made. He realized there existed across humanity, a common, species-wide anatomy of the soul. In other words, ego, Self, complexes, and archetypes are universal entities. Jung concluded that these complexes and archetypes hold not only what is taught to us; they exist in the psyches of each of us with a core content much like muscles and bones exist in each of our bodies. Nurture, education, and development bring about an infinite variety of how these entities manifest in each of us, but our psyches are not merely blank pages on which life writes. Rather, our psyches are comprised of entities with codes and energies; plus, we receive material fed through an under-the-surface network like a spring is fed by underground sources. These conclusions put new elements into a map of the psyche. Using the "Ego and Self" map above, picture complexes and archetypes scattered around in it and sources transmitting to them from "The Great Unknown." However we draw it on a map, what's important is to see that our capacities as humans go well beyond what either our personal history or the history of civilization show. OneEarth ways are not at all beyond our reach. Quite the opposite. They best express who we are as a species.

What Jung discovered to be universal in individual psyches, he also found in the collective psyche of cultures. As surely as cultures gather around rivers and trees and other structures of the natural landscape, the souls of cultures are defined by structures common to one another. Everywhere, these beneath-the-surface energies direct behaviors of humans and the civilization-shaping entities that we create. Jung's map helps us understand why we can fervently believe what we are saying and yet behave otherwise, sometimes without even being aware how far our behaviors have wandered from our declared intent. So it is that leaders of nations can speak passionately about peace while preparing to escalate war-making ability. Corporations can speak of bringing great good to humanity while using a production and economic model that destroys our common planetary home. Operating from ego centers of identity, we simply do not understand or recognize how the complexes and archetypes of our culture are influencing behaviors, how they take us in one direction while we are speaking of going in another.

The Soul Energies That Fuel the Heroic Journey

Becoming more aware of the psyche's energies and integrating their power into our lives was, for Jung, the journey to greater consciousness. He called it individuation, but not because it supported the individualism so characteristic in civilization. Though Jung recognized the anatomy of the unconscious as common to us all, he saw its energies and powers developing in limitless ways. Each of us "individuates" according to our own journey even as we are on a shared journey. Shifting our identity from the ego to the greater Self involves each of us entering greater consciousness according to our own undetermined way. Functioning from an identity of the

Self, what lives in our unconscious as undifferentiated and uncontrolled, a realm of untamed Spirit if you will, can be individuated, that is, transformed and integrated into what we need for our Great Work in the 21st century.

Individuation requires persistence. It is the humbling, arduous work of the heroic journey. The complexes and archetypes supply energies for the journey that we did not know we had, or know how to use. Living from our ego centers, these energies bring out-of-control chaos to our world. But living from our Self centers, the same energies bring impetus and assurance to our heroic journey. It's the kind of change that surprises us. Self works with energies of our complexes and archetypes that we'd known only as unmanageable before—not really knowing them at all.

Getting to know the complexes and archetypes active in our lives can, however, be as elusive as it is important. For example, the mother complex, which may be the most commonly referred to in everyday conversation, is rarely understood correctly or appreciatively. In popular understanding, having a mother complex means that we bring dynamics into other female relationships that were part of our relationship with our mother. Just how the mother complex influences our behavior can remain quite unconscious to us. In such a case, the mother complex holds us hostage. When its energies take possession of us, a dark, oppressive mood may settle over us. Or we lose the power to make important, freeing choices for our own lives because of the grip the complex has on us.

But popular understandings of the mother complex rarely include that all of us have one and that it brings necessary energies to our lives. What is necessary is that we individuate it. We do this by recognizing how the complex is at work in our relationships and decision-making. Some therapy may be necessary to help bring to light what we hadn't recognized about ourselves. By working consciously with the mother complex, benefits flow into our lives: our caring for others is richer, we develop a loving connection to Mother Nature, we can give ourselves sacrificially to a goal, and our sense of the divine is inclusive. Amid ecological crises, a positive relationship with our mother complex will empower practices to live interconnectively with all life in our eco-sphere. By individuating our mother complex, we immeasurably increase wellbeing in and around us.

Two other powerful complexes and archetypes weave themselves throughout this book: the Garden and the Heroic. The Garden is that universal structure and energy of the psyche intended to guide us in how to live OneEarth ways. The Heroic provides the inner drive to move us into the greater consciousness that can make the Garden a vibrant model for interdependent, Earth-size living. Chapter after chapter encourages each of us to individuate these complexes with their archetypal cores. As a contrast, Chapter Four describes how when the Heroic is suppressed, its energies act out in dark opposites, becoming the tyrant and weakling, usurper and manipulator, aggressor and withdrawer—energies which cannot embody the Earth-size living held vibrantly in the Garden complex and archetype.

Not only do our souls come with complexes and archetypes, they come with a built-in aid that brings these energies from their unconscious residence into our conscious worlds. I'm speaking of our dreams. We will not be able to benefit from our dreams—how they make us aware of our complexes and archetypes—unless we can get past the notion that they are weird. When we describe a dream as weird, it's merely our egos talking. Egos treat dreams lightly because their rational approach is too limited to understand the rich diversity of symbols that are the language in which dreams speak. Dreams are like plays enacted at night on the stage of our inner theaters. Our dream-maker ingeniously creates a cast of characters who symbolically present aspects of complexes and archetypes. These plays act out what's happening in the parts of our lives about which our egos remain quite unconscious. Despite their mysterious, and occasionally frightening, impressions, dreams communicate to the conscious mind what it has not yet grasped. The more we learn the language of our dreams—a language of symbols more than words—we will come to recognize the busy schedule our archetypes keep. Because the language of the archetype is universal, it can be heard and understood regardless of the language spoken by the dreamer or the culture in which she lives. Dreams facilitate individuation; their messages help us on the heroic journey.

The nutshell truth is that our ego identities feel overwhelmed by the likes of complexes and archetypes, but when we move our identity to the Self we have the capacity to interact positively with these psychic powers so important to the heroic journey. Self's use of these psychic powers gives us the potential to leave the ego Civilization Project for the greater work of OneEarth living. So much of what is impossible when we live from ego identity becomes natural when we live from Self identity. It is not that everything becomes perfect in Self identity living, but consciousness shifts to where the capacities of our human species transcend the constructions and practices of ego-centered living. Self identity cannot settle for MultiEarth living because it knows MultiEarth civilization is inferior to the OneEarth living we are capable of when we are consciously more attune to our complexes, archetypes, and symbols of our psychic, soulful world.

How Self Astutely Shapes OneEarth Living

Self is then far more than an interior experience. Self consciousness connects the personal with the cultural and geological. The confident humility of Self consciousness allows different kinds of interconnections than the anxious arrogance of ego consciousness. Jung came to see how the Self linked the personal and cultural when he recognized that the different myths of cultures are like the dreams of that culture. They speak in the same universal language that our personal dreams use.

Cultural myths tell common stories of the origin of the people, how their society came to be, and what they aspire to do. They tell stories of rulers and how the gods authorized them to rule. Overlooking for a moment how self-justifying such myths can be, when they are accepted by the people, they shape how the people think of themselves and their country. They reveal the unconscious energies of that culture. Such is the case in the U.S. with stories European-Americans tell around Thanksgiving Day. The myths of that Day include how the "pilgrims" came to the New World to seek religious freedom and opportunities, but leave out how they displaced First Peoples with tactics that resembled conquest far more than pilgrimage. Subsequently, mythology was created that told how European-Americans had a Manifest Destiny to settle the Wild West, but never said the land would need to be stolen and taken coercively from First Peoples through dishonest treaties. We also hear mythology about the rags to riches rise of people who arrive on U.S. shores as poor immigrants and become wealthy or powerful leaders. These myths help shape U.S. culture under the direction of egos that do not understand how to work with complexes and archetypes.

Societies never stop creating and adapting mythologies. One of the tricks in understanding the impacts of a particular myth is to discern whether it justifies those in power or reveals their underside, perhaps even poking fun at them. Both exist in a culture. Self has far greater capacities to make such discernment than ego does. The myths justifying those in power are used by them to inspire the citizenry. These myths typically strengthen MultiEarth egos; they do not show the way to Earth-size abundance. Myths of the underside reveal the deep structures of that society, structures that operate outside of the awareness of the leadership. Such myths can motivate rebellion. When they do, the powers that be will stop at nothing to reinstate the official mythology that justifies their power. However, if the people no longer believe the official mythology, the powers will tumble.

Such was the case in 1989–1991, in the breakup of the Soviet Union. Beginning with Poland, the countries who were Russian satellites in the Soviet Union, no longer believed the dream proclaimed in Soviet mythology, revolted, and created separate countries. The truth was that Soviet Premier Mikhail Gorbachev no longer believed the Soviet mythology either. It was a moment in civilization's story that illustrates how powerful the results are when cultural mythology changes. Because myths that justify egos have so much universality, a certain commonality can be seen around the world in how powers rise and fall within civilization. The same is true with myths that reveal the greater Self at work shaping cultures that contribute to OneEarth living.

We receive a big boost along the heroic journey when we understand how the energies of complexes and archetypes are expressed in the myths of civilization, and how those myths have a major say in what transpires in civilization. Our myths explain why we are locked into MultiEarth civilization and what dynamics in our culture might be drawn upon to urge people into OneEarth living. We will fail in the Great Work to which Earth and Self call us *unless* we continually access and integrate the limitless array of powers and potentials of these energies from the unconscious. If we do not bring these energies on board, and evaluate their merits consciously, they will fuel the darker capacities in our psyches and society, assuring that MultiEarth crises and disasters will intensify.

Accessing these immeasurable powers requires a major metamorphosis within us psychologically and spiritually. Our egos cannot continue as they have. They decrease in importance; Self radically increases. Egos just can't handle much of anything having to do with the unconscious mind or civilization's unconscious underworld. The heroic journey feels like one long metamorphosis for our egos, what Jung called quite simply, "defeat:" "The experience of the self is always a defeat for the ego."[92] Few of us take readily to defeat, even when this "defeat" takes us on the only journey headed for our survival within Earth-size consciousness and living.

The defeat of our egos in a role for which they are completely outmatched makes possible their reassignment to the role for which they are intended. A defeated and reassigned ego can see what part of a situation is its own responsibility instead of trying to do it all and then laying blame on others because their way is not working. When my ego tries to be the whole, it triggers the energies of complexes and archetypes that overwhelm it. But when my Self lifts energies of complexes and archetypes out of the unconscious with the intent that they become conscious, my ego can use them in the conscious world.

Take, for example, the results coming out of peace negotiations, legislative bodies, and climate summits. When egos seek final control of the outcomes, little changes. The personal and cultural complexes and archetypes of the participants dominate their behaviors and speech. They lose discernment whether another person, group, or nation is right or wrong. Nor do they seem to care. Control is what matters to egos that have not found their true role. Truth does not. Negotiations in which Selves replace egos proceed more genuinely. United Nations summits on climate change or legislative bodies enacting policies for a livable planet require participants who are on the heroic journey or who are being pressured by others who are.

Earth and Self are agreed: they will continue to send geological and archetypal energies that challenge and overwhelm a world led by ego consciousness. Inconvenient as it may be to egos everywhere, Earth and Self intend nothing less than calling us personally and collectively into our greater capacities. By embracing that Call we can express the universal Garden complex and archetype, evolving into a new Ecozoic age. Cultures of peoples across the seven continents have mythologies that sound the Call and empower us on the heroic journey which keeps Earth livable. In the Western world, Eden is one such myth, provided we tell the version that flashes its regained power. The archetype of the Garden, whatever name it is given, is being projected onto the mental screens of humanity by the many myths around the globe that tell their own versions of it. Collectively, the consciousness that results can impel us to make decisions that bring many versions of the Garden into being in the OneEarth world. Doing so is the work of the Self.

David Korten's Map: From Superpower
to OneEarth Consciousness

In *Blinded by Progress*, the first book in this Eden Series, I used David Korten's map of consciousness[93] to show the emotional, psychological, and spiritual immaturity of MultiEarth leadership and society. Here we unfold Korten's map again, but for a different reason: it helps us see the way out of the destructive MultiEarth Civilization Project and into topographies of OneEarth living. On Korten's map (see graphic below), Magical and Imperial topographies equate with the MultiEarth Civilization Project; Cultural and Spiritual consciousness are topographies of OneEarth living. The Socialized topography in the map represents a consciousness that has become uncomfortable with Magical and Imperial ways, but needs more persuasion to risk moving on.

Five Topographies of Consciousness

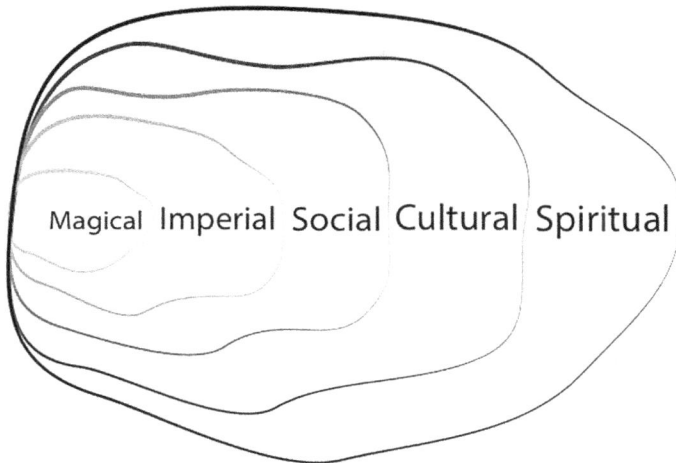

Magical Imperial Social Cultural Spiritual

The map represents MultiEarth consciousness as three or more sizes smaller than Spiritual Consciousness. Like Dr. Seuss' Grinch who stole Christmas because his heart was not one, not two, but three sizes too small, humanity steals and pillages Earth's beneficence because MultiEarth consciousness is too small. In the following paragraphs I briefly describe this map's five topographies of consciousness and how our relationship with Earth differs in each one. Traveling through these five topographies on the heroic journey compares to Jung's map in that the movement into greater topographies defeats and redirects the ego and befriends living with Self in charge. Because of what Self can do, the further we move into the larger topographies of consciousness, the more we are able to consciously use the energies and potentials of the complexes and archetypes.

Magical Consciousness—As children we do lots of magical thinking. We encounter the world, Korten says, as "fantasizers." Seeing the world with Magical Consciousness brings delight, not only to children but to the parents and adults around them. Children's eyes often open up our rationalized adult consciousness to where we feel wonder, explore imaginary spaces, and leave mysteries dangling in "I don't know." Responding to their questions prods us to think with imagination. Playing with them in their world, where they set the rules, gets us fantasizing. Their invitation, "Will you play with me?," can reconnect us to the creativity of imagining scenarios of life as we talk to toys and move them around.

Children connect naturally with Nature's magical playground, wondering and fantasizing about every bug and flower. When we value rather than laugh at or scorn a child's Magical Consciousness, we affirm their foundation for loving Nature and choosing One Earth living.

But Magical Consciousness has huge downsides when, as grown-ups, we act from its less responsible traits. Magical Consciousness can fantasize and play without cleaning up. It wants and takes without calculating accurately the cost. Responsibilities and duties not inherently part of Magical Consciousness need to be taught and grown into. Looking at this map for purposes of the heroic journey, we want to recognize that certain irresponsible traits of Magical Consciousness are widely practiced in MultiEarth civilization. MultiEarth consciousness leaves its messes for Mother Earth to clean up. It has the fantasy that we can live beyond Earth's capacities and that somehow, magically, everything will work out. MultiEarth consciousness engages in magical thinking about who pays the ecological costs when those are not factored into economic profits.

The heroic journey into greater consciousness does not consider Magical Consciousness as a thing grown-ups leave behind. Wonder and imagination are capacities we must hold onto and develop if we are to get into the topography of Spiritual Consciousness and keep Earth livable. Feeling magic in certain moments freshens our relationships and interactions with all our relations in the life community of our planet.

Imperial Consciousness—As childhood moves into adolescence, our relationship to the world shifts, Korten says, from "fantasizers" to "power-seekers." We increasingly engage the world with less dependence on parents and adults. We try to find our own resources, ideas, and relationships in our quest to establish a sense of independence. This highly challenging transition from dependence to greater independence does not happen evenly or without wounds and danger. Yet, it has its triumphs. We come to moments when we achieve a particular goal, know we're in charge of a piece of our environment, or finally depose a nemesis.

It's important to notice the imperial quality involved in becoming responsible for oneself, for others, for organizations, for areas where we have influence. Deeds once too big for us are conquered with growing strength. When we get some money and power, we feel the control they bring us. We criticize the way adults do life and check out alternatives. We push away from parents, yet depend on them. We come of age to do adult things—earn, drive, propagate, buy, trade, and fall in love. We can't wait to have greater freedoms, but understand only some of the responsibilities. As adolescents, many of us aspire to achieve and make our mark in studies, sports, art, or work, and try to hold our own with peers or influence and lead them. Our egos don't distinguish clearly between power and control, so in our adolescent years we become young emperors over a realm, vying with other emperors or forming alliances with them.

Important as adolescent Imperial Consciousness is as a topography for part of our journey, it proves difficult to leave. Consequently, it predominates in MultiEarth civilization. Korten underscores that in dominant, superpower cultures, we may never truly leave it. MultiEarth civilization rewards so many of the youthful, energetic characteristics that thrive in the topography of Imperial Consciousness that even the intended evolutionary process of our psyche gets arrested. The Civilization Project relies on the Imperial Consciousness quality of exercising power as a tool of control rather than to facilitate the wellbeing of all. Power is understood as more, bigger, and mightier than the rest. To emperors, if Nature can't serve their quest, then it's in the way. Egos, having gained some control, dig in their heels at the suggestion of moving into greater topographies of consciousness where they yield control to Self. Flexing muscles, egos want to show they can make it in the MultiEarth, imperial civilization they've grown up in. MultiEarth civilization lacks meaningful rites of passage that challenge our egos to undergo the depth of transformation necessary for moving into adult responsibilities with a deeper sense of Self.

With MultiEarth civilization and egos arranged around imperialism, the odds are stacked high to make Imperial Consciousness home. Still, the Earth-Self Call is heard in Imperial Consciousness and many, struggling, embrace the Call. Earth's insurgency and the inbuilt yearnings psychologically and spiritually stir the belief that we human beings are to be part of more than an imperial civilization. Korten's map shows that structuring the world according to imperial control through transnational corporations, economic domination, and superpower militaries cannot bring our best to the planet nor does it propel us into our greatest achievements as a species. Once our power-seeker behavior morphs into control, the heroic is suppressed. As the earlier chapter on "Turning from the Call" described, by continuing in the power-seeker topography of Imperial Consciousness as grownups, we shape life and society in the codependent polarity of manipulating withdrawers and bullying tyrants. To move into greater topographies of consciousness, Self needs to take over the power-seeking impulse from ego who has reduced power to life-draining control. With Self in charge, power-seeking finds the deep, life-generating power of the complexes and archetypes that move us along on the heroic journey.

Socializing Consciousness—Year by year in adulthood, we feel ideals of OneEarth living being overwhelmed by the duties of making a living in a MultiEarth world. In Socializing Consciousness, we are tugged in two directions. Do we socialize into MultiEarth civilization and delay Earth-size living? Or will we join with others to bring OneEarth living into the social fabric of how we live an alternative to the dominant economy and culture? We can go either way or feel a hybrid of both. Socializing Consciousness is an adaptive topography where we learn the skills of adapting and risk its pitfalls. Will we adapt our bigger ideals to the smaller topographies, or will we adapt to the Call of larger topographies in tune with Earth and the greater community of life that Earth continually regenerates?

If we can see a way to make imperial ways work for us, we may just hitch our identity to that plan. We ponder making a deal: *If I choose consciously to cooperate with more benevolent forms of superpower ways and MultiEarth living, will I not be able to do good and reconcile the conflicts with my ideals? Maybe I can bring change from the inside.*

But then, again, there's the tug to create the alternatives of Earth-size living by following those living more fully into larger topographies. In order to socialize in that direction, it helps to be in "their choir." By singing the music of greater consciousness, we are more likely to adapt in that direction. The music brings forth the best from us. The choir keeps us listening to the sounds of our deeper yearnings and Earth's unrelenting pursuit to keep the planet running on her terms. Without a choir, the dailyness of life can leave little time or energy to seek out and weigh options capable of moving us along on the heroic journey.

The competing pulls in Socializing Consciousness can have us adapting so many ways that we lose our way. With the imperial culture going strong, many hear the Call of Earth and Self as auxiliary, not urgent. To embrace it is to paddle upstream.

Everyone in the Socializing topography of consciousness has a lot to overcome. They are the oft-mentioned "swing-voters" in political campaigns. Many will swing in the direction of OneEarth living if they hear more compelling stories empowering OneEarth ways or see stronger, viable models of Earth-size living. Socializing Consciousness swings back and forth on many questions. *Am I ready to distance myself from the MultiEarth stories and culture— especially since some of its rewards of wealth and power are within my reach? Do I have the consciousness to break the habits of my own heart, habits molded by MultiEarth civilization? Can I stand up to power and truth, risking loss of what, on one level, I've worked for? Am I able to see how many academic and religious institutions treat OneEarth thinking and practices as outlier and unorthodox?*

Some will! They will find others more advanced in OneEarth ways and join in the Great Work. In doing so they will overcome the formidable obstacles presented by government policies, business profit-making, big money, controlled media, schooling with insufficient critical thinking, and compliant, non-prophetic dogmas of faith. Earth-size consciousness continues to call out from the streets and roads, and from the dwindling rainforests and aquifers: "Come out of MultiEarth configurations, trust OneEarth's promise." Many in the topography of Socializing Consciousness decide in favor of that Call. People in Socializing Consciousness get targeted as "swing-votes" in political campaigns. Similarly, they can swing away from or toward the OneEarth worldview. Many are swinging in the OneEarth direction, helping us get to a tipping point; others have yet to hear more compelling versions of OneEarth living or see examples of how they can be part of a society shaped by it.

Cultural Consciousness—In the topography of Cultural Consciousness, new ways of thinking imagine more inclusive cultures and bring them into being. Though the Civilization Project continues to imagine cultures where religions, empires, superpowers, and multinational corporations compete, in Cultural Consciousness the guiding moral principle for cultures becomes "all of us" together, not "me" or "my," not "us" versus "them," not "we" and "ours," but "all of us"—all species living, propagating, and dying within our planet's organic sufficiency and balance. Profits and power lose their enticement when a new order of greater inclusiveness takes hold in our thinking.

All who spend time in the topography of Cultural Consciousness inquire into other cultures, religions, and habits more than fearing them. Cultural Consciousness finds strength and greater wholeness through the inclusion of differences. How people respond to the current flow of human migration, the largest since World War II, provides a stark contrast between Cultural Consciousness and Imperial Consciousness. Imperial Consciousness wants to control the flow by enforcement. People in Socializing Consciousness may be of two minds. But people in Cultural and Spiritual topographies seek a more holistic and systemic response. Functioning from greater consciousness, we recognize more of the root causes of immigration—root causes that often stem from the policies of the imperially-oriented countries who, in many cases, are also most eager to restrict the immigrants from entering their borders. Larger topographies of consciousness recognize that differences in cultures help us re-imagine our world beyond the Civilization Project.

Most likely the numbers of people involved in such re-imagining of the world is greater than we think. In 2000, sociologist Paul Ray and psychologist Sherry Anderson published their book, *The Cultural Creatives: How 50 Million People Are Changing the World*.[94] Their study was only of Western civilization, but their criteria revealed that fully 25% of the U.S. population, or 80+ million people, are Cultural Creatives, with an estimate of 80–90 million more in Europe. Their study recognizes people migrating into greater consciousness and into a paradigm beyond what shaped Western civilization.

Living in Cultural Consciousness is not futuristic, idealistic, or utopian. Paul Hawken, entrepreneur and advocate for OneEarth living, writes in his book, *Blessed Unrest*, of coming to realize that globally millions of people and organizations manifest what Korten's map dubs Cultural Consciousness.[95] Hawken calls it the largest movement in the world, but also observed that many people who live at least part of the time in this larger topography do so unaware that they are part of this great movement of "blessed unrest." Whereas people in Imperial Consciousness find one another with the social and economic linkages of the dominant cultures, people in Cultural Consciousness have to create their own links apart from the dominant cultures. Social media is helping many connections to be made, but are there enough people in Cultural Consciousness that a tipping point has been reached, though yet undiscovered?

By tipping point, I mean somewhere up to 20% of the population who stop giving consent to societies and economies structured in smaller topographies. As cited in footnote 18 above, "scientists at Rensselaer Polytechnic Institute have found that when just 10 percent of the population holds an unshakable belief, their belief will always be adopted by the majority of the society." If the people strongly committed to the values of Cultural Consciousness sense solidarity with one another and all of Nature, then we can expect to see more and more cultures being imagined and created with stronger action on climate change, with livelihoods in balance with Nature, with cooperative economies, with inclusive Earth-centered spiritualities, and with wellbeing measured by a more reliable standard than economic growth. When we move around in the greater topography of Cultural Consciousness, it becomes inconceivable that humanity can be held back perpetually by superpower, MultiEarth thinking.

Spiritual Consciousness—Beyond Cultural Consciousness, the topography of Spiritual Consciousness beckons. There, the inclusiveness of Cultural Consciousness projects us further beyond the dualistic thinking that permeates Imperial Consciousness. Spiritual Consciousness unites the energies of differences into a cooperative, diverse whole. Korten speaks of this topography as being where we experience the Mystery of a true *uni*-verse. He echoes an observation from Aristotle: "nature longs for opposites and effects her harmony from them." The hemispheres scattered throughout a billion galaxies hold opposite poles in a single, greater sphere. It is that kind of One that we can imagine and make possible when our separate hemispheric ways of thinking do not become the last word—as commonly happens in smaller topographies of consciousness. Dualisms are not to be ignored. They are the penultimate in the holistic kind of thinking through which we can join Earth, rather than let dualisms like environment versus economy keep us apart and destroy us.

In present and past centuries of civilization, Spiritual Consciousness has been expressed mostly by sages, aboriginal rituals and myths, mystics with cosmic vision, some beneficent leaders, and spiritual luminaries. All show that it is accessible to our species but not to an ego-centered civilization. Korten's map shows that Spiritual Consciousness is what we are called to by Earth and Self. By calling this topography of consciousness "Spiritual," Korten recognizes how well that word serves when we want to talk about the core experience of this topography—the interdependence of all things. Thinking and living interdependently differs substantially from the independence that characterizes our thinking and living in the Civilization Project's Imperial Consciousness.

The interdependence of Spiritual Consciousness becomes possible when Self becomes our center of identity and our ego, fiercely independent, has sufficiently transformed to where it recognizes that collaborating with the Self is its rightful function. Jungian psychotherapist David Richo describes our choice for the heroic journey as one in which we make our departure from a world in which neurotic egos establish the norms. As the struggles of the heroic journey proceed and consciousness expands, our egos become healthier, less presumptuous, more able to walk humbly at Self's side. In the topography of Spiritual Consciousness, what presses most upon us is that in the struggle we are met by trans-formative gifts and a kind of wholeness we cannot achieve on our own. Richo says, "The gift we bring home is our own awakening to oneness with humanity and nature.... This realization makes the love we show universal and unconditional. Now we understand that love is our true identity beyond ego."[96]

Growing into Spiritual Consciousness promises to be an uneven struggle. We might, for example, function in Cultural Consciousness in a certain relationship, but then, without even thinking about it, move into power-seeking, Imperial consciousness regarding love of country. Or we might function with an adaptive Socializing Consciousness in how we dress, shop, vacation, or make political choices, but then move into Spiritual Consciousness regarding the environment. Korten quickens us with anticipation by making the point that when enough grownups constellate consciousness in Cultural and Spiritual topographies, a "Culture of Earth Community" inevitably manifests.

Taken together, the maps of Jung and Korten show us how to get out of the maze of MultiEarth civilization that traps so many of us. They show us that Imperial Consciousness imagines and creates MultiEarth living, but that our imaginations and creativity in Cultural and Spiritual Consciousness cannot settle until they bring about OneEarth community. In the Spiritual topography, we see how the pillars holding up the MultiEarth story are not part of the creational order after all. It is not true, for example, that we humans cannot really construct societies without having them sabotaged by greed and lust for more stuff and more power. We are not born with some sin meme or congenital condition passed along to us from our parents which makes Spiritual Consciousness impossible. Nor do we pass such a meme along to our children in a form that will inevitably sabotage their capacity to choose the heroic journey.

The Mystery inherent in evolution's, creative processes has nothing less in mind for us than to move into a topography of consciousness three sizes larger than what civilization's grinchiness knows. Daring to believe that we can live in OneEarth consciousness, and then showing our belief by what we do, puts us into the "revolution of human consciousness" that the Czech Republic President, Vaclav Havel, saw as essential for our planet.

Conclusion: Maps of Regions Beyond MultiEarth Civilization

The maps of this chapter show clearly that the Civilization Project is not the best humanity can do. They show regions beyond MultiEarth civilization where both our psychological-spiritual makeup as well as evolutionary processes expect us to go. Getting there requires more than resolve or information. Transformation is needed—a change in identity and a change in paradigm. Arriving in these greater topographies empowers us to imagine and create OneEarth cultures.

As I learned working with adults who sought education for transformation as well as information, transformational processes don't follow straight lines—not even bumpy straight lines. The topographies through which the heroic journey travels reveal enlarging expanses with wavy outer edges that invite us to move beyond their borders. Every added venture represents added consciousness and enlarges us. But it also introduces new vulnerabilities as the outer circumference pushes out against more of the unconscious, the unknown. This vulnerability we experience at the border raises our insecurity, and can tempt us to pull back, to build walls. Yet, our continuing growth and transformation depends on encountering what is out there.

Our *opus* is to expand our circle of consciousness to fit our planet. The emphasis is not on climbing the ladder or being at the head of the line. The heroic journey to greater consciousness does not ascend hierarchies; there are no preferred positions in a lineup; there are, however, expanding topographies.

Each map, in its own way, tells of big topographies beyond the control of MultiEarth's reach. Each map identifies regions that will open to us only as we get past the borders of our egos into that unknown Other. Encountering this Other with the capacities of Self and ego in conscious, loving, holistic relationship remains the essence of transformation.

The maps of this chapter picture what is possible for us. They imply the Great Work of the journey involved in making the possibilities real. A major series of events along the journey involve the struggle to leave Imperial Consciousness and the MultiEarth paradigm which has been our home. Leaving the independence that we achieve and value in Imperial Consciousness triggers fear, fierce resistance, and feels like loss. We need to exercise a major act of faith in order to believe that the interdependence inherent in Spiritual Consciousness is humanity's better way. Such faith happens, however, in the events that defeat the ego and bring us to a fuller embrace of Self as our identity.

What the maps cannot fully show about the heroic journey is the many sources along the way that bring us what we need once we commit to the Great Work and Self emerges. The Mysteries of the holistic Universe meet us as we continue to declare our intentions to stay on the journey and continue to let go of what have been our ways of thinking and acting. People in Spiritual Consciousness give witness to these sources of grace that come to strengthen and renew us like underground rivulets feed a spring, or like the refreshing breezes that blow from we know not where. These unpredictable, trans-egoic, spiritual sources repeatedly turn out to be fully sufficient for challenges on the heroic journey, even those we wonder how we can possibly meet.

The guides and maps inspire us with possibility as we realize that others have traversed this terrain before us and have weathered the storms. They, too, went through emptying and dismembering. Some have known shamanic experiences and have wondered whether they were going mad. Others have been taunted by inner demons or singled out by outer tyrants. Some saw Death coming for them. Through it all, their egos were met by the Self and they knew that the fullness of being human is experienced through *interrelationship* with all life instead of independence through lives of control. On the journey, they came to know unconditional grace and love as it met them in moments of transformation. The grace and love came from what they saw as the Source, God, the Way, the Divine, or whatever words they used to describe their experience.

People in Spiritual Consciousness learn how to feel the intensity of strong opposites. There we can find common cause beyond what in smaller consciousness feels divisive. In the topography of Spiritual Consciousness, we reduce the grip of past experiences or feared futures; we are able to focus on the present as we reimagine our lives and cultures in interdependent, Earth-size ways.

But not to get ahead of ourselves. We have far to go. So, with these maps and guides accessible, we cross the threshold of our ego-zone and push into what is, at the moment, Unconscious and Unknown. We're as prepared as we can be for all that will follow.

Ponder, Discuss, Act

1. Which of the maps do you see as helping you most to move into topographies of greater consciousness?

2. Pick a segment of your life where you'd like to be more aware than you are now. Where are you now on each of the maps with that segment of your life, and what kind of movement and choices go with the Call to greater consciousness?

3. Where on a map would you locate one of the MultiEarth practices in your life? in your culture?

4. What do you need to do so that you can reduce the grip of a MultiEarth situation most pressing in on you?

5. How can you move further into topographies of OneEarth consciousness even if your practice in the new topography falls short?

6. What's something you've discovered recently in your exploration of topographies of greater consciousness that has you most abuzz?

Metamorphosis to a New, Edenic Human

*I*s it even possible for us humans to change enough to keep Earth livable? Am I changing enough? What in my own soul, my own consciousness needs to change further? Am I functioning with a large enough consciousness to help bring the Garden archetype into OneEarth expression in the 21st century?

These are the questions of this Section. Every heroic journey arrives at the moment where people on the journey come into possession of the treasure that makes their world better even as it changes them further. Sometimes the treasure is hidden in a dangerous location filled with unknowns. Other times it's in the territory of adversaries and guarded by them. At this stage of the journey, it's do or die. We're looking for that solution, love, being, or way of relating that helps us make a whopping shift out of MultiEarth control and into Creation's OneEarth community. Where exactly can we find the treasure of interrelationship with all of Earth's community of life? Who or what is preventing us from making it ours?

My search follows this logic:

- The ways of civilization have separated our species from the treasure of OneEarth living.
- Civilization civilizes Nature's wild, interdependent, wilderness ways.
- Therefore, Nature's wildness, around us and in us, is the place to look for the OneEarth treasure.

So, Chapter Nine takes us into the wild, or more accurately, into the fascinating tension between taming and civilizing the wild or seeking the wild's capacity to "rewild" us. Rewilding aptly names this phase of the heroic journey. Shedding civilization's excessive civilizing influence continues to be necessary, and Nature's rewilding influence shows us the way to claim the treasure we seek.

In Chapter Ten the heroic journey moves to a climax. We enter the unconscious underworld and face our darkside more thoroughly than we've yet done. Our identity goes through yet another phase of metamorphosis from ego to Self. Only by coming to know better the parts of ourselves and society that we wish weren't so do we undergo the *additional change of mind and soul we need in order to fully handle the powers of the archetypal Garden within and Earth's uncompromising evolution beyond our control. To become capable of OneEarth living, we undergo rewilding and repeatedly make the passage from ego to Self. We metamorphose into a new, Edenic human with capacities of being that are impossible in civilization consciousness.*

CHAPTER NINE

From Taming the Wild to Rewilding Ourselves

We need the tonic of wildness—to wade sometimes in marshes where the bittern and the meadow-hen lurk…. We can never have enough of nature. We must be refreshed by the sight of inexhaustible vigor, vast and titanic features, the sea-coast with its wrecks, the wilderness with its living and its decaying trees, the thunder-cloud…. We need to witness our own limits transgressed, and some life pasturing freely where we never wander. —Henry David Thoreau, *Walden*

Wildness is a necessity…. Mountain peaks and reservations are useful not only as fountains of timber and irrigation rivers, but as fountains of life. —John Muir

Wilderness is not a place where humans don't live; wilderness is a place where humans live in harmony with the earth. —Scott Klinger

Stories of taming the Wild West lie deep in the mythology of how the United States came to be. But what does it mean to call the West "wild?" Did "white people" tame it? Does the Wild even need taming?

The First Peoples who lived in the geographies of the Wild West tell a story quite opposite to American mythology. Luther Standing Bear (1868–1939) was chosen as chief by the Ogalala Sioux in 1902. He authored books and articles that continue to be on college reading lists in anthropology, literature, history, and philosophy. Standing Bear says his people did not think of the West as wild.[97]

> Only to the white man was nature a "wilderness" and only to him was the land "infested" with "wild" animals and "savage" people. To us it was tame. Earth was bountiful and we were surrounded with the blessings of the Great Mystery. Not until the hairy man from the east came and with brutal frenzy heaped injustices upon us and the families that we loved, was it "wild" for us. When the very animals of the forest began fleeing from his approach, then it was that for us the "Wild West" began.[98]

Chief Standing Bear is one of many Indigenous voices that correct the views of civilization toward what is wild. The attitudes and actions of "white people" evoked a horror in the First Peoples that was too deep for words. First Peoples had roamed over great expanses of unowned lands for centuries. These lands were home; even more, these lands could not be separated from who they were. Then came U.S. westward expansion. The U.S. devised treaties to displace First Peoples from their vast lands and confine them within land reserves. Laws were devised to help settlers own the lands that had been a commons shared by First Peoples and all species. The U.S. military protected the settlements and enforced the containment of First Peoples. The takeover of the grand, unowned lands wrenched the souls of First Peoples. They were integral with the land. It was not real estate which could be appraised and given a dollar value. So when the U.S. forced tribes off their land, it was identity theft. First Peoples lost their way of life and who they were—a trauma from which recovery is wrenchingly difficult.

But First Peoples are not the only ones who've not recovered. The rest of U.S. civilization hasn't either. U.S. mythology continues the lie that westward expansion was a story of glory, perseverance, and daring that went into creating a great nation. In fact, it was a clash of paradigms in which First Peoples were methodically killed. First Peoples were living the OneEarth paradigm; westward expansion imposed the MultiEarth paradigm. Until "white people" and "white government" acknowledge that westward expansion was wrong in ideology and morally wrong in practice, the wound continues to bleed, fester, and ooze. European-Americans blew a marvelous opportunity to partner in living OneEarth ways on this continent. It could have worked for all.

Confessing the error would be a step in healing the psychological and spiritual wound in all who've separated from Earth's story. The wound is proving to be a savage hurt. The degree of its savagery becomes apparent in how European-Americans act toward species of the Wild and toward First Peoples. Non-Indigenous Americans have projected onto the First Peoples the wound they were not ready to heal in themselves. Rather than joining with First Peoples in learning the ways of living interconnected with Earth and her species, non-Indigenous peoples forced them into disconnected ways. Unconscious of how savage the wound of separation from the Wild actually is, First Peoples were called savage, rather than the people and systems responsible for inflicting the wound. European-Americans, unaware how extreme their belief was that Nature needed taming, saw how First Peoples connected with Nature and called them "wild." In their minds, First Peoples needed civilizing. Conforming this wild land and people to the MultiEarth paradigm was top priority. MultiEarth civilization in the U.S. is born out of the wound of separation from Earth and continues to be shaped by its pain.

Had "civilizers" moved beyond ego identities to ego-Self collaboration in greater topographies of consciousness, the outcome on this continent would have been much more Earth-size than we are today. Not only would civilizers have been healed of their own soul-wounds, they would have been enlarged in consciousness by learning from those they saw as standing in their way. It's a heroic journey that was never taken. Collaboration on an Earth-size paradigm could have brought the OneEarth treasure into a mixed race, continent-wide expression. Instead, we got MultiEarth on steroids through a European-American mythology that continues to be told even though it treats dehumanizing people and abusing Mother Earth as acceptable. It's a mythology that keeps this country outside of the many possible expressions of the archetypal Garden.

The Wild—Through MultiEarth or OneEarth Lenses?

Juanita, my spouse, Tyler, our grandson, and I packed up our camping gear before sunrise the day we left the Grand Tetons and headed for nearby Yellowstone National Park. For us, tent camping increases our intimacy with wildness. Even the "inconveniences" of camping help us experience more deeply our interdependence within Nature. In Yellowstone, we shared living space with bison, wolves, grizzlies, black bears, birds, and insects. We saw and felt steam from Earth's magma where it pierces the ground, forming geysers and springs. We witnessed the wild water and falls, treacherously beautiful, and flowing out of control with snowmelt after a winter with 200% normal snowpack. Many moments reminded us that we were in spaces where we were not in charge. We were welcome, but, clearly, we needed to learn the etiquette of relationships with the species and forces inhabiting these wild spaces.

Driving into Yellowstone early that morning, we headed toward the Norris Campground in search of a tent site. Suddenly, we had to brake to a dead stop. The road ahead was filled with a queue of stopped vehicles. What was going on? The question was quickly answered when a brawny bison ambled toward us in the lane of oncoming traffic. It's four legs seemed much too thin to hold up the great beast moseying along on them. There it was: an American icon of the Plains heading our way, and bringing to a halt a technological icon of our culture, the automobile.

During the next week we had many more bison moments. Marvelous beasts! So stunning, beautiful, and smelly; so dangerous when approached. What an opportunity we missed in U.S. westward expansion when we slaughtered vast herds of them rather than seeking interdependence!

Most often, when we saw bison in Yellowstone, they seemed unable to hurry (although they can run up to 35 miles per hour). They wandered through our campground daily and even into our tent site. Though the park service routinely warns visitors to get no closer than 25 yards, in the campsite they sometimes wandered nearer. In those instances, we did not need to move away; just to remain calm, give quiet respect, and show no movement of aggression. As long as we acknowledged their dominance, our subservience, all went well. Yet every year people are gored in Yellowstone because they violated a bison's space. Bison can whirl suddenly and attack.

We soon learned the attitude practiced by the park service. The animals live at Yellowstone permanently while we humans come and go. Humans may manage the park, and visitors may come throughout the year, but, in the park, we are the not the dominator species that we practice being outside the park. Yellowstone continually works at understanding interdependence and practicing it. Speed limits top at 45 mph throughout the park so that traffic can yield to the bison, grizzlies, wolves, and other mountain mammals. It's a really slow speed given the vast distances of the park. But even at that speed, animals get hit too often.

Other campground rules also brought home to us how we were sharing space with the animals. We were required to clear our campground table of all foods, drinks, and cooking gear after every use. We were to lock it all up in our car. We did this every night after dinner and again every morning following breakfast. Only our tent occupied the campsite all the time. To be sure, such chores were inconvenient. But they were a wonderful, strong reminder that we were not the boss. We were guests for a short stay, sharing space with other species and learning a bit about living interdependently with them.

Sharing space with wildlife as collaborating partners in Earth's community of life gets us into the OneEarth mindset of wilderness. How different this is from the more typical attitude characteristic of the MultiEarth paradigm where *Homo sapiens* expect preferential treatment, even regarding wilderness. There's a widespread attitude among us that we have an inherent right not only to protect ourselves from wild creatures and plants but to determine where they may live and how. Most of the time that dominance assures we can benefit economically from our position of power. As the graphics below show, in the MultiEarth paradigm *Homo sapiens* are the apex of the pyramid of life, an expression of egoistic civilization. In the OneEarth paradigm, *Homo sapiens* are within the circle of Earth's interdependent community of life.

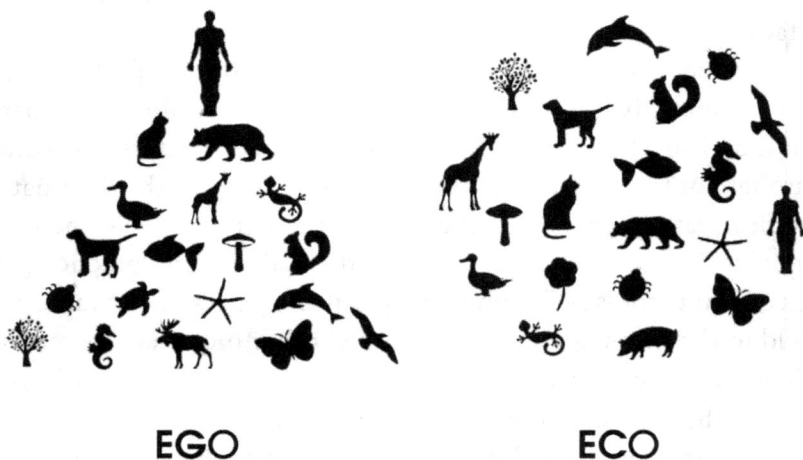

EGO   ECO

The worldview of OneEarth Creation perceives wildness as integral to the holistic connections that assure a life-sustaining ecosphere. We cannot move into the great challenges yet to come on our heroic journey if we keep the MultiEarth, egoistic mindset. If we catch ourselves wanting to cleanse our houses, yards, cities, and farms of all things wild and inconvenient, we can be sure that our attitude and consciousness are more ego than eco-focused. At this stage of the heroic journey it's important that we strengthen our understanding of the Wild's deep and mysterious interconnections *and become part of them.*

The worldview of MultiEarth civilization embodies a highly polarized and confusing attitude toward wildness. On the one hand, it perceives wildness in the natural world as a threat to suppress and defeat; on the other, it intentionally channels a type of wildness when it wages war, produces reality TV shows, and intimidates and tortures other humans through various enforcement and intelligence agencies.

MultiEarth civilization, ignoring its own extensive use of primal wildness in violent actions, makes much ado about the wild violence in Nature. Phrases like "red in tooth and claw"[99] and "the law of the jungle" underscore MultiEarth's jaundiced view that predation and killing are to be expected in the dangerous, brutal Wild. "It's a jungle out there" is the same kind of phrase about the predatory behavior of people competing against one another. Perhaps we understood the predation in Nature with more balance when we had to kill the meat we ate. Now that most of our meat comes already prepared or in sterile packaging, it's as if killing never had to happen for us to eat burgers, pulled pork, sushi, or chicken. Rarely does it cross our minds that every plant we eat has to die.

The Civilization Project cannot afford to see as pastoral and inspiring any area of Nature that humans want to claim for gain. If an area isn't Wild, then it doesn't need to be tamed and made productive. To civilize something, we need to believe it is dangerous or of no use, and that controlling it will improve it. First Peoples were repeatedly aghast at the brutality of the Europeans toward Nature. As Luther Standing Bear said, "We did not know the West was wild until the white man came." First Peoples were well aware of the natural predation among the species. They also practiced predation of their own. But consistent with their OneEarth views in general, First Peoples tended to kill only enough to meet their needs, assuring sustainability in the community of life across ecosystems and ecospheres.

The point is not the elimination of predation in OneEarth living, but to understand how it functions in the Wild and for what purposes. Except for species who make their food through the miracle of photosynthesis, predation is required by a wide range of plant and animal species to live. But because our species practices predation more destructively, more exploitatively than other species do, we need to figure out why. And why do MultiEarth predatory behaviors differ significantly from those of many First Peoples?

Part of the explanation is that the aggressive, wild violence of our predation often comes from the energies of the tyrant and bully, the dark archetypal energies that surface when we live ignoring the Earth-Self Call. Our egos, unable to handle those energies, become possessed by the desire for greater power and profits instead of greater consciousness. Under the influence of the dark archetypes, we bully our way into Earth's jungles, wetlands, grasslands, rivers, and oceans, evicting species from their homes. Animals and plants not only die through MultiEarth's predation, entire species become endangered and extinct because we take over their homes for profit-making beyond what we need. Such loss of proportion and balance is rare in the Wild, if it exists at all. But it's frequent among humans who turn away from the Earth-Self Call and live according to the standards of the MultiEarth paradigm. MultiEarth civilization, if it dares to do so, needs to ask itself, "Why has our civilizing the Wild been far, far more brutal to species than what they do to one another?"

Predation in Nature differs from wanton slaughter or clearing a wild region for MultiEarth productivity.[100] Everything killed in Nature is fully used by the killing species or scavenged and cleaned up by another. Nothing is wasted. Predation among some species does include infanticide and giving birth to far more babies than what will ever reach adulthood. We do not fully understand these practices, but we can see that they preserve the genetic health of a species and assure survival of that species, even keeping it in balance with all the other species that comprise the region. The predation we see in the Wild is part of a OneEarth world. As such, it functions in a topography of greater consciousness than what functions in MultiEarth domination. And with Earth moving inexorably into a new geological age, there's little reason to doubt that predation by humans will change from MultiEarth to OneEarth ways. On our part, we need a "Peoples Heroic Journey" like the many peoples marches happening around the globe that make public our concerns about climate change. Not that the next Earth era will eliminate predation. Eating continues. But, with the benefit of a OneEarth topography of consciousness, predation shifts from profit-making and imperial productivity to being part of the sustainable cycles of death and life.

The more we learn about predation in the life and death cycle of OneEarth living, the more we become ashamed and humbled that, in MultiEarth consciousness, our species practices gratuitous killing and wanton slaughter. The irony of civilizers behaving with less civility than those we call "wild" or "brutal" acutely reveals the limits of ego consciousness within which MultiEarth living proceeds. The unconscious influences of the Weakling-Tyrant (see Chapter Four) compound the ego's inclination to perceive the Wild with fear, and then subdue it—sometimes with rational courtesies, often with ruthlessness.

We will not succeed on our journey into the larger topographies of OneEarth consciousness without increased connections with the Wild. Henry David Thoreau opened others' eyes to this essential connection when he structured his life to include experiences of wilderness. Far from escapism, his connection with Nature kept fresh his Call to a OneEarth world. Nature often elicited eloquent words from Thoreau as he explained why we humans cannot develop fully within the consciousness of civilization. In his essay *Simply Walking*,[101] Thoreau wrote: "I wish to speak a word for Nature, for absolute Freedom and Wildness, as contrasted with a Freedom and Culture merely civil—to regard man as an inhabitant, or a part and parcel of Nature, rather than a member of society." Such a sentence distinguishes how MultiEarth civilization seeks civil "members of society" over the "absolute Freedom and Wildness" of OneEarth living. In the same essay, and in another strong claim for the priceless value of the Wild, Thoreau wrote, "In Wildness is the preservation of the world." Wildness, far more than civilized prowess, has the capacity to reverse climate change and keep Earth livable.

Our national and state parks can arouse and animate these wild energies that Thoreau recognized we need for preservation, but only to a degree. Despite all there is to love about them, the parks also reinforce a chronic pathology of the MultiEarth paradigm: they separate humans from other species.

I came to understand this about our national parks after Juanita and I delighted in watching the six-episode PBS special, "The National Parks: America's Best Idea," produced by documentarian Ken Burns and collaborator Dayton Duncan. It's a rhapsody of Nature and urges viewers to a conscious recognition of the sacred in the Wild. It praises the embodiment of democracy in Nature. But it falls significantly short of the OneEarth paradigm's understanding of our full relationship with Nature. I had missed this shortcoming until Scott Klinger, contributor to this book's Chapter Seven, sent me an eye-opening email that included these words:

> The national parks are a creation of the MultiEarth worldview. The MultiEarthers have divided the world into two pieces—the one to rape and pillage, and the other to maintain as pristine as possible. In the case of the national parks, "pristine" means without permanent human habitation. Most Indigenous Peoples I know have as negative a feeling about the parks as we white folks have a positive feeling for them. Not only were they displaced from the land which became the parks, but the U.S. government also turned the spaces sterile—banning the human species. There are not many places on earth where wilderness exists without human beings in it. Wilderness is not a place where humans don't live; wilderness is a place where humans live in harmony with the earth.

First Peoples acted consistent with their worldview of shared relationship with Nature in 2014, when Yosemite National Park celebrated the 150th year since the signing of the Yosemite Grant Act, the precursor to its becoming a national park. Les James

(Ahwahneeche), 79, and a tribal elder, said a blessing at an official ceremony in the Mariposa grove of sequoias, but he wasn't celebrating. He had worked in the park most of his life, being among those determined to keep a First Peoples' presence on that sacred land. But he also spoke candidly to the *Sacramento Bee* newspaper: "The changes, the destruction, that's what I don't like about it. You destroyed something that we preserved for thousands of years. In 150 years, you've ruined it."[102]

Helen Coats (Ahwahneechee) is descended from the First Peoples who were living in Yosemite Valley the day the U.S. Mariposa Battalion drove them out and burned their village. She now lives along Highway 140, just outside the park, and feels sad as she sees busloads of tourists heading into the park every day. Words from her wounded heart tell us bluntly: "They are just trampling my home to death."[103] Can the pain of MultiEarth's approach to the Wild, or the wounds it inflicts, be stated any more poignantly?

The Price of Taming the Wild: Our Wound of Disconnection

Les James and Helen Coats feel the pain of disconnection all the more keenly because they know how different interconnection feels. Their OneEarth traditions make them conscious of the wound whereas MultiEarth thinking has repressed the wound's pain into the unconscious world. From there it contributes to MultiEarth actions that cut Earth up into parts. Some parts are to be kept wild, meaning, free of human residences and certain other human activities. The rest is for human ownership, extraction of resources for gain, and pushing out whatever wildlife interferes with human purposes. But in all the parts under MultiEarth management, the pain from the wound of disconnection continues.

All of us devoted to, or under the influence of, MultiEarth thinking live with the wound that disconnects us from land's sacred power. As a result, our spirits, bodies, and souls receive less nourishment from the land than if we could sense its sacredness, as happens in OneEarth living. In MultiEarth's ways, land becomes real estate, something to be bought and sold according to values determined by how useful it is within the Civilization Project. Owning land conveys broad rights to the owner to profit from it and do with it what serves the owner. The sense of its sacredness vanishes.

What is true for land extends to all other species in the mysteries of Nature's untamed interactivity. Nature is bulldozed, blown up, and sprayed with chemicals so it will serve the money purposes of "civilized" humanity. Humans in the Civilization Project don't think of Earth as the Mother who feeds us or tends our home, nor think of the cells of their bodies as cells in the body of Mother Earth. Wounded and disconnected, humans act with aggression toward her and any of her wild things that encroach on us. We do the same toward the Wild within us. But despite ego's best effort to tame the exterior and interior Wild, the energies still take us over at times. The Wild has far too much voltage for our egos to handle. We deceive ourselves into believing that our disconnection from the Wild doesn't hurt us as much as it helps us. In our self-deception we remain in smaller topographies of consciousness, remain unhealed, and project outward onto others what we've not become conscious of in ourselves. So it is that we inflict our full wound onto the animals and vegetation we abuse and onto people who connect with Nature in ways we don't. Civilizers have yet to stop inflicting our full wound onto First Peoples, forcing onto them the same disconnection from Nature that wounds the psyches of everyone devoted to the Civilization Project. European-Americans dislocated First Peoples, forced them off their lands, and out of their wild and sacred places. Treaties solemnly made continue to be ignored and contested. This wound of disconnection will never stop wreaking havoc in the world until it is healed. And the only place where healing can happen is in topographies of greater consciousness that practice Earth-size thinking as the norm. There, new thinking and acting heal the wound. Prodigal civilizers return to reside within Nature. Earth's community of life welcomes them. A sacred bond is restored.

It may be that we become more aware of how severely the wound of disconnection impacts our world when we begin to heal from it. In MultiEarth consciousness humans stay stuck in the belief that the open wound is merely the cost of progress. It's the price required for greater benefits. The challenges of feeding and serving the growing human population, it is said, leave no option but to continue with actions disconnected from Nature. But any actions based in disconnection from Nature maintain the painful, basic disconnection of humans from our primal identity as people of Earth. "Humus," a word for Earth's topsoil, has the same linguistic root as "human." Scientifically, our bodies constantly exchange particles with everything around us, including soils and other species. The processes of our lives do not happen without Earth being involved. To deny or ignore these inescapable bonds of union with Nature and Earth violates our psycho-spiritual wholeness. It puts us, as well as the land and Nature we manage, at risk for abuse.

Many First Peoples and OneEarthers today live with the wisdom that to manage land means to learn all we can about living as *part* of the land. In their consciousness, humans are not outside of or superior to either the land or the species with whom we share it. But the Civilization Project pushes aside such traditional knowledge; the knowledge local people have about their regions bears the same fate. What matters most to the Civilization Project is that the lands be managed for whatever brings greater gain—"gain" being measured by the values of civilization. In its most altruistic moments the Civilization Project speaks of bettering humankind. Too rarely does that include bettering the environment—never mind that the two are inseparable. The Civilization Project may also speak laudably about conservation. But comprehensive conservation is repeatedly sabotaged by other forces in the MultiEarth paradigm which tilt sharply toward a utilitarian approach to land. The wound of disconnection is as old as the origins of civilization and as instant as the next decision made from a MultiEarth position *outside* the Wild.

No matter how we try to minimize the severity of the wound, its full pain is revealed in the magnitude of what it projects onto others: unending acts of killing First Peoples (genocide), choosing lifestyles that kill entire species and destroy habitats (biocide), and arranging systems that kill our Mother Earth (matricide). No pharmacology, policy, business, education, or religious experience contained within the MultiEarth worldview can heal the wound. Only changing to OneEarth thinking can. There we see ourselves within the matrix of the Wild. Taming the Wild gets countered with rewilding the human. Earth seeks connection. Across her systems, habitats, and species, she reveals to us a persistent energy to reconnect, to interconnect.

A bison powerfully illustrated this propensity of species to interconnect one night to Juanita and me while we were camping in the Norris Campground in Yellowstone. Though we had been following park guidelines to stay clear of bison by 25 yards, one of the 3,000–4,000 bison who roam the park seemed not to care about the rule and chose to be near us. Juanita awoke during the night to deep, loud breathing. She awakened me. Peering through our tent window, we could see that a bison was sleeping right beside our tent—right up alongside the wall of it. He was not annoyed with us, and we were hushed by his presence. We lay quietly, taking in the hallowed moments of intimate connection. It was a startling gift. By morning, he had gone off to graze. We rose, impacted anew by the lessons of the Wild. An ancient-contemporary icon of the Indigenous Peoples of the Great Plains had slept next to us and reconnected us with the abundance that has sustained peoples and species for millennia.

Do the wild bison of Yellowstone want to heal our disconnect from them just like all parts of a body seek healing with one another? We know that even when our bodies, minds, and souls are horribly traumatized, they still seek healing. If we can see Earth and her species as one body, everything being part of the same wild

Nature, then all parts understandably seek healing. The wild bison were traumatized unimaginably—nearly into extinction—when European-American settlers invaded the Great Plains and claimed the lands for themselves. Still, the innate behaviors of interconnection live on in the bison if we could understand them.

Our species can no longer maintain the posture of "taming the Wild." It is not possible for humans to ever pay the full price of conquering Nature. Theft has to be involved. MultiEarth debt—emotionally, financially, spiritually, and ecologically—exceeds human resources. Earth and her species, far from having been conquered, are reasserting their wildness and bankrupting the MultiEarth paradigm. We humans now face an overwhelming truth: Nature cannot be tamed, dominated, commandeered, subdued, or ignored in the ways of the MultiEarth Civilization Project. Our attempts to do so have resulted in Earth's immune systems rising up against us. Nonetheless, healing of the wound of disconnection is underway for all on the move toward OneEarth consciousness. A priority treatment for healing is the rewilding of humans, a treatment integral to our heroic journey. We can make rewilding a daily healing experience when we move into the topographies of greater consciousness because there we have eyes to see wildness actively interconnecting everywhere.

Finding the Wild in Today's "Civilized" World

Where is the Wild today? Where do we have to go to reconnect? Conveniently, we don't have to travel to a different geography; we just need to go into a greater consciousness. In OneEarth consciousness, the wildness of Nature shows up everywhere, always defying MultiEarth civilization's efforts to tame her. We see the urban Wild in the grasses that crowd through cracks in the sidewalks. It shows up as tree roots lift bumps into blacktop streets and buckle concrete sidewalks. Flowers color vacant, unkempt urban spaces. "Weeds" defy every manicured, monoculture lawn and field by insisting on adding their own choice of species. Viruses, bacteria, and fungi continually evolve new untamed versions, outwitting the medications and herbicides designed to kill them. Citified possums, skunks, raccoons, coyotes, and rats continually remind us, "We were here first. Like us or not. Displace us and we'll come back. We'll share space with you; we just insist that you share it with us too. We are the Wild and we defy your reign over your tamed spaces." Even the dirt and dust that invade our homes show that the Wild cannot be kept out. Anymore, when I am dusting shelves, I'm thinking: *The Wild has found its way here. I don't want this wild dust here, but I can't keep it away. I can remove it, but it keeps coming back. What is dust teaching me about living with the Wild?* I wouldn't say that these thoughts make the chore of dusting fun, but they do… well… make me smile.

John Elder, a Nature writer and past promoter of creative arts in the environmental studies program at Middlebury College, Vermont, (1973–2010), urged us to discover the Wild in all the places in our lives where it lives undiscovered. He wanted us to feel its erotics:

> Truth is, we live in undiscovered country. Wildness is not only about millions of roadless acres. You don't have to visit gates of the Arctic to be attuned to nature. New York City has the East River and the Hudson River. It's got the monarch butterflies that migrate down Fifth Avenue just above the heads of pedestrians. It's got the migratory-bird routes that come down over Staten Island and the Meadow-lands. It's got an incredibly dynamic, fast-moving sky….
>
> Detroit… is filled with urban grasslands where foxes and wild turkeys roam, some of them just two blocks from Tiger Stadium. Los Angeles is home to coyotes. They'll look you in the eye, and they are not tame animals. It's not as if the cities of the U.S. were brought here from outer space, or as if the residents didn't all evolve from hominids in the savannas of Africa. We're all in the thick of it.[104]

Elder's genius helps us all feel more in the Wild than we had thought we were. He so helpfully puts the emphasis on our consciousness, our ability to be discoverers and explorers of the undiscovered Wild in our daily lives. Understandings of the Wild that find it only in remote regions are misunderstandings. So too is any thought that urbanization must be reversed with back-to-the-land movements in order for us to experience the Wild. When we restrict how we think of wilderness, we make learning from the Wild as inaccessible as going to an expensive four-year, private university.

One way to see wilderness everywhere is to put it on a spectrum. Imagine pristine, proportionately populated settings at one end; blacktop roadways and parking lots at the other. Then find wilderness along the entire spectrum. There's a pricelessness to the Wild in edenic settings, and there's an indomitable sovereignty to the Wild wherever it shows up in the most urbanized centers. Rewilding can happen to us when we wipe dust from our shoes or feel the moisture in the morning air as well as on an ecotour to Katmai Preserve in Alaska. It depends on our topography of consciousness. Are our senses awake? Are our hearts healed enough to connect?

OneEarth consciousness changes how we feel and behave when spiders, ants, and innumerable crawling, flying, squirming things slip through the gates, doors, walls, and boundaries by which we intend to keep them out. In Earth's rewilding topographies of consciousness, we may still lament that dirt, dust, and mud soil our shoes, clothes, floors, windows, and cars, but we also recognize that dirt dirties civilization's attempts to reshape wilderness behavior to fit patterns designed in small consciousness. As a premiere member of the Wild's faculty, dirt teaches persistent dissent from the Civilization Project.

The same can be said for the air, creeks, fog, and trees that are part of our lives. They exert their wild interdependence without consulting civilization's managers. The moon and the sun move us emotionally whenever their light streaks through clouds in their own wild ways, never checking with civilization first. The sun holds our gaze in wild awe as he sky-paints while rising and setting, training civilization's artists as he does without ever being trained by them. We need only look up in areas where dark night skies exist away from cities in order to see the cosmic wilderness of planets and stars that do not consult us for their movements. The Wild is everywhere in our days and nights. The more we move around in topographies of consciousness where we are rewilded, the more we want to live within Earth's wild community of life—and the better we become at doing so.

Think of the Wild as a school of transformation. It specializes in expanding our consciousness, training us how to heal our festering wound of disconnection from Nature, equipping us for interdependent, OneEarth living, and enrapturing us with Earth-size mysteries. The sensuous Wild provides a feast of information for us to feel, see, hear, and handle. It floods our reason and stirs awe. Fortunately, this great school is everywhere. Its pedagogy continues through all seasons and weather. Its rewilding lab and library are accessible in the massive and the microscopic. When we become more interested in the Wild humanizing us than in our civilizing the Wild, when we see how the Wild and humans have mutuality in Earth-size living, then we know we are learning what the school of the Wild teaches.

On the global scene, rewilding counters the civilizing trends of urbanization, industrialized agriculture, and globalization. All appear unstoppable. All are hostile to the Wild. Each reinforces the other in a phalanx of MultiEarth aggression against Nature. The massive, global migrations from farms to cities, triggered by the industrialization of farming and the hope of finding jobs being created in urban areas, have continued hand-in-glove with modern globalization. That globalization proceeds according to a particular MultiEarth economic model based on growth requirements that Earth cannot sustain. These trends in the global context show us just how heroic rewilding truly is.

From the 1700s to the present (and continuing into the foreseeable future), industrialization and technologies of information have continued to disconnect us from many forms of wildness that can nurture and energize our bodies and souls. The more we've plugged into the matrix of globalization, the weaker our connection to the Wild has become. The disconnection crescendoed to a new fortissimo in 2010 when, for the first time in the civilization story, more people lived in urban settings worldwide than in rural ones. People arrive in urban centers wounded, having been dislocated from the land and Nature which shaped their identity. Urban centers are not prepared to treat such wounds. Their primary purpose is to be centers where Imperial Consciousness can concentrate wealth and power, not to foster movement from ego to Self, or from civilizing Nature to rewilding. The migration of people to cities, a direct result of globalization, creates more problems than solutions, more hurt than wellbeing. Because globalization is managed by transnational corporations and financial institutions following an imperial ideology of growth, profits, and control, it cannot do other than carry MultiEarth ways to a new extreme. Even in the context of this anti-Wild extremism rewilding can happen when urban dwellers take the heroic journey into greater consciousness.

Contrary to some critics, rewilding does not seek a return to hunter-gatherer living, nor to the pre-industrial 1600s. Though some humans may hang onto a romanticized image of an earlier rural and idyllic era, rewilding does not. Rewilding functions in a topography of consciousness where egos fear to go, where healing of the disconnection from Nature and Earth happens. Urbanization concentrates the problems generated by the expanding, imperial globalization. Rewilding pulls our thinking and acting out of globalization's matrix by changing us in a larger topography of consciousness. As we make a new connection with the Wild, we become capable of a OneEarth kind of globalism—not imperial globalization—that is right for the Earth-Self Call to engage the crises of the 21st century. OneEarth globalism includes decentralized collaboration, open source technologies, technologies scaled to a particular region and use, empowering local entities and economies, ruralism, and more—in a word, localization.

The current localization movement—local food, local businesses, local banks, local economies and currencies, resilient communities, and all efforts at local control of economic resources—fosters reconnection with the local biospheres of the natural world. When one or two localized efforts begin, two or three more spring up. Take farming as an example. An amazing number of small, organic farms continue to be formed in a kind of new ruralism. The Organic Farming Research Foundation reports that "The U.S. organic industry enjoyed robust growth in 2014, with the number of certified organic farms increasing by more than 5 percent over 2013, and domestic sales of all organic products soaring 11 percent to more than $39 billion."[105] In recent generations, young adults seldom saw much future in rural life. That, too, is changing. The numbers of young farmers has begun to increase as consciousness grows about where our food comes from and how it is grown.[106] Getting closer to the land and Nature is given as an important reason by young adults, female as well as male, for their choice to farm. Rural living holds values for them that urban living does not.

Seeing how rewilding and localization converge strengthens both for us as we seek to be reshaped into Earth-size living. Urban agriculture, community gardens in vacant plots, and gardening in yards connect us with the Wild under our feet. As soon as we grow some native plants and some vegetables—maybe add a few chickens—we learn not only about what we've planted, but also about the bugs, butterflies, birds, and microbes who find the changes we are making attractive to them as well. The ecology changes. We change. The food on our table changes. Author Michael Pollan, professor of journalism at the University of California Graduate School of Journalism, Berkeley, describes this in his book, *Second Nature: A Gardener's Education*. He emphasizes that the garden teaches the gardener the ways of wilderness if that gardener is open to such a OneEarth approach:

> Anthropocentric as [the gardener] may be, he [sic] recognizes that he is dependent for his health and survival on

many other forms of life, so he is careful to take their interests into account in whatever he does. He is in fact a wilderness advocate of a certain kind. It is when he respects and nurtures the wilderness of his soil and his plants that his garden seems to flourish most. Wildness, he has found, resides not only out there, but right here: in his soil, in his plants, even in himself…

But wildness is more a quality than a place, and though humans can't manufacture it, they can nourish and husband it…

The gardener cultivates wildness, but he does so carefully and respectfully, in full recognition of its mystery.[107]

To discover the Wild everywhere around us connects us half way with the significance of wildness for our heroic journey. Connecting to the Wild within is the other half.

The Wild Within: From Taming to Tending

MultiEarth civilization has zealously tamed Nature's wildness for economic benefit, but has remained unconscious of how Nature is in us too. And not just in us. We, too, are Nature. Jungian therapist Eugene Pascal writes: "Our psyches are part and parcel of Nature, a truth people in Western societies especially tend to forget."[108] He also quotes Jung as saying: "In spite of our proud domination of nature, we are still her victims, for we have not learned to control our own nature. Slowly but, it appears, inevitably, we are courting disaster."[109]

The result is that our inner wildness functions in service of MultiEarth purposes. When a MultiEarth corporation or person sees something they want, they wildly violate Nature and Earth, unconscious of the damage inflicted, including the damage to themselves. It is another instance of how the wound of disconnection from Nature replicates itself in MultiEarth's unconscious behavior.

Jung's approach to our inner Nature might better be described as tending than taming. He advocated vigorous effort to become aware of our many parts, to become conscious of the Wild within us. He did not believe that complexes and archetypes of the psyche could be eradicated. He advocated, instead, becoming conscious of them and tending them. Jung distinguished between conscious and instinctual energies in our psyches. The Wild connects us to the instinctual which provides us with essential powers for the heroic journey. But our instinctual energies cannot fully nor faithfully serve us unless we function from the center of Self. The ego is not a capable tender of instinctual energies. The Self-ego collaboration can tend them much like we tend a child, a garden, or tasks and people in a workplace. Tending instinctual energies means becoming more aware of them and noting how they are working within us. By bringing them into our conscious world, their energies bring greater capacities to our purposes. But outside of our conscious mind, they behave wildly, serving whatever impulses appeal to them.

Clarissa Pinkola-Estes (1945-)works as a Jungian analyst to bring fuller human capacities to life by turning trauma, ethnicity, gender, and marginalization to assets rather than liabilities. Her bestseller, *Women Who Run with the Wolves: Myths and Stories of the Wild Woman Archetype*,[110] provides lots of help on how to work with the instinctual, wild energies within us. The book was on the *New York Times'* bestseller list for 145 weeks when it came out in 1992. It fanned the flame of yearning that burns in both women and men for genuine inner power and freedom. Though written especially for women, men "translated" it into their own situation. Pinkola-Estes counters the taming obsession of MultiEarth civilization that imposes constriction, loss of power, and distrust of instinctual energies. In this debilitating context, the image of "running with wolves" awakens deep, instinctual energies that we regard as trouble or immoral, evil or uncontrollable.

Nor is "running with wolves" only an inner phenomenon. The reintroduction and spread of wolf populations in the U.S. since the

1970s has physically enacted what Clarissa Pinkola-Estes wrote about psychologically and spiritually. This synchronicity of outer and inner activity reflects the kind of deep structures Jung saw happening as our personal and collective unconscious brings material to the surface, expanding consciousness. For a century the U.S. had followed a policy of hunting wolves with the intention of exterminating them as vermin and pests.[111] That policy of open hostility ended in the 1960s with no more than 300 wolves running wild, limited to wilderness terrain in northern Michigan and Minnesota. Then the Endangered Species Act of 1974 came into play. Wolves were reintroduced into other places in the U.S. In 1995, Canadian wolves were released in the state of Idaho and in Yellowstone National Park. Those packs have been highly successful and their offspring have spread into surrounding states.

Symbolically, the success of wolf repopulation since the 1960s portrays the readiness of our instinctual and wilder energies to reawaken when given a chance, even though civilization's patterns repress wildness severely. As new wolf packs have formed, wolves have extended their ranges in the U.S. Not surprisingly, some ranchers have demanded government agencies responsible for managing wildlife give them permission to hunt and kill wolves. They cite livestock killings as their reason, though killing wolves to protect livestock often backfires. According to scientific studies, killing wolves fragments packs, and wolves from fragmented packs are *more* likely to kill livestock if it grazes nearby.[112]

In contrast to nervous ranchers, naturalists who manage areas where wolves have been reintroduced have been excited by the great improvement in the balance of plant and animal species resulting from the presence of wolves. Elk can no longer linger after drinking from streams, browsing down the vegetation growing there. They fear that a wolf pack may be watching nearby. So, after drinking, the elk seek cover. Consequently, willows and wetland species grow along waterways once again.

The tensions between ranchers and naturalists, between domestic animals and wildness continue in full drama as wolf populations expand. Their direct dialogue with one another mirrors a dialogue within ourselves. Both the rancher and the naturalist are parts of us. Connecting with our instinctual energies is essential to counter the captivity of civilization that would civilize our own wild energies into extinction. Just as certainly, our instinctual energies can run wild and bring harm to others and ourselves if they are not in dialogue with our parts that reason with them. Vigorous and ongoing dialogue is necessary to arrive at the kind of balance that thrives in topographies of greater consciousness. We need to learn to run with wolves in ways where authentic interdependence happens. Doing so assures connection with the wild energies we need to continue the heroic journey and transcend the Civilization Project for OneEarth ways.

Just as Clarissa Pinkola-Estes works with the archetype of the Wild Woman, psychotherapist, Jim Moyers, focusing in male psychology, depicts the essential role the Wild Man has in overcoming adversaries on our journey.[113] But there are challenges. The Wild Man acts according to instinct, not conscious choice. Moyers emphasizes that "the wild man is the shadow, the feared and despised opposite of civilized man. He is not easy to have around...."[114] He does not adjust to civilization's norms. But in his outside-the-box ways, he brings the very energy we need to go against civilizing, MultiEarth powers that would otherwise intimidate us into submission. Too much submission to MultiEarth ways paralyzes us and prevents progress on the heroic journey. However, once we've come to recognize that Wild Man is present, we want to shift gears to making choices consciously. Much as we need his instinctual wildness, we need *conscious choice* to guide us on the journey.

This interplay between wildness and conscious choice is often depicted as part animal, part human. Characters in myths combine human bodies with a horse, goat, bird, fish, snake, and others. In C. S. Lewis' book, *The Lion, the Witch, and the Wardrobe* (1950), subsequently adapted for television, stage, and movies, centaurs and fauns work in concert with humans to find their way through a dark forest by combining consciousness and instinct. In ceremonies, festivals, and rituals, humans may wear masks, makeup, particular jewels, select clothing or portions of animal skins in order to connect with instinctual energies that are necessary for tasks ahead. Given the disconnection that has shaped so many of us as we grew up in the Civilization Project, wearing items that align us with Earth and weather, soils and water, animals and plants, can galvanize our intentions to move further into OneEarth consciousness and action.

It takes a lot of intentional work to get beyond civilization's distrust and antagonism toward the Wild. Civilization's attitude is partly understandable in that the Wild is such a powerful interplay of energies—a kind of fire that needs to be tended so its great value can benefit us rather than left to burn at will. However, civilization's approach has been to suppress the fire more than tend it. The approach fails in us as it does in forests where managers have learned that if every fire is suppressed, Nature will gradually build up so much fuel that some future fire will burn with such intensity that it will overwhelm all efforts to suppress it. Similarly, no amount of civilizing can suppress "The Wild" out of us. Its unquenchable archetypal embers glow and flame in all humans personally and collectively.

The harder we suppress the Wild within, the more likely it is to make public appearances that sabotage us. Most of us have been caught, at one time or another, in acts of hypocrisy. In such moments, the Wild One within chose to disobey what our ego had proclaimed we'd obey. Left untended, the Wild One sooner or later violates our ego's morals, codes of business ethics, cultural norms, or religious virtues. Such episodes of the Wild One have ruined careers, but they have also brought people to greater consciousness and new life—awkward and embarrassing as the path may have been. The Wild has to be reckoned with, but taming is neither healthy nor ultimately doable. The better way is to continually seek conscious relationship with the Wild, a kind of tending that goes with becoming more conscious. Learning to interact constructively, consciously with the Wild is vital to our metamorphosis as humans and that of Earth.

What we want to leave on the heroic journey is a MultiEarth civilization that is Wild-phobic, whether it's the wildness of bacteria or beasts. Wildness makes no claim to be free of danger, disease, or death; nor does it seek to exterminate them. Wildness liberates what civilization enslaves in us. It fuels the inner drive that civilization has arrested. It stimulates our exploration of the unknown that civilization marginalizes. Wildness connects with the spirit of wholeness that civilization's rationalism and individualism are too small to comprehend. Wildness breaks us out of the addictive patterns, sociopathic leadership, and mundane workplaces that distort us. Wildness connects us to instinctual life that increases our capacities as we move into greater consciousness. In turn, we become more skilled as tenders of species and systems in Earth's community of life and more loving participants.

Does Earth Act Consciously?

The attitude of civilizing the Wild falls in line with thinking of Earth as inanimate. Both are commonplace in MultiEarth consciousness where egos shape our worldview. Thinking of Earth as dead, we have no feelings about extracting from "it" what we want. Had we been functioning in greater consciousness, where Self is our center, we'd have considered that Earth, too, might be alive as described previously in Chapter Six. As psychotherapist and philosopher James Hillman (1926–2011) put it, "It was only when science convinced us that Earth was dead that it could begin its autopsy in earnest."[115] Hillman sought to re-soul what civilization de-souls.

Is it possible that Earth is not only animate, but also acting with a form of consciousness? Are her reactions to carbon dioxide and methane in the atmosphere mechanistic, or organic? Does she have a kind of living consciousness that we have not yet perceived, but which factor into Earth's responses to Anthropocene abuse?

Rewilding opens us to consider questions about whether Earth's wildness behaves consciously or not. She is certainly making civilizers nervous as she outflanks the taming tactics of the Civilization Project, improvising new behaviors of weather extremes amid changing climates. We know her responses are organic, and not merely mechanical. But are they the result of information she takes in and then makes choices for one behavior or another based on some kind of conscious consideration or activity?

In the world of wild plants, such consciousness is being perceived. Herbologist Stephen Harrod Buhner observes plants communicating, showing feelings, and going in new directions—activities based on taking in information and processing it intelligently. Can this not be called a form of consciousness? And though consciousness in plants does not say anything about the same in planets, one wonders: *Maybe Earth is not an inanimate rock in space.* Egos may dismiss such a notion, but Selves, intent on journeying into OneEarth living, want to know. The exploration matters a great deal because it affects how we feel about our planet and bond with her. Buhner speaks from an identity of Self consciousness and a worldview in which Earth is "a living organism that modulates its own environment."[116] He watches how plants keep a bioregion livable by communicating with other plants around them. So, for example, bacteria under attack by antibiotics continue to revise themselves. They evolve organically to survive. In doing so, bacteria render ineffective many antibiotics that have been generated synthetically. The information on resisting an antibiotic travels rapidly throughout the bacteria community. Buhner explains:

> [Bacteria] are highly cooperative. As soon as a bacterium experiences an antibiotic, it begins generating possible solutions to it. Some people assume it's the few bacteria that are naturally immune that reproduce and create resistance, and in a minor way this might be true, but it's more accurate to say that the bacteria intentionally rearrange their genome to produce offspring that are resistant—and some of them

can spawn a new generation within twenty minutes. Every time a successful resistance mechanism is created, the bacteria then communicate it to all the other bacteria they meet, teaching them how to rearrange their genome to be resistant.[117]

Impressed as we are by how technology helps us find new solutions, Buhner cites James Shapiro, a bacterial geneticist at the University of Chicago, as saying that "bacterial information processing is far more powerful than human technology."[118]

When we recognize this kind of power in plant life, we can see that Nature and Self have better credentials for living a story that fits our only planet than anything civilization can conjure. Nature was doing it long before ego's Civilization Project took charge. So when we turn to the systems of biospheres for wisdom and guidance, we are coming home to a worldview with superior knowledge and a consciousness of greater maturity.

Being alive on a living Earth with a form of consciousness evokes feelings which bond us to Earth with caring and intimacy, whereas regarding her as an inanimate "it" does not. Though science and reason teach us to be cautious about leaping to conclusions, we can also err in presuming Earth has neither life nor consciousness. Our planet breathes carbon dioxide and oxygen as we do. Earth has intelligence in her hemispheres as do the hemispheres of our brain. She recoils when wounded, then regroups and generates healing. She has self-regulating systems that are continuously active. She adjusts to stimuli by continuously responding. The adjustments correct damage and imbalances in ways akin to a planetary immune system.

The enormous scale at which Earth's living processes happen boggle our perceptions. Because the vast scale has exceeded our mental frames to comprehend them, we've been slow to consider the possibility of Earth functioning with planetary consciousness. Wild Earth's responses to MultiEarth ways lumber along in a timeframe and size that are hard for our minds to calculate. We are trained to use civilization time, not geological time. Not surprisingly, then, we have been slow to believe that the geological stability which has been standard during the Holocene and Anthropocene epochs has been so deeply wounded by our behaviors that it is not likely to be re-established. Rather, a new and different epoch has begun to evolve. Civilization-thinking that holds Earth to be an inanimate object for our use has not had the consciousness to consider the implications of wounding Earth so savagely. Geologically, the relative quietness of Earth during the 12,000 years of those epochs has not challenged us to think of her as having some kind of living consciousness. Furthermore, the MultiEarth paradigm shuts off such inquiry. To ask whether Earth might be a living, conscious planet throws open the door to a different paradigm. The question also triggers sensitivities in us that want to halt MultiEarth's loveless, abusive wounding of our planet.

Considering if or how Earth has consciousness goes in different directions depending on how we think about Earth. If we think of her separate from all her inhabitants and her life-generating processes, then we are less likely to see consciousness at work. But if we shift to a holistic, integral picture of the planet that includes all the life forms she generates, *and also* considers the organic, interactivity as the processes of a single whole, then we are more likely to see consciousness at work. Thought of separately, as has been common in the MultiEarth paradigm, then humans have consciousness, maybe some other species, but the planet itself does not. But when everything is integrated into a holistic frame, the consciousness evolved in *Homo sapiens* as well as any other kinds of consciousness in other life forms all become integral to Earth's consciousness. As the parts of this planetary whole interact with one another—water and soil with plants, plants with air and insects, mammals (including humans) with planet, planet with bacteria, on and on—the relationships, organic and interdependent, show Earth functioning with consciousness that is diverse and mysterious.

The point is that as Earth's wildness continues to assert sovereignty over the MultiEarth Civilization Project, she may be acting more consciously than we've assumed. And, our own rewilding on our heroic journey to keep Earth livable involves us in increasing Earth's conscious capabilities as well as our own. Evolving an edenic interdependency between all species and systems, is not just what Earth does or we do, but what we do as one. Consciousness does not evolve separately. It requires us to think within interconnections instead of individualistically. Our rewilding and becoming part of Earth's wildness bears potentials that we cannot be explored except in larger topographies of consciousness.

These thoughts of rewilding into Earth's wildness and functioning in a diverse, unitary consciousness underscore again that our egoistic approaches to life have shaped a civilization too apart from Earth's processes. The MultiEarth paradigm does not consider whether or not Earth functions with an organic, responsive, and imaginative consciousness. But Earth's natural processes are wonderfully bigger and wilder than the MultiEarth paradigm had counted on. Frank Egler (1911–1996), a plant ecologist who worked with Rachel Carson on her renowned book, *Silent Spring* (1962), notes that natural, self-regulating "ecosystems are not only more complex than we think, they are more complex than we can think."[119] Egler speaks to the change happening in a lot of scientific inquiry which sees Earth's ways leading us to understand ourselves differently *within* Nature's wild and sovereign processes. Does Egler's understanding also open the door to discovering new forms of consciousness which facilitate keeping Earth livable? We are not able to pursue such a line of thinking within ego's capacities of consciousness; but Self is equipped and eager to go where we can think differently about the nature and consciousness of Earth, humans, and the whole, interacting community of life.

Rewilding Changes Human Nature

Rewilding is an essential process in reshaping and valuing our humanness given how being civilized into MultiEarth thinking stunts our most potent human capacities. Rewilding opens us to larger topographies of consciousness. Instead of people civilizing the Wild, the Wild naturalizes and humanizes people. Our glory is not in dominating Nature, but in being part of her glory. Rewilding heals us of the great wound of our disconnection from Nature, a wound that has turned us into civilizers and tamers of Nature instead of her lovers and tenders.

To rewild our lives is a choice to move out of being a civilized species with our egos in charge and into a space of consciousness beyond what our egos consider to be safe or possible. Trusting Self enough to put our identity there is an especially large risk, but the risk is immeasurably greater if we stay with ego in MultiEarth consciousness. Our independence from Nature has put us out of touch with what she can do. When we truly encounter Nature's wildness and creativity, the endless impacts of this encounter effect in us a conversion of how we see the world, ourselves in it, and our relationship to the sacredness of all Nature's processes. The more we experience the re-humanizing powers of rewilding, the more we realize how de-humanizing MultiEarth living is. We don't shed civilization in order to "go wild," as MultiEarthers might say, but to "go interconnected." The Wild reconnects us with essential human capacities and develops them. It moves us into greater Earth-size consciousness where we become integral with Nature's complex, conscious unity.

Conclusion: Wildness, a Teacher Unmatched by Civilization

To us who have undergone civilization, thinking of Nature as the great teacher sounds like a stretch. She's too wild and confusing. By contrast, traditional First Peoples recognize the species, waters, and landscapes as their teachers and their relatives. But civilization does not think of the crow, oak, river, mountain, or whale as relatives or teachers. Civilization looks for its teachers among those well-schooled in the disciplines of universities. Yet, when it comes to learning how to live the Earth-size way, the best possible credentials are found in the Wild. For hundreds of thousands of years, the Wild has been learning from failures and quantum-leap successes alike, revising and improving as she evolves. The Wild teaches us about the interconnecting systems that sustain our lives, though such a conviction has shallow roots in the consciousness of MultiEarth living.

Civilization can speak poetically and romantically of the natural world, and, when pushed, has taken steps to preserve large tracts of it. Praiseworthy as these actions are, even these reveal the MultiEarth proclivity to manage wilderness, not mimic her. Complete wilderness does not need to remove *Homo sapiens* who are practicing OneEarth living. But MultiEarth management has so far decided to do so, arriving at inferior alternatives.

Civilization stays detached from Earth's wildness, manages it, and, with frightening frequency, behaves with enmity toward it. The MultiEarth economy undervalues the Wild, harvests from it on the cheap, and often speaks about it condescendingly. At every turn, civilization reveals that it is largely unconscious of Nature's enormous wisdom. Instead of showing appreciation and turning to her for teaching, MultiEarth practices have thrown the waste of their production carelessly upon the face of Creation while presenting themselves as an improved, more evolved story. But the excrement of this "more evolved story" has fowled our nest.

Earth's wild processes regulate what happens on her and to her. In her wildness, Earth exhibits a sovereignty that is calling into question the dominance of the human species and MultiEarth's Civilization Project. In Earth's sovereignty lives a wildness that people cannot tame. It can, however, humanize, naturalize, and heal people.

The Wild, more than civilization, can teach us how to adjust to climate changes, reverse them, and arrange life to correct the crises in Earth's ecospheres. We humans have designed the problem. Wilderness has the wisdom to change us so that working and thinking as one we can solve it. Rewilding heals our wounds of separation, changes our attitudes from conqueror to learner, and tends the Wild around us and within us. It teaches us a new, integral view of ourselves with Earth and all interacting processes. Rewilding gets underway the process of creating a new human, to which we turn next.

Ponder, Discuss, Act

1. In what ways do you experience the "wound of disconnection?"

2. What are some ways you connect with the Wild in today's "civilized" society?

3. Do you feel intimacy or distance from your inner wildness? How so?

4. How do you contrast tending the Wild versus taming it?

5. Do you see any ways that civilization can teach OneEarth living without defeating its own project? Give your reasons.

6. What examples can you give of how the Wild teaches that the essence of life is interrelationships?

7. Talk with a friend about how each of you sees human nature. Discover where each of you is with the notion that rewilding changes human nature.

CHAPTER TEN

A New Human
(Underworld Included)

The historical mission of our time is to reinvent the human—at the species level, with critical reflection, within the community of life-systems, in a time-developmental context, by means of a story and a shared dream experience.[120]   —Thomas Berry, *The Great Work*

So if anyone is in Christ, there is a new creation: everything old has passed away; see, everything has become new![121]   —Apostle Paul

History insists that knowledge and good will are not enough; humanity must deal effectively with its darkside.[122]
                              —David Feinstein and Stanley Krippner

The head has become our fortified abode, and we hunker in there in the belief that our thinking will save us. But if science, for example, does on occasion seem to save the day, that just reinforces our illusion that we are separate from nature and have only to investigate and intervene in its workings in the right way, and all will be well. So the effect of relying exclusively on science is to more deeply validate our tyrannical tendencies.[123]   —Philip Shepherd, *The Sun*

Every heroic journey seeks and finds a treasure that malevolent forces want for themselves. Such treasure comes in many forms, but it always changes the people involved and the world around them. In *Lord of the Rings*, the treasure is a ring;

in *Raiders of the Lost Ark* it's an ark. These stories thrive on the heart-stopping adventures that happen as groups clash over the treasure. One group wants it for egoistic control and power; the other knows that its purpose is for the greater common good. But to claim it for the common good, they have to outwit and defeat many challenges from the ego-centered group. In adventure after adventure, they not only overcome the ego-centered group, but also their own egos. They move beyond their own ego consciousness into a greater consciousness capable of making good on the claim. This dynamic by which the outer action has transforming inner impact is what makes the journey heroic.

In our case, the treasure is Earth's interdependent community of life. It is a treasure of Earth-size living and a consciousness possible only with an identity centered beyond ego in our greater Self, and beyond civilization in Earth herself. So far our heroic journey has revealed to us that the treasure lives, to varying degrees, in the Wild, and that civilization, as shaped by MultiEarth thinking, relentlessly seeks to control the treasure. At this stage of the journey, the challenge upon us is to increase our capacities to live in the topographies of consciousness where Self and Earth are primary and interacting organically. We need to undertake the psychological and spiritual work that brings our soul-capacities up to what Earth is doing geologically. We need to get below the surface to see why Earth is rejecting civilization. For this work, the path of the journey takes us into the underworld, both our personal one and civilization's.

Ego and Civilization: Provisional Efforts, Not Our Best

Thomas Merton (1915–1968), a Benedictine monk, once said, "What can we gain by sailing to the moon if we are not able to cross the abyss that separates us from ourselves?"[124] It was a simple appeal for a new human from a person whose own engagement with the ego-Self struggle brought him to a consciousness large enough that he could cross into thoughts and actions too big for civilization. He learned from Nature, pursued interfaith spirituality, and earnestly believed that nonviolent societies were possible.

On the heroic journey, both our ego personality and civilization are understood to be provisional, not the end point—much in the way a caterpillar is provisional en route to a butterfly. Self knows how to meet Merton's appeal for a new human. It knows that the Civilization Project can be far surpassed by our species, and considers civilization's societies to be making do while our species figures out how to mature enough to move beyond them. Speaking of civilization in this intermediary way is analogous to how we develop from childhood. As children, we create a provisional personality, meaning we configure a personality to handle, as best we can, the "monsters" in ourselves and the overwhelmingly big and, too often, aggressive and hostile world.

Throughout adolescence as well, we continue to negotiate with life's forces from a more or less provisional identity. "Civilizing" the wild things inside and out is the best our ego consciousness can come up with given all of its past and developing fears. But what we created for the time being makes a poor choice for the long run. Similarly, civilization's ways with Nature do not make a good framework for practicing sustainable forestry, renewable agriculture, or planning urban centers with Earth's full community of life in mind. Provisional arrangements don't take in enough of the factors to create the more holistic policies and practices we need to mesh with Nature or to excite us about our full potential as humans. The result is a consciousness of adolescence that continues beyond its intended years and takes over shaping civilization from households to statehouses. Like an adolescent, civilization believes it already lives according to the greatest intelligence available. It does not seek the treasure that makes possible a new human able to live to our potential within a new paradigm of interrelatedness—especially since that paradigm is civilization's undoing en route to OneEarth living!

Nevertheless, because we are a species with open-ended possibilities for growing consciousness, the urge to go beyond these provisional arrangements stays alive in us. In addition, Earth's insurgency calls to those inner possibilities. The Earth-Self alliance urges us to transcend what is—to heal the wounds that gave birth to provisional arrangements and move on to where we can use our greater capacities. All of Earth's systems involved in evolutionary life groan and yearn for us to move beyond the provisional personality of our childhood and adolescence, and beyond the provisional civilization our egos have created. To go beyond the provisional, we must go where egos and civilization don't.

The Underworld's Attitude about Civilization

How often do we hear reports of events and wonder, *"Is that really what happened? What's behind this story?"* We know that to understand what's happening in our world we need to look beneath the surface for hidden and deeper reasons than the surface explanations we hear. The underworld of society, people, groups, businesses, and all entities holds the fuller story.

The underworld defies civilizing. And that's precisely why it's the ideal place to look for the energies and insight to take us beyond civilization. When Jung spoke of a psychological and cultural underworld, he understood that he was pushing a boulder uphill in a culture fond of rational explanations and scientific proof. Nonetheless, he continued to warn about the powers of the unconscious underworld, because he saw how much a civilization built on ego-centered rationalism is at risk from the very forces it represses. Jung warned that these forces will erupt out of our control, manifesting in demonizing enemies, irrational wars, degrading Nature, and a spiritual malaise so pervasive that rational approaches alone will never be able to correct them:

> Modern man [sic] does not understand how much his "rationalism" . . . has put him at the mercy of the psychic "underworld." He has freed himself from "superstition" (or so he believes), but in the process he has lost his spiritual

values to a positively dangerous degree. His moral and spiritual tradition has been disintegrated, and he is now paying the price for this break-up in world-wide disorientation and dissociation.[125]

Jung's warnings about the unconscious underworld came true on the world scene during his lifetime—most horrifically in World War I and World War II. Today, examples of the "disorientation and dissociation" Jung referred to show up constantly as we live in nations led by corporate-driven governments whose egos make decisions that conflict with Earth's systems. The heads of states, fossil-fuel corporations, and financial giants are among civilization's powers who have so dissociated from Earth that their energy policies miss the mark of Earth's demands. They refuse to put Earth's livability above their profits. The same dissociation prevents the new thinking and policies we need in agriculture, land management, ocean stewardship, and care of marine life. Many excellent people with considerable consciousness work in these fields, but when they function within the rationalism of the MultiEarth paradigm, their best efforts do not move us into OneEarth living. The dissociated, disoriented behavior of national and corporate leaders toward sensitive, life-sustaining eco-regions resembles the criminality of a serial killer who is able to outwit accountability far too long. All that MultiEarth ways don't like and think they don't need collect around archetypes in the unconscious where they generate a defiant attitude toward egos and civilization. In time they erupt.

Ambivalence and Cautions about the Underworld

MultiEarth's civilization and ego have a starkly different perspective on the heroic journey from how OneEarth and Self see it. Civilization and ego see it as foolish, nothing heroic to it. It's a descent into chaos. Choose it and we are sure to lose control— the very thing civilizing makes possible. Egoistic civilization sees the heroic journey as turning our backs on success and rejecting progress. To choose it is to joust with windmills and serve an impossible dream. It is a journey into some other world or underworld instead of advancing in the "real world." But Earth and Self see it as coming into the consciousness and power to transcend the Civilization Project, to reverse and correct the errors of the Project so that Earth's full powers can regenerate livable ecospheres. The heroic journey is a coming home to the greater truth of what it means to be human within Earth's cooperative community of life.

But it also carries risks. The epic movies in the *Star Wars* and *Lord of the Rings* series depict characters on heroic journeys that are able to function at new levels and upset dark empires, dark lords, and dark towers. But they also have characters who cannot handle the underworld. The temptation to go along with its powers and "make a deal with the devil" overcame Anakin Skywalker in *Star Wars*. Struggling to access the power to function with greater impact in the world, Anakin, Luke Skywalker's father, is tempted by the powers of the underworld and is taken over by them, becoming Darth Vader (Dark Father). Similarly, *Lord of the Rings* gives us the character of Gollum, whose ego-identity was not sufficiently strong to access the deep, archetypal powers of the ring without becoming "possessed." Both characters show us that going into the underworld carries no small risk.

In the preceding chapter I mentioned that the Wild within can get out of hand and carry us into the darkside. In the first chapter I detailed the dark abyss of Babylon where the story of Eden told of a OneEarth world that differed enormously from the MultiEarth world of Babylon and empires. In my previous book, *Blinded by Progress*, I have described the darkside of the MultiEarth story and economy—the darkside of corporations, economies, and nation-states, and how their darksides reinforce one another. Civilization's shadow lengthens along with its history. The MultiEarth paradigm continues out of balance over the millennia that it has been in preeminence. It has aborted the human, not allowing our fuller development. The official stories told by civilization's businesses and governments as well as schools and religious institutions have tilted far toward favoring civilizing rather than rewilding. Being a partner with all life forms and cooperating for the common good have been pushed down as priorities. They live, nonetheless, in our civilization's and soul's underworld. There is much for the heroic journey to expose us to there.

Why Self Can Create with Underworld Content, But Egos Can't

The underworld holds not only the treasure we seek, but energies to claim the treasure and capacities to live OneEarth ways. Clearly, we need to get beyond ego's dissociation from the underworld and identify with Self, the center able to connect creatively with this essential source. Before modern psychology, our ancestors and Indigenous cultures used ritual, ceremony, myth, and storytelling as their way to interact with the forces of the underworld. They knew the forces were there; their rituals and ceremonies sought constructive relationships with them. Carl Jung used psychology, a scientific approach, to seek constructive relationships with the forces of the underworld. Jung studied whatever the dominant paradigm neglected and rejected because he knew that was the paradigm's underworld. Every dominant paradigm goes out of balance and needs constructive relationships with its underworld if balance is to be restored.

Jung often spoke of the darkside, or "the shadow." Just as everything in the physical world casts a shadow, so does everything in the psyche. And, as in the physical world, the brighter a personality or civilization shines, the clearer and darker the shadow where its rejected energies and capacities hide. As Jung delved into personal and corporate shadows, he was surprised to discover that the shadow cast by our conscious worlds holds more than rejected or ignored experiences. It also collects inputs from many little underground tributaries which travel from sources far beyond an individual or cultural ego-identity. The shadows we cast are, then, more like wells fed by underground rivulets than cisterns that collect only waters from above the surface. All of us have, Jung determined, many of the basics of this collective unconscious. Its anatomy is with us from birth as surely as our birth-bodies come with anatomies.

Among the most influential parts of this underworld anatomy are the archetypes, providing psychic structures, energies, and potentials. They help us go beyond ego-identity, carry us toward greater consciousness, and increase our capacities—precisely where our heroic journey is taking us. Directing the archetypes requires the holistic capacities of the greater Self. The archetypal powers create havoc when egos try to manage them. Archetypes inflate egos into grandiose and manic behavior, or alternately, withdraw and leave egos without sufficient psychic resources to meet the day responsibly. With egos in charge, archetypal powers become dark powers running civilization and people.

To get a sense of the difference in capacity that we have when we identify with our greater Self, imagine holding a softball in your hands while in a grand ballroom. The softball is your ego; the ballroom is your greater Self. When we arrive in the consciousness of the ballroom instead of the softball, we enter into capacities for living OneEarth ways. The softball favors MultiEarth living. When the creational, evolutionary processes generated a psyche able to reconfigure who we are around the Self, it was a virtuoso achievement.

To bring back the treasure of OneEarth living from the underworld, Self and ego need to collaborate beyond what the journey has yet required. Ego identities cannot go into the same underworld that their limited consciousness and fears have created and made strong. So Self needs to be in charge. At the same time, Self needs a hand from the ego at the point where it wants to bring to consciousness what is unconscious about the OneEarth treasure.

When Self and ego collaborate, we understand ourselves, our workplace, and our country differently, because we are no longer repressing what we fear nor relying only on rationalism in our decisions. Self moves past the reactive, rigid, and small thinking of the ego. Centered in Self, we are able to navigate our civilization's and soul's underworld to bring the treasure of OneEarth living to the surface.

At the heart of civilization's and ego's inabilities to know their underworld lies their inability to look at polar opposites. Embracing both sides of a polarity is a key quality of Self's OneEarth consciousness, but a missing trait in ego's MultiEarth consciousness. Polarities are essential deep structures in the oneness of the Universe. But egoistic and imperial topographies of consciousness approach polarities with an either-or mentality. Unable to tolerate opposites coexisting in their consciousness, such topographies elevate one side and neglect, even demonize, the other. MultiEarth dominators, whether people, businesses, or nations, are in a topography of consciousness where their egos repress whatever side of a polarity is least advantageous to them. When a group dissents from their leadership, dominators commonly look for polarities among the dissenters which they then exploit to cause division in the dissent and weaken it. This old divide and conquer tactic appears commonly in the tyrant-weakling topography so widely spread across civilization.

Domination cannot perceive how a polarity actually has a deeper structure where it holds a uniting truth. Because dominators seek to handle polarities on the surface instead of including the unconscious depths, they claim one side as "truth" even though it's a one-sided distortion. Ironically for dominators, the side of the polarity they don't choose often contains the greater truth. Growth of consciousness happens when Self works with both poles of the polarities, even if one pole seems more right than the other. By holding their tension in the consciousness that they are part of a greater whole, the wisdom we need to transcend MultiEarth thinking emerges. In the language of Eden, when dominators eat the fruit of the tree of the knowledge of good and evil, polarity becomes primary in their consciousness. To eat the fruit of the tree of life, on the other hand, shows us a deeper holism. However, the

MultiEarth Civilization Project doesn't have access to the tree of life. That tree lives in larger topographies of consciousness.

Global Capitalism's Economic Underworld

The polarizing dynamics of capitalism and socialism illustrate the inability of MultiEarth consciousness to hold polarities in creative, transparent tension. As a result, the deeper unity that could result in a new economy for Earth-size living is never found. For much of the 20th century, the globe was sharply divided between the two. Capitalism was focused in markets; socialism was controlled by the state. Opting for one while vilifying the other brought incalculable animosity, warfare, death, and ecological destruction for decades. Both socialism and capitalism regarded the other as "The Enemy." Peace agreements mollified tensions at times, but didn't change the paradigm or move into a larger consciousness of shalom. There hasn't been the awareness that both capitalism and socialism are part of the same MultiEarth paradigm. Only by moving into topographies of consciousness that do not pick one over the other will we see the deep economy that can be surfaced for the greater OneEarth good.

Because economic ideas and decisions arguably rule the world, the underworld of economics holds special promise for our heroic search to find and claim the treasure of the new human and OneEarth living. After the Soviet Union's flag was lowered for the last time on December 25, 1991, Russia and all her satellite countries in Asia and Europe shifted their economies from state controlled socialism. They opened to capitalist practices. As a result, capitalist practices expanded their global reach. Though different countries shape models that they believe work best in their culture, as far as MultiEarth civilization can tell, no other macro-economy currently competes with capitalism's dominance. One pole of the polarity has won. But the more capitalism has been elevated, the larger its shadow has grown. The underworld continually collects what capitalism neglects and suppresses. Consequently, we can expect to find in the underworld of global capitalism's growth economy such components as the local economies it neglects and destroys, the cooperative business model it doesn't use, and the power of biodiverse, organic, and small farm agriculture that it defeats. All of these have powers that can reverse climate change and other ecological, economic crises. It's why OneEarth topographies of consciousness include these economic practices.

Capitalism's growth economy has rapidly lengthened its shadow in the last half century through accelerating practices that far exceeded the capacities of Earth's ecology. The situation is often framed, incorrectly, as a conflicted polarity: business versus the environment, with global capitalism favoring the business pole over the ecological one. Transnational corporations and chambers of commerce have sided with business despite the obvious truth that no economy can continue for long when it overextends its environment. Nonetheless, the MultiEarth economy committed to growth, and favoring capital expansion, has been so blinded by the need to put out favorable quarterly reports that it has been unable to stop operating beyond Earth's means.

The mindset in which business clashes with the environment has exposed a dark part of capitalism's shadow: capitalism has not been able to pay its own way. The costs of its profits have been greater by far than what it has been paying. Businesses typically report profits without including the amounts by which their profits diminished the value of the air, water, and soils in which they operated. From the vantage point of OneEarth consciousness and economics, capital economies stole many of their profits from the capital of the natural world.

The underworld of capitalism also holds a lot of energies of humans who've been mistreated by its practices. Though capital economies have benefitted many humans, its profits too often require cheap labor. Labor is often treated as a liability rather than an asset. Even slave labor is often welcomed. Some will argue that these consequences are not inevitable with capitalism; that they result from abuses by its users. But whether these abuses are

individual or systemic, capitalism has yet to show that it is an economic model that can find its place *inside* of Creation instead of
outside and over it. Socialism has had the same struggle. Neither
has been able to show that they are an economic model able to
get us to OneEarth living. Rather than choosing capitalism over
socialism or vice versa, holding the two in tension while looking
for the deeper structure of a unifying truth holds more promise for
moving to a new economy.

The massive extinction of species today adds still more length
to capitalism's shadow. The imbalances being created by the
die-offs, from microbes to mammals, continue to violate the ways
of the Wild. As a result, the energies of thousands of species, which
the MultiEarth capital economy has suppressed, inhabit its underworld. The heroic journey's passage through the underworld can
bring to the surface this suppressed interdependent community of
life—the community that brings great energy to OneEarth economic practices.

U.S. Capitalism's Big, Unjust Underworld

The underworld of U.S. capitalism includes pilfering land, paying
people too little for their labor or nothing at all, and pillaging Nature
while extracting resources. In the settling of the West (actually an
aggressive invasion), the U.S. gave land to people who were willing
to move west onto homesteads. But the land had to be stolen from
First Peoples who paid the actual cost of the westward movement
by people of European, African, and Asian descent. The U.S. forced
First Peoples to give away their land at a fraction of its value, restricting them to reservations arranged by treaties written in English. The
vast commons of the American West was enclosed as the settlers
became owners through laws made in Washington. The civilizing
MultiEarth economy expressed in those laws aggressively violated
the worldview and economy of Native Americans. For Indigenous
peoples, land was not a commodity that could be priced. It was part
of who they were. Moved off their land, they also lost their sacred

sites, their languages, and their cultures. Thousands lost their lives through new "white people's" diseases and armed conflicts with the U.S. Army and settlers. Official U.S. policies, driven by the capitalist economy, took away their economic abundance, pride, and dignity as sovereign people. Yet today, as in the past, the OneEarth ways of many of the First Peoples live on in capitalism's underworld. The emergence of a OneEarth economy brings to conscious practice what capitalism displaced—an economy based more in sharing and cooperation, wealth measured more in the commons than private ownership, and interdependence between humans, ecospheres, and all other species in a region.

The underworld of American capitalism also includes free labor coercively and violently imported from Africa where the economic abundance, cultural identity, languages, and the dignity of proud, black people were decimated. In holocaust proportions, half of those kidnapped from their land, communities, and culture lost their lives before ever reaching the Americas on the ships transporting them. The dead numbered in the millions. The survivors built a robust economy in the U.S. South without pay, but plenty of abuse. Nor has U.S. capitalism today stopped using tactics of worker oppression and slavery on the global markets.

Going still further into the underworld of American capitalism, the story of Latin America appears. Mexico was coerced militarily to give over half its territory—the Far West and Southwest of today's U.S. map—to the U.S. Our country continued to claim that such takeovers were part of this country's "Manifest Destiny." It was an aggressive geopolitical policy that was supported by a theology of entering and taking over the Promised Land. Politics and theology joined to assert that the U.S., not the imperial or colonial power of Spain nor the national powers of Mexico, would govern the Far West and Southwest U.S. Though owned by the U.S. since the end of the Mexican-American War (1846–1848), these vast lands continue to reveal capitalism's underworld by being a primary geography for cheap Mexican labor, the drug economy, and immigration battles.

Through various aggressions—from foot soldiers and imperial policy to paying a fraction of the real price of the land—the U.S. secured "the West," did it on the cheap, and handed the commonwealth over to capitalist enterprises largely as a gift. Sacred land became owned land. What was priceless became a commodity to be bought and sold. The full story of capitalism does not jive with an economic model built on high moral ground.

Metamorphosis: Passage to a New Economy

Because the system of capitalism, not just capitalists, has been unable to relate justly to ecospheres, humans, and other species, its underworld holds lots of gold to be claimed by all who risk the abuse and dangers of going after it. The MultiEarth economy's most ardent believers presume they can control the economy and keep its underworld under. So far, the world remains captive to an economy that must grow even though Earth's systems are collapsing under that growth. A growth economy no longer fits the configuration of ecological and species crises on today's planet. Earth is moving in a direction that leaves capitalism wanting. As more of us come to function with greater, Self-size understanding of the unconscious underworld, OneEarth living becomes stronger. Capitalism must adapt radically or be replaced.

But changing from capitalism stirs primal resistance in many. Just hearing about capitalism's shortcomings produces arguments from all who profit from it and believe it to be the best option. History shows that capitalism will go to great lengths to force its way. Wars are ignited when capitalism is threatened by cutoff of resources or political goals that threaten profits. Facing its shadow is capitalism's greatest challenge. Yet, Earth requires nothing less.

Capitalism is an economic system of ego consciousness. So Jung's observation that facing our shadow is as unwelcome and maddening for our egos as it is necessary, applies to capitalism as well. One of the best ways to get to know the shadow of an ego is to note when strong feelings arise about what we see in another person. Psyches project onto others what we don't acknowledge in ourselves. It's like looking at our projected image in a mirror. Though each time we have a strong emotional response is an opportunity to know more about our unconscious, we may resist what we discover. Jung and colleague, Marie-Luise von Franz, wrote:

> If you feel an overwhelming rage coming up in you when a friend reproaches you about a fault, you can be fairly sure... you will find a part of your shadow, of which you are unconscious.
>
> When an individual makes an attempt to see his shadow, he becomes aware of (and often ashamed of) those qualities and impulses he denies in himself but can plainly see in other people... such as egotism, mental laziness, sloppiness, unreal fantasies, schemes, plots, carelessness, cowardice, inordinate love of money and possessions... in short, all the little sins about which he might previously have told himself: "that doesn't matter."[126]

What Jung and von Franz said about discovering our personal shadow happens also for the systems egos have shaped. Capitalism has yet to face most of the "sins" about which it has been telling itself: "that doesn't matter." Unconscious of its underworld, capitalism continues to project it onto the world, and with uncalculated damage. Many who love the global capitalist economy argue—quite unconsciously—that the volatility of capitalism and its violations of Nature and people must be lived with the best we can; its downsides are justified by all the good it has brought to the world.

We need not, however, deny that capitalism has brought benefits to the world in order to explore its underworld. In the 21st century, the debate is no longer on the pros and cons of past benefits. The debate is whether an economy requiring growth can get us where we need to go. Earth's insurgency is telling us plainly, and the greater consciousness of Self is seeing clearly, that it cannot. All who insist that there is no better economic system are thinking in topographies of consciousness too small for Earth-size living. In larger topographies of consciousness, the energies that comprise capitalism's powerful underworld can be surfaced to configure an economy that regenerates life on our planet in the 21st century.

In the U.S., long the anchor of the global capitalism, the belief in capital growth has so many devoted advocates that looking into capitalism's faults is impossible without setting off a firestorm. It's also why our heroic journey must go there. Kudos to many people who articulate a new economy—Riane Eisler, David Korten, Gar Alperovitz, and the New Economy Coalition to name just a few from the thousands that exist.[127] Americans have much to learn regarding capitalism's underworld. U.S. capitalism has emphasized competition, but our greater capacities for cooperation and sharing go underused. It has created businesses that profit through cheap extraction, cheap production, mass consumption, and dumping of waste, but the welfare of the species that live where these businesses operate has been left out of their profit-loss equations. By excluding such powerful energies as cooperation and the interdependence of all species, U.S. capitalism is vulnerable to being succeeded by an economy that uses these greater energies as soon as more humans move into greater consciousness and product lines, such as the coal industry, collapse. The new, Earth-size economy will become more prevalent, using the powers that the capital economy has relegated to its underworld.

A widespread belief is that economics is too complex, so common people ask, "What can we do about it now anyway?" The answer is hard, but simple: we can bring capitalism's underworld to the surface. We can encourage one another to face consciously what capitalist egos shun, disown, and fear. The late Ray Anderson, the founder and CEO of Interface, Inc., the world's largest manufacturer of industrial flooring, spoke often about capitalism's underworld to his peers, once he'd faced it for himself. He came face-to-face with the darkside of his own capitalist practices, and the underworld of his company, while he prepared an address on sustainability in 1994. He did not feel he had the vision to deliver the address until a serendipity happened. He received a copy of

Paul Hawken's book, *The Ecology of Commerce: A Declaration of Sustainability.*[128] After reading it, he had what he called a "spear in the chest epiphany."[129] Hawken argues that leaders of industry are the only ones who can keep the industrial system from destroying the planet, and change it to operate within the planet. Anderson was convinced. He pivoted from where he'd been, developed a new vision of sustainability for his business, and delivered the speech.

In the 2003 Canadian documentary, *The Corporation,* Anderson addressed other CEOs at a convention and shared how he had become aware that he was a predator. He told his colleagues that they were predators too. All of them were prime predators of Earth's ecological resources. Facing this dark shadow, Anderson released great energy for good:

Anderson criticized the way economics is taught in many universities:

> We continue to teach economics students to trust the 'invisible hand' of the market, when the invisible hand is clearly blind to the externalities, and treats massive subsidies, such as a war to protect oil for the oil companies, as if the subsidies were deserved. Can we really trust a blind invisible hand to allocate resources rationally?[130]

Anderson's honest wrestling with his corporation's underworld energized an enlightened vision for his company to change all its practices and products that damage the Earth. Interface set a goal to have an environmental footprint of zero. Their website records their vision: "To be the first company that, by its deeds, shows the entire industrial world what sustainability is in all its dimensions: People, process, product, place and profits—by 2020—and in doing so we will become restorative through the power of influence."[131]

By looking at capitalism's underworld, Anderson accepted that the capital market is not inevitably guided by good. Anderson showed how greater honesty about our economic story would help us shift from our continuing practices of not paying the full costs of production. Hopefully, his company can achieve its goal of a zero footprint by 2020. En route they are taking bold leadership to eliminate or repair the environmental damage of their production. When the primary way to maximize profit is not to pay the full cost of production, the underworld of capitalism collects more and more energy for eruptions down the road. A successor OneEarth economy is sure to use that energy of the underworld to incorporate what capitalism can't handle.

Capitalism has not been able to come clean with the marketplace. It markets many products at low costs, but it does not admit that it hasn't paid the full costs of production. If capitalism cannot face its underworld with greater honesty and admit what it externalizes, then it cannot be the economy for Earth-size living. It will continue, instead, with land grabs, "free" slave labor, and coercive domination. Such behaviors are not the aberrations of a few companies; the dishonesty is in the system itself. Lowest possible costs plus unending growth in profits, even when our planet has limited capacities, is a capitalist recipe. It bakes Earth. As a result, the underworld of capitalism continues to elude the control of ego-shaped civilization. Its energies will continue to overwhelm our planet until they are claimed by us. We can make that claim by going into the Civilization Project's underworld. There, as our egos yield to Self, we become new humans that bring to the surface those energies that MultiEarth civilization and economics have suppressed. Dangerous? Yes. And highly promising.

Metamorphosis: Passage to a New Human

Each phase of the journey has a part in remaking us, beginning with the Call of Earth and Self to take a different path from the one civilization defines for us. Leaving where we've been and traveling into the in-between, liminal space means leaving much of who we've been to become more fully human. When we find the guides and maps that can show us the way into larger, ego and civilization-transcending topographies, we see more clearly how to move into greater consciousness. When we intentionally and responsibly engage in rewilding, the Wild further humanizes us; we learn to tend the Wild around us and within us instead of taming it. And with this chapter, the metamorphosis to becoming more fully human reaches the climactic moment: will we or will we not engage the underworld with full respect and daring intention? Engaging the unconscious and darkside of both our personalities and of civilization is essential to our metamorphosis to a new human. As described above, our egos must undergo severe reckoning because they have previously put all they couldn't handle into the unconscious. Will they, then, now reverse themselves? No, they aren't about to go into the underworld to engage what they've walled off. It's shakedown time for egos. They are humbled. Their only choice going forward is to serve the Self, the most capable archetype of all, and the one egos fear and avoid. Now egos fully yield control, and by serving Self help bring the transformation to a new human into the conscious world inside OneEarth's interrelational community.

Despite ego's great resistance to giving up being the center of our identity, if ego doesn't yield, then the journey will terminate in the underworld. That's what happened with Anakin Skywalker when he became Darth Vader in the movie series, *Star Wars*. If ego stays in charge, we will lead the rest of our lives as tyrants and weaklings. Ego must either give up the throne or be dethroned.

To the complete surprise of ego consciousness, the underground, though a habitat of dragons and foes for egos, is a habitat of partners for Self consciousness. In other words, we don't need to be saved from the underworld as much as we need to be saved by it. The shift from ego to Self, and from MultiEarth civilization to OneEarth societies, requires a death of one way so that a new way can come to life. Jesus put it succinctly: *Only those who lose their life will save it.*[132]

Psychotherapist James Hollis elaborates:

A mystery so profound that none of us really seem to grasp it until it has indisputably grasped us, is that some force transcendent to ordinary consciousness is at work within us to bring about our ego's overthrow.... That force, paradoxically, is the Self, the architect of wholeness which operates from a perspective larger than conventional consciousness. How could the ego ever come to understand, let alone accept, that its overthrow is engineered from within, by that transpersonal wisdom that has our being's interests at heart even in our darkest moments? This idea of beneficent overthrow is preposterous to the ego, for overthrow embodies the greatest threat to it, through the loss of sovereignty and the summons to live an agenda much larger and more demanding than the agenda of childhood adaptation and survival.

.... Stronger souls seek therapy; the more damaged seek someone to blame.[133]

Such a radical shift in our psycho-spiritual identities has stretched our use of language. Some speak of the death of the ego because it must surrender control. The radical shift of identity we need today for planetary impact must happen not only in people. Ego must surrender control of its cherished accomplishment, MultiEarth civilization, in order to serve the greater purpose that Self and Earth seek. But ego doesn't die in the sense that it can be buried and be superseded. Jungian analyst James Hollis says it more accurately: "When its [ego's] hegemony is overthrown, the humbled ego begins the dialogue with the Self."[134] After the overthrow, our species functions with an identity in which Self, along with a repurposed ego, directs life, we travel in a topography that civilization has not known how to gain. Self has the deep, inherent structures, along with archetypal energies and potentials, to handle the expansions our consciousness needs to make. Self can get us to Earth-size living by bringing powers from the underworld to the surface.

The importance of this moment when ego yields control and begins to serve Self cannot be overstated. Movie consultant Christopher Vogler, whose succinct summary of the heroic journey

I've loosely followed in these chapters, considers this to be where the magic of death-to-life happens, where we feel we're at the "brink-of-death" and then return, but have undergone change:

> This is a critical moment in any story, an ordeal in which the hero appears to die and be born again. It's a major source of the magic of the hero myth. What happens is that the audience has been led to identify with the hero. We are encouraged to experience the brink-of-death feeling with the hero. We are temporarily depressed, and then we are revived by the hero's return from death.[135]

What Vogler calls "the ordeal" of the heroic journey happens as intense drama somewhere "near the middle of the story…. the hero enters a central space in the Special World [in contrast to the Ordinary World left behind] and confronts death or faces his or her greatest fear. Out of the moment of death comes a new life."[136] This death can be physical. It can also be dying to privilege and assets, the death of a key relationship, the death of a community, or any other ending that feels deeply threatening and grief-evoking.

The metamorphosis of a caterpillar into a butterfly, one of Nature's many rites of passage, is a familiar analogy for human transformation. What is less familiar, however, is that inside the chrysalis, the caterpillar turns into a mushy soup, entirely losing its previous form and identity. Only then do elemental buds go to work from within the chaos of the soup to evolve the image and life of a butterfly. By analogy, our ego identity turns to mushy soup before elemental buds in our souls align with Self as our identity passes into a new form which transcends all the capacities of what came before it. This kind of form-transcending passage is the core of religious experience. The Apostle Paul enthusiastically described how anyone who would make the passage into divine consciousness would be a new form, a new creature. He further urged us to undergo this passage so that we would not be conformed to the reigning culture, but could transcend it and be transformed to have greater capacities through a new way of thinking.[137]

When we are in the ordeal, much of how we are accustomed to handling threatening situations doesn't help anymore. We are in the "mushy soup" inside the chrysalis. The powerlessness of what is familiar to us leads us to risk making different choices. We become willing to try what civilizers considered abnormal, false, or far out. What is happening, though it's largely out of our control, is that a new identity is forming under the direction of Self, an identity capable of living Earth-size lives and shaping OneEarth societies. So we exit one identity and participate in reconfiguring a new one, personally and collectively, internally and externally. There is farewell and exodus. Ego dies to its former exaggerated tasks. We take the risk of losing relationships, a job, and privileges we value. These, too, need to undergo reconfiguring. We likely risk financial status or turn from potential economic profit. Spiritually, some of the language and beliefs we long affirmed fall away. They just don't fit what's happening in the new topography of consciousness. New theology, words, and spiritual views feel more genuine—and far more exciting. A very different way of being, the way of the Self, becomes possible. We understand what happened when Siddhartha experienced "enlightenment" and became known as Buddha. We connect with epiphanies such as the "burning bush," or being "in Christ," or any of the phrases used in religions and spiritualities which transcend ego's polarities in a deeper One. Ambivalence and paradox abound. One moment we feel emancipated; the next moment, we are swimming in grief. Out in society, powers of civilized consciousness fight us as they feel threatened by our changing; they take on the task of bringing us back in line or, failing that, to wipe us out. We are passing from civilization into naturalization.

Egos and civilization, of course, don't acknowledge that they can't make the size changes that our Great Work calls for. They tout their achievements with chest-thumping pride and use them as evidence that they can meet the challenges. But history shows that civilizers have been unable to break us out of the MultiEarth paradigm. It takes more than added education in civilization's schools to become new humans able to partner in creating a new economy. We need to make the journey from smaller topographies of consciousness to greater ones—a journey to which more education may contribute but does not complete.

There is no disagreement that the heroic journey is a journey into the underworld that our egos and civilization have rejected or ignored. But whereas ego and civilization avoid such darkness, Earth and Self see it as the darkness that is a necessary part of evolving a new human with greater consciousness. Mythology scholar Joseph Campbell, in *The Power of Myth,* the series for television that he did with host Bill Moyers, emphasized the role of the underworld in creating a new human: "One thing that comes out in myths is that at the bottom of the abyss comes the voice of salvation. The black moment is the moment when the real message of transformation is going to come. At the darkest moment comes the light."[138]

While egoistic civilization avoids the abyss and the darkest moment as much as possible, the Self and those with OneEarth eyes see it as akin to the darkness of the womb before we transition to life beyond it. In the dark moments of the abyss, when ego consciousness dissolves into soup, buds for a metamorphosed life configure themselves. From these the new Self-human grows, one as different from the ego-human as the butterfly is from the caterpillar. Yet they are connected. As the boundaries of the soul familiar to the ego are transgressed, new regions of the soul's greatness are found.

This metamorphosis into a new human enables us to claim the OneEarth treasure. That's not, however, the end of the journey. Beyond claiming the treasure, the tests of living it amid MultiEarth's determination to stay in charge are still to come.

Living as New Humans

It's possible to live with some consistency as a new human when we live in OneEarth topographies of consciousness! Below are three approaches to life in such topographies. The core of each one has us interacting within the interdependent, interactive, and intelligent organisms and systems of all of Nature. In such consciousness, new capacities evolve in us. We transcend where we've been and become new creatures centered in Self, seeking our fullest meaning within Earth-size living.

1. The Tao of Interdependence—Fritjof Capra (1939–), a physicist and founding director of the Center for Ecoliteracy, Berkeley, California, uses what he's learned from Nature to challenge the science of the past 300 years. As a systems thinker, Capra has searched for the essential principal of life in Nature's systems, not in her parts and particles. His widely acclaimed book, *The Tao of Physics* (1975), boldly named this essential life force as "the Tao," the word used for it in Eastern mysticism, philosophy, and religious thought. Tao is "the way," as in the way to go in life or the way of all things. It can be conceptualized only in part. To know the way is a matter of intuiting its dynamic in daily living. Life is known in the living, in its changes and interactivity. Throughout the Cosmos, Tao is the essential force and interactive dynamism of everything. Being attune to that dynamic force is the way to go in life.[139]

Once he sensed the active, interacting dynamic of Nature, Capra shifted the focus of his research from material things themselves to the movements and interactions of things. He urges us to lay aside Francis Bacon and the 17th century science that made controlling Nature the aim. This older science approached Nature as a machine in motion. Though that mechanistic approach has brought new understanding of many things, it now prevents understanding the essence of things—the Tao, the way to go. By reducing life to mechanics, the older science misses that the essence of life is happening in the interrelating processes. But by using an organic, yin-yang model of singular totality, Capra sees that all parts of the whole—all the way to the cells—function cognitively, consciously, and cooperatively. Capra emphasizes, "We urgently need a science that recognizes the fundamental interdependence of all phenomena, acknowledges nature as a mentor and model and reconnects us with the living world."[140]

A consciousness of the Wild as sovereign and finally untamable facilitates the conversion of thought and paradigm that Capra urges. Powers of the Wild work on us to deprogram us from the mechanistic model of science, while simultaneously rewilding us, retuning us to the Tao, those deeper structures of Nature that are life's principles. Self resonates with the Tao. Centered in the consciousness and capacities of Self, we are continually renewed by those deeper structures, by the Tao as it pulses its life throughout Earth's evolving community of life in which we live as new humans. Living in the planetary community of life is not possible for people in topographies of consciousness where ego is the center. Egos ever look for openings to break from the community to control it. But Self, conscious of the Tao that egos miss, knows that living as new humans with greater capacities of consciousness and action happens within every ecosphere's interdependent community of life. It's the Tao.

2. An "Ecological Civilization" of Interconnections in Process—
China is taking strong initiatives to clean the soot, toxins, and pollutants out of its air, soil, and water. Given they are also pursuing growth in their economy, the Chinese state is managing conflicting aims. Nonetheless, from within these tensions, China's 17th Communist Party Congress announced, in 2007, a goal to shape an "ecological civilization." Details for implementing the slogan, "Building an Ecological Civilization," are given by the Central Committee in a 2015 policy document, "Further Promoting the Development of Ecological Civilization."[141] No other country has yet stated an official ecological goal as broad as this one. China knows it must find a more congenial relationship between capital and Nature in order to address its multiple crises in public health and depletion of natural capital.[142]

The concept was quickly taken up by the Institute for Postmodern Development in China which had been formed just two years earlier in 2005, to "integrate classical Chinese philosophy with progressive forms of Western thought."[143] When the

Central Committee announced its ecological initiatives, the Institute focuses its mission more precisely: "to find global pathways to ecological civilization." The Institute coordinates the study of postmodernism at centers in over 30 universities. All search for solutions to Chinese and global problems. Studies proceed within frames of thought coming from Chinese philosophers, from Karl Marx, and from Alfred North Whitehead. A shared interest in Whitehead and process philosophy links the Institute closely with the Center for Process Studies in Claremont, California—the center formed in 1973, by two members of the faculty at Claremont School of Theology, John Cobb, Jr. and David Griffin.

Cobb and Griffin recognized that the philosophical paradigm explicated by Whitehead differed dramatically from the thinking that created the problems inherent in MultiEarth thinking.[144] The Center for Process Studies approaches the crises of the 21st century as a crisis in thinking. True to its name, "process thought" gives its primary attention to process instead of matter, to the organic and constant changing of things rather than to the things themselves. It approaches Nature as an organism with its own life-changing capacities instead of an inanimate machine with moving parts. Cobb says:

> The sciences have thus far focused on explaining organisms in terms of mechanisms. They have assumed that when one fully explains an organism, one will account for it by "matter in motion." Whitehead's philosophy of ecological relations, in contrast, taught that when one fully understands matter, one will account for it in terms of the "organisms" of which it is ultimately composed.[145]

Cobb has been quick to see how Whitehead's thought opens up new, life-sustaining thinking about the major issues of the environment and economy, writing a book about each one.[146]

Whitehead pushed away from the philosophies that have shaped and undergirded the Civilization Project, seeing the gaping incompleteness of their focus on matter while leaving organic process neglected. In effect, Whitehead went into the underworld of the Civilization Project and claimed process as the more significant factor. Grasping the treasure of process thinking, Whitehead guides us into topographies of consciousness where we focus on interrelationships and Earth community, on the organic aliveness of our world more than the materiality and stuff of it.

Making an "ecological civilization" our aim counters the language I use in this book in that I define our aim as transcending "civilization." I consider civilization to be a provisional project of ego consciousness, and make our aim OneEarth living. My logic is that a different relationship with Nature from the one that civilizes her can better be called something other than "civilization." But the Chinese government, seeing itself as the shaper of an advanced society intent on coping with ecological crises, put the two words together. I understand why process studies see this as an opening from a major world government and have quickly picked up on it to advance ecological thinking. We can hope that the process paradigm with which the Center for Process Studies and the Institute for Postmodern Development in China frame "ecological civilization" takes it out of the paradigm of the Civilization Project and into the consciousness of OneEarth living. Process thinking certainly has the power to reframe many slogans and concepts on the interconnectivity at the heart of our Great Work to keep Earth livable.

I sensed such a thoughtful reframing going on at a conference I attended in June, 2015. The Center for Process Studies was the primary sponsor and a sizable contingent of the 1000+ attendees came from China through the Institute for Postmodern Development in China. The aim of the conference was to change our way of thinking, to move to an Earth-size paradigm and process. The concept of an "ecological civilization" was an integral part of the sessions. If that conference, entitled "Seizing the Alternative: Toward an Ecological Civilization," is indicative, then the power of a new paradigm based philosophically in process thinking will move us along into OneEarth ways, and the language of "ecological civilization" may prove to be more help than hindrance.

Both the Institute for Postmodernism in China and the Center for Process Studies show how process thought and its language, generated from within an academic discipline at an institution accredited by civilization's standards, can contribute a lot to our understanding of the treasure we need for Earth-size consciousness. Will these centers, like yeast changes grape juice to wine, change the paradigm throughout their institutions of learning and throughout their countries? Such a yeasty fermentation happens in larger topographies of consciousness. Capacities of the new human, centered in Self, are awakened and sustained so that we are able to think and act in Earth-size ways. Though new humans are not flawless, being grasped by the powers of Self and the Wild empower us to live and think in substantially different ways, in particular, in sustainable interdependence.

3. The Intelligence of Interconnecting Organisms—Herbologist Stephen Harrod Buhner speaks of the intelligence exhibited in the behaviors of interconnecting organisms. Buhner works with what he calls living or botanical medicines. He has studied the healing properties of hundreds of plants, shamanic healing practices, and a variety of healing modalities. He has especially sought out healing practices not used, or little used, in allopathic medicine which dominates Western approaches to healing. In other words, Buhner has gone into the underworld of the medical practice in the West to rediscover what's been ignored, rejected, and suppressed.

In an interview in *Sun* magazine (2014), Buhner talks about how living medicine comes from using a different paradigm, one that understands Nature and humans differently from Western approaches to healing. Buhner's paradigm is more Nature-centered and approaches healing as proceeding via interactive processes that restore balance among the energies of life, trusting that as balance happens, healing happens. Buhner's work knows that the "reductionist, mechanistic approach to nature, such as the one our culture has inherited from scientists of the early to mid-twentieth century, is deeply flawed," and regrets that, although science is increasingly rejecting such thinking, "this oversimplified model is still taught in schools. Children are told that humans are the most intelligent organism on the planet, while other organisms are mostly unintelligent and do not possess complex language or make tools or have empathy."[147]

Buhner's OneEarth worldview approaches all organisms as having intelligence, not just humans. He listens for their language and observes their empathy. He follows the researchers who "continue to find evidence of spontaneous self-organization in matter, such as occurs in living creatures. If molecules, for instance, are packed tightly into a closed container, they will synchronize and begin to act as a unified whole."[148]

In the MultiEarth paradigm, such self-organizing has long been attributed only to humans. But close observations of plants, animals, and matter show activity that we call "intelligence" when humans do it. Buhner continues:

> A biological organism is something more than the sum of its parts.... We intuitively understand this to be true with human beings, but we have been trained not to apply it to every other substance and life-form on the planet.
>
> When spontaneous self-organization occurs in a biological organism, the organism immediately begins working to keep its new self-organized state intact. It analyzes incoming data and generates responses. In other words, intelligence arises in the system. It does not matter if this is a bacterium or a plant or a person or an ecosystem. The organism becomes extremely sensitive to all incoming data, because anything that touches it might destabilize it. Tiny inputs can create huge changes in self-organized systems.[149]

We're in a new way of thinking about all that is around us when we consider that every change generates new intelligences to respond to that change. If we can stop civilizing what's around us, and open to their knowledge and activity, we recognize how they want to interconnect with us. That's exactly what we do when we live in greater consciousness as new humans.

In *The Dream of the Earth*, Thomas Berry speaks of these energies that work to our benefit even though they are not under our control:

> Our best procedure might be to consider that we need not a human answer to an earth problem, but an earth answer to an earth problem. The earth will solve its problems, and possibly our own, if we will let the earth function in its own ways. We need only listen to what the earth is telling us.[150]

Berry urges us to turn our attention to Earth's dream, Earth's consciousness, and reconfigure our consciousness and practices to synchronize with her. Earth's dream has been cast aside by the MultiEarth dream, but that dream is now struggling against overwhelming crises and sophisticated death. At this stage of the heroic journey, having experienced the tectonic shift from ego to Self, our Selves have reconnected with the dream of Earth. Our Selves want nothing more than to use their enormous capacities of intuition and imagination to reconfigure our psyches and societies to synchronize with Earth and interdependent life. It's where the journey takes us next.

Conclusion: Metamorphosis to OneEarth Living

MultiEarth powers are scrambling to gain control of processes discovered in larger topographies of consciousness. The thinking among MultiEarth powers is that if humanity really insists on living ecologically on our planet, then MultiEarth powers intend to be in charge of green energy, local economies, and sustainable uses of forests and food supplies. But can they deliver? They are not facing their underworld, but continually projecting them outward in their economic, social, and environmental behaviors; they continually miscalculate the size of Earth's pushback to their decisions; and their huge profits weigh them down to where they can't keep up with the speed at which Earth is changing. These liabilities, coupled with more people moving into topographies of consciousness that create a new human, doom MultiEarth control. Be it through collapse or conversion, the MultiEarth paradigm is sure to be transcended the more Self and ego join in creating a new human re-centered out of civilization and into Earth-size. To experience the treasure of OneEarth living is to experience a metamorphosis of the human to our fuller capacities able to thrive in a regenerating, intelligence-creating Earth. A major reason given for why we can't change the current trends engineering an unlivable world is that human nature isn't capable of changing sufficiently to shape societies and lives that share cooperatively in Earth-size living. The heroic journey believes otherwise, and this chapter has shown the passage through the underworld by which we become human beings with greater consciousness—new humans, centered in Self and Earth.

Finding in ego's and civilization's underworld what we need for OneEarth living metamorphoses us into capacities neither ego nor civilization believe are there. We cannot continue being the domesticated pets of a dangerous economy designed by those benefiting from the illusion that the resources of more than one planet can be ours if we just acquire enough power, wealth, blessing, or status.

Having traveled this far on the journey, we can see how MultiEarth ways snooker us, tempting us out of our position inside of Nature. As such, the Eden story describes up to the minute events. We leave the Garden; our choices opt for the Civilization Project and stunt our innate drive to live with greater consciousness. But these larger topographies of consciousness are our destiny. As we continue experiencing rewilding along the heroic journey, we realize that larger topographies are not out of reach, they only require passage through the underworld, that which our egos and the Civilization Project have ignored and cast aside. The journey has enlarged our consciousness enough so that Self recognizes the underworld as a habitation of resources for Earth-size thinking and living, not as wilderness of adversaries, as ego does.

Our egos are outmatched by the inequalities, paranoia, intimidation, surveillance, torture, and violence of civilization. Ego efforts to address these will always be subverted by the energies in our underworlds. Without a full metamorphosis of consciousness, the changes we make will remain contained within the paradigm of MultiEarth living; we will not make it all the way to living with Self at the center. Only then can we achieve the Earth-size changes we need.

The psychological and spiritual shifts from ego to Self, and from civilization to Earth, do not happen casually, though they are the intended metamorphosis of our species as we move from infancy to adolescence to early adults to middle adults and to elderhood. If we don't get bought off by civilization, the Tao will include us in her way. Living in OneEarth's interactivity, organisms and systems that MultiEarth thinking considers machines in motion, we recognize as living entities in processes that constantly create life and intelligence.

Through the journey's transformative processes, we arrive in consciousness where plants, microbes, and animals function with intelligence and empathy. The transformative process we undergo is analogous to the planted seed that dies en route to becoming a fruit-bearing plant, and the caterpillar that dies in a chrysalis only to emerge as a butterfly. Without the ordeal of metamorphosis to new consciousness, we do not know how to live inside Earth's community of life as part of it.

The heroic movement is a life-or-death act of faith. We choose to believe that we can survive, albeit in a form beyond anything our egos imagine, and move into a topography of consciousness in which we experience for ourselves a healthy, Ecozoic interrelatedness of all elements in Earth's biospheres. We believe that organisms and systems have intelligence, that they are alive in ways we do not fully comprehend. We believe that our own being will be more fully realized in such a larger consciousness, ecosystem, and cosmology.

We've decided to move with the fullest knowledge science and reason provide, but not to limit ourselves to them. New humans include the knowledge of intuition, imagination, and faith in the unknown mystery. Submitting to the larger movements of Earth and Self, we put our faith in them. It's a kind of sacred dare.

Ponder, Discuss, and Act

1. What pros and cons carry the most weight with you regarding whether or not our species can become new humans?

2. Carl Jung said, "Everyone carries a shadow, and the less it is embodied in the individual's conscious life, the blacker and denser it is. At all counts, it forms an unconscious snag, thwarting our most well-meant intentions." How have you been able to understand yourself (or another) better by learning about the shadow (underworld) all of us have?

3. Why do you avoid the underworld, or what parts do you avoid? Why do others avoid the underworld as you observe them or hear them explain their reasons?

4. Why or why not is the economic underworld a helpful example of the underworld's function and potentials? What other example(s) have power for you?

5. Describe a passage through the underworld that you have experienced. Or describe one that you avoid.

6. Give your thoughts on the three approaches to living as new humans:
   - Finding the Tao in Nature and tuning to it.
   - Implementing policies for an ecological civilization.
   - Joining in a community of life where communication includes all species.

7. What in this chapter invites you most strongly to act?

SECTION SIX

Living in the
Topographies of Eden

Completing the heroic journey brings us home, but everything looks different. It looks different because we are different. The eyes of Self and the eyes of ego see the same scenes differently. We have metamorphosed into new humans with capacities to live in the topography of Spiritual Consciousness.

Yet, expressing Spiritual Consciousness in the MultiEarth world challenges us. For me, each day has moments in which I'm learning to act from an identity of Self rather than ego. Being aware of the choice I have in that moment, and going with Self, connects me with the capacities for living within Earth's interdependent community of life. Answering the question, "What is Spiritual Consciousness?," teaches me more about living there. To stay with the metamorphosis analogy, the butterfly doesn't learn its new life sitting on the branch outside the chrysalis. We need to explore the topography. The final two chapters make the case for the important roles imagination and myth play in making it possible for us to live in Spiritual Consciousness, implementing OneEarth ways.

Chapter 11 makes the case for imagination. Like a third eye, imagination sees much of what is otherwise invisible. What our third eye sees regarding MultiEarth civilization is apocalyptic as the Civilization Project unravels in the face of Earth's insurgency. But then the eye also sees the images of the new, interdependent Earth community. Imagination shows us a plethora of images of OneEarth living and powers us into living them.

Chapter 12 brings myth alongside imagination as another key to living beyond ego's MultiEarth civilization. Symbols and myths with psychic power and spiritual meaning sustain our capacities as new humans, Self-directed, who desire deeply to live OneEarth ways. Living with Spiritual Consciousness in Earth's interdependent community requires us to use these two empowering capacities as fully as possible.

I have come to believe that the myth or story we imagine ourselves to be living has greater impact on us and on the world than does the past. I believe the proverb: "Change the story, change the future." Eden, when changed into an imaginative story about The Garden that lives *in every human's soul, is a story able to guide us and energize a new world out of the crises of our century.*

CHAPTER ELEVEN

Seeing Beyond Civilization's Apocalyptic Breakdown

We are all apocalyptic now, or at least we should be, if we are rational.
—Robert Jensen

[The unconscious] has two natural pathways... to the conscious mind: One is by dreams; the other is through imagination.... The unconscious has developed a special language to use in dreams and imagination: It is the language of symbolism.... Inner work is primarily the art of learning this symbolic language of the unconscious.[151]
—Robert Johnson, *Inner Work*

The passage to being new humans does not complete the heroic journey. It does, however, equip us with greater capacities for living with OneEarth consciousness, what Korten calls Cultural and Spiritual Consciousness (see Korten's map, Chapter Eight). Those capacities are being fully tested in the decades of the 21st century as the Civilization Project tries every way to stay in charge of the world, claiming it can save what it is destroying. Civilization is unwilling or incapable of facing the apocalyptic scenario it is responsible for setting in motion.

The heroic journey has brought us into a consciousness where we can imagine transcending civilization's scenario. The challenge is: can we live Cultural and Spiritual Consciousness effectively? The answer is positive: we can because it's not an individualistic effort. Inherent in these two topographies of greater consciousness is living not only in kinship with other new humans, but also in radical interdependence with all of Earth's community. That interdependence is embedded in how we think and act as new humans in topographies where consciousness is managed by Self. In Spiritual Consciousness, interdependence functions across our daily activities—how we parent children, see ourselves within the Wild, shift the thinking of the workplace and organizations we participate in, and engage in conversations with people on shaping OneEarth living.

In these larger topographies of consciousness, we also see deeper into scenarios than what is possible in ego topographies. In the case of climate change, for example, egos respond with behaviors that show they're under the influence of tyrant-weakling archetypes. Tyrants deny it with bravado, or broker "solutions" far smaller than the scale of what's evolving ecologically; weaklings don't want to talk about it, or make some surface changes as their contribution. Egos ever protect their own convenience, profits, and control. The Self manages effective responses with the abilities and courage to work with higher skilled tools such as apocalyptic thinking and imagination.

Our Current Apocalypse

Prime stuff for apocalypse hangs in the air today and has spread like an epidemic throughout MultiEarth civilization. Apocalypse carries with it the idea of the world coming to an end. And it is true: the world that we know is ending. Global temperatures have already risen 1° Celsius above preindustrial levels (1850–1900 is the base timeframe) and are sure to rise at least one more in this century—maybe even 2° or more.[152] The melting ice of Greenland, the Arctic, and Antarctica is raising sea levels, and will continue to do so throughout this century, to where migrations of people, plants, and animals from coastal areas will bring incalculable dysfunction to those areas and their economies. Higher seas intensify normal coastal events such as King Tides. As these tides come further inland, they affect areas around the world, from Florida to islands in the Pacific and Indian Oceans. The United Nations Environment Programme monitors fifty-two island nations, home to 62 million people, for the impacts of rising seas. Even though the peoples of these islands have contributed virtually nothing to global climate change, their worlds are ending. Tuvulu may be the first island nation to disappear.[153] Residents have begun migrating to New Zealand. The nations of Kirbati (Pacific) and Maldives (Indian) will likely disappear completely by the middle of the 21st century.[154]

Non-human species are well into an apocalyptic extinction as they leave us at the rate of dozens of species per day, a trend that means 30–50% fewer species will be alive by mid-century.[155] With them goes a whole library of knowledge on how to live interdependently in their regions. Meanwhile, the human species continues to explode, nearly quadrupling in less than a century, from two billion in 1930 to 7.4 billion in 2016. We're displacing other species and magnifying all the ways that the MultiEarth civilization paradigm is unsustainable. As more people want to live at a MultiEarth scale rather than an Earth-size one, solving the overload that our species places on Earth becomes less possible. The responses by MultiEarth leaders to these multiple crises are typically apocalyptic in that many decisions on energy via fossil fuels, food production through industrial agriculture, and military expansionism take us deeper into the very apocalypse that they claim to be preventing. Climate summits have been particularly inept at keeping us below 2° Celsius, a rise that will be disastrous for MultiEarth civilization.[156]

Rising seas, temperatures, rates of species extinctions, and human population expansion illustrate how the assumptions on which civilization has proceeded are being upset. In light of this intensifying situation, journalist Robert Jensen urges us to see "apocalypse" as a helpful word to describe what's happening: "We are all apocalyptic now, or at least we should be, if we are rational."[157] Jensen, professor of journalism at the University of Texas, Austin, challenges thinking that apocalyptic talk is extremist or whacky and urges us to see it as a most rational way to talk about events that push well beyond the boundaries of what civilization has known as "normal cycles." One of the features of apocalypse as a literary genre is a dexterity with images that allows it to describe events we'd never thought would happen. Genres less adept with images cannot accurately convey the truth of all the ways ego-shaped civilization is deluding itself, or the intensity with which Earth is taking charge ecologically. Apocalypse provides the verbal means to bring reason and imagination together for sane conversations about how we can make our way forward in this emergency. Jensen continues:

> It is time for a calm, measured apocalypticism that recognizes that the ecosphere sets norms, which we have ignored for too long, and that we need to develop a new sense of solidarity among humans and with the larger living world. So, speaking apocalyptically need not leave us stuck in a corner with the folks predicting lakes of fire, rivers of blood or bodies lifted up to the heavens. Instead, it can focus our attention on ecological realities and on the unjust and unsustainable human systems that have brought us to this point.[158]

Thinking of ourselves as apocalyptic may take some getting used to, but it definitely makes possible more powerful speech about what's happening. Apocalyptic thinking engages our imaginations with all that science is telling us; then it finds the metaphors and language to convey more accurately the projected end results of the irrationality underway as civilization's MultiEarth paradigm unravels. Empires and superpowers posture and bully. Financial markets boom and bust. Have-nots suffer the greatest casualties while have-lots acquire worthless extreme wealth. Redistribution of wealth geysers upward, creating apocalyptic disparities in power. Corporations displace governments and people as the ones in control of water, land, seeds, food supplies, and democracies. They relentlessly continue the centuries-long takeover of the commons, becoming owners of what, in reality, belongs to us all. And through it all, greenhouse gases increase to where they are now the largest weapon of mass destruction we humans have ever created. Oppression rolls toward a death count for millions of species with no one able to predict how many more species can die before the web of life on which we humans depend collapses for our species as well. And still, leaders and all who live in ego consciousness behave as if ego-centered topographies are all there is. Speaking of these developments apocalyptically gives us frames of speech that are neither hostile nor restrained. We find ways to speak accurately and urgently about what's ending.

As Nature responds to human civilization in the Anthropocene Epoch, Earth's self-regulating processes have begun to rebalance the unsustainable imbalance generated by *Homo sapiens'* oppression. The consequences of such rebalancing need apocalyptic language to describe them as the macro-forces of OneEarth Creation clash with the macro-forces of MultiEarth civilization. Earth raises the stakes for MultiEarth's staying in charge. MultiEarthers put more money on the table in order to continue their gamble. But as they take their controlling, dominating model to an unprecedented level, they simultaneously guarantee that crises will intensify, crescendoing to civilization's own catastrophic undoing.

It is in this apocalyptic context that what's happened on the heroic journey matters big. New humans functioning in topographies of greater consciousness see more clearly not only the systemic breakdown of civilization, but also the breakthrough to new worlds where the capacities of the new human are part of Earth's emerging epoch. We are able to see that the metamorphosis from ego to Self, and the journey by our planet from civilizations to a new Creation, are the personal and planetary way to living potentials we've not yet experienced in their fuller, breakthrough expression.

Both Halves of Apocalypse:
Breakdown and Breakthrough

Media, movies, and literature are only half right about apocalypse when they focus on devastation and trauma so great that words fail—other than to call it the "end of the world." The other half is that apocalypse also opens to a new world. This dual dynamic of apocalypse is its genius. It holds the end and the beginning in a single word, in a single genre.

Seeing apocalypse as describing a period of tumultuous transition to Earth's next chapter—not only a relentless, monstrous destruction of what is—corrects the word to its core meaning. Coming from the Greek language, *apokalupsis* literally means "uncovering." It lifts a veil; reveals something hidden.[159] Apocalypse lifts the veil from the efforts of MultiEarth and ego consciousness to make the world better, revealing the impossibility of doing so while using an anti-Earth paradigm. At the same time, apocalypse *reveals* the OneEarth alternative that was practiced before the Civilization Project and continues to unfold amidst all the MultiEarth death.

Earth's *opus* during the past 4.5 billion years has seen a number of apocalyptic moments. The five mass extinctions that appear in Earth's fossil record are examples. In each of these extinctions, about 75% of the species were lost in a period lasting from a few centuries to two million years. The fifth mass extinction, 67 million years ago, was likely triggered when an asteroid six miles in diameter collided with Earth at a speed 150 times faster than a jetliner. It set off incalculable seismic and geological disruption. The atmosphere quickly filled with dust and particulates, hiding the sun for months. The climate changed so rapidly that the dinosaurs simply couldn't adjust quickly enough to survive.

But with that apocalyptic event, Earth did what she'd done previously. Her deep evolutionary processes responded resiliently and moved Earth into her next chapter. Then as now, Earth behaved from a geological intelligence comprised of systems and processes intent on evolving life forms and livable habitats. It was a tumultuous transition. Yet, the end to the way the world had been for millennia also unveiled the beginning of the next era. The current apocalyptic transition is likely to be similar. It will proceed according to geological precedent and timelines. There being no precedent in civilization's history for the scale of this transition, egos and civilization see it only as breakdown. Meanwhile, Earth, with her deep evolutionary role in the Cosmos, has gone into the travail of birthing something new, unlike anything she's yet brought forth. Concurrently, humans centered in Self and functioning in larger topographies of consciousness are developing the capabilities for living interdependently in what Earth is evolving.

However, the trauma for us, the planet, and all the rest of her species cannot be overstated. Apocalypse describes an insurgency by both the planet and the energies of the underworld. Earth undoes civilization; the unconscious underworld undoes ego. The metamorphosis to a new human in the womb of the soul is paralleled by Earth's processes into a new epoch, which is also a new Earth. Earth deconstructs civilization's reign over ecospheres and networks of species. The chaos involved is like an abyss, but it acts like the dark womb of Mother Earth, where life buds gestate into the birth of new and continuing Creation. Apocalypse refers to this entire sequence; not just the trauma of deconstruction.

As such, apocalypse reveals what egos and civilization have hidden, but also what greater consciousness keeps secret from smaller consciousness. Our current situation is becoming increasingly revelatory in a true apocalyptic sense. Earth is revealing limits that make it impossible for MultiEarth ways to continue. Earth's abundant creational order cannot sustain over seven billion people living at MultiEarth levels, let alone that many people plus the rest of Earth's species. The numerical dominance of *Homo sapiens*, plus the adversarial and antagonistic attitude this species holds toward Nature, have driven MultiEarth civilization off of Earth's evolutionary highway. The Civilization Project has proceeded in its basic violation of planetary possibilities and has revealed that it is unable and unwilling to configure itself *within* Earth's systems and life community. Humans have transitioned Earth out of the Holocene epoch and into a highly unstable sequel, the Anthropocene. The details can be argued, but the overarching revelatory truths of the apocalyptic time we have entered become increasingly clear to all of us who open our eyes in a topography of consciousness where we're not blinded by MultiEarthism. Equally revelatory, with opened eyes we can see that many peoples have lived OneEarth ways under the radar of the Civilization Project. These alternatives are foundational for apocalyptic reimagining of life. Or as Mayan Indigenous Peoples have been saying for some time, while continually reshaping resistance to MultiEarth ways, "We want a world where many worlds can coexist."

"Imagine!… It Isn't Hard to Do"

Central to the apocalyptic way of seeing the world is its reliance on imagination as a way of knowing. Its imaginative prowess generates images able to describe Earth's massive push-back to the MultiEarth paradigm, but it's just as able to wow us with how interdependence and interrelatedness constantly evolve new Creation. Apocalyptic thought and speech gets its effectiveness from these images, not from statistics and graphs, nor by marshaling the facts, though such data have a place in the logical arguments we raise against the damaging, life-threatening activities of MultiEarth powers. Apocalyptic imagination grabs our emotions in ways statistics, graphs, and facts do not.

Despite its many powers, imagination doesn't generally hold the same authority in MultiEarth civilization as does science, reason, and logic. The common phrase, "It's just your imagination," shows that imagination is not considered a bonafide way of knowing. Nonetheless, our imaginations provide an effective way of seeing through the breakdowns of civilization to the better alternative. Physicist Albert Einstein was significantly countercultural in believing that "imagination is more important than knowledge." He added, "For knowledge is limited, whereas imagination embraces the entire world…. It is, strictly speaking, a real factor in scientific research."[160] At the time, physics was locked in the Newtonian paradigm. Einstein recognized that it would take imagination for science to break into new frames. Without an infusion of imaginative new possibilities, scientific knowledge would continue to function inside its chosen paradigm. Similarly today, if we treat imagination as "not real" in comparison to how MultiEarth civilization uses science, math, and economic orthodoxy, then we are far less likely to see through civilization's breakdown to OneEarth solutions.

"Imagination" names the highly valuable image-making faculty of our species. It comes from the Latin *imago* or *image*, and is the faculty by which the bigger part of our minds, the unconscious part, becomes available to us. Imagination transforms the content of our unconscious minds into images that we see as they flash onto the screens of our minds. Ideas we've rejected, moods that possess us, a potential we didn't know we had—all of these can be intentionally or spontaneously accessed by our imaginations. With the help of meditative states of mind, we can call up images purposely. We can sketch them, paint them, compose their music, or project them into the artistry of a stage play. But images also appear unsolicited, as when we say, "That just came out of nowhere." In Charles Dickens' *A Christmas Carol* (1843), Ebenezer Scrooge is encountered by unsolicited images. The story illustrates how we can interact with images. In dialogue, they will tell us who they are and why they appear—all of it making conscious what has previously been in our unconscious world.

My own way of working with images is to write down what I say to them. Then, as I give them time and attention, the images talk through my imagination. A conversation ensues. They speak with moods and attitudes. Sometimes we argue; sometimes we're thoughtful or caring. After the conversation, be it brief or long, I know more about myself than I did before taking time to benefit from my imagination. We don't have to become experts or fully understand how imagination works in order to use our imaginations effectively to transcend our ego personalities or ego-shaped civilization.

World-renowned music artist, John Lennon (1940–1980), highly experienced in artistic imagination, made the case for universal use of imagination in his song "Imagine." He disrobed the idea that imagination is "difficult" to do and urged all of us to join him in using our imagination as a vehicle to transcend where ego's civilization has become stuck:

> Imagine there's no countries, It isn't hard to do;
> Nothing to kill or die for, And no religion too;
> Imagine all the people, Living life in peace…
>
> You may say I'm a dreamer, But I'm not the only one.
> I hope someday you'll join us, And the world will be as
> one.

American psychologist Rollo May (1909–1994) also urged us to break out of subordinating imagination to rational forms of knowing. He posed two questions: "What if imagination and art are not, like many of us might think, the frosting on life, but the fountainhead of human experience? What if our logic and science derive from art forms, rather than the other way around?"[161] May's insight sets on its head the common assumption employed in civilization that science and math are the best tools to advance human wellbeing. His questions give plenty of reason for schools to develop skills in imagination and arts rather than to make them expendable in the budgets that treat science and math preferentially. In an apocalyptic century, a skillful use of imagination as a way of knowing is especially important. Without access to the vast regions of our unconscious or underworld through images, we cannot transcend the current apocalypse of ego-shaped civilization.

Despite this urgent need for imagination, relying on imagination can sound risky to all who believe that we make our best decisions on rock-hard data derived by scientific investigation and with careful processes of rational thinking. Truth is, however, that every arrangement of data happens according to some paradigm, and that paradigm has been conceived by our imaginations. But once we become accustomed to the paradigm, we live within it unconscious of it. We forget that it was once imagined and that, as a basic structure within which we live and think, we continue to believe in it—a constant re-imagining of it. Regarding the MultiEarth paradigm, civilization has forgotten what a boldly imagined proposal it is. Imagined out of the unconscious world, egos have grabbed hold and run with it. Or, more accurately, egos were grabbed and have been run by it. Our conscious minds look at the world through the lenses of whatever paradigm we have in place, and then arrange what we see, think, and do to fit the questions and solutions of that paradigm. The MultiEarth paradigm shows us that while imagination is wholly essential, it also surfaces images that egos cannot handle without reducing them in size and energy. The Civilization Project is an example of how egos took OneEarth images and reduced them to what they could handle. Self is far better equipped to sort out the images, choose which ones to use, and how.

What I want to be clear about is that both MultiEarth and OneEarth paradigms are imagined constructs within which to live. And that Self, not ego, is the center with sufficient consciousness to dialogue with the images brought forth by our imaginations and decide which can best serve life. The larger topographies of consciousness into which the heroic journey takes us, identifies us with the Self and its capacities. The abilities of Self and imagination to work together makes apocalyptic imagination a highly potent tool to critique what is, unveil deeper structures, and reveal possibilities of what can be. In the smaller consciousness of egos, apocalypticism is a jumble of incomprehensible images. Egos mishandle the images. A common mistake is to literalize them as predictions of doom, at which time evil is punished and good rewarded.

The foundational use of imagination in apocalyptic knowing in no way closes out the importance of rational thinking. We need strong rational thought to decide whether or not a particular paradigm serves us best in our current situation. The rational works best when it serves the imaginal, not prevents it. This book makes the case that the MultiEarth paradigm has served the ego's Civilization Project well, but has been devastating to Earth, and has stunted our species from evolving our greatest Self capabilities. We can reject the MultiEarth paradigm on rational grounds, and invoke imagination to see the way to live a OneEarth paradigm. We need reason and imagination working together in this century of apocalyptic breakdown and breakthrough. At times, imagination gives us the frame in which to see the picture most accurately. At other times, reason configures the data in ways to show that the picture needs a different frame.

Using Apocalyptic Imagination to Undercut MultiEarth Dominance

The primary reason that apocalyptic descriptions can be so effective in undercutting MultiEarth dominance is that they emerge from below the surface of that dominance. Apocalyptic descriptions challenge the official messaging by which nations and corporations zealously control the conversation and promote the story they want their audience to believe. Now that Earth's insurgency has intensified to apocalyptic proportions, message-control by corporations, governments, and media becomes ever more difficult. Earth's apocalyptic events burst the confines of controlled messaging and the apocalyptic genre becomes an ideal vehicle for describing them accurately.

Two strong examples of how apocalyptic imagination have undercut the dominant powers in the past come from the Bible: the New Testament book of *Revelation* (1st century CE) and the Old Testament book of *Daniel* (2nd century BCE). Both of these examples show the dual power of apocalyptic revelation—its excellent ability to describe civilization's breakdown as well as its inspiring ability to see the new Creation emerging. The authors of *Revelation* and *Daniel* spoke to their audiences with highly dramatic symbols that came to them while in meditative, altered states of mind. Both authors had learned how to access the world of the unconscious and invite its energies and entities to manifest in images. Their practice of mindful, visual prayer is a form of what Jung called "active imagination." Through its use, the Self opens to Divine Consciousness.[162]

With their imaginations in full bloom, and open to the Divine Spirit mediated through their altered states of consciousness, the authors of *Daniel* and *Revelation* broke through imperial double-speak and spin. They sought to encourage everyone who wanted to live an Earth-size paradigm amid MultiEarth empires. Daniel encouraged resistance against the Hellenistic empire; John wrote *Revelation* to encourage alternatives to the Roman empire. Their images of monsters ruling the world portrayed the pain inflicted ruthlessly by sociopathic people and oppressive, feelingless struc-tures—monstrous behaviors of imperial governments and eco-nomics. They wanted to give people images able to express primal emotions against the MultiEarth oppressions too horrific for civil words.

But apocalypticism doesn't stop there. Daniel and John went on to describe powers at work that were greater than those of Hellenism and Rome. Painting from a colorful palette, they described an Almighty One, a cosmic Sovereign, and a truly Human One—all wild and uncontrolled by empires with their dominating systems. The author of the biblical *Revelation* presents the "One on the throne" as surrounded by a devoted, musical, and cosmolog-ical entourage who continually break into primal and transcend-ing exultations affirming that no power of civilization is greater than "the One," and no story is greater than the cosmological story which "the One" inhabits.

These apocalyptic authors show a consciousness that the sto-ries of the cultures they live in do not have. The stories of *Revelation* and *Daniel* breakout beyond the limiting stories of imperialism to remind us of our evolutionary purpose, our Great Work, and the heroic journey to full humanness. Through apocalyptic writing, they unveil reasons for love and hope that tie to the story of the Cosmos, not the story of civilization.

The writings in *Daniel* and *Revelation* have an irrationality that is antithetical to empire's rational, bureaucratic releases. The apocalytpic symbols fly into the hearts of those resisting empires, bearing encouragement to remain strong and faithful. They call to all fence-sitters to throw themselves into the cause of living in accordance with the Spirit of the One, the Almighty. The apocalyptic writings do not defeat empire through strength as MultiEarth thinks of strength. Instead, they undercut empire with powers from the MultiEarth's own underworld brought to the surface through imagination.

In these two apocalyptic stories the Great Story does not get told by civilization's superpowers. The Great Story revolves around One called "Ancient of Days," a mysterious Presence older than time who is also the Creator of the New Heaven and New Earth, the buds of which apocalyptists, past and present, see functioning in greater topographies of consciousness. This New Creation is not the next empire, but the peaceable, shalom community of all Earth's inhabitants, a community that only the greater topography of spiritual, cosmic consciousness has the dimension and maturity to embrace. This New Creation—then, now, or anytime—is the result of both the Great Work of consciously maturing humans and the unquenchable evolutionary processes of Earth. Both express the incarnate and transcendent nameless One.

Using your own apocalyptic "eye," imagine the New Creation as a grand, inclusive commons of the planet, with all inhabitants living in peaceable wellbeing and economic democracy. It is not utopian, as MultiEarth alternatives are. The New Creation is the dream of Earth. It is inherent in the DNA of the planet and the consciousness of Self to move toward such Creation, what Berry called the Ecozoic Era. By imagining that Era, we add a way of knowing to our repertoire that helps us live toward the archetypal Garden, and, with the capacities of greater consciousness, give shape to OneEarth living.

Avatar: A Movie Mimicking Current Apocalypse

In 2009, *Avatar,* the epic science fiction film written and directed by James Cameron, gave us an example of apocalyptic imagination breaking through MultiEarth's entrancement. *Avatar's* high drama positions Earth and the Wild as a counter story to civilization and technology. Their economies clash, as do their views of Nature, humanness, the sacred, Indigenous peoples, technology—all that comprises a paradigm to live by.

The plot of *Avatar* imagines us in the 22nd century and takes us to Pandora, a moon in the Alpha Centauri star system. With this science fiction leap, the movie gets in our face about the dramatic struggle happening today between the MultiEarth and OneEarth ways of living—to put it in the language of this book. In the movie, those who have been shaped by the story of civilization regard their story as the ONLY way, and feel sure they are advanced beyond all other models for living well. They proceed with superior science, futuristic technologies, and shockingly dehumanized consciousness. The year is 2154, and natural resources on Earth have been depleted. Humans seek a valuable, rare mineral, aptly named unobtanium, which they have discovered under the soils of Pandora where the Indigenous Na'vi people live.

Intending to land in force on Pandora and mine the mineral with an armada of technology, the civilizers regard the Na'vi as relics of the past, an irrelevant, inconvenient obstacle to civilization's Progress and modernization. The Na'vi live intimately connected with their natural world. Their deity lives throughout Pandora's Nature and is intimately experienced there. The civilized people from Earth reveal personal and systemic antagonism to the Na'vi and their OneEarth living. In tragic irony, their ruthless and savage aggression proceeds in the name of being "civilized" and devoted to Progress. In stark contrast, the Na'vi respond out of their love for the Nature of Pandora. It is mutual love. Pandora's natural world loves them as well. It is this love, strong as a rushing stream, that arouses opposition to the invaders.

Pandora's invaders mimic the mythology that shapes MultiEarth life on planet Earth. Human civilization has become so separated and so alienated from the realities of evolutionary Creation that it regards the Wild as nothing more than a source for materials that have commodity value. People whose worldview is shaped by Creation are seen as special interests, environmentalists, a step behind, or anti-business. They are nuisances to be pushed aside—bulldozed along with the trees, animals, and streams that stand in their way.

But the commodifiers of Nature, whether in *Avatar* or on Earth, have not fully comprehended its Wildness. The invading techno-armada of civilization believes it has superseded the powers of the Wild and can overrun the Na'vi. But Pandora's Wild is interconnected by deeper realities than such rational thought discerns. The Na'vi, functioning with greater consciousness, plug into the Wild and resist the civilizers. The Wild is aroused to action and, with full mythic capacities, the Na'vi and the Wild defeat the techno-armada. The devotion of the Na'vi to their deity and Nature proves wiser than the civilizers' belief in technology and a worldview intent on using Nature for their ends. The precious element unobtanium remains unobtainable. Though the Na'vi suffer losses from the clash, their worldview proves to be more aligned with the powers of the natural order. The outcome of *Avatar* reaffirms that civilization's story is a kind of parenthesis contained within Earth's transcending story of evolutionary Creation.

A subplot in *Avatar* portrays the heroic journey of Jake, a leading character sent to Pandora by the civilizers to gather intelligence on the landscape and the Na'vi inhabitants. Jake becomes attracted to the ways of the Na'vi, and soon senses that there's far more to the Na'vi than what his technological colleagues and he had thought. He's enchanted by the profound connection the Na'vi have with their forest and land. The influence of one of the Na'vi females, Neytiri, mentors him to see what his science-trained eyes had been missing. The key indicator of his transformation is when he can *see* what he was blind to as a civilizer. The adversarial attitude toward the Na'vi and Pandora with which Jake began his mission, changes to love once he sees with the same consciousness with which the Na'vi see. Jake's conversion is consummated when he looks at Neytiri and says the poignant and simple words, "I see you." His new and greater consciousness gives him the capacity to plug into Pandora's natural order and wild powers. As a new, naturalized male, Jake joins the Na'vi to battle against the civilizers when their technologically sophisticated armada arrives to take over Pandora.

The battle that ensues is apocalyptic. Two worldviews clash. Technology clashes with the Wild. Civilization breaks down and Creation breaks through. The suffering, loss, heroism, and transformation that happen reveal how dangerous the ego consciousness of civilization is—how incapable it is of seeing that there are greater topographies of consciousness from which to think, act, and live.

Becoming Seers—Imagining Our Way to the New

Fittingly, the name, Na'vi, is Hebrew for "prophet" or "seer"—a significant subtlety not revealed in the movie. Like the shamans of Indigenous peoples everywhere, Hebrew seers develop skill in using their imagining eye. With that skill, they see beyond the vision of ego consciousness—an ability often mistaken for predicting the future. Seers value the images that rise from the underworld, whereas ego consciousness can't make sense of them and dismisses them. Once we recognize that these images hold meaning of a different and often greater kind than rational thinking can decipher, we are on the way to developing our seer abilities.

The Little Prince, first published in 1943, is a classic for seers. French aristocrat, poet, and author, Antoine de St. Exupery (1900–1944), wrote this masterpiece after the ordeal of fleeing France for the U.S. just before France fell in World War II. It continues to be one of the world's top sellers. In this adult fable, which cleverly maintains a children's style, a fox points out to the Little Prince (who has fallen to Earth from an asteroid) some of

the strange ways adults think and behave. The best known teaching
of the fox has to do with seeing. "It is only with the heart that one
can see rightly," says the fox. "What is essential is invisible to the
eye." His own life torn up by war, St. Exupery wrote a corrective
to a warring civilization which was lopsided with empirical knowledge, science, and technologies. He ached with the knowledge that
imagination could have made peace when, instead, reason argued
for war—the very hell that sent him scurrying out of his home and
homeland. That hell killed tens of thousands and culminated with
the first ever atomic bombs dropped on two Japanese cities.

St. Exupery saw that we could not transcend war with ego consciousness and rational thought, but that we could do so through
images from the unconscious that transcend war's arguments.
Two centuries before *The Little Prince*, another seer, English poet
William Blake (1757–1827) spoke to this same power of imagination: "Imagination denied, war governed the nations."[163] Blake
saw how devaluing imagination keeps us from committing to the
images that call out our greater capacities for the arduous work of
making peace. Without imagination, we are left with the apocalyptic breakdown that war delivers on people, species, landscapes, and
societies. And despite claims and rational arguments that fighting
a certain war will end wars and violence, no such war has been
discovered. By treating the knowledge garnered from imagination
on par with, or more valuable than, the knowledge of reason, and
integrating the two, we discover and live the images that make for
peace amid conflicts.

The role imagination plays in transcending civilization's
wars is also its role in transcending MultiEarth civilization. Once
the heroic journey brings us to where we trust our imaginations
enough to see OneEarth possibilities, and to see them as viable in
the face of the challenges, then we can live those possibilities—not
perfectly, but faithfully. It is not reason's forte to see the possibilities that are outside of the current frame of consciousness, but
imagination's. It is most important, therefore, to regard imagination
as another primary way of knowing. Imagination and reason are,

then, two poles in an integral epistemology. Once our imaginations give us a new OneEarth frame in which to see the world, then our reason can work within that new frame to help us go beyond the MultiEarth experiences of the past. To do so is the apocalyptic breakthrough we need to keep Earth livable.

The Spiritual Nature of Apocalyptic Seeing: Unity of Dualisms

Apocalyptic breakdown includes violent clashes between the dualisms into which smaller topographies of consciousness see the world divided. Apocalyptic seeing unveils deeper and transcendent unity. It

- reveals to us deeper understandings of dominating powers that we hadn't seen before, understandings that undercut their authority;
- connects us with imagination as a way of knowing in addition to and beyond rational knowing;
- unveils a viable Earth-size alternative to ego's Civilization Project; and
- reveals that, as new humans centered in Self (with ego in a supporting role), we are capable of living in the OneEarth, interdependent community of life.

All of these actions of apocalyptic seeing have a transcending quality, transcending ego and civilization polarities while incorporating them. The actions connect us with a greater, animated whole, which is to say, with a spiritual way of being in the Universe.

A word of caution and clarification needs to accompany all promotions of imagination. A major reason for imagination's effectiveness is that many of its images are expressions of archetypes. The primal, spiritual nature of archetypes, when they are misunderstood, can bring havoc, chaos, crime, war, and death to the world. The violence of mass killings, suicide bombings, and terrorist wars so ubiquitous in today's news are examples. So, also are many of the tyrant-weakling behaviors discussed earlier (Chapter Four). The images that rise from the archetypes are far too often taken as guidance for literal action—a tragic misunderstanding of the symbolic language of imagination. Pathological, psychopathic, and sociopathic behaviors result and can happen even in people who we generally regard as emotionally healthy. People with certain mental illnesses have to take extra precautions regarding the powers of the unconscious. As already stated, our egos inflate or withdraw when they function within the overwhelming energies of the archetypes. To understand and use the symbolic language of imagination as responsible seers requires getting far enough along on the heroic journey that we operate in larger topographies of consciousness—topographies where the capacities and humility able to work with powerful archetypal images prevails. In smaller topographies of consciousness, people who claim to be seers may also have access to the archetypal energies and may make spiritual claims based on that access, but they cannot be trusted to work with them responsibly. The best way to protect against the horrific evil arising from mishandling of apocalyptic seeing is to access the spiritual nature of archetypes within a community in the greater topography of Spiritual Consciousness—a topography that will be more fully described in the next chapter.

Not surprisingly, "seeing" figures prominently in the scriptures of all religions as a metaphor to speak of lesser or greater consciousness. To be blind is to operate from smaller topographies of consciousness. To heal blindness, though sometimes referring to physically seeing, most often refers to becoming more conscious, to see what had been invisible.

Seeing is central in the ancient myth of Eden. It's core question asks: are Eve's and Adam's eyes truly "open?" In which paradigm or topography of consciousness were they functioning? After the serpent asked Eve and Adam whether they were allowed to eat of all the fruit of the Garden, they said, "Yes, with one exception: the Tree of Knowledge of Good and Evil in the middle of the Garden is off limits. If we eat from it, we will die."

"Seeing" as Consciousness in
Scriptures of World Religions

The truth has come, and falsehood has vanished away. Surely falsehood is ever certain to vanish. —Qur'an 17.85

The holy Preceptor by the Word lighted a lamp;
Thereby was shattered darkness of the temple of the self,
And the unique chamber of jewels thrown open.
Wonderstruck were we in extreme on beholding it—
It's greatness beyond expression.
                —Sikhism, Adi Granth, Bilaval, M.5, p.821

The Atman is the light: the light is covered by darkness; this darkness is delusion; that is why we dream. When the light of Atman drives out our darkness, that light shines forth from us; A sun in splendor, the revealed Brahman.
                —Hinuduism, Bhagavad Gita 5.15–16

I am blind and do not see the things of this world; but when the light comes from above, it enlightens my heart and I can see, for the Eye of my heart sees everything; and through this vision I can help my people. The heart is a sanctuary at the center of which there is a little space, wherein the Great Spirit dwells, and this is the Eye. This is the Eye of the Great Spirit by which He sees all things, and through which we see Him. If the heart is not pure, the Great Spirit cannot be seen.   —Black Elk, Sioux Tradition

The Self within the heart is like a boundary which divides the world from That. Day and night cross not that boundary, not old age, nor death; neither grief nor pleasure, neither good nor evil deeds. All evil shuns That. For That is free from impurity; by impurity can it never be touched. Wherefore he who has crossed that boundary, and has realized the Self, if he is bland, ceases to be blind; if he is wounded, ceases to be wounded; if he is afflicted, ceases to

be afflicted. When that boundary is crossed night becomes day; for the world of Brahman is light itself.
—Hinduism. Chandogya Upanishad 4.1–2

Perfect knowledge is attained on the destruction of deluding karmas, of karmas which obscure knowledge and perception, and of karmas which obstruct faith. With the absence of the cause of bondage, the annihilation of all karmas is liberation.   —Jainism. Tattvarthasutra 10.1–2
[note: Karma (Sanskrit), translated in English is "Action."]

To know the eternal is called enlightenment. Not to know the eternal is to act blindly to result in disaster. He who knows the eternal is all-embracing. Being all-embracing, he is impartial. Being impartial, he is kingly [universal]. Being kingly, he is one with Nature. Being one with nature, he is in accord with Tao. Being in accord with Tao, he is everlasting. And is free from danger throughout his lifetime.
—Taoism. Tao Te Ching 16

But the serpent wasn't so sure. He surmised that if they ate from it, the magical powers of the fruit would make them like God, giving them the power to discern good from its complicated entanglement with evil. The serpent assured them that if they ate from this tree, they would not suddenly die. Instead, their eyes would still be open. Indeed, their eyes would be more open than before, because they would see the world differently. As it turns out, what they saw was a world divided into competing dualisms. The knowledge of good and evil was just the start of seeing the world in polarities.

How insightfully this myth conveys that MultiEarth civilization, functioning in ego consciousness, tries to make sense of the world by seeing it in terms of good and evil, matter and spirit, body and soul, us and them, friends and enemies, systems and individuals, women and men, environment and economics, and on and on. That greater consciousness that is able to hold the dualisms in a larger, regenerative unity is lost. But we can regain that power by becoming new creatures centered in Self. Then the inner eye of the heart, that is, greater consciousness, can see the transcending unity within which dualisms function. The dualisms can then energize the unity of OneEarth thinking and living. In Earth-size, Spiritual Consciousness, we see the interdependent whole—the yin and yang energies of all the dualisms fuel regenerative interactivity to keep Earth livable.

One of Jesus' distinguishing characteristics was how he worked with dualisms such as rich-poor, male-female, empire-Creation, and Human-Divine. The Human-Divine dualism came up when he was asked about where his powers came from, when he explained his relationship with God, or when he urged others to claim their capacities in union with God and stop setting him apart. In ego consciousness, the Human and Divine are seen as poles apart. But not so in Self consciousness. To cross the bridge from psychological language to religious language, "Self" can be understood as equivalent to important meanings of "Messiah" and "Christ" in Judaism and Christianity. Apart from when the Greek word "Christ," or its Hebrew equivalent "Messiah," are used as proper nouns, they mean "anointed" or "smeared." These words were used to talk about how the Divine is present within Human lives, relationships, and activities. To be "christed" or "christened" means that you have the capacities for a consciousness that is smeared or anointed with the Divine. It's metaphorical language to describe a consciousness in which the Divine and Human are not poles apart but smeared together. Religious rituals involving anointing with perfumed oils or water enact ritually what people profess to believe about that person, or possibly even see in them with their inner or third eye— which is that the Divine and the Human are one in this person and must not be polarized but treated as a regenerating whole.

Because Jesus developed the abilities to speak and live from this consciousness with such fullness, "Christ" came to be used freely by his followers as a proper noun and name for him. Jesus, on the other hand, hardly used it at all to define himself. He much preferred the phrase "son of man," a term emphasizing a consciousness of being fully Human. Why? Because Jesus recognized that people were struggling to be Human in the face of acute dehumanization by Rome's imperial control of people. Furthermore, the Temple's religion, rather than being a source of Human strength amid imperial rule, had developed rules and teachings which further dehumanized people—especially people at the low end of the social hierarchy. So Jesus made being fully Human a cornerstone in how he urged people into larger topographies of consciousness and fullness of life. Developing the Human, he believed, also developed Divine consciousness, bringing about oneness of Human and Divine in people. He greatly desired to see people develop a union of the Divine-Human dualism for themselves—a point often missed when Jesus, the Christ, is elevated into an extraordinary person. To be more true to his own intent, consider him a model of ordinary persons who move into the consciousness where the Human and Divine join in a dynamic, deeper unity.

After Jesus was gone, his followers began to speak of being "in Christ" as a way of expressing the Christ or Divine-Human consciousness in our lives. The alternative is to live in ego consciousness. Moving into Christ involves what I have described earlier as shifting our identities from our ego center to the greater Self. This Great Work of psycho-spiritual development moves us toward our fullest capacities as the Human. We become able to live divinely interdependent with all Creation. When Jesus spoke of "Messiah," he rejected the cultural ideas of the term associated with political leadership. He made that point several times. Once he held up a lily that had grown as a wildflower in the field. He said that to be Messiah meant being able to see more glory in that wildflower than what could be seen in Solomon (referring to Israel's great and infamous monarch whom the Jews expected a political messiah to emulate). Jesus further taught that developing this ability to see with the third eye required losing our life in order to save it. Or, in the language of this book, losing our lives as shaped by our egos in order that we might save life through the enlightenment of the greater Self, or the Messiah consciousness.

Some spiritual communities, including those of Eastern Christian expressions, call this intentional, ongoing process of moving toward greater consciousness "divinization." They understand the shifting of identity from ego to Self as a journey that includes dying and living again, a version of shedding the skin of one identity for a new one, or of metamorphosing from an earlier form into a more developed one. The strong idea shining out of "divinization" is that becoming more fully Human cannot be separated from becoming more Divine. Unpacking our Human-Divine capacities carries out our evolutionary purpose. When we see and experience the Human-Divine unity, we can also see the Divine-Creation unity, that is, we see the Divine in all species and things and all species and things in the Divine. We no longer see our species as dualistically separate from other species but as integral to the unifying processes of Earth. Any strong lines we've drawn between Human and Divine, or material and spiritual, become perforated; the two dance together in a dynamic wholeness able to generate the changes Earth calls us to make.

Another religious story, the story of the Buddha, evolves from the experience of Siddhartha Guatama, whose capacities to use his third eye blossomed while sitting under a Bodhi tree following a long search for truth. The word "buddha" in Sanskrit, the classical language of India and the liturgical language of Hinduism, Buddhism, and Janism, translates as "to see," or "awake." Siddhartha became Buddha as he came to an enlightened consciousness that allowed him to see the oneness of the world—a vastly different view from the dualistic vision that he learned in the MultiEarth civilization of his time and culture had. The idea is not to set Siddhartha Buddha apart from the rest of us, but for us all "to see" and be "awake," i.e., to be "buddha."

These examples from Judaism, Christianity, and Buddhism illustrate how religions value seeing with the third eye. Each religious expression brings its own nuances; all contribute descriptions of enlightenment, of moving through the ordeal of ego "death" to being a new human with an ego-transcending center that connects to divine consciousness. Because this transforming mystery is beyond rational explanation, the language religions use can sound excessive to the rational mind, or not as deserving as "factual" information. The experiences described can also seem unattainable except for a few.

The key to gaining an appreciation for these experiences has to do with topographies of consciousness. The smaller topographies of ego consciousness literalize and otherwise distort ego-transcending experiences. Cultural and Spiritual Consciousness, able to use the third eye of imaginative seeing, appreciate that these experiences are less about exceptional attainment and more about being on the heroic journey. When we stay on the journey, we move to Self consciousness and use imagination's ways of knowing. Doing so inevitably connects us with greater capabilities. What we could not do in a civilization shaped by egos we can do in the OneEarth topographies shaped by Self and Creation. The greater capabilities that emerge for us in greater topographies of consciousness make possible radical changes. These basic changes in how we see things show us ways through crises where our egos could see only the closing down and caving in of things.

Currently, with Earth's insurgency responding to ecological crises generated by MultiEarth living, there's an urgency for broad and capable use of the third eye both in general imagination and in apocalyptic analysis. We need to see clearly which dualistic clashes are destroying Earth's inhabitability. Mistaken diagnoses only add to the chaos of who's clashing with whom. When the topography of consciousness we are in thinks dualistically, there's no guarantee that we correctly identify the actual dualisms of a conflict. As an example, blaming migrant farmworkers and service people for the loss of jobs in the U.S. doesn't come close to understanding or identifying the dualisms that energize the larger globalized economy. In Cultural and Spiritual Consciousness we are able to see more correctly which dualisms are the actual source of particular struggles. Plus, with the third eye of imagination, we see how the energies of that dualism are part of a greater unity. Apocalyptic seeing unveils dualisms accurately and finds the openings in Earth's open-ended processes.

Hope and Expectations During Apocalypse

As Earth pursues the Ecozoic Era, humans are the holdouts. But we are also creative centers of unquantifiable energy and potential for moving into Ecozoic living. This paradox puts us in a fingernail-biting race with time as to whether the scale of paradigm conversion that's needed will happen. If we do not miss the moment, the result will be wide conversion to new life as MultiEarth civilization fails and OneEarth living, already vibrant but suppressed, emerges.

Naturally, civilization works to suppress any forces of apocalypse that would be its undoing. Though suppression may delay full-scale apocalypse, it ultimately intensifies the events that will see the demise of the Civilization Project. In this sense, suppressing the apocalyptic undoing of civilization is analogous to suppressing wildfires in an old forest. The combustible material in the forest builds because the natural, intermittent fires that would clean it out for new growth are being suppressed. Finally, a fire ignites that burns so intensely with all the fuel on the forest floor that it breaks through all efforts to suppress it and burns what the many suppressed fires did not. Only then can the forest regenerate with a spectrum of post-fire species.

Apocalyptic events are that fire. They move across Earth bringing death to MultiEarth's civilizing ways that continue trying to suppress the Earth-size ways. Civilization is only capable of creating new empires, new world orders, and doing so on its own MultiEarth terms. Earth and Self have the extraordinary capacity to co-create a new Earth and a new human, shifting us into a new OneEarth story.

Living the OneEarth story and economy does not allow us to escape the apocalyptic events of the 21st century. All of us get carried into the tribulation of the struggle, even death, along with all other species and life-systems of the planet. At the same time, apocalyptic seeing finds the breakthroughs beyond the out-of-date structures of MultiEarth living as they break down. The new emerges both from and beside the death of the former. The *breakdown* of civilization proceeds with apocalyptic shaking of its foundations and beliefs, a drama with trauma and death; the *breakthrough* of this apocalypse happens as all who've come to Earth-size consciousness make possible the new life with Earth-size foundations and beliefs that see the unity inherent in polarities.

Vaclav Havel, who spoke to the U.S. Congress in 1990, about a necessary revolution of consciousness (see "Conclusion" of Chapter 3), was a Czech playwright, essayist, poet, dissident and politician active during a time when his country was shifting from a Communist government to a democracy with a market economy. To his surprise, he became the tenth and last President of Czechoslovakia (1989–92) and the first President of the Czech Republic (1993–2003). He spoke often about hope in ways that resonate with apocalyptic seeing amid Earth's manifold crises today. What does it mean to live with hope in our current situation?

> Hope is definitely not the same thing as optimism. It is not the conviction that something will turn out well, but the certainty that something makes sense, regardless of how it turns out. Hope, in this deep and powerful sense, is not the same as joy that things are going well, or willingness to invest in enterprises that are obviously heading for success, but rather an ability to work for something because it is good.[164]

Working for success in MultiEarth civilization differs sharply from working for what OneEarth thinking sees as good. When we work for success in MultiEarth civilization the rewards are whatever civilization offers. As the apocalyptic breakdown of civilization continues, the rewards civilization confers lose value like a descending stock market. But when we work for the good of Earth's community, we are pulled along by hope. What we do makes sense, regardless of how it turns out, because it is part of the apocalyptic breakthrough to new Creation. That is not the same as saying "everything will be all right after all." It is rather a conviction, an expression of faith that transcends my own wellbeing and transcends all that I currently understand about the world. It is an expression of faith that a new Creation is underway and that we are called to be co-creators. Our link to it in any moment is to do love, justice, and good—all acts deepened to transformative levels by living in a topography of Spiritual Consciousness.

Conclusion: What Apocalypse Reveals

Apocalypse uncovers extremes where civilizers try to keep the lid on. Weather extremes disrupt and kill. Extremists defy governments. Volatile stock markets and vulnerable investments drive fears of the next economic collapse. But apocalypse also draws back the veil on innovations of entrepreneurs with the consciousness to work at Earth's scale.

In 1996, I was given a shocking health diagnosis. I had two cancers simultaneously: the right testicle and the right kidney. Aggressive damage was underway in my body and I could not wind back the clock to undo it. Both of these tumors were on course to grow, grow, grow until they killed me. I was their unwilling host. I had lost control of my health. How was I to live while I awaited surgery and all the treatments and trauma that would happen after? What is more, Juanita and I had been married for only a month. How was she to live during those days? Radical intervention was the only path for me, but just what that would require of us was disturbingly uncertain.

MultiEarth living has brought us to a similar moment in the health of our planet. Earth is our host, but MultiEarth civilization lives the myth that if "you aren't growing you're dying." MultiEarth's economy continues its hell-bent tilt to "grow, grow, grow," even when Earth's immune system is overwhelmed. Either we will make the radical intervention needed to save ourselves or Earth will intensify her current intervention, end the Anthropocene's MultiEarth civilization, and move on. The 21st century is apocalyptic—not that it will become apocalyptic by midcentury, but that it's been so from the start as the apocalyptic tendencies of the 20th century balloon. Saying so is not being dramatic or exaggerated; it's just choosing an accurate word to describe what civilization has habitually understated.

Continuing with the analogy of my personal health, surgery removed my testicle, kidney, and thirty-plus lymph nodes. I am alive today only because chemotherapy is especially effective with testicular cancer and because the kidney tumor was still encapsulated. At one point, my surgeon, James Giblin, M.D., after explaining there were no guarantees of successful surgery, encouraged me wryly, "Lee, I think you'll have to find something else to die from." He could see through to an outcome that I could not—an analogy to apocalyptic imagination which can see not only the breakdown of what is but beyond it to the breakthrough of the new.

The kind of imagination involved in apocalyptic imagination differs from "Oh, you're just imagining that." Apocalyptic imagination is not making up something, but a process of discovery and coming to knowledge that differs from empirical observation and rational deduction. The cancer of MultiEarth living has moved into apocalyptic proportions. Some devastations can't be undone, even as they continue. Earth strains. The Civilization Project cannot outlive the sixth mass extinction based on current trends. But in this traumatic situation, the knowledge that comes through imagination envisions different frames in which to arrange data, possibilities not revealed by observation or deduction.

This seeing below the surface and beyond the seen or observable distinguishes imagination. Apocalyptic imagination is a species of imagination focused especially in the intense kinds of breakdown underway in the macro-changes on our planet and a human civilization in greater imbalance than ego consciousness can see.

In the function of imaginative knowing, and seeing the invisible with the third eye, that which is called spiritual especially impinges on us. In particular, the polarities so visible and operative in smaller topographies of consciousness become parts of a larger unity in larger topographies where polarities operate within a transcending unity. This transcendent experience happens anytime we identify with Self as our center and ego is brought into the role for which it is intended. The human pole is joined by the divine pole in more experiences of One. Working with an interdependent unity in which polarities are consciously seen as interacting parts is the forte of greater topographies of consciousness. Love is the experience of polarities resolving in deeper or transcending union. Consequently, love is pandemic in the greater topographies of consciousness necessary for OneEarth choices. Apocalypticism helps us live with that unity not only as a viable vision of the future, but also as a highly useful, loving way to work with the polarizing events of the present. Apocalyptic imagination grows the conviction in us that OneEarth living is plausible at a scale to reconfigure the world. It's the kind of revelation we need. Do we not all need more of the consciousness in which the results of such imagination are unveiled?

Ponder, Discuss, and Act

1. Respond to Robert Jensen's perspective that we are all "apocalyptic now."

2. What are your thoughts on Einstein's conviction that "imagination is more important than knowledge?"

3. Do you consider imagination, empirical observation, and reason to be balanced in your life? If so, what influences, either internal or external, brought that balance about? On the other hand, if you feel that you are out of balance, how do you think you got that way?

4. Which of the statements from religion that describe "becoming seers" or "seeing with the third eye" resonate most with you?

5. How can use of the apocalyptic genre help our communication about extremes?

6. Which polarities especially challenge you? What is a deeper or transcending structure in which they contribute to a larger One?

CHAPTER TWELVE

Arriving Home: Living OneEarth Consciousness During Civilization's Unraveling

The three phases of this journey—departure, struggle, return—are a metaphor for what happens in us as we evolve from neurotic ego through healthy ego to the spiritual Self. The neurotic ego insists on staying in control and fears the emergence of the Self which says yes to 'what is.' The ego's fear of the Self is conditionality fearing unconditionality. Ironically, this is fear of fearlessness! How the ego can sabotage our integration again and again![165] —David Richo

Sometimes the hero returns and her world does not want what she brings. Her old community finds it difficult to use what she brought back, "it doesn't know how to receive it" (quoting Joseph Campbell, The Power of Myth, 141). Apart from difficulties of the hero sharing her boon with her world, she also must come to grips with being a transfigured being in a world that is not. She walks in both worlds. "Freedom to pass back and forth across the world division… [and] not contaminating the principles of the one with those of the other, yet permitting the mind to know the one by virtue of the other—is the talent of the master." (p. 229). She is a master of two worlds.[166] —William Hart

The urgent challenge to protect our common home includes a concern to bring the whole human family together to seek a sustainable and

integral development, for we know that things can change.... Humanity still has the ability to work together in building our common home.
—Pope Francis, *Laudato Si'*, 2015

Our heroic journey takes us home—our OneEarth home that is. It is a home of consciousness that feels deepening love for our planetary home. It is the home a new, greater consciousness builds amid the unraveling of the civilization built by former, smaller consciousness. We arrive in what one of our maps (see Chapter Eight) calls Spiritual Consciousness. We could not have arrived in this topography without the changes that the heroic journey brought about in us; nor can we live in this topography without continuing to make real those changes. Important changes resulting from the journey include:

- Our minds have changed—we think and imagine primarily in a OneEarth paradigm.
- Our identities have changed—we've moved out of ego to Self as primary.
- We have capabilities for OneEarth living we didn't have before.
- We have added imagination as a way of knowing alongside empirical observation and rational thinking; our ability to see through what is to what can be and must be is increased.
- Our hearts love what our imaginations tell us can be; we are drawn with all our hearts to make real the images rising from the unconscious, embracing them as symbols and myths to live by.
- We live with a sense of the sacred in all that is and throughout our activities; we have a sense of transcending where we've been.
- We distrust ego's and civilization's rejection of the underworld, and respect it as a vast world that is home to resources we need for OneEarth living. We also respect it as a world of powers beyond what our ego can handle.

- We live with a continuing sense of Call to our Great Work to keep Earth livable amid civilization's advancing apocalyptic breakdown.

This chapter is about how we live these changes that have remade us into different people with greater capabilities. It is about living on Earth, our planetary home, a consciousness she's been yearning for us to make real for her. Not to be overlooked is how the great power of love works, tough and tender, animating politics, economics, art, education, households—whatever activities of society and life that keep Earth's community of life viable.

When Spiritual Consciousness Is Home

Living in Spiritual Consciousness evokes the relief and satisfaction of arriving home after completing a hard trek. But shortly, disconcerting feelings arise whenever our greater consciousness encounters life being lived captive to smaller consciousness. Living in two different worlds, we feel the tugging, even the animosity between them. We know we've left the consciousness of MultiEarth civilization, but it's still ongoing. We understand ourselves to live in a community with all species, but around us much of daily life stays focused on individuality and humans only. We know our ego has undergone humiliation and changed from wanting to run the show to being Self's assistant—a healing and right-sizing of the ego to be sure—but around us, egos that make civilization tick continue. Re-identified from ego to Self, we continue to explore the underworld, but ego-living in civilization continues to suppress it.

Looking again at the maps in Chapter Eight, we know we've moved into new topographies and the Self consciousness with which we are to live. Jung's map gives us a picture that assures us of greater powers once our identity undergoes metamorphosis from ego control to the Self. Self is positioned to interface with the underworld and see polarities within a greater One, giving us a new identity. Ego helps out by adding some rational thought to the images and energies Self pursues and receives. Self has the lead role and ego a supporting one. Korten's map in the same chapter gives us a picture of several topographies of consciousness, a sequence we move through en route to Spiritual Consciousness. Our Self is restless until it arrives there; our egos can't handle it except in a supporting act.

My belief is that we can live primarily in the topography of Spiritual Consciousness because we are now bonded with other species and a Divine Presence as the One in every polarity and the animating mystery in every process of interdependence. This consciousness makes possible such actions as shaping OneEarth societies. Making our home in this topography of consciousness—not just visiting it, but living there as our ongoing residence—is essential to reshaping life on our planet to OneEarth ways.

Life in the Topography of Spiritual Consciousness

Arriving home is not arriving at perfection. It's arriving in a consciousness where our fuller humanness is constantly called forth in "good enough" ways to achieve OneEarth living. In the topography of Spiritual Consciousness we live with an expectation that we will fulfill the evolutionary processes for our species. Neither more, nor less. We are expected to function with a kind of consciousness other species don't have. It may or may not be greater or better, but it's different, necessary, and wanted. We are to pursue that consciousness, and we are to receive it as it comes toward us. Earth and the entire community of life count on us. The topography of Spiritual Consciousness does not seek ideal standards of living but a community of life to which we bond in interdependent processes—that life which our planet is so miraculously equipped to bring forth.

Arriving "home" in Spiritual Consciousness integrates us tighter in thought, being, and action with Earth. Living in this topography as thoroughly as we can during the prolonged sunset of the Civilization Project involves us in recurring experiences of the themes and mythic elements that comprise the journey itself.

They can look a little different from how they did on the journey itself because of the vantage point Spiritual Consciousness gives us. The processes and symbols carry a charge that empowers the capabilities for which we've evolved as a species and which we've journeyed to achieve. They describe what living in Spiritual Consciousness looks like but what MultiEarth civilization doesn't call forth.

1. Living Interdependently, the OneEarth Treasure

The biggest difference for us as we take up living in the topography of Spiritual Consciousness is how thoroughly the treasure of interdependence with all of Creation's community of life affects our daily thought and action. Martin Luther King, Jr., is quoted as underscoring our interrelatedness during a 1967 Commencement Address at Oberlin College:

> All life is interrelated, and we are all caught in an inescapable network of mutuality, tied in a single garment of destiny. Whatever affects one directly, affects all indirectly. For some strange reason I can never be what I ought to be until you are what you ought to be. And you can never be what you ought to be until I am what I ought to be—this is the interrelated structure of reality.[167]

King went on to say that this interrelatedness is why nonviolence and peace work—two kinds of thinking and acting that do not happen successfully in ego consciousness where violence and war are relied upon to control MultiEarth civilization. But the results of the heroic journey, during which we metamorphose from a human of the ego to a human of the Self, make nonviolence and peacemaking a first response, not something we hope for. In Spiritual Consciousness, living interdependently transforms many ideas and behaviors that we'd previously thought of as ideals to daily practice. The normal procedure thinks and acts in terms of "all of us" instead of "me."

In a community of Spiritual Consciousness, we reinforce for one another that interdependent relationships are the Tao of the physical world. They are the locus of life's renewing energy. Disconnect from the Tao and we disconnect from what sustains us. Or to say it in the frame of process thought: reality is in the interdependent process we are part of more than in the physicality of that process. Our primary focus is on what happens among us and on aligning that with the processes of all of Creation. We live in the knowledge that we cannot do any one thing without triggering consequences elsewhere. Furthermore, we approach the ongoing processes of plants and animals as having intelligence; often it is intelligence that we do not have. So too with Earth's processes that MultiEarth thinking regards as inanimate. In Spiritual Consciousness we open to the animation of all things and the intelligence of the interactive processes that we see ourselves inside of. Since we are no longer superior to these intelligences or outside of these processes, we are far more attentive to them. Even when we can't understand them, we respect them enough to seek the best interaction with them that we can.

The world of Spiritual Consciousness is enchanted by a living Earth, our Self-directed souls, and the Spirit of One moving through the interactive, interdependent community of all life. We live eager to understand more of the interactive Creation we are in; at the same time we recognize that what we understand is a fraction of all that is happening, and that, even with rapidly expanding knowledge, we can know only a fraction, albeit perhaps a bigger one. Self lives with a humility about living within the whole of Creation that ego does not. Self feels the awe, wonder, and love. Self senses the sacredness of the interactivity and relishes this way of being beyond the enchantments that ego's Civilization Project offers. We see wealth as in the relationships and processes of Earth's community of life not in extraction from them. As a result we increase our sense of wealth by seeking the fullest possible participation of all who are impacted by a decision, including all the species and generations impacted by a decision.

All of these changes, many of them beyond our reach before the heroic journey, become possible and expected when we arrive home in Spiritual Consciousness. Living interdependently, interactively in the processes of Earth's living community tests the thoroughness of our passage from ego-humans to Self-humans and gives us daily opportunities to increase practical, holistic living in Earth's intra-activity.

2. The Vision and Actions that the Inner Garden Stirs

In Spiritual Consciousness symbols and myths renew what we make conscious in daily life in this topography. The primal image of a verdant Garden that lives within all of us archetypally is especially important to our Call to keep Earth livable. The Garden is an evolved, healthy ecosphere, local and planetary, which we aspire to and which Earth appears bent on evolving. In the consciousness of MultiEarth civilization, the Garden lives mostly in the underworld because egos and civilization have judged it too utopian to be practical. Any belief that this Garden is a deep, archetypal model of Earth's intent and human potentials frightens the bejesus out of egos and civilization which could never control its operations. But in Spiritual Consciousness, centered around the larger core of Self and a living Earth, the Garden is a profound symbol rising repeatedly from our souls. It animates our imagination and gives us a spectrum of images which motivate us to shape lives and societies of sustainable, interactive wellbeing. Eden, meaning "delight" in Hebrew, is one of the names for this Garden. Neither magical nor innocent, Eden throbs with numinous energy that motivates us to embody OneEarth ways in all we do, from food to finance, education to entertainment.

Eden is a symbol that lives in humans of all times and cultures, whatever its name. It manifests in art, how we tend ecospheres, and in the Wild everywhere. It guides what we manifest in Spiritual Consciousness because it eloquently symbolizes an ecological system in which balance and interdependence operate as regulators in a creational order. We long for Eden. We know intuitively that the greatest fulfillment for our species happens within that order. Even if we can't articulate it consciously, our unconscious knows that we need to be in a participatory and relational community of all of Earth's species and regulating processes to actualize our lives and the evolutionary purpose of our species in Earth's family of species.

Ego's MultiEarth civilization distances us from our inner Garden precisely because it lives in us so deeply and with such great power and potential that OneEarth lives and societies are what we shape when not distracted. Neither our souls nor the soul of society can be separated from this inner archetype. Only the consciousness of MultiEarth civilization believes that Eden is utopian and beyond our reach. In Spiritual Consciousness we know better. When Eden stirs, our imaginations bring to consciousness images of how to tend Creation; we know how to do what ego's MultiEarth civilization does not. We keep Earth livable.

3. Continuing Attention to *The Voice* that Calls

A most important voice in Spiritual Consciousness is the Voice that calls us to be full participants in the interactivity of Creation. Though we hear many voices tugging us in one direction or another, in Spiritual Consciousness we know to give special value to the Voice that Calls us to our fuller capacities. The Eden story recognizes this Voice as God calling to humanity (the word *adam* is a complex word that includes generic meanings such as "humanity," as well as gender specific usage[168]). In other words, the Divine calls not just to the prototypical, archetypal male, Adam, but also to the prototypical, archetypal Eve. And, if we treat the story like the myth it is, then that Voice calls out to all humanity across all centuries and cultures. None of us can escape this Voice. We may suppress it or deflect it with distractions and substitutes, but we hear it in our souls. We hear it speak to us through Earth's grandeur and pain, through the integral and hurting Earth community of life, and through the events and stillness of our interactive ways.

The Voice calls us out of topographies of lesser consciousness and into our Great Work. From within the topography of Spiritual

Consciousness the Voice and Call continue to guide our energies to reverse climate change, restore Earth's soils and waters, balance human population among the species, transcend nation-states with Earth-centered governance, imagine the world that the symbols in our souls tell us is possible, and recognize the sacred in all processes.

Such a Call might have paralyzed us in smaller topographies of consciousness, but not in Spiritual Consciousness. Though it still stretches us, we take to the Call because of what we've become part of and want more of. We want to be part of what Earth is doing and to experience that larger, sacred Presence in all the processes we undertake, all relationships in which we partner. We want to be part of the Call in action as we work amid the breakdown of civilization to make real the images of OneEarth living for which we and all of Creation yearn.

4. Handling Polarities as Sources of Unity beyond Division

The interplay of polarity and unity, dualism and oneness define cultures. Every culture has myths telling how these primal powers struggle against one another. Others tell of bringing forth a unity beyond the struggle. The Eden myth presents this great issue in the symbols of two trees, the Tree of the Knowledge of Good and Evil and the Tree of Life. The Tree of Life is a symbol valued across cultures as the center around which all that lives gathers. No matter how various species may struggle with one another, they come together in a peaceable kingdom around the Tree of Life. The tree is integrative whereas the Tree of the Knowledge of Good and Evil separates wholes into parts.

The Tree of the Knowledge of Good and Evil does not disappear from our inner Eden as we journey into greater topographies of consciousness. Dualistic thinking and the polarities of knowledge are primal powers that cannot be eradicated; the Self, however, sees how they are essential to the greater One. Whether symbolized as a tree or otherwise, they stay with us in Spiritual Consciousness. They grow lusciously and appear to give great power to understand life. But if we pursue them far, we soon leave the greater topography of Spiritual Consciousness, heading in the direction of ego consciousness. Seeing the world dualistically divides and separates what are actually integrative, interactive processes of a unified Nature and a single planet. When we divide the processes and relationships of Earth's interdependent community into good and evil, physical and spiritual, individualism and community, East and West, and science and religion—just to cite a few—without seeing them as two poles of a greater, regenerating whole, we have left the topography of Spiritual Consciousness. Seeing the world dualistically is not the problem. It is when we are unable to see it as two poles of the greater whole that we know we've slipped into egoistic consciousness. Spiritual Consciousness sees the One which the dualisms energize, though in smaller consciousness they appear to separate. Acting on that appearance of smaller consciousness keeps the world in crises of ecology, war, and disparity. Then ego has returned as central to our identity; we've turned from Self.

Because ego consciousness handles dualisms separately and divisively, not holistically, MultiEarth civilization cannot deal with the crises of climate change. Economics and business, for example, function with unnecessarily high antagonism toward the environment and ecospheres because of dualistic consciousness. Thinking dualistically prevents them from acting on the obvious: healthy ecospheres are prerequisites for the best possible economics and businesses.

The Tree of Life speaks more of participating in life fully than of knowledge about it. The leaves of the tree heal even the polarizing divisions among nations. It continually bears fruit, different in every season. In Spiritual Consciousness, primal, archetypal energies rise through our imaginations with images that reveal to Self not only the polarities but the One that the polarities are parts of. When we engage with polarities so that they interact with one another, they open up to a whole that neither can be on its own. The capacity to handle paradox, polarity, and dualism so that they energize the One in which they reside is one of the great experiences of living in Spiritual Consciousness and makes OneEarth living real. It is a topography vibrant with continual emergence.

5. Tricksters and Subtleties Influence Our Conscious Choices
One of the legacies of the Civilization Project is that we humans can't handle the subtleties of the trickster well enough to achieve OneEarth living on a significant scale. As history shows, plenty of evil has hidden in the use of new technologies such as pumping oil, atomic energy, pharmaceutical drugs, television, printed words, and social media. Such mysterious and powerful alluring energies exceed what rational ego consciousness can comprehend, so ego consciousness in solitary individualism is highly vulnerable to them. When an especially alluring choice, dressed up by certain charismatic, beautiful people or enticing technology, shines brightly, ego is after it. MultiEarth civilization is the victory of the trickster, be it the serpent in the Eden myth or other trickster images in various mythologies and cultures.

Not that tricksters are inherently evil. They are just tricky in how they challenge our assumptions. In Spiritual Consciousness as elsewhere, the Trickster influences us to look at things the opposite of what we're doing. Consequently, turning from the Call to lesser constellations of identity is ever possible. Many of our choices have such subtle differences that they may not become clear until we've lived into them for awhile.

Spiritual Consciousness does, however, empower us with capacities better able to sort through choices. What lures egos does not lure Self. Earth community is infused with balance and many spiritual, wise energies. OneEarth community expects Evil's presence and, like an immune system in our body, acts with a repertoire of responses that baffle ego's capacities. Debt is a pervasive experience handled differently by ego and Self, MultiEarth consciousness and OneEarth consciousness. The OneEarth response when hardship or injustice puts someone into debt is to keep the debt short term. The aim is to restore the debtor to full participation in the community as soon as possible. But the MultiEarth response has been to create an economy based on debt. The current student debt totaling over one trillion dollars is an intolerable consequence of this egoistic response. OneEarth thinking works to prevent debt from creating divisions in the community of life. Maximizing interactivity in that community is OneEarth's goal. OneEarth practices would rather cancel debt than destroy any person's or group's ability to participate in Earth's community. But MultiEarth's dualistic thinking separates debtor from lender. The debt becomes primary, not the community of life; the thing takes over rather than the processes of life. Ego-thinking is not able to factor in both accountability for a debt and processes to sustain full participation for all in the community of life. But Self-thinking functions from within the bonds of interdependence, where it can creatively balance accountability for debt with the cancellation and forgiveness of it, preserving the treasure of the interrelated community. The biblical jubilee exemplifies a strong economic model able to handle debts and debt-forgiveness in just such a community-empowering way.

6. Repeated Departures: Letting Go as Normal

As we continue in Spiritual Consciousness to affirm the Call to our Great Work, we also continue to experience Departure. That is, we repeatedly let go of ego's attempts to construct realities itself instead of serving our new identity configured around Self. When we first embraced the Call, we felt the overwhelming odds we faced in leaving MultiEarth civilization for a new way of thinking and living. Now, with Self identity, every new opportunity to re-embrace the Call presents a fresh opportunity to face the daunting complex of past moments and integrate them into the topography of Spiritual Consciousness. Once we know that "for this we are in the world," we can give a hug of love to every fear that arises and get on with life in ways that keep Earth livable.

We can no longer be stopped from pursuing our path because others do not understand us or because we cannot answer all the voices inside and out who question whether we've gone mad or really have what it takes. We know that we must keep faith with the Voice too deep, too strong, too connected, and too loving to turn down. We cannot be halted by such things as wondering what will happen if we fail. We must make an all-out effort to develop the capacities, the opportunities this greater consciousness gives us. Our compelling desire is to be full participants in what Earth requires.

7. Exploring the Unconscious Continues with Wise Guides and Maps

The outer edges of consciousness never stop expanding. The boundaries of Spiritual Consciousness only mark where we are, not the limits of where we can go. The atmosphere in this way of thinking and being is one of sharing, interacting. We appreciatively inquire of one another. OneEarth living is inclusive. Diverse people and thinking discover synapses firing on how to move past ego and work constructively with the mighty forces of the unconscious. We're looking to develop fuller humanness, not to be something other than human. We want to explore the depths of the human mystery, not cave to shallow definitions that need civilization's fixes. The solidarity brings to consciousness just how myriad our individualistic tendencies are. Our thinking is changing the more time we spend in Spiritual Consciousness. The mystery of our own humanness is revealed as we test our skills in sharing, leaning on others, coming through when they lean on us, and so much more. Without coming to know ourselves and others as humans-in-process, moving into greater being and awareness, we confine others to our own little box rather than liberate them and ourselves to know the greater treasures of Earth's abundance as well as her limits.

8. Rewilding That Renews Humanness and Balance

Even as we cannot remain ego-centered and individual in Spiritual Consciousness, we cannot remain within only human relationships. Practicing being *part of* Nature and Wilderness, and taking instruction from natural, wild teachers around us and in us integrates us into the whole, the One. Moving into deeper relationships within Nature assures us that we are becoming more adept in choosing

Self as our identity. We become better able to sense the difference when ego is not in control, though present. Being present within Nature and Wilderness enchants the mythology we bring to consciousness for OneEarth living. Knowing that we are Nature and Nature is us is different from merely liking Nature's beauty and setting aside pristine expressions. Understanding ourselves as part of Nature radically changes the story we live by and grows our capacities for OneEarth ways.

9. Earth Is Animated, Alive, and Mother-like

Earth remains an inanimate object for much of MultiEarth civilization, but in the OneEarth paradigm we see Earth adjusting with life-like responses to wounds and crises. Wherever Earth falls on the spectrum of inanimate to animate, what is clear is that Earth shines in the Universe as a special life-supporting sphere. Mythologies of many cultures speak of Earth as Mother and link her intimately with feminine birthing, productivity, and caring. The deep unconscious energies of Earth have risen into consciousness through our imaginations and been perceived as the Earth goddess. Earth attracts love and stirs awe, elicits gratitude and prompts reverence for her teachings and wisdom. We cannot understand what Earth means to life without opening ourselves to her symbolic power. Earth speaks and we speak to her. Geology and mythology are both needed to grow our interactions with Earth, our feeling for her and with her. We cannot reverse climate change with statistics about an inanimate planet, or with science alone. We must also tap into our *feelings* for Earth. Like the Na'vi in our earlier example of the movie *Avatar*, we must feel our love for her and our sense that we are loved by her. The more we tune into Earth energetically as well as geologically, the greater becomes our strength to throw off civilization's reductionist ways of thinking about our planet, and the more Earth will reinforce our courage to live in Spiritual Consciousness and undo the damage we've caused. Science and myth are stronger when they join in conveying that our relationship with Earth has a pulse, and that feelings and facts make strong partners in Earth's community of life.

10. Remembering Ancient Wisdom That Guided Old Ways

OneEarth mythology includes primal energies of The Old Way—energies that MultiEarth memories have forgotten, but which shaped the lives of our species for tens of thousands of years before the Civilization Project. Many First Peoples have been torn between these "traditional ways" and the coercion or allure of civilization's modernizing powers and peoples. All who know something of the Old Way and who live inside of Nature, not above her, help strengthen contemporary OneEarth mythology. All who hone the art and skill of listening to Earth's speech, all whose reverence for Earth considers her wisdom to be greater than the knowledge of science, all who can bring some of this Old Way to the new Earth can contribute to our common path towards interdependent living with all species.

11. Imagination, a Valued Way of Knowing

Without using imagination as a way of coming into knowledge, we cannot continue to live in the topography of Spiritual Consciousness. The rest of this chapter focuses on the language of our imaginations, symbol and myth, so that we can better appreciate their great influence on our lives and their prominence in Spiritual Consciousness.

Myths and Symbols—Essentials for Living Spiritual Consciousness

Jung said that after fifty years of working with symbols that arose from his unconscious and that of his clients, as well as the symbols comprising the myths of various cultures, he had become convinced that these were front and center in what guided human existence, both individuals and whole cultures:

I have spent more than half a century in investigating natural symbols, and I have come to the conclusion that dreams and their symbols are not stupid and meaningless. The results, it is true, have little to do with . . . buying and selling. But the meaning of life is not . . . explained by one's business life, nor is the deep desire of the human heart answered by a bank account.[169]

"The deep desire of the human heart," as Jung calls it, directs us to seek deeper connection with life than what is offered on the surface. Mythologist Joseph Campbell, who was greatly influenced by Jung, repeatedly said that myths connect us with the experience of life—a deeper connection than only understanding it. So much of life is lived outside of understanding. The rite of passage from ego consciousness to Self consciousness described in the previous chapter is an intense experience of life that supersedes understanding. The symbols of caterpillar, chrysalis, and butterfly, along with the mythic process of metamorphosis, parallel the ordeal we undergo when our identity center changes from ego to Self. But neither process is fully understood, but they connect us with an experience that transforms life from one form to another. Meditate on it, and we feel in our bellies and hearts the shifting. Whatever we understand about metamorphosis, the belly and heart sensations go beyond it.

In Spiritual Consciousness we live more conscious of how images and myths function. Jung's conclusion that dreams and symbols are not merely weird movies on the screens of our minds is the conclusion of Self, not ego. It remains unusual in MultiEarth ego consciousness for us to turn to dreams, myths, and symbols in order to connect with a greater wisdom than ego-thinking provides. Rarely do we make key decisions based on the message of a symbol from a dream or waking imagination. They remain a foreign language. We are as unable to interact significantly with them as we are with a person whose language we don't understand. Consequently, because we in modern society have such limited ability to understand symbolic speech, we are significantly hampered from sustained living in the topography of Spiritual Consciousness.

The images our imaginations bring us will expand our lives and consciousness if we interact with them. They correct any one-sided focus on science, math, and empirical knowledge that we've adopted from MultiEarth thinking. The images our imaginations bring to us connect us with another world we can aptly call "The Other"—meaning, all that we do not know or are unaware of, but which, nonetheless, lingers at the edges of our consciousness and intrudes into our lives as it wills. To get a picture of The Other at work, imagine it coming into our imaginations from beyond the topographies of consciousness. Imagine it coming from beyond the Self, and coming through the Self into our consciousness.

Much of The Other is unknowable to rational thinking so our imagination's ability to work with images and myths becomes invaluable. The most profound dimensions of The Other remain beyond words, even though we speak of it as best we can. So, for example, "God," or "the gods," has been an important way to speak of some experiences of The Other. In Spiritual Consciousness, we want to know what the symbols and myths are saying in order that they can influence our conscious choices, not just our unconscious ones.

Though our capabilities to rationally understand The Other are seriously limited, our experience of The Other exceeds our understanding. Where our rational minds falter, our imaginative minds make a contribution. The Other comes to us through the images created by our imaginations—symbols that are essentials in the Spiritual Consciousness to which the heroic journey has brought us. It is critical, however, that we forever remind ourselves that symbols *are* pointers to The Other; they are not actually "it" itself. This is true for both visual symbols and word symbols. "God," for example, is not the name of a specific entity or object but a pointer to what is beyond entity and object. Michelangelo's painting on the ceiling of the Sistine Chapel shows the arm of God, with the index finger, reaching out to touch the human. It stirs in us that moment just before an electrifying touch happens between us and another. We revere the artistic genius with which Michelangelo has portrayed such a numinous moment, and we can use that symbol to experience such moments in our memory and in anticipating such in the future. But it remains a pointer to those moments. The experience of being touched by another subject unites the human and the divine, working change in us in ways that the image as object does not.

Even though the image gives us access to the experience of The Other, the Other itself remains forever unknowable to us in anything but a partial way because, in our three-dimensional world, we are limited to knowing objects. We are *subjects* gaining acquaintance with *objects*. The Other, however, is beyond the subject-object dualism. It is the One. It is the ocean, not the waves. One of the continuing fascinations of living in Spiritual Consciousness is that The Other continues to be explored, not unlike we continue to explore the Universe with our telescopes or travel to regions of the world where we haven't yet been.

Though the spirituality and sacredness of OneEarth living do not fully reveal the Spirit and the Divine Presence that remains as the One, we do experience connection with the One through silence, intentional meditation, and deepening our sense of interdependence with the full community of Creation. Through art, movies, dance, rituals, and many other forms, we express something of it. When we are able to share it vulnerably from our souls, transformation happens in us and in others. All involved may be drawn into a sense of unity with all things. The enchantment and transformative power of OneEarth living depends on our inclusion of elements that connect with the Mystery permeating our planet. In Spiritual Consciousness, experiencing the Mystery, The Other, sustains life and keeps the processes Earth's ecospheres functioning.

Myths Direct Our Lives

We don't spend our days thinking of how we live inside of air. We just breathe it. But the air has enormous influence on our lives. Myths are like that. We are mostly unaware of them and their influence in our lives. Both the myths of civilization and our personal mythology influence not only what we consciously aim for in our lives, but also how our lives play out differently from where we were aiming. The notion that a myth can direct our lives from outside of our awareness may cause us to bristle. We definitely don't like the thought that our lives live the role of a character in a universal myth. So we minimize in our mind the influence of civilization's story, Earth's story, the tyrant's story, the heroic story, the older child's story, the middle class story, or any other.

It's true that within any of the myths influencing us unconsciously, we make thousands of choices, resulting in smaller life stories of infinite variation. The kicker, however, is that these mini-stories never transcend the macro-story. Going beyond that macro-story requires us to become conscious of how we're living it, and then to be aware that we can change to another one. Such a change happens when we leave the MultiEarth mythology for the mythology empowering OneEarth living. Because MultiEarth mythology has implanted into us unconsciously as well as consciously that we are *not* capable of Spiritual Consciousness, that we are too flawed, changing out of that mythology likely requires us to become more conscious of how it affects our thinking. Holding that myth up to the light of greater consciousness allows us to reject it and put our faith, instead, in the OneEarth mythology which holds that Self is fully at home in Spiritual Consciousness.

In the documentary about himself, "Finding Joe," Joseph Campbell emphasizes that myth and metaphor teach us to go beyond what we thought possible within history. Metaphors and symbols carry us into the genre of myth, which is a kind of meta-history. Our egos work more comfortably with history, but our greater Self is fully able to work with myth.

In Spiritual Consciousness, history, science, symbols and myths all intermingle in a community of life where we experience a new way of being. Myths distinguish themselves in this community by their power over history and ego consciousness, a power based in the deeper structures of life which Self is far better able to handle. Myths and symbols are more primitive than history, for example, in that they are more primary, older, and primal.

The powers of myth and the trans-rational Self were presented to the public by Campbell and journalist Bill Moyers in the 1988 PBS series, "The Power of Myth." Of the six episodes in that series, the first five were filmed at filmmaker George Lucas' "Skywalker Ranch" during the final years of Campbell's life. Lucas was heavily influenced by Campbell while creating the *Star Wars* movies. One of the goals of *Star Wars* is to develop a contemporary mythology able to challenge our entrancement with "the mythic power of the industrial vision," as Thomas Berry called it. *Star Wars* emphasizes powers different from those of ego thinking. Luke Skywalker, for example, learned to trust the Jedi ways of acting from intuition and deep feelings rather than try to defeat the Empire's industrial might and ingenuity with rational thinking alone. Skywalker also learned that the enemy on the outside has its counterpart within himself, and that dealing with the enemy within grew his consciousness to the point that, when he encountered his adversaries, better results were possible. In the end, even his scary Dark Father (Darth Vader) could be redeemed in the greater topography of consciousness where Skywalker had come to live.

Both *The Power of Myth* series and the *Star Wars* movies underscore that our species has suckled at the breast of the mother of rationalism way beyond weaning time. Mothers in the animal kingdom know when to wean their young. We're overdue as a culture to wean ourselves away from excessive reliance on ego's rational thinking. In Spiritual Consciousness we trust ourselves in the wilder and messier realm of symbol, myth, imagination, and the unconscious—all flush with layers of living, being, and meaning that rationalism alone cannot give us.

While much of society keeps history and myth compartmentalized and thinks rational ways of knowing are better than non-rational, Spiritual Consciousness breaks through these boundaries. In Spiritual Consciousness, we give priority to how symbol and myth connect the unconscious and conscious mind, the Self and the ego, using both the rational and the non-rational throughout the curriculum of living. As we guide youth and young adults to find vocation, not just a job with income, we need to teach the practice of listening to the inner Voice revealed in symbol and myth. Without learning to recognize and trust the inner Voice, the outer voices drown out what's inside. Then civilization's macro-story runs our lives. We choose jobs based on where the most money can be made. We lead by exercising control. The cycles of civilization continue as endlessly as they are blind. But by breaking into Spiritual Consciousness, where we can consciously work with the powers of myth, we could quickly come to a tipping point in human consciousness—in time to be part of the Ecozoic Era. Studying only history, and trusting only rational ways of knowing, cannot get us there.

Myths Impact Us Through Mystique

Mystique is about the non-rational, the meta-history, and the mythic. Thomas Berry understood the importance of perceiving and telling the mystique of a myth. In speaking of Earth's Dream, Berry spoke of the mystique of Earth, not just the facts of its history or geology or biota. Just the existence of our planet, its powers to generate and regenerate life—unique among the spheres of this solar system—can stir our emotions. Earth's Dream needs to be more compelling and enchanting than the vision of living with greater industrialization or better technology. So too with the nationalistic dreams that are invoked in political and military speeches. The most persuasive, inspiring speeches are those that can tap into the mystique that myths hold more than facts. The mystique held in the Dream of Earth can challenge the mystique of any MultiEarth dream. Berry taps into that mystique with such words as "taste," "fascination," "grandeur:"

> A taste for existence within the functioning of the natural world is urgent. Without a fascination with the grandeur of the North American continent, the energy needed for its preservation will never be developed. Something more than the utilitarian aspect of fresh water must be evoked if we are ever to have water with the purity required for our survival. There must be a mystique of the rain if we are ever to restore the purity of the rainfall.[170]

Imagine for a moment that world leaders in government and business have come under the spell of the mystique of the natural world and Earth so strongly that they move beyond the mystique of their country, products, and profits. And imagine a global forum of these leaders at which they take turns at the podium to talk about how the mystique of Earth is impacting them and their work. It could be a United Nations Assembly or the World Economic Forum at its annual meeting in Davos, Switzerland. The audience includes leaders of nations, an array of women and men who are CEOs of business and finance, leaders in academia and religion, and leaders of nonprofits. Speeches tell about the mythology of Progress that encircles the globe and manifests as increased technology and consumption of goods in more countries. The U.S. president, after speaking of the needs of a rapidly growing human population, the desire to foster strong economies, and the wellbeing of citizens, speaks to how our decisions are impacting Earth, our common home. The president continues:

> In the U.S. we are now eager to change the mythology we live by. We are eager at this Forum to join with all nations and economies to shift to mythologies that fit our one beautiful planet. Doing so is our most urgent business. We have begun shifting from the American Dream to a bigger dream that calls on our best capacities as humans. We

have recognized that having a dream for our nation only is too small a dream in the 21st century. All of us must now be planning to live according to the Dream of Earth, the amazing planet that has birthed us and sustains us.

Changing our mythology implies many changes in how we live and how we relate to one another on our planet. Those challenges are great and require a mythology greater than any of our nations now lives by. The Dream of Earth provides us immediately with a universal mythology, an inspiring source for all our cultures and economies. It guides us to make real what we know to be true: that all of us live interdependently with all species on our spectacular planet. Earth's Dream holds a mystique that none of us can match with the mythologies of our countries, businesses, religions, careers, institutions, or profit-making. Our species, the human species, has not been called to our greatest potentials through the myths or dreams we've been using. We need to feel the pull of Earth's mystique to help us live more fully into such innate, soulful capacities as cooperation and sharing.

We know that Earth's vast abilities to regulate her systems have provided life. Now they also push back on our economic model, creating ecological crises everywhere. Earth is rejecting the American Dream, and other nationalistic dreams. They are too small for our planet and for her inhabitants, including us. Even as she rejects the mythologies we've been living by, she calls all of us on the planet to find our most powerful identities, the identity of "we" and of "all of us," and join her in her desire to see life flourish. Her life-generating powers aren't finished yet. She is evolving a new Earth with a new community of life. But our old mythologies are completely missing out on this evolutionary dream.

Because the U.S. has led the world in the achievements of industrialization and the excesses which are destroying our planet's inhabitability, I assure us gathered here that we are rushing to participate in these macro-changes. No longer can we encourage a world in which people look at the American example or that of any so-called First World economy. Earth will no longer tolerate peoples or nations whose identity is wrapped up in being the best at anything that takes more from our planet than what we give in return. Turning from what has brought us to where we are, all of us together are redirecting our aspirations to Earth's far better dream.

During this event, we are showing the world that we are joining in the unity of our planet's community of life. We have all agreed to seek changes in our flags so that their most prominent symbol is one from Nature. We are strengthening our economies, not through growth, but through localization. Many tribes of First Peoples and other groups and individuals in many lands have long traveled the path of living sustainably on Earth. Today we confess that we have treated them horribly. We ask for forgiveness. We affirm their persistence, resilience, and ingenuity as all of us undertake our Great Work of moving together into full participation in the metamorphosis to which Earth calls us all. Thank you.

The mystique of Nature and Earth is what we breathe and feel daily in the topography of Spiritual Consciousness. It is a Sacred Presence we cannot ignore, nor do we have any desire to. That mystique makes it less likely that we will submit to smaller thoughts or practices of nations, businesses, or systems held under the sway of MultiEarth ways. Our excitement is with the challenges of OneEarth living.

Symbols Keep Spiritual Consciousness Enchanting

The more we tune into imagination's symbolizing powers, the more we gain confidence that new mythology has the power to bring about the huge social changes that we need. Psychologists David Feinstein and Stanley Krippner speak to the social, not only the personal, transformational power of mythology:

> Because it is our myths, more than our genes, that have gotten us into our current dilemmas, it is our potential for formulating more highly effective mythologies that offers the greatest protection against our following in the wake of the dinosaur.[171]

Berry agrees:

> The main difficulty in replacing the industrial order is not the physical nature of the situation, but its psychic entrance-ment. This mythic commitment preceded the actuality of the industrial achievement. It was, rather, a condition for, not the consequence of, the industrial achievement. So, too, with the ecological pattern: the myth is primary, though its early realization must be achieved and valid indications established for its possibilities for the future.[172]

It is most certainly not inevitable that we humans will always yield to aggression, greed, or ease. Mythologies and spiritualities that say so are highly suspect in the light of Spiritual Consciousness. Our evolutionary, creational purpose and all of the world's spiritual traditions believe that we can transcend our lower instincts and actions.

To illustrate only from the spiritual traditions of Judaism and Christianity, both of these traditions testify to the union of the Divine-Human and Divine-Nature polarities. As a result, their mythology of the Human and of Nature hold a mystique that transcends the reductionist views held by MultiEarth mythology. Though words fail to describe the mystique involved—Divine image, Messiah or Christ consciousness are used—it becomes most real when we arrive in the topography of Spiritual Consciousness. Efforts to make it real in ego consciousness are partial at best. The mystique carries too great a voltage for ego consciousness to handle. But in Spiritual Consciousness, the mystique of experiencing the union in which polarities are held results in new dimensions of being, including capacities to love. Love permeates the mythology of Spiritual Consciousness—a lubricant that facilitates all the interactivity of Earth's interdependent community of life. Our stories switch to align with Earth's dream, with the deepest spiritual energies at work within our souls, and with all Creation. The best of soul and science come together. Enchantment thrives.

Into the Future with Spiritual Consciousness

All of us who long for the change from ego's MultiEarth Civilization Project to the OneEarth living of Self and larger topographies of consciousness can't help but want change to hurry. The questions intensify around the globe: *Why have our various cultures not yet been caught up in a collective ecological vision? Why has the ecological movement not captured the imaginations of people around the globe?* Thomas Berry gave us his answers in *The Dream of the Earth* (1988) over 25 years ago:

> If this movement has not yet achieved its full efficacy in confrontation with the industrial vision, it is not primarily because of the economic or political realities of the situation, but because of the mythic power of the industrial vision. Even when its consequences in a desolate planet are totally clear, the industrial order keeps its control over activities because of the energy generated by the mythic quality of its vision. We could describe our industrial society as counter-productive, addictive, paralyzing manifestation of a deep cultural pathology. Mythic addictions function something like alcohol and drug addictions. Even when they are

obviously destroying the addicted person, the psychic fix-
ation does not permit any change, in the hope that continued addiction will at least permit momentary survival. Any
effective cure requires passing through the agonies of withdrawal. If such withdrawal is an exceptional achievement in
individual lives, we can only guess at the difficulties on the
civilizational or even the global scale.[173]

Berry's words underscore that going on the heroic journey to
Spiritual Consciousness really is a big deal. Think of it. To leave the
addictive MultiEarth civilization, rewild our dehumanized lives,
recover the treasure of interdependent, interactive relationships in
the underworld, metamorphose from being centered around ego
to being centered in the Self, and move on into the topography of
Spiritual Consciousness where imagination joins rational, empirical scientific thinking in greater ways of knowing—such a journey
is the kind of achievement that changes how we want to live. We
can't be who we once were. In Spiritual Consciousness, the mythic
power of the industrial vision recedes and the mythic power of the
ecological vision blooms.

Living in Spiritual Consciousness as best we can continues
to change us and our planet. Its enchanting wildness and Spirit
enchant us. Enchantment is not a sentimental weakness, but a transcending strength. Not a fairy tale kind of thing, but the living reality of Spiritual Consciousness. It activates the cure for what ails us.
The wound of disconnection across Nature and Earth heals.

Withdrawal from "mythic addiction," as Berry calls it, is
underway. To borrow a saying from Alcoholics Anonymous, many
are getting sick and tired of being sick and tired. Their stories of
being delivered from MultiEarth addiction have impact. Vignettes
include refusing higher paying promotions in favor of living more
simply and relationally, turning away from nonorganic eating,
embracing low-meat diets, tending native plants organically, and
so many more. These small actions matter in a big way if we do
them as acts on the journey, acts that grow our participation in

the mythic vision of OneEarth ways. They can orient us to our evolutionary purpose. In the hands of ego, these actions become no more than green dressing on our lives. Ego consciousness and the systemic dynamics of civilization are too limiting to hold, live, or tell the grandeur of OneEarth mythology. Only in the hands of our greater Selves do these small acts accumulate into transformation. It is our greater Selves that equip us with what we need in order to work more skillfully with the symbols that increase the mythic power of the OneEarth vision and help us enter more fully the Dream of Earth. It is the breakthrough which these apocalyptic times reveal.

Does arriving in the greater topography of Spiritual Consciousness after our heroic journey, end our journeying, or might we take more than one heroic journey in our lifetime? In part, the answer depends on how we think of the journey. If we think of it as a process that extends over a lifetime, one is quite enough; if we see it as a process that we go through in a chapter of life, then other chapters may well include a further journey. In the framework of a lifetime, arriving home is to be an elder, sage, and spiritual guide as a participant within Earth's community. In the framework of a life chapter, we can see how the journey equips us for our work in the prime of life. Most likely, it isn't important whether we see ourselves taking more than one heroic journey. What is important is that we take at least one. When the Call comes to us, nothing matters more than that we embrace it.

Conclusion: Inhabiting Eden

Each chapter of this book moved us along on the heroic journey to arrive in a larger consciousness. Along the way we shed the egoistic mythology of civilization that continues headlong into dark tragedy for Earth and life. Instead, we became attentive to the symbols and mythology rising from the unconscious. Far from a new mythology, it has long been shaping and energizing a living Earth community. But it may be new to us if we've been captive to MultiEarth living and assumed it was the way to go. Once we live inside of Earth's life community instead of dominating it, we experience a mythology previously unfamiliar to us. It empowers us to transcend the limited capacities of our ego identities to live new lives with the greater capacities Self incorporates into our being and behaviors.

I have entitled this conclusion "Inhabiting Eden." I am speaking of inhabiting the mythology of Spiritual Consciousness and doing it now in the apocalyptic turmoil of the 21st century. I do so first of all with the full confidence that we are capable of it. Second, I believe that by inhabiting Eden consciousness and framing our story within Earth's Garden, we will contribute to Earth community as interdependent participants, enacting the drama of this evolving sacred, OneEarth myth. Doing so brings us the deepest feeling of being. It fulfills our evolutionary, creational purpose. It is not utopian perfection; nor life without flaws and struggle. It is 21st century Eden. It is the awe of living within a bigger something that knows how to balance life's polarities in ways that are more than we can fully comprehend. It is what being human feels like, a kind of humanness that is fully alive. Through this we experience love, beauty, reverence, wellbeing—a sense of the sacred in all the struggle and anticipation that comes with being a part of the great generating processes of our Cosmos. It is the journey of the Universe and the journey of the Soul.

This heroic journey equips us for far more than what we've achieved in the Civilization Project. The Spiritual Consciousness into which this journey moves us equips us to shape lives and societies structured in dynamic interdependence with all species and ecosystems. Together, as OneEarth-minded people, we can generate policies and standards that incarnate the OneEarth mythology— cooperation, competition that's in balance, interactive community with all life, sharing resources, wellbeing, love, nonviolent resolutions, spiritual reverence, a sense of wonder, a participatory democracy that mimics Nature, and a mystique about all of Creation. If this sounds like a tall order, it only reinforces the significance of change that happens in living Spiritual Consciousness.

Everyone seeking to live the OneEarth mythology as defined by Nature, Earth, and Spiritual Consciousness can benefit from such a positive, high-profile action. Given the reluctance of so many people in positions of global leadership to act on climate change, the rest of us can invoke statements such as Pope Francis' encyclical on ecological conversion, *Laudato Si* (2015), in support of policies and actions, translating it into the real movement Earth needs.

Both the heroic journey and our Great Work to keep Earth livable proceed unevenly today. People and groups have traveled various distances. That the journey and Work challenge us more deeply than we wish speaks not just of the diabolical intent of many MultiEarth powers who advance MultiEarth propaganda and ideology but also the fact that we have further to go ourselves than we may want to admit. We are often guilty of wanting so much to bring change on the outside (lead programs, change policy, march in the street, educate others) that we neglect the reshaping we need to do within. We hesitate to let go of thoughts that justify some of the MultiEarth choices we want to hold onto. We resist facing up to the archetypes and complexities of the underworld that we know we must redirect. Pope Francis in his welcome environmental encyclical, *Laudato Si*, in 2015, called the continuing changes we need to make as "ecological conversion."

Almost certainly, getting into topographies of greater consciousness involves us in continuing with our inner work along with our interrelationships with all people and species. Without doing so, we remain highly vulnerable to being sabotaged by the energies of the unconscious underworld. Bringing these energies into the light of day and integrating them into Spiritual Consciousness never ends. It keeps *us* growing—a far better focus than requiring an economy that keeps on growing. If we do not direct these energies in the light of Spiritual Consciousness, they will direct us.

The topography of Spiritual Consciousness presents us with demands and graces exceeding anything we could have imagined or thought we could handle, even though arriving in that

Consciousness is our evolved destiny as a species. Because of this interweaving of challenge and grace, psychologist David Richo describes the heroic journey as an "ambiguous effort:"

> Every hero who makes this ambiguous effort also receives the aid of a god, a metaphor for grace, a guidance not of our own making, a power that cannot be willed. Consciousness elicits grace to match every accepted challenge with new-found adequate strength. (These graces are the equivalent of 'quantum leaps' in physical evolution.) Our effortful steps are thus advanced by an effortless shift. This felicitous combination precisely defines the truly heroic, i.e. to put out the effort to live through pain and to be spontaneously transformed by it.[174]

In the topography of Spiritual Consciousness, we live into the new capabilities by which we redirect our choices. We do so radically and quickly enough that Earth can provide a livable habitat, albeit greatly changed, for at least some of the millions of species for whom she provides. OneEarthers do not aspire to destinations of the past, seeking some imagined older, simpler times. But blending ancient wisdom with 21st century science and evolution's unfolding freshness make sense. Earth is evolving, then, not only under the impacts of the smaller consciousness of the Civilization Project, but also the many expressions of greater consciousness. The worldview imagined and shaped by our greater Self is being practiced. In that terrain, rich and poor, male and female, competition and cooperation, matter and spirit, science and religion live in the yin-yang awareness that neither is complete without the other.

This book has taken us from understanding ourselves far too exclusively in terms of our egos to the immense landscapes of the greater Self. The sequel to this book will provide broad contours of OneEarth living and specific examples of what such living looks like, completing this three-part Eden Series.

The processes detailed in this book, if we undertake them and not just read them, will set our feet on the threshold of living lives radically metamorphosed and capable of Eden. What has lived in the unconscious realm will be made conscious every day in OneEarth ways. In these lives, we will express more profoundly than we have so far our interdependence with all others.

Ponder, Discuss, Act

1. Tell your personal myth to one or more people. Invite them to do the same. This is the story in which you talk about your origins and childhood, your motivations, your Call, your connections and relationships, what you're feeling and doing amidst the crises provoked by the MultiEarth civilization story, a sense of where you're going in your life, and how you think about your transition from this life (i.e. your death). Don't worry about sounding incomplete; move past any shyness about sounding silly to ego's rationalistic judgments as you tell your story.

2. The unconscious realm is an unfathomable source, a mystery desiring to make life fuller and more human. Below, Einstein identifies it as the source of true art and science; Hollis sees it as the source of mature spirituality. Respond to the following quotations from Einstein and Hollis about its mystery. How does this mystery inform your life?

   The most beautiful thing we can experience is the mysterious. It is the source of all true art and all science. He to whom this emotion is a stranger, who can no longer pause to wonder and stand rapt in awe, is as good as dead: his eyes are closed.
   —Albert Einstein

   The whole purpose of science and art is to awaken the cosmic religious feeling of reverence.
   —Albert Einstein, *Ideas and Opinions*

   Finding a mature spirituality will only occur when we internalize the fact that our egos are only a small part of a larger mystery. It is a mystery at work outside of us, in the cosmos, in nature, in other people, and in ourselves as well.
   —James Hollis, *Finding Meaning in the Second Half of Life*

3. Review the graphic of the heroic journey earlier in the book. Which stage of the journey is especially important to you at this time?

4. If you have experiences in the topography of Spiritual Consciousness, give examples.

5. Respond to the following from the introduction to Section Six:

   I have come to believe that the myth or story we imagine our- selves to be living has greater impact on us and on the world than does the past. I believe the proverb: "Change the story, change the future."

   And also:

   Eden, when changed into an imaginative story about The Garden that lives in every human's soul, is a story able to guide us and energize a new world out of the crises of our century.

APPENDIX I

Table Contrasting MultiEarth and OneEarth Worldviews

(Repeated from the first book in the series, "Eden for the 21st Century," *Blinded by Progress: Breaking Out of the Illusion That Holds Us* (OneEarth Publishing, 2013)

This table shows that worldviews impact all of our structures and behaviors throughout society. The table is not comprehensive, but illustrative. The six contrasting points in the first section give a general "Overview," followed by subsections that elaborate on other contrasts between the two overarching worldviews so determinative of two different ways of living on our planet.

Overview

Multi Earth Worldview	One Earth Worldview
The human species strives for **lifestyles** that use more resources than available on one planet	The human species aims for **lifestyles** within the abundant resources of one planet
All **systems** from food production to finance, commerce, and government designed to extract more and more despite creational order and limits	All **systems** from food production to finance, commerce, and government designed with a sense of abundance within creational order and limits
Ecological footprint exceeds one planet	**Ecological footprint** fits within one planet

Multi Earth Worldview	One Earth Worldview
Emphasis on individualism socially and economically reflects the effort to understand all of reality by finding, separating, and examining every particle of matter in search of the basic building block for the whole; energy, community and spirit/Spirit are in a sidebar to essential reality	**Emphasis on the entire community of life** socially and ecologically reflects the effort to understand all of reality by observing the interdependence of all things, and the energy and spirit/Spirit that holds all systems in vibrant, evolving interconnection
Timeframes shaped by rewarding those who act most quickly to gain advantages in economics and power	**Timeframes** shaped by rewarding those whose actions consider other species, future generations, nature's seasons, and Earth's eco-region cycles
Technology brings convenience, speed, improvement, health, wealth, and scores of advantages in overcoming obstacles to human life and progress; optimism abounds because of wealth created by new products and how they fix, save, and advance human enterprises	**Technology** brings benefits when it is to scale within the parameters of planetary and species wellbeing; skepticism comes from destruction of the planet and people that result from manufacture and use of many technologies

Religion and the Sacred

Multi Earth Worldview	One Earth Worldview
God is believed in, usually as the God or deities of a religious tradition, is restricted to the private sphere; is invoked to address personal needs and bless human endeavors	**God** is the experience of The One—beyond and behind all religious traditions—inherent in and beyond the evolutionary processes of Earth and Cosmos and seeks co-creativity from all life
Gods of civilization receive daily devotion and are the deities of functional religion	**Gods of civilization** are relativized to the cosmic God of continuing Creation
Sacred and secular have separate realms; sacred reduced to religious sphere and absent as a living Spirit or Mystery from economics, politics, business, and elsewhere	A deep sense of the **sacred** so infuses everything, everywhere, that even the term **"secular"** loses meaning; no realm is separate from sacred presence
Religious power of nationalism and economics goes unrecognized and functions uncontained when sacred is confined to realm of religion	**Religious power of nationalism and economics** is recognized and contained within the greater sacred wonders
The **primary revelation of the sacred** comes through sacred texts, temples, and priesthoods or teachers	The **primary revelation of the sacred** comes through the natural world, the interactive, evolutionary processes of continuing Creation
Having more than enough materially is considered a sign of divine blessing; giving back to the community in some ways an act of generosity and, perhaps, spiritual practice	**Having more than enough materially** is seen as a violation of the creational order, taking what rightfully belongs to others or the entire community of life

Economics

Multi Earth Worldview	One Earth Worldview
Belief that Earth's great assets generate the greatest **wellbeing** when **private ownership** develops them; publicly held assets of air, water, and land are ever subject to well-conceived plans of private ownership	Belief that Earth's great assets generate the greatest **wellbeing** when **private ownership** develops them; publicly held assets of air, water, and land are ever subject to well-conceived plans of private ownership
Profits are maximized for corporate and private benefit; profits trump people rights and needs, social good, and eco-systems' balance necessary for continued thriving	**Profits** are calculated based on good accomplished within eco-systems, for the social good, and for the wellbeing of people and all species
Sense of **scarcity** takes over consciousness as everyone competes for Earth's limited resources; ads urge us to unlimited accumulation of more; no notion that having enough or being enough feels like abundance	Sense of **abundance** evolves in our consciousness as efforts focus on living within the generous limits of our planet's life-giving productivity; the abundance of enough displaces the sense of scarcity and pursuit of more
Growth is the primary indicator that an economy is healthy and functioning for the greatest good of all; when stock exchanges and GDPs of countries are growing, the world is a better place for all	**Growth indicates health in an economy only** when it fits within eco-systems of a region, generates a stronger, locally-integrated economy, and serves the wellbeing of all people and species there; steady state economy
Economic structures designed for **export-import flow of money** as managed by non-local, large, and multinational corporations, most often weakening local economies	Economic structures designed for **money to flow through local enterprises** fostering strong, local economies

Multi Earth Worldview	One Earth Worldview
Debt is an instrument of economic growth and may be structured for whatever terms serve the lender's growth goals; some regulations apply	**Debt** helps a community only if structured for the short term such as seven years; longer terms quickly shape wealth hierarchy and undermine community; economic growth cannot be linked to debt
Land is real estate, a basic tool of wealth creation, and held by title to give primary decisions for its use to the private owner; considerations of use by other species are often overridden	**Land** is sacred and must be held in ways that steward it as commonwealth for all life; primary decisions regarding it are made by community structures with a view that includes generations to come
Distribution of wealth moves to where power concentrates and more wealth accumulates leaving behind areas of poverty both among people and Creation	**Distribution** of wealth moves throughout local regions as power purposefully remains decentralized and cooperative, facilitating widespread sufficiency among people and Creation
Consuming, owning, accumulating, and saving are core economic activities shaping the lives of people and driving the economy	**Sharing, giving, cooperative holding, and stewarding wealth of the commons** are core economic activities shaping the lives of people and driving the economy

Government

Multi Earth Worldview	One Earth Worldview
Decisions made as egos and ego-systems vie for power, influence, control, and dominance	**Decisions** made as people live out of a deeper sense of Self than ego and within the context of eco-systems, seeking cooperation and the common good

Multi Earth Worldview	One Earth Worldview
Power and assets continually centralize and structure into hierarchies	**Power and assets** continually decentralize and structure into cooperatives and confederations
Hierarchies arrange value, concentrate power, and determine control	**Hierarchies** assure fulfillment of function so that all parts exercise their power and fullest value of each part benefits all
Corporations shape corporato-cracies in which they rule; democratic forms are maintained but so controlled that people are denied real power; control remains in the most powerful, richest corporations	**People shape democracies** in participatory forms so that "we the people" exercise real power within a worldview to protect all life forms as the real wealth of a region
Corporate model is best model, not only for business, but also for education, healthcare, food supply, incarceration, and other social and economic sectors; its track record of productivity and efficiency have benefited all	**Corporate model** is one model among others to use in organizing business, education, healthcare, food supply, incarceration, and other social and economic sectors; its track record is marred by ecological and human exploitation that counterbalance benefits

Nature and Maturity of Human Species

Multi Earth Worldview	One Earth Worldview
Development of **human consciousness** gets stunted and thus functions primarily as ego-centered, ethnic-centered, and imperially oriented	Development of **human consciousness** encouraged to mature and thus function primarily as world-centered, cosmos-centered, and spiritual

Multi Earth Worldview	One Earth Worldview
Humans have evolved to the apex of all Earth forms; our capacities separate us from other forms and equip us to govern and rule all Earth life and systems, assuring life rises above savagery and is civilized	**Humans have evolved interdependent** with all Earth forms; our capacities equip us for deepening the living consciousness throughout all Earth life and systems, seeking the deepest expressions of wellbeing already inherent throughout evolutionary, creational wisdom
Achieving strong independent individuality and self-reliance are praised as essential to **thrive as persons**	Achieving deep interrelatedness with all life is the context where individuality matures and we **thrive as persons**
Security experienced through accumulation of private assets	**Security** experienced through relationship with all of Earth's community of life
Higher capacities of humans seem too weak to compete with capacities such as greed for more power and wealth so social and economic powers such as markets must be designed to control base behaviors, bringing into play such self-regulating dynamics as competition to facilitate positive results	**Higher capacities of humans can prevail** over such capacities as greed when systems are designed to reward higher capacities of interdependence, love, and cooperation and consciousness is encouraged to mature to where "we" is more important than "I," "us," and "them"
Meaning and significance of life defined by our roles and success in civilization's ways	**Meaning and significance of life** defined by our interdependence with Earth's entire community of life

Attitude Toward Nature

Multi Earth Worldview	One Earth Worldview
The **value of nature** lies in whether or not it is useful; does it have resources that can produce commodities	The **value of nature** is inherent in what she teaches us, for the evolutionary wisdom she holds, for her capacities to bring essential inspiration to the human spirit
Nature is an "it," subservient to humans in a hierarchy with humans at the top (males at the apex), living species arranged in descending order with inanimate matter at the bottom	**Nature is a "she,"** a Great Mother with creational energy and Spirit; each animate and inanimate part inter-connected and fulfilling its purpose in her community of life
Sacredness of nature is confined to certain areas established as parks; elsewhere sacredness is excluded and nature is a resource from which to extract products for sale and profit for owners, including the land itself	**Sacredness of nature** is everywhere revered and celebrated in seasonal rituals and festivals; extraction of resources proceeds only as needed and with respect for the wellbeing of all species and future generations
Wildness (wild-erness) is savage, filled with dangers to the human species and needs to be taught, tamed, ordered, civilized	**Wildness (wild-erness) is a great teacher** of the evolutionarily successful ordering of Creation, keeps us connected with our own urges for freedom

RELATED READING

Anderson, M. Kat. *Tending the Wild: Native American Knowledge and the Management of California's Natural Resources* (Berkeley and Los Angeles, CA: University of California Press), 2006.

Barnet, Richard J. and Ronald E. Muller. *Global Reach: The Power of the Multinational Corporation* (New York: Simon and Shuster), 1974.

Berry, Thomas. *The Dream of the Earth* (San Francisco: Sierra Club Books), 1988.

Berry, Thomas. *The Great Work: Our Way into the Future* (New York: Bell Tower), 1999.

Black Elk, Wallace and William Lyons. *Black Elk, The Sacred Way of a Lakota* (New York: HarperOne), 1991.

Brown, Lester R. *Eco-Economy: Building an Economy for the Earth* (New York: W.W. Norton), 2001.

Brown, Lester R. *Plan B 2.0: Rescuing a Planet under Stress and a Civilization in Trouble* (New York: W. W. Norton), 2006.

Brueggemann, Walter. *The Prophetic Imagination* (Minneapolis: The Fortress Press), 2001.

Buchbinder, Amnon. "Out of Our Heads," *Sun*, (April, 2013), 7–14, an interview with Philip Shepherd.

Daly, Herman and John Cobb. *For the Common Good: Redirecting the Economy Toward Community, the Environment, and a Sustainable Future* (Boston: Beacon Press), 1989.

Deloria, Vine, Jr. *God Is Red* (New York: Dell Publishing), 1973.

Duchrow, Ulrich and Franz J. Hinkelammert. *Transcending Greedy Money: Interreligious Solidarity for Just Relations* (New York: Palgrave MacMillan), 2012.

Edinger, Edward F. *Ego and Archetype: Individuation and the Religious Function of the Psyche* (Boston: Shambala), 1992.

Fox, Matthew. *Original Blessing: A Primer in Creation Spirituality* (Bear and Company), 1983. Revised edition (San Francisco: Jeremy P. Tarcher/Putnam), 2000.

Ghosh, Amitav. *The Great Derangement: Climate Change and the Unthinkable* (London: Allen Lane/Penguin Books), 2016.

Hawken, Paul. *Blessed Unrest: How the Largerst Movement in the World Came into Being and Why No One Saw It Coming* (New York: Viking Press), 2007.

Hawken, Paul, Amory Lovins & L. Hunter Lovins. *Natural Capitalism: Creating the Next Industrial Revolution* (New York: Little Brown & Co), 1999.

Hollis, James. *Finding Meaning in the Second Half of Life* (New York: Gotham Books), 2005.

Howard-Brook, Wes. *"Come Out, My People!" God's Call Out of Empire in the Bible and Beyond* (New York: Orbis Books), 2011.

Jensen, Robert. *We Are All Apocalyptic Now: On the Responsibilities of Teaching, Preaching, Reporting, Writing, and Speaking Out* (Robert Jensen in conjunction with MonkeyWrench Books), 2013.

Johansen, Bruce. *The Native Peoples of North America: A History* (Westport Connecticut: Praeger Publishers), 2005.

Johnson, Robert. *Inner Work: Using Dreams and Active Imagination for Personal Growth* (San Francisco: Harper), 1986.

Jung, Carl and Marie-Luise von Franz. *Man and His Symbols* (New York: Doubleday), 1964.

Kaza, Stephanie. *Hooked!: Buddhist Writings on Greed, Desire, and the Urge to Consume* (Boston: Shambhala), 2005.

Kimmerer, Robin Wall. *Braiding Sweetgrass: Indigenous Wisdom, Scientific Knowledge, and the Teachings of Plants* (Minneapolis, Minnesota: Milkweed Editions), 2013.

Korten, David. *The Great Turning: From Empire to Earth Community* (San Francisco: Berrett-Koehler Publishers, Inc.), 2006.

Mander, Jerry. *In the Absence of the Sacred: The Failure of Technology and the Survival of the Indian Nations* (Sierra Club Books), 1991.

Moore, Kathleen Dean and Michael P. Nelson, editors. *Moral Ground: Ethical Action for a Planet in Peril* (San Antonio: Trinity University Press), 2010.

Moore, Robert and Doug Gillette. *King, Warrior, Magician, Lover: Rediscovering the Archetypes of the Mature Masculine* (San Francisco: Harper), 1990.

Moore, Robert and Doug Gillette. *The King Within: Accessing the King in the Male Psyche* (New York: William Morrow and Company), 1992.

Moore, Robert and Doug Gillette. *The Lover Within: Accessing the Lover in the Male Psyche* (New York: William Morrow and Company), 1993.

Moore, Robert and Doug Gillette. *The Magician Within: Accessing the Shaman in the Male Psyche* (New York: William Morrow and Company), 1993.

Moore, Robert and Doug Gillette. *The Warrior Within: Accessing the Knight in the Male Psyche* (New York: William Morrow and Company), 1992.

Nelson, Robert H. *The New Holy Wars: Economic Religion versus Environmental Religion in Contemporary America* (University Park, PA: Penn State University Press), 2010.

Pagels, Elaine. *Adam, Eve, and the Serpent* (New York: Random House, Inc.), 1988.

Pascal, Eugene. *Jung to Live By* (New York: Warner Books), 1992.

Quinn, Daniel. *Ishmael* (New York: Random House), 1995.

Richo, David. *How to Be an Adult: A Handbook on Psychological and Spiritual Integration* (New York: Paulist Press), 1991.

Shepherd, Philip. *New Self, New World: Recovering Our Senses in the Twenty-first Century* (Berkeley, CA: North Atlantic Books), 2010.

Sponsel, Leslie. *Spiritual Ecology: A Quiet Revolution* (Santa Barbara, CA: Praeger), 2012.

Van Ham, Lane. *A Common Humanity: Ritual, Religion, and Immigrant Advocacy in Tucson, Arizona* (Tucson, Arizona: University of Arizona Press), 2011.

Van Ham, Lee. *Blinded by Progress: Breaking Out of the Illusion That Holds Us* (San Diego: OneEarth Publishing), 2013.

Van Ham, Lee. "Unmasking the Gods of the Marketplace," *Nurturing the Prophetic Imagination*, edited by Jamie Gates & Mark Mann, 91–102. (Eugene, OR: Wipf & Stock), 2012.

Weatherford, Jack. *Indian Givers: How the Indians of the Americas Transformed the World* (New York: Fawcett Columbine), 1988.

NOTES

CHAPTER ONE

1. I use the word "topography" to refer to size of consciousness. "Topography" is my metaphor of choice because it gives "consciousness" a space on an imaginary map. Others use "level" or "order." By using "topography," references to smaller and greater consciousness can be readily pictured in a spatial, but non-hierarchical, way.

2. Chris Vogler, "Hero's Journey," accessed May 19, 2014, http://www.the writersjourney.com/hero's_journey.htm.

3. Berry, Thomas, *The Great Work: Our Way into the Future* (New York: Random House, 1999), 159.

4. Much of how I present the Eden story in this chapter follows Wes Howard-Brook, *"Come Out, My People!" God's Call Out of Empire in the Bible and Beyond* (New York: Orbis Books, 2011).

5. Elaine Pagels, *Adam, Eve, and the Serpent* (New York: Random House, Inc., 1988), 150.

6. "Revolution" is somewhat of a misnomer here, but it does call attention to the enormous changes that evolved during the Neolithic Era (10,200–2000 BCE). Great changes in agriculture included irrigation, domestication of animals for labor, and other improved technologies. Many nomadic lifestyles settled into a location to grow crops. As production brought surpluses, villages and cities formed. Gradually city-states and city-based empires became possible as MultiEarth civilization took shape. See the following chapter for a broad brush summary of Neolithic times. See also "Neolithic Era," *Wikipedia*, accessed November 3, 2014, http://en.wikipedia.org/wiki/Neolithic.

CHAPTER TWO

7. Thomas Berry, *The Great Work*, 3.

8. James Hollis, *Finding Meaning in the Second Half of Life* (New York: Gotham Books, 2005), 65.

9. Thomas Berry tells why he uses the term "Ecozoic" in an essay posted on the website of the Center for Ecozoic Societies, accessed July 26, 2016, at http://www.ecozoicsocieties.org/ecozoic-reader-archive/. "This new mode of being of the planet I describe as the Ecozoic Era, the fourth in the succession of life eras thus far identified as the Paleozoic, the Mesozoic, and the Cenozoic. But when we propose that an Ecozoic Era is succeeding the Cenozoic, we must define the unique character of this emergent era. I suggest the name 'Ecozoic' as a better designation than 'Ecological.' Eco-logos refers to an understanding of the interaction of things. Eco-zoic is a more biological term that can be used to indicate the integral functioning of life systems in their mutually enhancing relations."

10. Berry, *The Great Work*, 3.

11. The dates and descriptions of all the geological periods are given further elaboration in the helpful articles in *Wikipedia* that are referenced in other footnotes in this chapter.

12. "Neolithic Revolution," *Wikipedia*, accessed March, 28, 2014, http://en.wikipedia.org/wiki/Neolithic_Revolution.

13. "Civilization," *Wikipedia*, accessed March 28, 2014, en.*wikipedia*.org/wiki/Civilization, provides a highly readable introduction to how early civilization evolved, the rise and fall of various centers of civilization, and differing theories about how civilizations emerge and collapse.

14. Ulrich Duchrow and Franz J. Hinkelammert, *Transcending Greedy Money: Interreligious Solidarity for Just Relations* (New York: Palgrave Macmillan, 2012), 9–11. Duchrow and Hinkelammert provide a history of the continuing impact of the money, private property, interest, debt economy on humanness, ecology, and societies from the 8th century BCE to the present.

15. Elizabeth Kobert tells this story in her article, "Enter the Anthropocene—The Age of Man," *National Geographic,* (March, 2011).

16. Edward Wilson had a career as professor of biology at Harvard. He considers the evolutionary myth to be the grandest story that we can know, accessed February 10, 2014, http://en.wikipedia.org/wiki/E._O._Wilson. His calculation of human biomass that I mention here comes from the same article in *National Geographic* named in the previous footnote.

17. Daniel Quinn, *Ishmael* (Bantam/Turner Books, 1992).

18. Berry, *The Great Work*, 3.

19. "Minority Rules: Scientists Discover Tipping Point for the Spread of Ideas," Rensselaer Polytechnic Institute website, accessed April 9, 2016, http://news.rpi.edu/luwakkey/2902#sthash.wCE1qDlm.dpuf. "Scientists at Rensselaer Polytechnic Institute have found that when just 10 percent of the population holds an unshakable belief, their belief will always be adopted by the majority of the society."

CHAPTER THREE

20. Berry, *The Great Work*, 7–8.

21. I use the words "soul" and "psyche" interchangeably, psyche being Greek for soul.

22. This quote is taken from a short essay by Berry that can be found online at the Center for Ecozoic Societies website, accessed July 26, 2016, http://www.ecozoicsocieties.org/?s=Ecozoic.

23. I use the words "Call" and "Invitation" interchangeably.

24. Robin Wall Kimmerer, *Braiding Sweetgrass: Indigenous Wisdom, Scientific Knowledge, and the Teaching of Plants* (Minneapolis, Minnesota: Milkweed Editions, 2013), 48–49.

25. See the online calculator of world population and other population data at "Worldometers," accessed September 6, 2015, http://www.worldometers.info/world-population/.

26. To calculate your ecological footprint see the online calculator at the Global Footprint Network, accessed March 5, 2016, http://www.footprintnetwork.org/en/index.php/GFN/page/calculators/.

27. The Port Huron Statement came from the student activism of the 1960s. It was written primarily by Tom Hayden who completed it June 15, 1962, during a convention of Students for a Democratic Society which Hayden served as Field Secretary at the time. The statement was a manifesto for the organization. It took its name from Port Huron, Michigan, which was near where they were meeting. Hayden later served in the California State Assembly and California Senate.

28. In the *Wikiquotes* entry on Einstein quotes, accessed August 1, 2013, https://en.wikiquote.org/wiki/Albert_Einstein, Alice Calaprice, editor of *The New Quotable Einstein* (2005), could not find a source for this exact quote but offers that it may be a paraphrase of a 1946 quote in the New York Times, May 25, 1946. The article was entitled "Atomic Education Urged by Einstein" and quoted Einstein: "A new type of thinking is essential if mankind is to survive and move toward higher levels." The radical new consciousness he said was necessary following the invention and use of the atomic bomb has new relevance today when applied to the catastrophic possibilities of ecological collapse.

29. "Velvet Revolution," *Wikipedia*, accessed March 3, 2916, https://en.wikipedia.org/wiki/Velvet_Revolution.

CHAPTER FOUR

30. Philip Shepherd, "Out of Our Heads," an interview conducted by Amnon Buchbinder for The Sun, (April 2013), 10.

31. Robert Moore and Doug Gillette, *The King Within: Accessing the King in the Male Psyche* (New York: William Morrow and Company, 1992), 160.

32. Philip Shepherd, "Out of Our Heads," 13.

33. Joseph Campbell, *Hero with a Thousand Faces* (Princeton, NJ: Princeton University Press, 1973), 15, as quoted by Philip Shepherd, *New Self, New World: Recovering Our Senses in the Twenty-first Century* (Berkeley, CA: North Atlantic Books, 2010), 31.

34. Philip Shepherd, *New Self, New World: Recovering Our Senses in the Twenty-first Century* (Berkeley, CA: North Atlantic Books, 2010), 34.

35. Robert Moore focused on the male psyche because he sought (1) to understand the wounds and fears pervasive in males, (2) to show paths of healing, and thereby (3) to regain male-female balance in society. He recognized that patriarchy, so dominate in the human Civilization Project, is a product of masculine fear and wounding. He and Gillette give detailed descriptions of the four archetypes in four books: *The King Within* (1992), *The Warrior Within* (1992), *The Magician Within* (1993), and *The Lover Within* (1993)—all published by William Morrow (New York).

36. For a more complete description of mature archetypal behaviors and immature bipolar behaviors, see Jim Warner, "Our Inner Advisors and Shadows—Summary," *OnCourse International*, accessed April 29, 2016, http://www.oncourseinternational.com/onlineLibrary/pdfs/Inner_ Advisors_Overview_Document.pdf. Warner coaches businesses and individuals on transitions.

37. "Why We Can't Wait," *Wikipedia*, accessed January 2, 2015, http:// en.wikipedia.org/wiki/Why_We_Can%27t_Wait, explains: "*Why We Can't Wait* is a book by Martin Luther King, Jr. about the nonviolent movement against racial segregation in the United States, and specifically the 1963 Birmingham campaign. The book describes 1963 as a landmark year in the civil rights movement, and as the beginning of America's 'Negro Revolution'."

38. The Hebrew myth of Cain and Abel can be read in Genesis 4:1–16, accessed April 30, 2016, https://www.biblegateway.com/passage/?search=Genesis+4&version=NRSV.

39. These four Hebrew letters are commonly pronounced "Yahweh." Jewish readers substitute the word "Adonai" because of the belief that the Divine cannot be named without reducing that Presence. The very inconvenience of not naming the Presence reminds us of the greatness of Being, a most significant reminder given how MultiEarth powers presume greatness and might as they rule Earth.

40. The complexities of the BP spill in the Gulf of Mexico can be read online; an example is "Deepwater Horizon Oil Spill," *Wikipedia*, accessed April 30, 2016, https://en.wikipedia.org/wiki/Deepwater_Horizon_oil_spill.

41. Robert Moore's website, accessed June 23, 2014, http://www.robertmoore -phd.com/index.cfm?category=17, presents details of his continuing research, including diagrams that help picture the structure of our souls, the movement toward greater maturity, and how male and female journeys are similar and different.

CHAPTER FIVE

42. David Richo, *How to Be an Adult: A Handbook on Psychological and Spiritual Integration* (New York: Paulist Press, 1991), 3.

43. Carl Jung, "Commentary," in Richard Wilhelm translation of *The Secret of the Golden Flower* (London: Kegan, Paul, Trench, Trubner & Co., 1947), 93.

44. Willis Harmon, *Global Mind Change* (Berrett-Koehler Publishers, 1998).

45. Richo, *How to Be an Adult*, 7.

46. Taken from Henri J.M. Nouwen, *Reaching Out: The Three Movements of the Spiritual Life*, (1975), 54, who cited as his source, *Zen Flesh, Zen Bones*, comp. by Paul Reps (Garden City, N.Y.: Doubleday, Anchor Books, 1961), 5.

47. For a fuller description of the "Way of the Negative" (Via Negativa), see Matthew Fox, *Original Blessing: A Primer in Creation Spirituality* (Bear and Company, 1983). A revised edition was published in 2000 (New York: Jeremy P. Tarcher/Putnam). This highly influential book describes in contemporary context the four spiritual paths taught by Meister Eckhart (1260–1328): Via Positiva, Via Negativa, Via Transformativa, and Via Creativa.

48. See the website www.jubilee-economics.org for details of this work on a fair economy that fits sustainably with the resources of one planet.

49. Lane Van Ham, *Civil Religion in Tucson Immigrant Advocacy Groups*, an unpublished doctoral dissertation (University of Arizona, 2006), 155–156. The quotes from Victor Turner come from, *From Ritual to Theatre: The Human Seriousness of Play* (New York: PAJ Publications, 1982), 47, 51.

50. Chhaganlal, Bankey Behari Lala, trans., *Fiha-Ma-Fiha: Table Talk of Maulana Rumi* (New Delhi: DK Publishers, 1998), 84.

CHAPTER SIX

51. Albert Einstein, from the New Paradigm website, accessed October 18, 2015, http://www.newparadigmjournal.com/Oct2008/newhuman.htm.

52. For the broad brush story of human arrival on the planet, I used the posting "Human Evolution," *Wikipedia*, accessed October 18, 2015, https://en.wikipedia.org/wiki/Human_evolution.

53. The history of written languages has the complicating factor of what is meant by "written language." For example, pictographs and petroglyphs are much older than a language with an alphabet. Before alphabets we could not replicate in writing what someone said orally. William Schneidewind, professor of Semitic languages at UCLA, says writing in the Mesopotamian region took off between the 8th and 6th centuries BCE with officials and elites writing as early as 1000 BCE. See website accessed May 16, 2013, http://www.pbs.org/wgbh/nova/ancient/origins-written-bible.html posted on 11-18-08.

54. Many images exist online to visually represent Earth's history on a 24 hour clock. An excellent one is *Deep Time: A History of the Earth—Interactive Infographic*, accessed February 21, 2016, http://deeptime.info/.

55. See the *Wikipedia* entry, accessed May 17, 2016, http://en.wikipedia.org/wiki/Geologic_time_scale for color graphic tables clearly defining this chronology of Earth time and events.

56. Critics have challenged the origins of theso-called "Seventh Generation Principle." The exact wording of *The Constitution of the Iroquois Nations*, Law No. 28, is as follows: "In all of your deliberations in the Confederate Council, in your efforts at law making, in all your official acts, self-interest shall be cast into oblivion. Cast not over your shoulder behind you the warnings of the nephews and nieces should they chide you for any error or wrong you may do, but return to the way of the Great Law which is just and right. Look and listen for the welfare of the whole people and have always in view not only the present but also the coming generations, even those whose faces are yet beneath the surface of the ground – the unborn of the future Nation." See "Seven Generation Sustainability," *Wikipedia*, https://en.wikipedia.org/wiki/Seven_generation_sustainability accessed 5/17/2016.

Oren Lyons, Faithkeeper and Chief of the Onandoga Nation, one of the Iroquois Nations, does not hesitate to use "seventh generation" language in interpreting the Iroquois tradition: "We are looking ahead, as is one of the first mandates given us as chiefs, to make sure and to make every decision that we make relate to the welfare and well-being of the seventh generation to come. … What about the seventh generation? Where are you taking them? What will they have?" quoted in the same *Wikipedia* article and taken from "An Iroquois Perspective" Pp. 173, 174 in *American Indian Environments: Ecological Issues in Native American History*. Vecsey C, Venables RW (Editors). Syracuse University Press, New York.

57. The excerpt above is from the presentation David Brower gave to the E.F. Shumacher Society, 1992, Stockbridge, MA. It can be read in full at the website, accessed March 16, 2016, http://www.wildnesswithin.com/heal.html.

58. "Gaia Hypothesis," *Wikipedia*, accessed March 16, 2016, https://en.wikipedia.org/wiki/Gaia_hypothesis, informs us of the history of this hypothesis and the extensive scientific attention that continues to be given to various parts of it.

59. Kimmerer, 55–56.

60. Kimmerer, 56.

61. Kimmerer, 56–57.

62. Thomas Berry, *The Dream of the Earth* (San Francisco: Sierra Club Books, 1988), xiv-xv.

63. Albert Einstein, *Out of My Later Years*, (Castle Books, 2005), 9.

64. Thomas Berry, "The New Story," *Teilhard Studies*, (Autumn, 1977), publication of the American Teilhard Association for the Future of Man, Inc.

65. Berry, *The Dream of the Earth*, 10.

66. The Center for Process Studies has been a primary center for carrying forward Whitehead's thought into the 21st century. See their website, accessed October 29, 2015, http://www.ctr4process.org/.

67. Stephen Jay Gould, 1942–2002, was one of the most widely read authors of popular science due to his 300 essays in *Natural History.* His field was evolutionary biology. He taught at Harvard and worked at the American Museum of Natural History in New York.

68. For a peer-reviewed and helpful integration of religion, science, and spirit, see David Korten, "Religion, Science, and Spirit: A Sacred Story for Our Time," Yes! Magazine blog, accessed March 18, 2016, http://www.yesmagazine.org/happiness/religion-science-and-spirit-a-sacred-story-for-our-time.

CHAPTER SEVEN

69. For the life and wisdom of William Commanda (1913–2011), see many online sources including "William Commanda," *Wikipedia,* accessed July 28, 2016, https://en.wikipedia.org/wiki/William_Commanda, and "Keeper of the Wampum: William Commanda, Algonquin Elder," by Jennifer Clibbon for CBC News, August 3, 2011, accessed July 28, 2016, http://www.cbc.ca/news/canada/keeper-of-the-wampum-william-commanda-algonquin-elder-1.988042.

70. Berry, *The Dream of the Earth,* 5.

71. Jerry Mander, *In the Absence of the Sacred: The Failure of Technology and the Survival of the Indian Nations* (Sierra Club Books, 1991), 2.

72. Mander, *In the Absence of the Sacred,* 220–221.

73. See the "Jubilee Economics" website for more information on this work on alternative, OneEarth economics, accessed March 22, 2016, http://www.jubilee-economics.org/.

74. "Indigenous Peoples of Mexico," *Wikipedia,* accessed July 4, 2016, https://en.wikipedia.org/wiki/Indigenous_peoples_of_Mexico.

75. Far from being backward as is often assumed, many in Mayan communities understand neoliberal economics well and strategize their resistance to its policies of privatization, free trade, deregulation, and fiscal austerity—all of which are used against them. They also understand that one of the strongest strategies of resistance is to live alternatives. So they maintain common land instead of owning it privately, grow organic coffee and market it in fair trade, not free trade, venues, and much more. See "Neoliberalism," *Wikipedia,* accessed March 22, 2016, https://en.wikipedia.org/wiki/Neoliberalism.

76. NAFTA became the trade rules for Canada, the United States, and Mexico, in January 1, 1994. In preparation, Mexico changed an article in their Constitution which had forbidden private ownership of the *ejidos*, the large tracts of land used by Indigenous peoples. Through NAFTA, these lands could be privatized by Indigenous peoples, transnational corporations, or others. Indigenous peoples, of course, did not have the financial means to compete for land given the prices that wealthy corporations and others could pay. Nor did their worldview agree with owning land. But with the loss of lands, their resources, livelihoods and wealth were lost—a regrettable practice of systemic genocide.

77. See the Smithsonian Museum publication, *Do All Indians Live in Tipis: Questions and Answers from the National Museum of the American Indian* (New York: Harper Collins, 2007).

78. Scott Klinger and Rebecca Adamson, "The National Parks: America's Best Idea?" posted October 5, 2009, on *Commondreams*, accessed November 30, 2015, http://www.commondreams.org/view/2009/10/05-6.

79. See *The Menominee Forest-Based Sustainable Development Tradition 1997*, an archived document of the Environmental Protection Agency, accessed November 30, 2015, http://archive.epa.gov/ecopage/web/pdf/ menominee-forest-keepers-1997-25pp.pdf; also, Menominee Tribal Enterprises, accessed November 30, 2015, http://mtewood.com/Forestry/ Forest%20Overview/Forest%20Management.html.

80. This story is derived from oral presentations by Tashka Yawanawa and David Hircock of Aveda given at the United Nations in New York City in April, 2008. Additional information on this innovative partnership can be found in "Aveda and the Yawanawa: CSR Chief to Chief" by Alice Kornfield, posted March 24, 2010, in *Fast Company* magazine online, accessed November 30, 2015, http://www.fastcompany.com/1596661/ aveda-and-yawanawa-csr-chief-chief, and at the Aveda company's website, accessed November 30, 2015, http://www.aveda.co.uk/discover/index. tmpl.

81. Christopher Vogler, *A Practical Guide to Joseph Campbell's "The Hero with a Thousand Faces,"* accessed February 23, 2015, http://www. thewritersjourney.com/hero%27s_journey.htm.

82. For a summary of the 20-point paper that gave the rationale for this action, see "Trail of Broken Treaties," *Wikipedia*, accessed July 15, 2016, https:// en.wikipedia.org/wiki/Trail_of_Broken_Treaties.

83. Vine Deloria, Jr., *God Is Red: A Native View of Religion* (New York: Grosset & Dunlap, 1973), 49–50.

84. First Peoples Worldwide website, accessed February 17, 2014, http://www. firstpeoples.org/who-are-indigenous-peoples. A comparison of the First People Worldwide website to "Indigenous Peoples," *Wikipedia*, accessed February 17, 2014, http://en.wikipedia.org/wiki/Indigenous_peoples, reveals some differences in statistics and in definitions of "indigenous."

85. *Indian Country Today Media News*, http:// indiancountrytodaymedianetwork.com/, an online media since 2011, is a great news source on events today involving First Peoples in the United States and Canada, and now expanding beyond.

86. See "Anishinaabe," *Wikipedia*, accessed July 10, 2016, https://en.wikipedia. org/wiki/Anishinaabe.

87. Kimmerer, one of "the people of fire" herself, describes the importance of fire among her people and gives details of the prophesies of the Seven Fires. So that these sacred prophecies can be described in her voice, the extensive quotes here come from the chapter in *Braiding Sweetgrass*, entitled, "Shkitagen: People of the Seventh Fire," pages 360–373,

88. For the full text of this important presentation, see *Akwesasne Notes*, accessed July 15, 2016, https://ratical.org/many_worlds/6Nations/ BasicCtC.html.

CHAPTER EIGHT

89. James Hollis, *Creating a Life: Finding Your Individual Path* (Toronto: Inner City Books, 2001), 68. Quoted from C. G. Jung, "Mysterium Coniunctionis," *Collected Works* 14, par. 778.

90. Paul Riceour, *Freud and Philosophy* (Yale University Press, 1970), 27.

91. Morton Kelsey was an Episcopal priest who experienced healing personally through a Jewish Jungian therapist and went on to write over a dozen book on spirituality, understanding of dreams, healing, spiritual direction, meditation, myth—all from a Jungian worldview.

92. Hollis, *Creating a Life*, 68. Quoted from C. G. Jung, "Mysterium Coniunctionis," *Collected Works* 14, par. 778.

93. David Korten, *The Great Turning: From Empire to Earth Community* (San Francisco: Berrett-Koehler Publishers, Inc., 2006), 41–56. Korten's first footnote in the chapter acknowledges in some detail his indebtedness to various prominent scholars on how human consciousness matures, and that the work of Robert Kegan, Harvard University, has framed his own presentation. What I call "topographies," Korten calls "orders."

94. Ray, Paul H. and Sherry Ruth Anderson, *The Cultural Creatives: How 50 Million People Are Changing the World* (New York: Harmony Books), 2000.

95. Paul Hawken, *Blessed Unrest: How the Largest Movement in the World Came into Being and Why No One Saw It Coming* (Viking Press), 2007. Also, see http://en.wikipedia.org/wiki/Blessed_Unrest, accessed 12-10-15.

96. Richo, *How to Be an Adult*, 7.

CHAPTER NINE

97. "Luther Standing Bear," *Wikipedia*, accessed February 25 2015, http://en.wikipedia.org/wiki/Luther_Standing_Bear.

98. Luther Standing Bear, *Land of the Spotted Eagle*, 1933, quoted in *Quotery*, accessed February 25, 2015. http://www.quotery.com/quotes/only-to-the-white-man-was-nature-a-wilderness-and/.

99. The phrase is from *In Memoriam* (Segment LVI), by Alfred Lord Tennyson (1809–1892). Accessed online 1-3-15, http://www.online-literature.com/tennyson/718/.

100. The important debate over the role of predation in Nature far exceeds what can be covered here. Scientists continue robust study of its purposes. Their various conclusions do not confirm wanton slaughter or gratuitous killing by any species, though specific instances may sometimes appear to be such. For example, the claim that wolves engage in slaughter is doubtful as shown by Brian Palmer, "Do Wolves Kill for Sport?" accessed February 17, 2015, http://www.slate.com/articles/news_and_politics/explainer/2009/11/do_wolves_kill_for_sport.html. For a review of infanticide among species, see "Infanticide," *Wikipedia*, accessed February 17, 2015, http://en.wikipedia.org/wiki/Infanticide_%28zoology%29.

101. See Mark Stabb's online comments about *Simply Walking*, accessed January 3, 2015, http://thoreau.eserver.org/simply.html. *Simply Walking* began as a lecture to the Concord Lyceum (1851) and became an essay published in the *Atlantic Monthly* a month after Thoreau's death in 1862.

102. *Sacramento Bee* online edition, July 8, 2014, accessed July 8, 2014, http://www.sacbee.com/2014/06/29/6520426/yosemites-anniversary-for-indians.html. The entire article clearly describes how the First Peoples' worldview differs from the paradigm that has shaped the national parks.

103. Ibid.

104. An interview with John Elder by Leath Tonino, "The Undiscovered Country: John Elder on the Wild Places Close to Home," *The Sun Magazine* (June, 2013), 14–15;online posting accessed July 28, 2016, http://thesunmagazine.org/issues/450/the_undiscovered_country.

105. Organic Farming Research Foundation website, accessed January 5, 2016, http://www.ofrf.org/news/organic-sales-farm-growth-soar-2014.

106. Many articles are reporting this new trend on youth and farming. One example is "In New Food Culture, a Young Generation of Farmers Emerges," reported by Isolde Raftery in the *New York Times*, March 5, 2011, accessed January 5, 2016, http://www.nytimes.com/2011/03/06/us/06farmers.html?_r=0.

107. Michael Pollan, *Second Nature: A Gardener's Education* (New York: Grove Press, 1991).

108. Eugene Pascal, *Jung to Live By* (New York: Warner Books, 1992), 57.

109. Pascal, 91.

110. Clarissa Pinkola-Estes, *Women Who Run with the Wolves: Myths and Stories of the Wild Woman Archetype* (New York: Ballentine, 1992).

111. Gray Wolf Conservation is a wolf education website by Annie Hunter. She provides a brief history of the great ambivalence humans show toward wolves, accessed January 7, 2016, http://www.graywolfconservation.com/Wild_Wolves/history.htm.

112. "Killing Wolves to Protect Farm Animals Backfires," The Wolf Center website, accessed April 11, 2016, https://www.thedodo.com/wolf-hunts-backfire-856736320.html.

113. James Moyers, on his website, *Attending the Soul*, accessed March 4, 2015, http://jimmoyers.com/index.html.

114. Moyers, accessed March 4, 2015, http://jimmoyers.com/articles/wildman-to-king-i.html.

115. Quoted by Stephen Harrod Buhner in an interview with Akshay Ahuja, "Living Medicine," *The Sun Magazine* (December, 2014), 12.

116. Buhner, 12.

117. Buhner, 7.

118. Buhner, 13.

119. "Frank Edwin Egler," *Wikipedia*, accessed March 4, 2015, http://en.wikipedia.org/wiki/Frank_Edwin_Egler.

CHAPTER TEN

120. Berry, *The Great Work*, 159.

121. II Corinthians 5:17, New Revised Standard Version.

122. David Feinstein and Stanley Crippler, "Bringing a Mythological Perspective to Social Change" *ReVISION* (Summer 1988), 27. An article adapted from their book, *Personal Mythology: The Psychology of Your Evolving Self,* (Los Angeles: J.P. Tarcher, Inc., 1988), 30.

123. Philip Shepherd, "Out of Our Heads," 13.

124. Jonathon Motaldo (Ed.), *Choosing to Love the World: On Contemplation* (Boulder, Colorado: Sounds True, Inc., 2008), is a book of quotes from the writings of Thomas Merton.

125. Jung, "Commentary," 84.

126. Carl Jung and Marie-Luise von Franz, *Man and His Symbols* (New York: Doubleday, 1964), 174.

127. Jubilee Economics Ministries, www.jubilee-economoics.org, a nonprofit which I've been part of since 2000, has provided focus for my own learning about what a new economy looks like, its possibilities, and obstacles.

128. Paul Hawken, *The Ecology of Commerce: A Declaration of Sustainability* (New York: HarperCollins), 1993.

129. The Ray C. Anderson Foundation website, accessed January 22, 2016, http://www.raycandersonfoundation.org/rays-life/.

130. Cited in *Plan B 2.0*, Lester R. Brown, (New York: W.W. Norton &Co, 2006), 253. Brown's footnote tells us that this quote comes from a speech, "A Call for Systemic Change," given by Anderson at the National Conference on Science, Policy, & the Environment: Education for a Secure and Sustainable Future, Washington, D.C., Jan. 31, 2003. See Interface, the company website, accessed July 28, 2016, www.interfaceglobal.com/Sustainability.aspx.

131. Interface, the company website, accessed January 19, 2016, http://www.interfaceglobal.com/Company/Mission-Vision.aspx, and also the Ray Anderson website, accessed January 23, 2016, http://www.raycandersonfoundation.org/rays-life/.

132. Gospel of Matthew 10:39.

133. Hollis, *Finding Meaning in the Second Half of Life*, 70–71.

134. James Hollis, *The Middle Passage: From Misery to Meaning in Midlife* (Toronto, Canada: Inner City Books, 1993), 27.

135. Vogler, quoted from his Story Tech Consulting website, accessed March 17, 2015, http://www.thewritersjourney.com/.

136. Vogler, Ibid. Refer to the "Introduction" of this book for Vogler's brief outline of the heroic journey.

137. See II Corinthians 5:17 and Romans 12:2 in the New Testament.

138. Joseph Campbell and Bill Moyers with Betty Sue Flowers (Ed.)*The Power of Myth*, (New York: Doubleday, 1988), is a book that was released at the time Moyers interviewed Campbell during a six-episode series on PBS that carried the same name as the book. The quote is from Chapter 2, "The Inward Journey."

139. "Tao," *Wikipedia*, accessed January 26, 2016, https://en.wikipedia.org/wiki/Tao. See also "The Tao," accessed January 26, 2016, http://www.thetao.info/.

140. Quote taken from Jay Walljasper, "The Wow of Physics", *Ode Magazine*, November, 2007.

141. Sam Geall, "Interpreting Ecological Civilization," posted 6/7/2015 on the *China Dialogue* website, accessed April 20, 2016, https://www.chinadialogue.net/article/show/single/en/8018-Interpreting-ecological-civilisation-part-one-.

142. See the "China Daily," 10-24-2007, accessed January 27, 2016, http://www.chinadaily.com.cn/opinion/2007-10/24/content_6201964.htm. See also Zhang Chun, "China's New Blueprint for an 'Ecological Civilization,'" *The Diplomat*, September 30, 2015, accessed January 27, 2016, http://thediplomat.com/2015/09/chinas-new-blueprint-for-an-ecological-civilization.

143. See The Institute for the Postmodern Development of China website, accessed January 28, 2016, http://www.postmodernchina.org/cgi/index.php.

144. In addition to the process thought of Alfred North Whitehead (1861–1947), who taught at Cambridge and Harvard, the Center of Process Studies also gives attention to other process thinkers. These include Charles Hartshorne (1897–2000), who taught at University of Chicago, Emory University, and University of Texas), and Henri Bergson (1859–1941), who taught at French universities and was awarded the Nobel Prize in Literature in 1927.

145. John Cobb, on the website for the 2015 conference, "Seizing the Alternative," which was sponsored by the Center for Process Studies and others, accessed April 23, 2105, http://www.pandopopulus.com/whitehead-pando-and-a-philosophy-of-ecological-relations/.

146. John Cobb, *Is It Too Late? A Theology of Ecology* (1971, revised 1995); *For the Common Good: Redirecting the Economy for Community, the Environment, and a Sustainable Future* (1989, revised 1994), co-authored with economist Herman Daly; and *Sustaining the Common Good: A Christian Perspective on the Global Economy* (1994), which challenged classical economists' zeal for the god "Growth."

147. Stephen Harrod Buhner as interviewed by Akshay Ahuja, "Living Medicine," *The Sun Magazine*, (December, 2014, Issue #468), accessed January 14, 2016, http://thesunmagazine.org/issues/468/living_medicine.

148. Buhner, Ibid.

149. Buhner, Ibid.

150. Berry, *The Dream of the Earth*, 3.

CHAPTER ELEVEN

151. Robert Johnson, *Inner Work:Using Dreams and Active Imagination for Personal Growth*, (San Francisco: Harper, 1986), 4.

152. "Global Climate in Context as the World Approaches 1° C above Pre-Industrial for the First Time," Met Office website, accessed April 24, 2016, http://www.metoffice.gov.uk/research/news/2015/global-average-temperature-2015.

153. Jonathan Adams, "Rising Sea Levels Threaten Small Pacific Island Nations," *New York Times* (May 3, 2007), accessed June 13, 2016, http://www.nytimes.com/2007/05/03/world/asia/03iht-pacific.2.5548184.html.

154. "Sea Level Rise" is a peer-reviewed article posted on the Smithsonian Institution website, accessed June 13, 2016, http://ocean.si.edu/sea-level-rise, that sorts through how climate change is affecting normal ocean patterns. It projects impacts on coastlines in the 21st century.

155. The Center for Biodiversity describes impacts of species loss on its website, accessed January 31, 2016, http://www.biologicaldiversity.org/programs/biodiversity/elements_of_biodiversity/extinction_crisis/.

156. The Climate Emergency Institute website provides a highly comprehensive summary with exhaustive links regarding our climate emergency, accessed April 24, 2016, http://www.climateemergencyinstitute.com/index.html.

157. Jensen, Robert, "Rationally Speaking, We Are All Apocalyptic Now," posted February 8, 2016, to Truthout website, accessed June 2, 2015, http://www.truth-out.org/opinion/item/14322-rationally-speaking-we-are-all-apocalyptic-now. Jensen has also authored *We Are All Apocalyptic Now: On the Responsibilities of Teaching, Preaching, Reporting, Writing, and Speaking Out* (published by Robert Jensen in conjunction with MonkeyWrench Books), 2013.

158. Jensen, "Rationally Speaking."

159. "Apocalypse," *Wikipedia*, accessed February 5, 2016, https://en.wikipedia.org/wiki/Apocalypse.

160. This quote has been challenged as inauthentic. But the Quote Investigator website, accessed February 4, 2016, http://quoteinvestigator.com/2013/01/01/einstein-imagination/, has verified it as part of an interview recorded in *The Saturday Evening Post* magazine (1929). It also appears in Albert Einstein, *Cosmic Religion and Other Opinions and Aphorisms* (New York: Covici-Friede, Inc.), 1931.

161. Rollo May, *The Courage to Create* (New York: W. W. Norton, 1975).

162. For extensive descriptions of the process of accessing Divine Consciousness through active imagination, see Robert Johnson, *Inner Work:Using Dreams and Active Imagination for Personal Growth*, (San Francisco: Harper, 1986) and Morton Kelsey, *The Other Side of Silence: Meditation for the 21st Century*, (Costa Mesa, California: Paulist Press, 1997). Both use Jung's concept of "active imagination." Kelsey, an Episcopal priest, was especially interested in showing a Christian audience how to use imagination in prayer and spiritual practice to balance Western Christianity's excessive attention to rational theology and verbal prayer.

163. The full quote as Blake inscribed it around an image of the Laocoon sculpture is "Art Degraded Imagination Denied War Governed the Nations" and can be seen at the website, accessed July 1, 2016, https://en.wikisource.org/wiki/Laocoon_(Blake).

164. Havel, Vaclav. *Disturbing the Peace* (New York: Vintage Books, 1990). The quote is translated from Chapter 5 which is entitled "The Politics of Hope," excerpts, accessed June 11, 2015, at http://en.wikiquote.org/wiki/V%C3%A1clav_Havel.

CHAPTER TWELVE

165. Richo, *How to Be an Adult*, 3.

166. William B. Hart, "The Intercultural Sojourn as the Hero's Journey." on the Myths-Dreams-Symbols website, accessed February 6, 2116, http://www.mythsdreamssymbols.com/heroadventure.html.

167. Martin Luther King, Jr., "Remaining Awake through the Revolution," a commencement address give at Oberlin College, 1967. From the Oberlin College Archives, http://www.oberlin.edu/external/EOG/BlackHistoryMonth/MLK/CommAddress.html, accessed June 18, 2016,

168. "Adam," *Wikipedia*, provides etymological data and usages of the word that show it is a common noun as well as a specific proper name, sometimes gender specific and sometimes not, https://en.wikipedia.org/wiki/Adam, accessed 6/21/2016.

169. Jung and von Franz, *Man and His Symbols*, 93.

170. Berry, Ibid.

171. Feinstein and Krippner, "Bringing a Mythological Perspective to Social Change," 27.

172. Berry, *The Dream of the Earth*, 32–33.

173. Berry, *The Dream of the Earth*, 31–32.

174. Richo, *How to Be an Adult*, 7.

INDEX

H

XYZ

JOHN AUGUST SWANSON, COVER ARTIST

John August Swanson's art has been wonderfully acclaimed by museums and galleries in many countries, including the Smithsonian, Washington, D.C., which hosts two of his pieces in its permanent collection. His painting, "The Procession," was selected by the Vatican to be part of the Vatican's Museum of Contemporary Religious Art. He is included in print collections in the U.S. and Europe. What a treat, then, that he agreed to have his "Into the Forest" be the cover art for this book.

I met John in 2010 at a conference in San Diego, where he was the conference artist. There I learned more about his process of serigraph-making. He draws the prints, then silkscreens. The complexity of his serigraphs can require 40 to 60 different silk screens—even more.

Born of a Mexican mother and Swedish father, John's art reflects the storytelling of them both. His website tells of the influence of Corita Kent on his art, and that "his unique style is influenced by the imagery of Islamic and medieval miniatures, Russian iconography, the color of Latin American folk art, and the tradition of Mexican muralists."

Much of John's art expresses his deep understanding of what it means to "do justice" today. His spiritual life is united with his art. He's taken many of his pieces and put them onto posters where he juxtaposes them with poignant quotes from people who make prophetic witness to a better world. Some of these are on his website as well. You can purchase any that fit your purposes.

Beyond giving permission to use his art on the book cover, John believes in what's between the covers. He prays and acts to keep Earth livable and does so with great Spirit and deep love.